Management Control Systems and Tools for Internationalization Success

Nuno Miguel Teixeira
Instituto Politécnico de Setúbal, Portugal

Joaquim Silva Ribeiro
Instituto Politécnico de Setúbal, Portugal

Ana Bela Teixeira
Instituto Politécnico de Setúbal, Portugal

Teresa Godinho
Instituto Politécnico de Setúbal, Portugal

A volume in the Advances in Human Resources Management and Organizational Development (AHRMOD) Book Series

IGI Global
DISSEMINATOR OF KNOWLEDGE

Published in the United States of America by
IGI Global
Business Science Reference (an imprint of IGI Global)
701 E. Chocolate Avenue
Hershey PA, USA 17033
Tel: 717-533-8845
Fax: 717-533-8661
E-mail: cust@igi-global.com
Web site: http://www.igi-global.com

Library of Congress Cataloging-in-Publication Data

Names: Teixeira, Nuno Miguel, 1974- author. | Ribeiro, Joaquim Silva, 1950- author. | Teixeira, Ana Bela, 1953- author. | Godinho, Teresa, author.
Title: Management control systems and tools for internationalization success / by Nuno Miguel Teixeira, Joaquim Silva Ribeiro, Ana Bela Teixeira, and Teresa Godinho.
Description: Hershey, PA : Business Science Reference, [2020] | Includes bibliographical references and index. | Summary: “”This book examines internationalization processes and their costs, advantages and risks, and concepts, techniques and management control tools, and organizational performance evaluation instruments”--Provided by publisher”-- Provided by publisher.
Identifiers: LCCN 2019035699 (print) | LCCN 2019035700 (ebook) | ISBN 9781799820079 (hardcover) | ISBN 9781799820086 (paperback) | ISBN 9781799820093 (ebook)
Subjects: LCSH: International business enterprises--Management. | International trade.
Classification: LCC HD62.4 .T44 2020 (print) | LCC HD62.4 (ebook) | DDC 658/.049--dc23
LC record available at https://lccn.loc.gov/2019035699
LC ebook record available at https://lccn.loc.gov/2019035700

This book is published in the IGI Global book series Advances in Human Resources Management and Organizational Development (AHRMOD) (ISSN: 2327-3372; eISSN: 2327-3380)

British Cataloguing in Publication Data
A Cataloguing in Publication record for this book is available from the British Library.

Advances in Human Resources Management and Organizational Development (AHRMOD) Book Series

Patricia Ordóñez de Pablos
Universidad de Oviedo, Spain

ISSN:2327-3372
EISSN:2327-3380

Mission

A solid foundation is essential to the development and success of any organization and can be accomplished through the effective and careful management of an organization's human capital. Research in human resources management and organizational development is necessary in providing business leaders with the tools and methodologies which will assist in the development and maintenance of their organizational structure.

The **Advances in Human Resources Management and Organizational Development (AHRMOD) Book Series** aims to publish the latest research on all aspects of human resources as well as the latest methodologies, tools, and theories regarding organizational development and sustainability. The **AHRMOD Book Series** intends to provide business professionals, managers, researchers, and students with the necessary resources to effectively develop and implement organizational strategies.

Coverage

- Organizational Development
- Employee Relations
- Training and Development
- Diversity in the Workplace
- Compliance
- Process Improvement
- Organizational Behavior
- Entrepreneurialism
- Executive Compensation
- Succession Planning

IGI Global is currently accepting manuscripts for publication within this series. To submit a proposal for a volume in this series, please contact our Acquisition Editors at acquisitions@igi-global.com or visit: https://www.igi-global.com/publish/.

The Advances in Human Resources Management and Organizational Development (AHRMOD) Book Series (ISSN 2327-3372) is published by IGI Global, 701 E. Chocolate Avenue, Hershey, PA 17033-1240, USA, www.igi-global.com. This series is composed of titles available for purchase individually; each title is edited to be contextually exclusive from any other title within the series. For pricing and ordering information please visit https://www.igi-global.com/book-series/advances-human-resources-management-organizational/73670. Postmaster: Send all address changes to above address.

Titles in this Series

For a list of additional titles in this series, please visit:
https://www.igi-global.com/book-series/advances-human-resources-management-organizational/73670

Handbook of Research on Positive Organizational Behavior for Improved Workplace Performance
Elif Baykal (Istanbul Medipol University, Turkey)
Business Science Reference • ©2020 • 445pp • H/C (ISBN: 9781799800583) • S $295.00

Analyzing Workplace Deviance in Modern Organizations
Naman Sharma (Entrepreneurship Development Institute of India, India)
Business Science Reference • © 2020 • 354pp • H/C (ISBN: 9781522599968) • US $205.00

Recent Advances in the Roles of Cultural and Personal Values in Organizational Behavior
Zlatko Nedelko (University of Maribor, Slovenia) and Maciej Brzozowski (Poznan University of Economics and Business, Poland)
Business Science Reference • © 2020 • 420pp • H/C (ISBN: 9781799810131) • US $225.00

Handbook of Research on Social and Organizational Dynamics in the Digital Era
Efosa C. Idemudia (Arkansas Tech University, USA)
Business Science Reference • © 2020 • 667pp • H/C (ISBN: 9781522589334) • US $295.00

Corporate Governance Models and Applications in Developing Economies
Otuo Serebour Agyemang (University of Cape Coast, Ghana) Abraham Ansong (University of Cape Coast, Ghana) and Ben Kwame Agyei-Mensah (Solbridge International School of Business, South Korea)
Business Science Reference • © 2020 • 330pp • H/C (ISBN: 9781522596073) • US $195.00

Macro and Micro-Level Issues Surrounding Women in the Workforce Emerging Research and Opportunities
Başak Uçanok Tan (Istanbul Bilgi University, Turkey)
Business Science Reference • © 2020 • 309pp • H/C (ISBN: 9781522591634) • US $195.00

Cases on Learning Design and Human Performance Technology
Jill Stefaniak (University of Georgia, USA)
Business Science Reference • © 2020 • 362pp • H/C (ISBN: 9781799800545) • US $195.00

Organizational Culture and Achieving Business Excellence Emerging Research and Opportunities
Rassel Kassem (Abu Dhabi Judicial Department, UAE) and Mian M. Ajmal (Abu Dhabi University, UAE)
Business Science Reference • © 2019 • 143pp • H/C (ISBN: 9781522584131) • US $165.00

IGI Global
DISSEMINATOR OF KNOWLEDGE

701 East Chocolate Avenue, Hershey, PA 17033, USA
Tel: 717-533-8845 x100 • Fax: 717-533-8661
E-Mail: cust@igi-global.com • www.igi-global.com

Table of Contents

Preface

The growing globalization, both in economic as in social terms, allows an easier movement of goods, people and capital around the world, establishing countless opportunities for companies from different countries to reach new markets beyond the domestic one, contributing to corporate and business development, as well as to the establishment of partnerships, previously less accessible.

Conversely, the current context of uncertainty and permanent innovation at the level of products and processes and, in particular, the development of new information and communication technologies (ICT), it changed the way and the rapidity of conducting businesses, approaching markets and partners, and making it possible for a more effective monitoring of companies' chain value.

Effectively, management control systems, which ICT potentiate, have been expanding and becoming more effective and fast. It provides accurate information about the market, the competitors and organizations' internal functioning. Thus, ICT are becoming a key strategic resource for business success, playing a prominent role in organizations' accomplishment, backing a more rational, updated and, consequently, informed decision-making, at lower risk.

Also, the organizations' success happens not only through the strategies' definition but, fundamentally, by aligning their workers with its organizational goals. In this sense, management control tools are also an important means for disseminating both the mission and the strategy defined by different hierarchical levels and several functional areas. Along with property facts' accounting, and enlightening about the activity evolution and its competitive environment, management control systems contribute to a greater human resources' involvement in goals' establishment and actions. This is unconditionally critical to business' success, as well as to organizational readjustment initiatives.

This book, titled *Management Control Systems and Tools for Internationalization Success,* wants to help its readers to deepen their knowledge on the various internationalization processes and its costs, advantages and risks, as well as concepts, techniques and management control tools and organizational performance evaluation instruments.

Chapter 1 is dedicated to the theoretical framework of the internationalization strategy. It intends to reflect on the main theories and studies, encompassing the key motivations behind the internationalization decision, as well as aspects related to the success and risk associated with it. It also presents some financial instruments, as the internationalization decision implies greater financial needs, which can leverage business activities in international markets. Some tools are still described, to support the initial decisions that companies face in this type of projects, namely, where to and how to internationalize.

In the internationalization process, within their operational cycle, companies have to decide about credit, interest rate and exchange rate risks in the commercial and financial operations on a daily basis. Considering this, Chapter 2 describes some risk management techniques at credit, currency and interest rate.

Chapter 3 conveys the importance of management control systems to business success. Its prominent role in credible, timely and personalized information to decision-makers influences value creation or destruction. Chapter 4 describes and analyses different management control instruments and organizational performance assessment. It also discusses its potential contribution to a more effective response to the current challenges of competitive context. Several basic themes are also described in Chapter 5 about management control definition and necessary monitoring information, as well as competitive context and management control adequacy at the different stages of business development.

Linking described concepts and theories with experience and business practice is crucial to achieve knowledge. Therefore, to illustrate both good and bad practices, we present an empirical study and its critical analysis about a Portuguese ICT company, which has been through an internationalization process and has implemented a management control system with a very interesting complexity level. Chapter 6 characterizes the information and communication technologies' sector on a worldwide, regional and Portuguese level, in order to enable the understanding of the competitive environment.

Chapter 7 characterizes the company and its national and international advancement, as well as the implemented management control system, with reference to the instruments developed in the previous chapters.

Lastly, Chapter 8 carries out the company's financial performance, critical analysis, internationalization process and management control system.

The empirical study shows that the company has launched its activity into new external markets, particularly in countries with high growth rates (Angola and Brazil). These countries, very similar in economic development, were both, at the time, very sustained in oil extraction, consequently representing little diversification risk, which jeopardized the success of the internationalization strategy.

Effectively, despite the internationalization process having provided an important growth in the company's activity and its organizational growth, the challenges associated with this decision led to a high increase in the investment level and to a financial degradation, in the last years under analysis.

Also, at the level of the company's control system, it was found that, despite being quite developed in terms of information and its support, it did not respond adequately in the sense of a risk anticipation and other variables of strategic scope. If it had been different, it would have allowed monitoring the competitive context and providing guidance to demand improvement in more attractive international areas. In turn, this would have led to better development level and more adjusted internal structures, as well as to competitive advantages creation and to ascertained accomplishment.

The company's control system, which also functioned as organizational and employee performance assessment, was very oriented towards financial results, with managers' evaluation and respective premiums resulting mostly from local goals commitment valuation and not associated with organizational performance, with reference to the predicted values and existing deviations. That is, the system should seek to better align the action of intermediate managers to the organizational goals, sharing business risks with them and leading them to decide accordingly to corporate interests and not so much to the units' short-term results for which they were responsible, because this meant to care more about results than with business sustainability.

Chapter 1
Internationalization Strategy

ABSTRACT

This chapter, devoted to the theoretical framework of internationalization strategy, intends to perform a reflection on its main theories and studies. The authors discuss the main motivations that firms face to internationalize their activity as well as the aspects related to the success of approaching new markets. Then it also characterizes the main risks associated with the decision of internationalization and international trade. The authors will also present developed tools to support the two starting decisions that companies face in this type of projects: where and how to internationalize. They also intend to go into the decision of direct investment in international markets, providing knowledge about different perspectives, as several empirical studies show a more detailed vision of this strategic option and its main financial impacts on business. Finally, it discusses the main conclusions about the relation between internationalization and the performance of companies.

INTRODUCTION

Products, services, currencies and cultural values are constantly changing, moving restlessly around the world, from Continent to country, from city to village and from group to person. What was once considered as a foreign issue is now considered ours.

In our daily routines, we handle with products and services of various nationalities, from clothing and food that we consume, to the most sophisticated technological equipment. Indeed, gone are the times where organizations worked only for domestic markets and faced only national competitors. Organizations are changing worldwide. Nowadays, we live in a so-called knowledge society, with instant communications and global businesses, where changes occur so rapidly that are imperceptible.

As such, today we face a global market, characterized, in the first place, by many companies offering similar or equivalent products, and secondly, by a more exigent demand that is increasingly looking for differentiating factors in the consumed products. Thus, it is not surprising that choice constraints, such as price, are being replaced by certified quality, ecofriendly label, design, technical assistance expertise, packaging, branding, etc.

DOI: 10.4018/978-1-7998-2007-9.ch001

This competitive reality required a major change in the organizations' activities. In fact, modern managers focus their attention on the market, its players and business' critical factors. This is because the company is an open system constantly interacting with the environment where it operates.

Nowadays, business success depends on customer value' creation, as well as on the strength of the relations with the various actors upstream and downstream, and also on operational and strategic inefficiencies' elimination, as both contribute to lower competitiveness. As such, there is a relentless pursuit of competitive advantages' achievement, through either product differentiation or process efficiencies.

Thus, new business context is an assiduous challenge to the organizations, due to players' very different skills, which could jeopardize the competitive advantages established over time.

However, this new scenario that allows goods, people and capital to move easier around the world, also represents the emergence of numerous opportunities for companies in different countries to reach new markets, more attractive and with higher growth rates, allowing them to develop business and strategic partnerships previously unreachable by distance and by domestic focused markets management. In this sense, the use of such opportunities also enhances companies' size and competence increase, which strengths the creation of sustained competitive advantages.

This chapter, assigned to theoretical framework of internationalization strategy, intends to perform a reflection on its main theories and studies.

We discuss the main motivations that firms face to internationalize their activity, as well as the aspects related to the success of approaching new markets. Then, it is also this study's intention to characterize the main risks associated with the decision of internationalization and international trade.

Furthermore, the decision of internationalization also implies greater financial needs. Then, we will present some financial instruments that could leverage the activity of enterprises in international markets. We will also present developed tools to support the two starting decisions that companies face in this type of projects: where to and how to internationalize.

Crossing markets' attractiveness with organizations' expertise leads us to discuss the existence of a logical internationalization "by stages", and the forms of approach to new foreign markets – exports, projects' development, whose achievement is limited in time – or permanent presence in target markets. Usually, the latter option represents bigger investment and therefore greater risks. Therefore, we also intend to go into the decision of direct investment in international markets, providing knowledge about different perspectives, as several empirical studies show a more detailed vision of this strategic option and its main financial impacts on business.

Finally, it will be discussed the main conclusions about the relation between internationalization and the performance of companies.

Internationalization Importance in the Current Business Environment

In a globalization context, the geographical activity area is the key to good business strategies. Internationalization has been leveraged due to two factors (Knight & Cavusgil, 2004):

- economies and markets' globalization, which provided more consistency to consumer preferences worldwide, making global business easier, simplifying production and different markets' positions; and

- technological information and communication innovation, as well as improved production methods, logistics and transportation, which decreased trade costs and favored international turnover increase.

Thus, regardless generic policy options, companies' internationalization is an important issue that has generated intense and diverse reflections on literature, in the last decades. The intention of this work is not to do an extensive literature review; however, it is impossible not to mention its important contribution to business success.

This contribution may occur, according to Freire (1998) through capitalizing central competencies and competitive advantages developed over time in domestic markets; location savings through easier access to raw materials or cheaper production factors; increasing scale economies; and experiencing business growth in more attractive markets, reducing unitary production costs.

Hence, internationalization may be a way to make business viable; businesses that otherwise would not survive inside national borders. However, the internationalization processes can be slow and difficult, involving considerable resources. Nevertheless, there is not only a way to achieve it. On the contrary, it depends on the activity, on the company's characteristics (size, age, etc.) and on the available resources (Knigh & Liesch, 2016).

The Stages of Internationalization and Innovation

Several authors (Johanson & Wiedersheim-Paul, 1975; Johanson & Vahlne, 1977; Bilkey & Tesar, 1977; Cavusgli, 1980; Reid, 1981; Czinkota, 1982; Andersen, 1992; Hennart, 2014; Bruneel & De Cock, 2016) describe the internationalization process' stages, according to markets' knowledge and the ability to allocate resources to those markets, sequential domestic stage transition, local independent representatives, commercial subsidiaries and subsidiaries with all activities:

Step 1: Do not realize regularly exports;
Step 2: Export through independent local dealers;
Step 3: Open commercial subsidiaries in target markets;
Step 4: Open subsidiaries in target markets, integrating all activities.

Nonetheless, in recent years, many companies internationalized shortly after its establishment, contradicting the internationalization models developed by Johanson and Wiedersheim-Paul (1975) and Johanson and Vahlne (1977), originating the Born Global Firms (BG) and International New Ventures (INV) concepts (Hennart, 2014; Schueffel, Baldegger & Amann, 2014; Zander, 2015; Bruneel & De Cock, 2016).

On one hand, one can consider BGs as being business organizations that aim to reach competitive advantages by using resources and selling products in numerous markets (Weerawardena et al., 2007; Covielo 2015; Ribau, Moreira & Raposo, 2018). INVs, on the other hand, may be considered as business organizations which, from the very beginning, pursue competitive advantages using their internal resources and international sales (Oviatt & McDougall, 1994; Furtado et al, 2019; Fernandes et al, 2019).

These companies had a common feature: strong competitive advantages in innovation (Filipescu, 2006). Thus, studies on the relationship between internationalization and innovation have been approached from two perspectives:

- International Performance of countries and industries, where, in both cases, it was evident that technological innovation is a key in the internationalization capacity. This is because the technological gap between countries is a source of competitive advantage for those who are in the most favorable position, contributing to the internationalization of its industries and businesses (Soete, 1987; Fagerberg, 1988; Dosi *et al.*, 1990; Boitani & Ciciotti, 1992; Meliciani & Pianta, 1995; Archibugi *et al.*, 1996; Olejnik & Swoboda, 2012; Beugelsdijk, et al, 2018);
- International Performance of companies, which aims to assess the impact of innovation in internationalization. Several studies have confirmed a strong correlation between innovation and internationalization: Hirsch and Bijaoui (1985); Pucik and Ito (1993); O'Farrell *et al.*, 1993; Kumar and Siddharthan (1994); Braunerhjelm (1996); Merino and Brown (1996); Rodriguez (1999); Melle and Raymond (2001); Eusébio and Rialp (2002), Filipescu (2006), Kafouros *et al.* (2008), Furtado et al, 2019 and Fernandes et al, 2019. However, other studies did not show any relationship between these variables, like Willmore, (1992), Wakelin (1998), Lefebvre *et al.* (1998) and Alonso Harmful (1998) Sterlacchini (1999) and Valenzuela (2000). Filipescu *et al.* (2009) justify their less positive research results due the fact that, in most studies, innovation is measured by research and development expenses. Therefore, many companies, especially the smaller ones, choose to put these values in operating costs, losing many information for that item.

As refered by Filipescu *et al.* (2009) and by Vlacic, González-Loureiro and Eduardsen (2019), progressive internationalization will also allow to better understand target markets and their specificities, which contributes to a continuous logic improvement and increases supply adequacy to consumer needs. So, it can be said that there is a cause-effect relationship between innovation and internationalization.

Indeed, innovative countries, industries or companies, will easily become references in their area, through their own know-how and new solutions.

Johanson and Vahlne (2003) revised their early work – the Uppsala model – founded on international markets' fluctuations. In this new study, the authors referred how important it is to collect information and knowledge by establishing networking relationships, both with customers and suppliers. This Network-based Theory has already been proposed in their first model, because this type of relationship increases commitment among the participants, which allows companies to better identify business opportunities abroad, with no incremental process (Johanson & Vahlne, 2003).

Figure 1. Relationship between innovation and internationalization
Source: Adapted from Filipescu, 2006

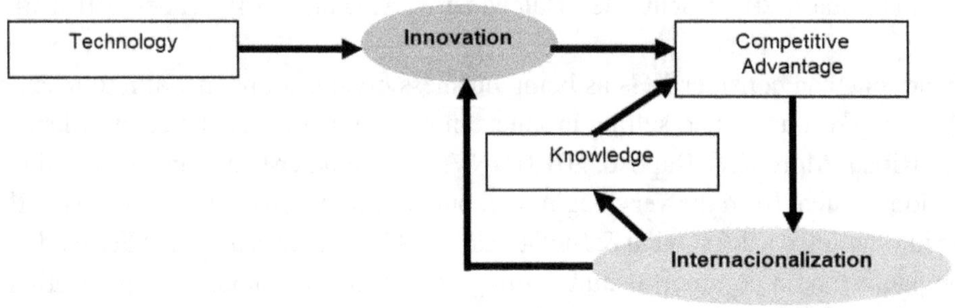

The relational-based outlook among market players has also been significant in explaining how SMEs succeed in international markets. According to (Håkansson, 1982; Håkansson & Johanson, 1984; Andersson, Evers & Griot, 2013; Furtado et al, 2019; Fernandes et al, 2019), the network-based perspective relays both on knowledge and on innovation on products and processes.

The Risk and Internationalization Strategy

According to Simões (1997), even taking into account innovation and attractiveness, an internationalization process is much too risky to investors. Hence, it should usually start with more accessible and less demanding markets, geographically and culturally closer, with less resource allocation. The model previously referred by Johansson and Vahlne (1977) includes five steps that can be followed to minimize the risk: Casual export, experimental exports, regular export, commercial subsidiary and productive subsidiary.

Moving in stages, systematically, allows the internationalization process to be carried out in a sustainable way, letting the organization to acquire expertise, gradually increasing the adjacent business risk, which favors risk management techniques development and maximizes organizational growth.

Smithson (1998) stated that risk management decreases cash flows volatility, increasing its value due to greater protection, interest rate fluctuations, exchange rates and commodity prices. Companies may maintain cash flows balance, without losing value and competitive position.

Managers, according to Neves (2012), have distinct behaviors facing risk. They may be risk averse, risk indifferent or players, and may decide on a policy of non-coverage, a systematic coverage policy or a selective coverage policy. Campbell and Krakaw (1993) referred that, if the option is risk coverage, it must be evaluated later, in a report, which analyzes the strategy performance and deviations between expected and verified events. In addition, possible gains and losses resulting from not covering the risks must be evaluated, as it might be covered regarding continuous performance improvement.

Thus, risk coverage needs to improve techniques as well to introduce more efficient ones. Vis-à-vis its type, risk can be divided into systematic and unsystematic. According to Ross *et al.* (1995), systematic risks are unexpected events that affect almost every asset and cannot be easily eliminated.

Non-systematic risks are unexpected events affecting only individual assets or small groups of assets. Non-systematic risks and often called specific risks. A perfect diversification of assets can remove the specific risk but keep continuing the exposure to market risk. It is called diversification effect emphasized by Markowitz (1952). The secret is investing in little correlated assets or negative correlations, taking advantage of contrary trends (when one decreases, the other one increases). This combination allows each assumed risk profile to optimize profitability.

In addition, companies' internationalization can be important because the negative impact of certain markets can be mitigated with gains in another market, as different countries have different economic cycles. Diversification may, then contribute to the existence of a short-term financial balance and to cash flows sustainability over time.

The Types of Risk in International Markets

According to Boczko (2005) the sources of risk in international markets are divided into four categories: country risk related to their own government acts, credit risk associated with the possibility of non-payment of client debts, risk of ownership, related to possible assets loss or damage due to foreign location and foreign exchange risk caused by the volatility of the exchange currencies' rate.

Neves (2012) also notes risk commodity prices, coupled with goods or raw materials' volatility and interest rate risk related to interest rates' volatility.

Briggs (1998) argues that country risk can be divided into political risk associated with governments' actions; organizational risk associated with the country current practices and procedures (corruption, etc.); and economic risk associated with the economies' growth rate and external payments balance. We may say that, according to this author, country risk is closely related to money supply and its impact on economic variables such as inflation rates, interest and exchange rates.

Credit risk happens whenever there is some probability that a counterparty fails to pay the other party a future due cash flow.

Credit risk also relates with country's risk, as some government policies make companies experience difficulties sending payments to their suppliers or receiving from their customers.

Exchange risk is associated with transactions performed in foreign currency, and it has a strong interdependence with other types of risk. According to Cornell and Shapiro (1983), exchange risk has two distinct components:

- transactional exposure, usually affecting the short-term which can be defined as the possibility of incurring in exchange rate gains or losses, at a future date; and
- operational exposure, whose effects are usually felt on the long term, which is the conversion risk that results from fluctuations in the currency value, along with price adjustments.

In this way, the risk of exposure to foreign exchange does not depend only on the number of international transactions that a company performs, but also on the degree of exposure to external influences that the economy of the countries in which it operates is exposed, like for example, the interest rates.

The country risk through the development of the economies and its impact on inflation and interest rates, as well as credit risk due to monetary fluctuations which may mitigate future cash flows (Alves *et al.*, 2007) are, then, very much related with exchange risk.

According to Dhanani (2004), this risk is the uncertainty over the value of an asset or liability in a future period, when the latter is expressed in other currency. The volatility of a currency, i.e. the own value' oscillations suffered, defines the uncertainty degree. There are currencies whose maximum and minimum values are far their average value, as well as others where fluctuations are smaller. The different values can be dispersed, and variations may be completely random or seasonal. The behavior of the foreign exchange markets is therefore an uncertainty and the tendency of various currencies is often unpredictable, and its next quotation unknown.

For Matos (1992) exchange rates are influenced by economic and financial, political, technical and speculative factors. The first will be the most important in a long-term perspective and include the balance of payments of a country, its inflation rate, its budgetary position and its interest rates. The political factors include government events with national and international impact; technical are those who have short-term effects and are related to regulatory changes; finally, speculative factors are short-term and come from the speculators agents' movements, who use the markets as a way to take advantage of favorable trends and monetary imbalances, for financial gain. According to the author, these four types of factors influence the balance between currency supply and currency demand, causing price fluctuations.

Additionally, the exchange rate and the interest rate are closely related and have a negative correlation, i.e. opposed behaviors. Strong currencies have low interest rates, and weaker currencies have higher interest rates. Economic reasons justify this. When the growth is lower, companies tend to raise prices in order to compensate for lower quantities sold, the inflation rate rises having direct impact on interest rates, also under pressure to grow in order to remain attractive to investors placing capital in financial institutions. Simultaneously, exchange rates tend to depreciate to offset the rise in domestic prices from international customers. On the other hand, when the economic growth is positive, the trend is to observe the same kind of relationship between the variables, but in reverse. Obviously, these relations must ultimately aim to manage the quantity of money available in the financial system, to avoid breaks or cash excesses.

Exchange risk can be divided, according Eitman *et al.* (2005), in three different types: conversion risk, transaction risk and economic risk.

Conversion risk corresponds to the difference in exchange rates that have an impact on the Balance Sheet and Income Statement, through trade and financial transactions in foreign currencies and the subsidiary accounts' consolidation (Rupeika, 2005).

According to Dhanani (2004), transaction risk is the conversion of the cash flows expected in foreign currency to local currency and has direct impact on treasury. It is the most obvious and easily identifiable currency risk. According to Rupeika (2005), this is based on future activities and checks on the competitive position of the company.

For Matos (1992) this exists from the moment that there is a commercial or financial transaction with a foreign entity, and this entails foreign currency inflows or outflows in later periods. This can occur in purchases or sales of goods and services in foreign currency borrowings or funds applications made in foreign currency or other funds transfers in foreign currency, such as dividends or royalties.

The economic risk, also called strategic risk exposure, results from the developed business, the attractiveness of the exploited markets, but also the influence of other markets through competition, production costs, selling prices and interest and foreign exchange rates fluctuations. This risk may include the other two types of foreign exchange risk, and is the potential loss of value and the deterioration of the competitive position in the medium and long term duc to the volatility of foreign currencies in international markets, which may decrease margins, due to sales prices or costs of production (Rupeika, 2005).

The interest rate risk relates to uncertainty about interest rates variation, namely in variable rates transactions. Take a loan at variable rate, for instance: if the interest rate rises, the amount due to the Bank will augment, constraining treasury management, which may cause liquidity problems. Conversely, an interest rate reduction would result in favorable treasury management. On the contrary, on treasury applications, an interest rate cut will constrain the available resources, because the amount of interest periodically received will decrease, whilst the opposite situation would result in favorable amount of interest received (Ferreira, 2008b).

According to this author, an interest rate exposure' evaluation allows companies to analyze the strictness and uncertainty of open positions, as well as potential losses. He also states that organizations should apply more suitable risk management methods, when there is uncertainty about potential losses. These methods may have three purposes:

- To balance fixed and variable rates' exposure;
- To reduce risks, both on loans and investments;

Figure 2. Risk management curve
Source: Adapted from Ferreira (2008b)

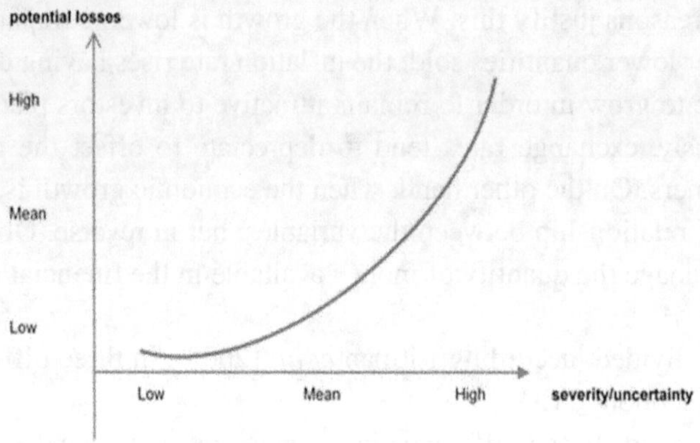

- To protect against adverse interest rates changes on the yield curve (generally, lending money for a longer period, requires a higher interest rate to the financier).

Still according to Ferreira (2008b), interest rates matter for the whole economy, since any value change may affect it in several ways. On one hand, an interest rate increase reduces both consumption and investment, slowing down the economy. On the other hand, an interest rate decrease makes financing easier, allowing companies to expand, generating higher production and wages' growth potential. Naturally, this causes greater economic dynamics and a more favorable business environment, which positively influences companies' results. Thus, on a business level, interest rate risk not only focuses on financial transactions (loans and applications) performed by companies, but also on business evolution itself, by conditioning the potential market's characteristics.

Therefore, there are several types of international trade risk to be properly studied by companies when deciding about internationalization and markets approach. Thus, the internationalization business plans should identify the different risks companies are subject to, as well as possible alternatives to mitigate their impact on business success.

The Selection of Markets and Internationalization Approach

Considering the various risks referred, a company internationalization strategy, involves two decisions to make: **where to internationalize** and **how to internationalize**.

For an analysis of foreign markets and the decision of **where to internationalize**, companies should consider three types of factors that may influence the future performance (Freire, 1998; Kuivalainen, 2012):

- Business factors associated with markets characteristics, particularly market size, growth rate, sales channels, potential partners, prices and similarities in consumption habits over the domestic market;
- Operational factors associated with regular business operation, such as legal and fiscal constraints, fund repatriation possibilities, cultural habits with implications in organizations management, available resources and its costs, utilities practices, customs tariffs, among other;

- Risk factors that may cause damage to the company's assets, as country risk related to economic and financial conditions and political stability, foreign exchange risk and interest rate, existing and potential competitors.

Regarding this, Collis and Montgomery (1997), reported that markets selection should include the integrated analysis of the various factors mentioned above, in order to obtain an overview of the internationalization success prospects and the main activity constraints that are likely to occur. For this, they propose to use business portfolio management tools, as those developed by consulting firms Boston Consulting Group (BCG), McKinsey and Arthur D. Little (ADL).

The BCG Matrix connects the attractiveness of different businesses or markets with the company's competitive position in those markets or business. To measure the attractiveness, it uses the growth rate of the market / industry, considering the high rates that are above the growth of the national economy. As to the competitive position, the indicator used is the relative market share, which is given by the ratio between the market share of the company and the market share of their largest competitor in every business (Nunes & Cavique, 2001).

Basically, there are businesses providing growth in the short term (stars - high growth rates business leaders), businesses generating cash flows to finance other businesses' investments (cash cow - low growth rates business leaders), business ensuring sustainability in the medium and long term (question marks - no leadership, high growth rates) and abandoning other businesses (dogs - no leadership, low growth rates). The goal is to generate short-term profits without jeopardizing business success in the medium and in the long term.

Table 1. BCG Matrix

		Market Share	
		High > 1	**Low < 1**
Market Growth	High	**Star**	**Question Mark**
	Low	**Cow**	**Dog**

Source: Adapted from Lambin, 2000

Figure 3. Possible strategies in BCG matrix
Source: Adapted from Ribeiro, 2003

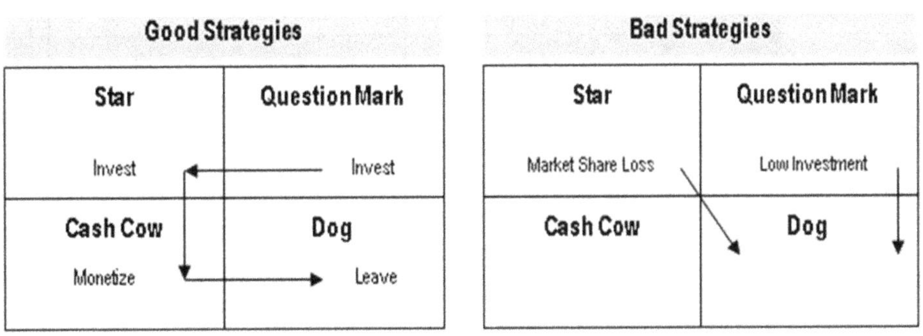

The BCG matrix main criticism summarizes business attractiveness by linking growth rate and competitive position to companies' market shares. As known, there are several factors that influence business attractiveness and companies' competitive position, such as alternative products or new competitors, which affect business profit level. Otherwise, reputation, quality, innovation and process efficiency, clearly favor the competitors that dominate these skills.

In response to these criticisms, the General Electric / McKinsey matrix was drawn. It classifies business or market attractiveness and competitive position not only by relating growth rate and market share, but also by the use of several quantitative and qualitative factors, equalizing business evolution and market competitiveness.

According to these criteria, other factors directly affect cash flow formation beyond size and growth dynamics, such as cost structure (profitability) and competitive intensity. Whenever competitive intensity is high, it usually leads to price wars or activity costs increase, through more advertising campaigns or larger payment terms. In addition, generic markets characteristics are punctuated associated with economic, technological, social and political-legal contexts that may conditioned the activity of the various players.

In respect of the criteria relating to the company competitive position, it intends to measure both commercial and production capacity, as well as partnerships with adequate service level (suppliers and human resources) and skills renewal capacity over time (research and development).

It is to point out that, over the years, the list of criteria and weightings have been adjusted according to users' objectives and the business features or markets in question. Based on the scores, there is a framework of the various businesses or markets, in areas, as defined in the matrix depicted in Figure 4.

As for the business portfolio management model developed by ADL consultant, which also crosses business and markets attractiveness with competitive position, several qualitative and quantitative factors, like those used in the previous matrix are also taken into account. Attractiveness is evaluated through businesses or markets lifecycle, as the company should know how to harmonize it in their initial stage, which requires high investments, with a maturity phase which, by liberating higher cash-flows, should contribute to activity financing.

Table 2. Market attractiveness analysis (grade 1-5)

		Markets					
Description	**Coefficient**	**Market A**		**Market B**		**Market C**	
		Points	**Weighted Points**	**Points**	**Weighted Points**	**Points**	**Weighted Points**
Market Dimention	20%						
Growth Rate	20%						
Profitability	15%						
Competitive intensity	15%						
Technology Requirements	15%						
Inflation Vulnerability	5%						
Energetic Requirements	5%						
Environment Impact	5%						
Total	**100%**						

Source: Adapted from Nunes and Cavique, 2001

Table 3. Company competitive position analysis (grade 1-5)

		Markets					
Description	**Coefficient**	**Market A**		**Market B**		**Market C**	
		Points	**Weighted Points**	**Points**	**Weighted Points**	**Points**	**Weighted Points**
Market Share	10%						
Growth Rate	15%						
Quality	10%						
Brand Image	10%						
Distribution Net	5%						
Production Capacity	5%						
Production Efficiency	5%						
Unit Costs	15%						
Suppliers	5%						
I&D Performance	10%						
Human Resources	5%						
Total	**100%**						

Source: Adapted from Nunes e Cavique, 2001

Figure 4. General Electric / McKinsey Matrix
Source: Adapted from Lambin, 2000

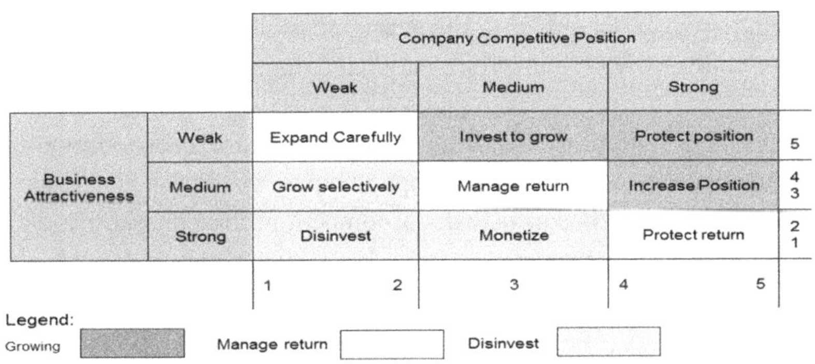

Regard the decision of **how to internationalize**, Daniels and Radebaugh (1986) and Hennart (2014) report several methods that should be chosen, once again, in view of markets attractiveness and company potential competitive position, in those markets:

- Transactions of products, services, patents and trademarks, occasional or frequent, exporting or importing directly in their own name or through agents and distributors;
- Specific projects for defined time periods that may include the first two forms of internationalization - transactions and direct investment.
- Direct investment in foreign countries through subsidiaries, production plants or distribution centers and marketing.

Figure 5. ADL Matrix
Source: Adapted from Freire, 1998

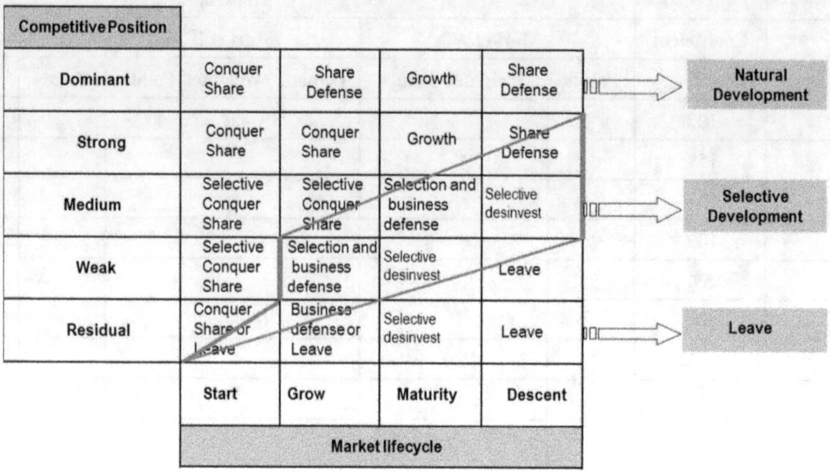

The choice for each internationalization mode assumes certain benefits but also many risks. For example, the greater the target markets activity increase, the greater the penetration degree and the turnover potential to be increased. However, this greater intervention also implies a greater direct investment, increasing financial risks of any business outputs for incompatibilities with local authorities or less market success.

Otherwise, internationalization through projects implementation has the benefit of limiting the company's investment. Even so, there is also the strong possibility to using its know-how in facilities construction for other entities, creating new international competitors with very similar skills (Daniels & Radebaugh, 1986).

In this sense, Freire (1998) proposes that the internationalization decision mode, is taken based on the analysis of the attractiveness - international competitiveness matrix, which crosses potential markets attractiveness to competitiveness, comparing to direct competitors, based on an evaluation criteria similar to the General Electric / McKinsey matrix.

Figure 6. Attractiveness Matrix - international competitiveness
Source: Adapted from Freire, 1998

		Company Competitive position		
		Weak	Medium	Strong
Business Attractiveness	Strong	Desinvest / Joint-Venture	Direct Investment Growing	Direct Investment Growing
	Medium	Desinvest / Transactions/ Projects	Selective Invest/Projects Transactions	Direct Investment Growing
	Weak	Desinvest / Transactions/	Desinvest / Transactions/	Selective Invest/Projects Transactions

Thus, it appears that markets selection and internationalization process depends on market attractiveness and its potential to create favorable conditions to add value, either through its current size, either through its future growth and competitive conditions, such as negotiation, competition between competitors, etc. Another important factor in making decisions about which markets to address and the input mode in these markets, relates to the company's ability to create sustainable competitive advantage from their resources.

So is the permanent link between the potential attractiveness of the markets and the company's ability to create competitive advantages, which should guide decision-making on target markets and how they should be addressed.

Direct Investment Across National Borders - Conditions

Thus, abroad direct investment, i.e. the acquisition of local companies or implementation of new companies in target markets, has been an important issue studied over the years by several researchers as a way of to minimize the risk of such a decision.

Such research identifies a number of factors that can serve as reference to companies in the choice of how to conduct direct investment abroad. The most frequent conditions by the various studies are associated with transaction costs, organizational learning capability, the specificities of mergers and acquisitions, the company's growth level, the industry structure characteristics and institutional theory (practices carried out by if copying behaviors reference organizations recognized as models).

With respect to **transaction costs**, affect the decision of direct investment abroad, through costs related to changes in activity of inputs because of the option by entering new markets (Williamson, 1975; Hennart, 1982; Buckley & Casson, 1998; Hennart, 2000; Hennart, 2014; Shahzad, 2019). On this topic, the researchers point out various behaviors of reference over the years.

Whenever the company has a unique understanding of the technology and it prefers to perform the core of investments for acquisitions, it can easily transfer technological knowledge for new plants and carefully select the required workforce (Hennart, 1982; Hennart & Park, 1993). Nevertheles, less dependent technology companies have greater propensity for holding acquisitions (Hennart *et al.*, 1996; Larimo, 2003; Hennart, 2014).

Companies from countries with more international experience easily choose direct investments, while companies from countries with lower international tradition, opt for acquisitions as a way to gain more experience (Hennart, 1982; Hennart & Park, 1993; Caves, 1996; Hennart, 2014; Beugelsdijk et al, 2018).

Companies that internationalize its business through quite different production base, choose to purchase other companies to acquire the necessary skills; on the contrary, companies that internationalize its business through similar products, tend to make greenfield investments, as it is easier to transfer the accumulated knowledge (Hennart & Park, 1993; Caves, 1996; Hennart, 2014; Beugelsdijk et al, 2018).

Many companies prefer acquisitions, usually, because it hold advanced management control systems, which makes controlling easier (Caves & Mehra, 1986; Zejan, 1990; Hennart & Park, 1993; Larimo, 2003; Hennart, 2014; Beugelsdijk et al, 2018).

On the other hand, purchases usually require high financial values, which are more accessible to large companies than small ones (Pennings *et al.*, 1994; Caves, 1996; Larimo, 2003; Hennart, 2014; Beugelsdijk et al, 2018).

Finally, companies that internationalize to markets with greater cultural distance (concept that measures the amount of values shared by two cultures - Hofstede, 2001) tend to opt for the realization of new investment, because the costs of acquisitions generally increase because of cultural incompatibilities (Cho & Padmanabhan, 1995; Hennart et al, 1996; Larimo, 2003; Hennart, 2014; Beugelsdijk et al, 2018).

In relation to **organizational learning capabilities**, the decision about the form of direct investment abroad is conditioned by the fact that companies operating in various fields of activity are exposed to a wide variety of events and ideas that strengthens their knowledge base and technological capabilities (Huber, 1991; March, 1991; Hennart, 2014; Beugelsdijk et al, 2018).

Thus, companies with international experience in many countries and in many industries, generally have a body of knowledge and very broad technological capabilities, being the acquisitions attractive by the lack of complementarity of new knowledge and the accumulated expertise transfer costs for new entities (Cho & Padmanabhan, 1995; Vermeulen & Barkema, 1998; Hennart, 2014; Beugelsdijk, 2018). However, Barkema and Vermeulen (1998). From a certain level of diversification, companies prefer to make purchases to reduce the level of complexity to cope with management.

Additionally, researchers also refer that the choice about direct investment depends on previous experience of internationalization through acquisitions and new investments (Cho & Padmanabhan, 1999).

Related to **mergers and acquisitions**, the literature identifies two types of problems directly associated with the lack of knowledge about the acquired entity that may have an impact in the form of direct investment: difficulties in determining their fair value and formulation of an accurate vision of the ease of integration of the new entity (Ravenscraft & Scherer, 1987; Hennart, 2014).

Therefore, companies that are more familiar with the culture and the contexts of target markets, opt more easily for acquisitions because they have a more realistic picture about the fair value to be paid and the difficulties of integration of the new entity, derived from cultural differences (Hennart & Park, 1993; Hennart *et al.*, 1996; Hennart, 2014; Beugelsdijk et al, 2018).

Furthermore, mergers and acquisitions problems associated with lack of knowledge of the acquired entity, still stands out more when internationalization is based in very different products. In this situation, ignorance is even greater on any entities that potentially may be acquired and companies choose new investment more easily, because of acquisitions benefits (Hennart and Park, 1993; Hennart, 2014; Beugelsdijk et al, 2018);

As for the **company's growth level**, it also conditions direct investment, because of the possibility of contracting managers is limited. So, when companies want to open large subsidiaries to respond quickly to demand, it generally choose to purchase a locally existing entity with workforce and managers (Caves & Mehra 1986; Hennart & Park, 1993; Hennart, 2014).

In the case of small subsidiaries, involving fewer resources, companies easily opt for internationalization through new investment (Caves & Mehra, 1986; Hennart & Park, 1993; Shahzad, 2019);

The **industry structure** also influences the form of direct investment abroad by entry barriers in the destination markets' industry (Caves & Mehra, 1986; Zejan, 1990; Hennart & Park, 1993; Meyer & Estrin, 1997; Shahzad, 2019).

When the target industries are highly concentrated, companies prefer internationalization through acquisitions to avoid a response from competitors, due to the resulting increase in the supply of entry of a new company, affecting the profitability of the various players (Caves & Mehra, 1986). However, the target markets of governments can be opposed to acquisitions as a way of protecting existing monopolies, forcing companies to carry out the internationalization through new investment (Hennart & Park, 1993; Hennart, 2014).

Companies wishing to internationalize to industries with a high maturity degree mostly choose acquisitions, in order to avoid responses from other competitors (Zejan, 1990; Hennart, 2014).

In parallel, in target industries where there are very high growth rates, it is common the option for internationalization through acquisitions, because installing a subsidiary involves some time, and that could lead to loss of market penetration opportunities (Caves & Mehra, 1986; Hennart, 2014).

On the other hand, in emerging economies is difficult to find interesting entities for possible acquisitions, and companies choose to do new investments (Caves, 1996; Hennart, 2014).

Finally, researchers who use **institutional theory** to explain reference behavior on direct investment abroad, argue that multinational companies' subsidiaries suffer both internal pressures (from the owner) and external (from the governments where they are installed) which often collide. That usually happens because global integration agreement with group policies is not always consistent with the interests of local economies (Prahalad & Doz, 1987; Rosenzweig & Singh, 1991; Kostova & Zaheer, 1999; Vlacic et al, 2019).

Thus, companies that aim to reach a similar group policy in all markets, prefer internationalization through new investment, because of practices integration and globally shared values (Harzing, 2002; Vlacic et al, 2019).

Companies that apply different management policies in the various markets in which they operate, give priority to acquisitions due the fact that the acquired entities are more familiar with the rules and interests of local governments (Harzing, 2002; Vlacic et al, 2019).

Several factors influence the decision on the form of direct investment abroad. Although there is no unanimity on behavior patterns, it is possible to conclude about what may condition the decision on foreign investment through acquisition or through new companies' formation. Namely, issues associated with the technologies used and the specific nature of the offer, the previous experience in the international markets approach to cultural differences among people, the company growth rate, the industry structure and corporate governance policy (more or less uniform procedures of business groups) (Hennart, 2014).

Internationalization and the Financial Performance of Companies

Considering the several risks which international trade exposes the companies to, several studies have been developed, which tend to show the connection between internationalization and the financial performance of the business context.

Regarding the impact of internationalization on company performance, there are some studies where there were found no link evidences between internationalization and performance (Buckley et al., 1977 and 1984; Kumar, 1984; Morck & Yeung, 1991; & Gerpott Jakopin, 2005) or where the correlation was negative (Brewer, 1981; Siddhartan & Lal, 1982; Michel & Shaked, 1986; Chang & Thomas, 1989; Collins, 1990; Dragun, 2003; Lu & Beamish, 2006). Nevertheless, most studies show performance increment by increasing the capacity of internationalization (Vernon, 1971; Errunza & Senbet, 1981; Kim & Lyn, 1987; Grant, 1987; Dunning, 1988; Grant et al., 1988 ; Geringer et al., 1989; Czinkota & Wongtada, 1997; Lu & Beamish, 2001; Hsu, 2005; Chiao et al., 2006; Elango, 2006; Kuivalainen & Sundqvist, 2006; Martinez, 2006; Bausch & Krist, 2007; Pangarkar, 2008; Hsu & Pereira, 2008; Zeng et al., 2009; Kiederich & Kraus, 2009; Fernandes et al, 2019; Furtado et al, 2019).

Still, most studies that have shown a positive relationship between internationalization and performance also observed that the success of this strategy clearly depends on the domain of unique skills in some specific areas. These areas are product innovation or production technologies, reputation, managers experience in internationalization, know-how transfer to subsidiaries, logistics efficiency in freight transport, cooperation with local authorities (most knowledge of the market, operators and inputs) or with national companies who shared resource distribution, marketing and facilities to the target market (Harrigan, 1988; Geringer et al., 1989; Czinkota & Wongtada, 1997; Wolff & Pett, 2000; Lu & Beamish, 2001; Chiao et al., 2006; Elango, 2006; Martinez, 2006; Chiao et al., 2008; Hsu & Pereira, 2008; Kafouros et al., 2008; Slangen & Hennart, 2008; Kiederich & Kraus, 2009; Fernandes et al, 2019; Furtado et al, 2019).

However, several authors noted that internationalization was beneficial to performance only to a certain level. Management complexity and associated organizational costs of a wide range of operations progressively decreases companies' profitability (Rumelt, 1974; Daniels & Bracker, 1989; Geringer et al., 1989; Sullivan, 1994; Hitt et al., 1994; Ramaswamy, 1995; Al-Obaidan & Scully, 1995; Belkaoui, 1998; Gomes & Ramaswamy, 1999; Boggs & Hsu, 2003; Martin & Papadopoulos, 2006; Kumar & Singh, 2008; Lavie & Miller, 2008; Cadogan et al., 2009).

In addition, there are also a considerable number of studies about the importance of the characteristics of the company's country of origin for financial success of the internationalization strategy. In fact, these studies show that countries with greater tradition of internationalization and with more resources available in the areas of technological knowledge and innovation, promote successful internationalization (Wan & Hoskisson, 2001 and 2003; Wan, 2005; Elango & Sethi, 2007; Hennart, 2014).

We can conclude that the internationalization strategy may also have an important role in business success, and should be properly framed with an overall strategy of mastered skills and competitive advantages created. Thus, it is important that the international order is carefully supported a detailed analysis of the attractiveness of the markets and the competitiveness in each country.

CONCLUSION

This chapter aimed to reflect on the main issues associated with companies' process of internationalization and the impact on its administration and financial performance.

For such purpose, in chapter one, it was debated the main theoretical frameworks on the internationalization strategy.

First we noted the opportunities that internationalization may place to business and the importance of innovation in this process, demonstrating that there are numerous studies that empirically evidence a close relationship between the ability of internationalization and the degree of innovation of the companies. This put into question the classical model of internationalization based on successive steps.

Then, it was conducted a reflection on the main types of risk associated with internationalization decision and international trade. In addition, it was found that one of the most critical risks is the foreign exchange risk that can be classified into three types, conversion, transaction, and economic.

In sequence, we studied some decision instruments, including portfolio management matrices (BCG, General Electric / McKinsey and ADL), which can be used for market selection and for the methods of approaching foreign markets.

Among the various methods of approach to foreign markets (transactions, projects and direct investments), it was documented that the concretization of direct investments abroad is the one with higher associated risk. Therefore, we focused on the main studied theories on this subject, demonstrating several factors that may influence the decision of investing abroad through companies' acquisition or creation.

Particularly, issues relating to the used technologies and the specific nature of the offer, the previous experience in international markets, the approach to cultural differences between people, the rate of growth of the company, the industry structure and the corporate governance policy.

Finally, several studies were analyzed regarding the internationalization and financial performance, and it was evident that, most part of the results of those investigations, show that there is a positive relationship between the degree of internationalization and the evolution of financial indicators of the companies.

REFERENCES

Al-Obaidan, A., & Scully, G. (1995). The theory and measurement of the net benefits of internationalization: The case of the international petroleum industry. *Applied Economics*, *27*(2), 231–239. doi:10.1080/00036849500000029

Alonso, J., & Donoso, V. (1998). *Competir en el exterior. La empresa Española y los mercados internacionales*. Madrid: Edições Icex.

Alves, M., Teixeira, N., & Rita, R. (2007). *A gestão do risco cambial, as fontes de risco e as técnicas de pagamento: um estudo de caso*. Paper presented at XXI Congresso Anual AEDEM, Universidad Rey Juan Carlos, Madrid, Spain.

Andersen, O. (1992). On the internationalization process of firms: A critical analysis. *Journal of International Business Studies*, *24*(2), 209–231. doi:10.1057/palgrave.jibs.8490230

Andersson, S., Evers, N., & Griot, C. (2013). Local and international networks in small firm internationalization: Cases from the Rhône–Alpes medical technology regional cluster. *Entrepreneurship and Regional Development*, *25*(9/10), 867–888. doi:10.1080/08985626.2013.847975

Archibugi, D., Ceccagnoli, M., & Palma, D. (1996). *Innovazione e internazionalizzazione nel modello competitivo italiano. Cuaderni di Politica Industriale, 8.*

Barkema, H., & Vermeulen, F. (1998). International expansion through start-up or acquisition: A learning perspective. *Academy of Management Journal*, *41*(1), 7–26.

Baum, M., Schwens, C., & Kabst, R. (2015). A latent class analysis of small firms' internationalization patterns. *Journal of World Business*, *50*(4), 754–768. doi:10.1016/j.jwb.2015.03.001

Bausch, A., & Krist, M. (2007). The effect of context related moderators on the internationalization performance relationship: Evidence from meta analysis. *Management International Review*, *47*(3), 319–347. doi:10.100711575-007-0019-z

Belkaoui, A. (1998). The effects of the degree of internationalization on firm performance. *International Business Review*, *7*(3), 315–322. doi:10.1016/S0969-5931(98)00013-4

Beugelsdijk, S., Kostova, T., Kunst, V. E., Spadafora, E., & van Essen, M. (2018). Cultural Distance and Firm Internationalization: A Meta-Analytical Review and Theoretical Implications. *Journal of Management*, *44*(1), 89–130. doi:10.1177/0149206317729027 PMID:30443095

Bilkey, W., & Tesar, G. (1977). The export behavior of smaller Wisconsin manufacturing firms. *Journal of International Business Studies, 9*(1), 93-98.

Boczko, A. (2005, Mar.). International Payment Risk. *Financial Management*, 35–37.

Boitani, A., & Ciciotti, E. (1992). *Innovazionne e competitivitá nell'industria italiana*. Bologna: Il Mulino.

Braunerhjelm, P. (1996). The relation between firm-specific intangibles and export. *Economics Letters, 53*(2), 213–219. doi:10.1016/S0165-1765(96)00898-1

Brewer, H. (1981). Investor benefits from corporate international diversification. *Journal of Financial and Quantitative Analysis*, *16*(1), 113–124. doi:10.2307/2330669

Brigs, P. (1998). *Principles of International Trade and Payments*. Oxford, UK: Blackwell Publishers.

Bruneel, J., & De Cock, R. (2016). Entry Mode Research and SMEs: A Review and Future Research Agenda. *Journal of Small Business Management*, *54*(S1), 135–167. doi:10.1111/jsbm.12291

Buckley, P., & Casson, M. (1998). Analyzing foreign market entry strategies: Extending the internalization approach. *Journal of International Business Studies*, *29*(3), 539–562. doi:10.1057/palgrave.jibs.8490006

Buckley, P., Dunning, J., & Pearce, R. (1977). The influence of firm size, industry, nationality and degree of multinationality in the growth and profitability of the world's largest firms. *Weltwirtschaftliches Archiv*, *114*(2), 243–257. doi:10.1007/BF02696473

Cadogan, J., Kuivalainen, O., & Sundqvist, S. (2009). Export market-oriented behaviour and export performance: Quadratic and moderating effects under differing degrees of market dynamism and internationalization. *Journal of International Marketing*, *17*(4), 71–89. doi:10.1509/jimk.17.4.71

Campbell, T., & Kracaw, W. (1993). *Financial risk management: fixed income and foreign exchange*. New York: HarperCollins Publishers.

Caves, R. (1996). *Multinational Enterprise and Economic Analysis* (2nd ed.). New York: Cambridge University Press.

Caves, R., & Mehra, S. (1986). Entry of foreign multinationals into U.S. manufacturing industries. In M. Porter (Ed.), *Competition in Global Industries* (pp. 449–481). Boston: Harvard Business School Press.

Cavusgil, T. (1980). On internationalization process of firms. *European Research*, *8*(November), 273–281.

Chang, Y., & Thomas, H. (1989). The impact of diversification strategy on risk-return performance. *Strategic Management Journal*, *10*(3), 271–284. doi:10.1002mj.4250100306

Chiao, Y., Yang, K., & Yu, J. (2006). Performance, internationalization and firm specific advantages of SME's in a newly industrialized economy. *Small Business Economics*, *26*(5), 475–492. doi:10.100711187-005-5604-6

Chiao, Y., Yu, J., Li, P., & Chen, Y. (2008). Subsidiary size, internationalization, product diversification and performance in an emerging market. *International Marketing Review*, *25*(6), 612–633. doi:10.1108/02651330810915556

Cho, K., & Padmanabhan, P. (1995). Acquisition versus new venture: The choice of foreign establishment mode by Japanese firms. *Journal of International Management*, *1*(3), 255–285.

Collins, J. (1990). A market performance comparison of US firms active in domestic, developed and developing countries. *Journal of International Business Studies*, *21*(2), 271–287. doi:10.1057/palgrave.jibs.8490335

Collis, D., & Montgomery, C. (1997). *Corporate Strategy – Resources and the Scope of the Firm*. McGraw-Hill.

Czinkota, M. (1982). *Export development strategies: US promotion policies*. New York: Praeger Publishers.

Czinkota, M., & Wongtada, N. (1997). The effect of export promotion on US trade performance: An analysis of industry internationalization. *The International Trade Journal*, *11*(1), 5–37. doi:10.1080/08853909708523871

Daniels, J., & Bracker, J. (1989). Profit performance: Do foreign operations make a difference? *Management International Review*, *29*(1), 46–56.

Daniels, J., & Radebaugh, L. (1986). *International Business: Environments and Operations* (4th ed.). Reading, MA: Addison-Wesley Longman, Inc.

Dhanani, A. (2004). The Management of Foreign Exchange-Rate Risk: A Case from the Manufacturing Industry. *Thunderbird International Business Review*, *46*(3), 317–338. doi:10.1002/tie.20011

Dosi, G., Pavitt, K., & Soete, L. (1990). *The economic of technical change and international trade*. New York: Harvester.

Dragun, D. (2003). *Challenging the rhetoric: internationalization, size and financial performance*. European Retail Digest.

Dunning, J. (1988). The eclectic paradigm of international production: A restatement and some possible extensions. *Journal of International Business Studies*, *19*(1), 1–32. doi:10.1057/palgrave.jibs.8490372

Eitman, D. K., Stonehill, A. I., & Moffett, M. H. (2005). *International Financial Management* (9th ed.; V. Pezerico, Trans.). New York: Bookman.

Elango, B. (2006). An empirical analysis of the internationalization performance relationship across emerging market firms. *Multinational Business Review*, *14*(1), 21–44. doi:10.1108/1525383X200600002

Elango, B., & Sethi, P. (2007). An exploration of the relationship between country of origin and the internationalization performance paradigm. *Management International Review*, *47*(3), 369–392. doi:10.100711575-007-0021-5

Errunza, V., & Senbet, L. (1981). The effect of international operations on the market value of the firm: Theory and evidence. *The Journal of Finance*, *36*(2), 401–417. doi:10.1111/j.1540-6261.1981.tb00455.x

Eusébio, R., & Rialp, A. (2002). *Innovación tecnológica y resultado exportador: un análisis empírico aplicado al sector têxtil-confección Español.* Working paper nº4, Departamento da Economia da Empresa, Universidade Autónoma de Barcelona.

Fagerberg, J. (1988). International competitiveness. *Economic Journal (London)*, *98*(June), 355–374. doi:10.2307/2233372

Fernandes, L., Pereira, C., Simões, D., & Moreira, A. (2019). Challenges of the Internationalization Strategy of a Technology-Based International New Venture. In N. Teixeira, T. Costa, & I. Lisboa (Eds.), *Handbook of Research on Entrepreneurship, Innovation and Internationalization* (pp. 419–438). Hershey, PA: IGI Global. doi:10.4018/978-1-5225-8479-7.ch018

Filipescu, D. (2006). *Innovation and internationalization. A focus on exporting firms. Paper presented in IV Jornadas Business Economics*. Autonomous University of Barcelona.

Filipescu, D., Rialp, A., & Rialp, J. (2009). Internationalisation and technological innovation: empirical evidence on their mutual relationship. Advances in International Marketing, 20, 125-154. doi:10.1108/S1474-7979(2009)0000020008

Freire, A. (1998). *Estratégia – Sucesso em Portugal*. Lisboa: Verbo.

Furtado, J., Pereira, A., Pereira, I., & Moreira, A. (2019). Does Theory fit real Life Situations? A Case Study on the Internationalization Process of a Technological Service-Based Firm. In N. Teixeira, T. Costa, & I. Lisboa (Eds.), *Handbook of Research on Entrepreneurship, Innovation and Internationalization* (pp. 419–438). Hershey, PA: IGI Global. doi:10.4018/978-1-5225-8479-7.ch016

Geringer, J., Beamish, P., & DaCosta, R. (1989). Diversification strategy and internationalization: Implications for MNE performance. *Strategic Management Journal*, *10*(2), 109–119. doi:10.1002mj.4250100202

Gerpott, T., & Jakopin, N. (2005). The degree of internationalization and the financial performance of European mobile network operators. *Telecommunications Policy*, *29*(8), 635–661. doi:10.1016/j.telpol.2005.06.003

Gomes, L., & Ramaswamy, K. (1999). An empirical examination of the formo f the relationship between multinationality and performance. *Journal of International Business Studies*, *30*(1), 173–188. doi:10.1057/palgrave.jibs.8490065

Grant, R. (1987). Multinationality and performance among British manufacturing companies. *Journal of International Studies*, *18*(1), 79–89.

Grant, R., Jammine, A., & Thomas, H. (1988). Diversity, diversification and profitability among British manufacturing companies, 1972-1984. *Academy of Management Journal*, *31*(4), 771–801.

Håkansson, H. (1982). *International Marketing and Purchasing of Industrial Goods: An Interaction Approach*. Chichester: Wiley.

Håkansson, H., & Johanson, J. (1984). Heterogeneity in industrial markets and its implications for marketing. In I. Hagg & F. Wiedersheim-Paul (Eds.), *Between market and hierarchy*. Uppsala: Department of Business Studies.

Harrigan, K. (1988). Joint ventures and competitive strategy. *Strategic Management Journal*, *9*(2), 141–158. doi:10.1002mj.4250090205

Harzing, A. (2002). Acquisitions versus greenfield investments: International strategy and management of entry modes. *Strategic Management Journal*, *23*(3), 211–227. doi:10.1002mj.218

Hennart, J. (1982). *A Theory of Multinational Enterprise*. Ann Arbor, MI: University of Michigan Press.

Hennart, J. (2000). Transaction costs theory and the multinational enterprise. In C. Pitelis & R. Sugden (Eds.), *The Nature of the Transnational Firm* (2nd ed.). London: Routledge.

Hennart, J., Larimo, J., & Chen, S. (1996). *Does National Origin Affect the Propensity of Foreign Investors to Enter the United States through Acquisitions?* Discussion paper no. 189. University of Vaasa.

Hennart, J., & Park, Y. (1993). Greenfield vs. acquisition: The strategy of Japanese investors in the United States. *Management Science*, *39*(9), 1054–1070. doi:10.1287/mnsc.39.9.1054

Hennart, J.-F. (2014). The Accidental Internationalists: A Theory of Born Globals. *Entrepreneurship Theory and Practice*, *38*(1), 117–135. doi:10.1111/etap.12076

Hirsch, S., & Bijaoui, I. (1985). R&D intensity and export performance: A micro view. *Weltwirtschaftliches Archiv*, *121*(2), 138–251. doi:10.1007/BF02705822

Hitt, M., Hoskinsson, R., & Ireland, R. (1994). A mid range theory of the interactive effects of international and product diversification on innovation and performance. *Journal of Management*, *20*(2), 297–327. doi:10.1177/014920639402000203

Hofstede, G. (2001). *Culture's Consequences: Comparing Values, Behaviors, Institutions, and Organizations Across Nations* (2nd ed.). Thousand Oaks, CA: Sage Publications.

Hsu, C. (2005). Internationalization and performance: The S curve hypothesis and product diversity effect. *Multinational Business Review*, *14*(2), 29–46. doi:10.1108/1525383X200600007

Hsu, C., & Boggs, D. (2003). Internationalization and performance: Traditional measures and their decomposition. *Multinational Business Review*, *11*(3), 23–49. doi:10.1108/1525383X200300015

Hsu, C., & Pereira, A. (2008). Internationalization and performance: The moderating effects of organizational learning. *Omega*, *36*(2), 188–205. doi:10.1016/j.omega.2006.06.004

Huber, G. (1991). Organizational learning: The contributing processes and literatures. *Organization Science*, *2*(special issue), 88–115. doi:10.1287/orsc.2.1.88

Ito, K., & Pucik, V. (1993). R&D spending, domestic competition and export performance of Japanese manufacturing firms. *Strategic Management Journal*, *14*(1), 61–75. doi:10.1002mj.4250140107

Johanson, J., & Vahlne, J. (1977). The internationalization process of the firm – a model of knowledge development and increasing foreign market commitments. *Journal of International Business Studies*, *8*(1), 23-32.

Johanson, J., & Vahlne, J. (2003). Business relationship learning and commitment in the internationalization process. *Journal of International Entrepreneurship*, *1*(1), 83–101. doi:10.1023/A:1023219207042

Johanson, J., & Wiedersheim-Paul, F. (1975). The internationalization of the firm – four Swedish cases. *Journal of Management Studies*, *12*(3), 305–322. doi:10.1111/j.1467-6486.1975.tb00514.x

Kafouros, M., Buckley, P., Sharp, J., & Wang, C. (2008). The role of internationalization in explaining innovation performance. *Technovation*, *28*(1-2), 63–74. doi:10.1016/j.technovation.2007.07.009

Kiederich, A., & Kraus, S. (2009). Investigating new technology-based firm internationalization: The impact on performance, the process and the antecedents. *International Journal of Business Research*, *9*(2), 1–12.

Kim, W., & Lyn, E. (1987). Reverse investments in US manufacturing industries. *Journal of International Business Studies*, *18*(2), 53–67. doi:10.1057/palgrave.jibs.8490406

Knight, G., & Cavusgil, T. (2004). Innovation, organizational capabilities and the born global firms. *Journal of International Business Studies*, *35*(2), 124–141. doi:10.1057/palgrave.jibs.8400071

Knight, G. A., & Liesch, P. W. (2016). Internationalization: From incremental to born global. *Journal of World Business*, *51*(1), 93–102. doi:10.1016/j.jwb.2015.08.011

Kostova, T., & Zaheer, S. (1999). Organizational legitimacy under conditions of complexity: The case of the multinational enterprise. *Academy of Management Review*, *24*(1), 64–81. doi:10.5465/amr.1999.1580441

Kuivalainen, O., & Sundqvist, S. (2006). Profitability of rapid internationalization: The relationship between internationalization intensity and firms export performance. *Journal of Euromarketing*, *16*(1-2), 59–69. doi:10.1300/J037v16n01_05

Kuivalainen, O., Sundqvist, S., Saarenketo, S., & McNaughton, R. (2012). Internationalization patterns of small and medium-sized enterprises. *International Marketing Review*, *29*(5), 448–465. doi:10.1108/02651331211260331

Kumar, M. (1984). *Growth, acquisition and investment: an analysis of the growth of industrial firms and their overseas activities*. Cambridge University Press.

Kumar, N., & Siddhartan, N. (1994). Technology, firm size and export behavior in developing countries: The case of Indian enterprises. *The Journal of Development Studies*, *32*(2), 288–309.

Kumar, V., & Singh, N. (2008). Internationalization and performance of Indian pharmaceutical firms. *International Business Review*, *50*(5), 321–330.

Lambin, J. (2000). *Marketing Estratégico*. Lisboa: MacGraw-Hill.

Larimo, J. (2003). Form of investment by Nordic firms in world markets. *Journal of Business Research*, *56*(10), 791–803. doi:10.1016/S0148-2963(02)00467-8

Lavie, D., & Miller, S. (2008). Alliance portfolio internationalization and firm performance. *Organization Science*, *19*(4), 623–646. doi:10.1287/orsc.1070.0341

Lefebvre, E., Lefebvre, L., & Bourgault, M. (1998). R&D related capabilities as determinants of export performance. *Small Business Economics*, *10*(4), 365–377. doi:10.1023/A:1007960431147

Lu, J., & Beamish, P. (2001). The internationalization and performance of SME's. *Strategic Management Journal*, *22*(6-7), 565–586. doi:10.1002mj.184

Lu, J., & Beamish, P. (2006). SME internationalization and performance: Growth vs profitability. *Journal of International Entrepreneurship*, *4*(1), 27–48. doi:10.100710843-006-8000-7

March, J. (1991). Exploration and exploitation in organizational learning. *Organization Science*, *2*(special issue), 71–87. doi:10.1287/orsc.2.1.71

Markowitz, H. (1952). Portfolio Selection. *The Journal of Finance*, *7*(1), 77–91.

Martin, O., & Papadopoulos, N. (2006). Internationalization and performance: Evidence from Spanish firms. *Journal of Euromarketing*, *16*(1-2), 87–103. doi:10.1300/J037v16n01_07

Martinez, J. (2006). Do industrial districts influence export performance and export intensity? Evidence for Spanish SME's internationalization process. *European Planning Studies*, *14*(6), 791–810. doi:10.1080/09654310500496115

Matos, J. (1992). *Finanças Internacionais*. Lisboa: Editorial Presença.

Meliciani, V., & Pianta, M. (1995). Specializzazione tecnologica e crescita economica nei paesi OCSE. *Rivista Internazionale di Scienze Economiche e Commerciali*, *42*(7-8), 565–588.

Melle, M., & Raymond, J. (2001). *Competitividad internacional de las pymes industriales Españolas*. Paper presented at XI Congreso de ACEDE, Zaragoza, Spain.

Merino, F., & Moreno, L. (1996). Actividad comercial en el exterior de las empresas manufactureras españolas y estrategias de diferenciación de producto. *Papeles de Economia Española*, *66*, 107–123.

Meyer, K., & Estrin, S. (1997). Privatisation acquisition and direct foreign investment: Who buys state-owned enterprises? MOCT-MOST. *Economic Policy in Transitional Economies*, *7*(1), 159–172.

Michel, A., & Shaked, I. (1986). Multinational corporations vs domestic corporation: Financial performance and characteristics. *Journal of International Business Studies*, *17*(3), 89–101. doi:10.1057/palgrave.jibs.8490435

Morck, R., & Yeung, B. (1991). Why investors value multinationality. *The Journal of Business*, *64*(20), 165–187. doi:10.1086/296532

Neves, J. (2012). *Análise e Relato Financeiro – Uma visão integrada de gestão (5th ed.)*. Lisboa: Texto Editora.

Nunes, J., & Cavique, L. (2001). *Plano de marketing – estratégia em ação*. Lisboa: Dom Quixote.

O'Farrell, P., Hitchens, D., & Moffat, L. (1993). The competitiveness of business services and regional development: Evidence from Scotland and the South East of England. *Urban Studies (Edinburgh, Scotland)*, *30*(10), 1629–1652. doi:10.1080/00420989320081631

Olejnik, E., & Swoboda, B. (2012). SMEs' internationalisation patterns: Descriptives, dynamics and determinants. *International Marketing Review*, *29*(5), 466–495. doi:10.1108/02651331211260340

Pangarkar, N. (2008). Internationalization and performance of SME's enterprises. *Journal of World Business*, *43*(4), 475–485. doi:10.1016/j.jwb.2007.11.009

Pennings, J., Barkema, H., & Douma, S. (1994). Organizational learning and diversification. *Academy of Management Journal, 37*, 608–640.

Porfírio, J. (2001). *Finanças Internacionais*. Lisboa: Universidade Aberta.

Prahalad, C., & Doz, Y. (1987). *The Multinational Mission*. New York: Free Press.

Ramaswamy, K. (1995). Multinationality, configuration and performance: A study of MNE's in the drug and pharmaceutical industry. *Journal of International Management, 1*(2), 231–253.

Ravenscraft, D., & Scherer, F. (1987). Mergers, Sell-Offs, and Economic Efficiency. Washington, DC: Brookings.

Reid, S. (1981). The decision maker and export entry and expansion. *Journal of International Business Studies, 12*(2), 101–112. doi:10.1057/palgrave.jibs.8490581

Ribau, C., Moreira, A. C., & Raposo, M. (2015). Internationalisation of the firm theories: A schematic synthesis. *International Journal of Business and Globalisation, 15*(4), 528–554. doi:10.1504/IJBG.2015.072535

Ribeiro, J. (2003). *Modelo de identificação de grupos estratégicos para a indústria metalomecânica de produção, por encomenda, de bens de equipamento* (Unpublished doctoral dissertation). ISCTE, Lisboa, Portugal.

Rodriguez, D. (1999). Relación entre innovación y exportaciones de las empresas: Un studio empírico. *Papeles de Economia Española, 81*, 167–180.

Rosenzweig, P., & Singh, J. (1991). Organizational environments and the multinational enterprise. *Academy of Management Review, 16*(2), 340–361. doi:10.5465/amr.1991.4278953

Ross, S., Westerfield, R., & Jaffe, J. (1995). *Administração financeira*. São Paulo: Editora Atlas.

Rulmet, R. (1974). Diversification strategy and profitability. *Strategic Management Journal, 3*(4), 359–370.

Rupeika, A. (2005). Nowadays Approach to Foreign Exchange Risk Management. *Management of Organizations: Systematic Research, 35*, 151–164.

Schueffel, P., Baldegger, R., & Amann, W. (2014). Behavioral patterns in born-again global firms. *Multinational Business Review, 22*(4), 418–441. doi:10.1108/MBR-06-2014-0029

Shahzad, F. (2019). An Analysis of Internationalization Theories and Behavior of Finnish Retail SME's in Russia. In N. Teixeira, T. Costa, & I. Lisboa (Eds.), *Handbook of Research on Entrepreneurship, Innovation and Internationalization* (pp. 419–438). Hershey, PA: IGI Global. doi:10.4018/978-1-5225-8479-7.ch019

Siddhartan, N., & Lall, S. (1982). Recent growth of the largest US multinationals. *Oxford Bulletin of Economics and Statistics, 44*(1), 1–13. doi:10.1111/j.1468-0084.1982.mp44001001.x

Simões, V. (1997). *Internacionalização das Empresas Portuguesas: Que papel para a cooperação?* Lisboa: Economia & Prospectiva.

Slangen, A., & Hennart, J. (2008). Do foreign greenfields outperform foreign acquisitions or vice versa? An institutional perspective. *Journal of Management Studies*, *45*(7), 1301–1328. doi:10.1111/j.1467-6486.2008.00794.x

Smithson, C. (1998). *Managing financial risk*. New York: McGraw-Hill.

Soete, L. (1987). The impact of technological innovation on international trade patterns: The evidence reconsidered. *Research Policy*, *16*(2-4), 101–130. doi:10.1016/0048-7333(87)90026-6

Sterlacchini, A. (1999). Do innovative activities matter to small firms in non-R&D intensive industries? An application to export performance. *Research Policy*, *28*(8), 819–832. doi:10.1016/S0048-7333(99)00023-2

Sullivan, D. (1994). Measuring the degree of internationalization of a firm. *Journal of International Business Studies*, *25*(2), 325–342. doi:10.1057/palgrave.jibs.8490203

Valenzuela, A. (2000). Modelo de capacidades para la internacionalización de la empresa exportadora Española. *Cuadernos de Economía y Dirección de la Empresa*, *5*, 91–109.

Vernon, R. (1971). *Sovereignty at Bay: the multinational spread of US enterprises*. New York: Basic Book.

Vlacic, B., González-Loureiro, M., & Eduardsen, J. (2019). The Internationalization of SME's: Strategic Choices Under a Cognitive Approach. In N. Teixeira, T. Costa, & I. Lisboa (Eds.), *Handbook of Research on Entrepreneurship, Innovation and Internationalization* (pp. 419–438). Hershey, PA: IGI Global. doi:10.4018/978-1-5225-8479-7.ch017

Wakelin, K. (1998). Innovation and export behaviour at the firm level. *Research Policy*, *26*(7-8), 829–841. doi:10.1016/S0048-7333(97)00051-6

Wan, W. (2005). Country resource environments, firm capabilities and corporate diversification strategies. *Journal of Management Studies*, *42*(1), 161–182. doi:10.1111/j.1467-6486.2005.00492.x

Wan, W., & Hoskinsson, R. (2001). Country resource environments, corporate diversification strategies and firm performance. Academy of Management Proceedings, 27-45. doi:10.5465/apbpp.2001.6133450

Wan, W., & Hoskinsson, R. (2003). Home country environments, corporate diversification strategies and firm performance. *Academy of Management Journal*, *46*(1), 27–45.

Williamson, O. (1975). *Markets and Hierarchies: Analysis and Antitrust Implications: A Study in the Economics of Internal Organization*. New York: The Free Press.

Willmore, L. (1992). Transnationals and foreign trade: Evidence from Brasil. *The Journal of Development Studies*, *28*(2), 314–335. doi:10.1080/00220389208422234

Wolff, J., & Pett, T. (2000). Internationalization of small firms: An examination of export competitive patterns, firm size and export performance. *Journal of Small Business Management*, *38*(2), 34–47.

Zander, I., McDougall-Covin, P., & Rose, E. (2015). Born globals and international business: Evolution of a field of research. *Journal of International Business Studies*, *46*(1), 27–35. doi:10.1057/jibs.2014.60

Zejan, M. (1990). New ventures or acquisitions: The choice of Swedish multinational enterprises. *The Journal of Industrial Economics*, *38*(3), 349–355. doi:10.2307/2098503

Zeng, S., Xie, X., & Wan, T. (2009). Relationships between business factors and performance in internationalization – an empirical study in China. *Management Decision*, *47*(2), 308–329. doi:10.1108/00251740910938939

Chapter 2
Risk Management Strategies in International Markets

ABSTRACT

On an operational level, companies with processes of internationalization are confronted with credit risks, interest rate risks, and foreign exchange risks in trade and financial operations that they perform daily within their operating cycle, transforming sometimes great opportunities into financial catastrophes. As these risks strongly affect companies' normal activities in international markets through higher financial costs arising from receipts that don't occur, from unfavorable exchange differences or negative evolution's in the interest rates, different strategies to manage these risks will next be addressed. At first, the payment techniques and sources of financing in international trade that allow to mitigate the credit risk and to protect the company's treasury will be presented. Then, the techniques to hedge exchange risk and interest rate risk will be studied to highlight how they could improve the international businesses' margins.

INTRODUCTION

As mentioned in the last chapter, the decision of internationalization, involves a series of risks, amongst other, the entry mode in foreign markets, company's competitiveness, markets context and the risks of the countries involved in the companies' business.

As such, the decision of internationalization must be the result of the strategic analysis, to assess both the economic and financial viability, to approach new markets, as well as the potential benefits to be obtained given the associated costs.

Also, and on an operational level, companies are confronted with credit risks, interest rate risks and foreign exchange risks, in commercial and financial operations that they perform daily within their operating cycle, transforming sometimes-great opportunities into financial catastrophes. As these risks strongly affect companies' normal activity in international markets through higher financial costs, arising from receipts that do not occur, from unfavorable exchange differences or negative evolutions in the interest rates, we will address next different strategies to manage those risks.

DOI: 10.4018/978-1-7998-2007-9.ch002

At first, the payment techniques and sources of financing in international trade, that allow to mitigate the credit risk and to protect the company's treasury, will be presented. Then, the techniques to hedge exchange risk and interest rate risk will be studied, to highlight how they could improve the international business' margin.

CREDIT RISK MANAGEMENT TECHNIQUES

Payment Techniques

These instruments, if properly used, can make international operations not only safer but also less expensive, thus contributing to their development and strengthening. (Porfirio, 2003, p. 121)

Gogoski (2012), mentions that, as far as economy proper functioning is concerned, payment systems are a requisite for every organization. It allows money to fulfill its function in goods or services' exchange.

Regarding modern monetary economies, money is its essence, and monetary procedures are what makes the payment system circulate. A well-conceived payments infrastructure contributes to the smooth functioning of the markets, and helps to eliminate friction in trade, by ensuring financial stability to those same markets (Gogoski, 2012).

Bolt and Chakravorti (2010), mention that payment systems choice must assess several factors, such as transaction features, stakeholders' location and cost structure.

Porfirio (2003), refers several payment systems applicable to foreign trade, that can be gathered into two broad categories, depending on documents' transaction:

- Direct settlement operations, in which documents are directly sent to the buyer. It comprises two means of payment: foreign cheque and money transference order.
- Documentary operations, in which document' transmission is carried out through financial institutions. They include two payment methods: documentary remittances and documentary credits.

The parties, considering operations' safety, may choose the procedures that best serve its interests.

On the assumption that acquisition is not instantly paid, and considering international trade good practices in this field, as well as the growing number of economic agents it involves, documentary credit has become the most widely used secure payment mean, on the best interest of the various international trade parties involved (Agência para o Investimento e Comércio Externo de Portugal [AICEP], 2010).

Bank draft is a payment document issued by a Bank, over an owned account or an account on another financial institution that, unlike documentary credit, has a significant timeline between the moment of the cash withdrawal on the importer's account and the cash deposit on the exporter´s account (Banco Português de Investimento [BPI], 2018).

Bank draft is a product designed for companies that develop an import/export activity, to be used in transactions abroad, with high confidence' suppliers or customers. The exporter sends the documents along with the respective goods, directly to the importer. The importer instructs the bank to issue a foreign cheque by withdrawing in favor of the exporter, over a bank account within the exporter's country. The issuing bank withdraws the total amount plus expenses from the account of origin and delivers the cheque to the beneficiary, for submission. The beneficiary then presents the cheque to a bank where it has an account, for trade or collection.

Foreign payment orders or international transferences are banking operations that involve credit institutions from different countries, permitting funds transmission among accounts, in any currency. These transferences are made at the initiative of a company or individual payer, that requests a financial institution to withdraw from its account and to deposit in another, that of the beneficiary, in a financial institution abroad. These operations' advantages are convenience, rapidity and safety. It is a way to send funds abroad which reduces both costs and administrative burden associated with payments' implementation and control (Instituto de Apoio às Pequenas e Médias Empresas e à Inovação [IAPMEI], 2011).

Consignment is the most elementary documentary operations' mean of payment, but is also the least secure to the exporter, since the importer may access the goods before fulfilling bank obligations (Banco Português de Investimento [BPI], 2018). It consists in an order given to the bank by the exporter, to send bills of exchange or other financial documents, for payment or acceptance by the importer. As a rule, these financial documents relate to goods' shipment. The exporter begins by subscribing the agreement and sending the acceptance to the importer. Then, the issuing bank directs the acceptance to the correspondent bank, instructing it about the acceptance and maturity payment. After acceptance, the correspondent bank sends it to the issuing bank, that sends it back to the exporter or, keeps it for collection at maturity (BPI, 2018).

As for documentary remittance "it is a more expounded process than consignment, which requires a higher involvement of financial institutions (…), thereby providing a safer form regarding international trade operations' liquidation (…)" (Porfírio, 2003, p. 102).

The fundamental difference with consignment has to do with the simple fact that, through the documentary remittance, the importer only gets effective possession of the shipped merchandise after payment or acceptance, which corresponds to the actual value of the operation in question. (Porfírio, 2003, p. 102)

Documentary remittance is a procedure in which the seller dispatches the goods, but not the transfer ownership' documents. Generally, those are sent through the seller's bank to a bank in the buyer's location, that will only hand out it under certain conditions. Eventually, it may happen the remittances' discount contained in the issued bill of exchange. If it is that so, the funds on the transaction value are advanced by the Bank on the exporter's behalf, maintaining the right of recourse, in case of buyer's default (IAPMEI, 2011).

The documentary credit, originally "credit letter" (L/C), defines the primary form of swapping messages among financial institutions via a letter, that comprises all terms inherent to a documentary credit. The technological information' evolution in general and, especially, the SWIFT entity' creation (Society for Worldwide Interbank Financial Telecommunication), changed this exchange, which began to be comprehensively carried out, through SWIFT system. As such, the "credit letter" designation fell in disuse in some way, assuming the name of documentary credit" (Porfirio, 2003.p.102).

The documentary credit is a payment' guarantee for goods/services' transaction, that consists in an bank order given by the importer. From that point on, that bank will assume, towards the exporter, the obligation to pay, accept or negotiate the goods/services' value, provided that the beneficiary submits all the required documents in accordance with all the terms defined in that commitment (letter of credit). It was designed to companies with international activity that need to perform collections or payments with meager degree of trust among parties (Montepio, 2014).

In a documentary credit with payment against documents presentation (spot), the importer requests the bank to open a credit, whose conditions are sent to a bank in the exporter's country, for its notification. The exporter reviews the terms of the credit letter (previously agreed with the importer) and ship the goods to designated destination in it. Within the stipulated term, the exporter delivers the required documentation to the notifier bank; If it confirms the documentary credit, and if the documentation submitted fully complies the stipulated conditions, the credit value is paid to the exporter, who sends the received documents to the issuing bank. Otherwise, the credit is only notified, and the exporter's Bank sends the documentation to the issuing bank, requesting immediate reimbursement. In either case, the issuing bank checks documents' compliance with the credit letter' terms, and, no divergence found, it reimburses the bank that sent the documentation, delivering it to the importer, against due payment. Upon possession of the documents, the importer collects the goods. In case of a documentary credit against acceptance or deferred payment (term), the process is identical, except for the payment, which is replaced by the acceptance of an effect or payment deferral to an agreed deadline (IAPMEI, 2011).

Besides payment techniques, it is important to mention the importance of companies' financing forms in international markets, since its proper use can be crucial to any company's expansion strategy, as it may allow cash flows' balancing.

Financing Forms

Financing in international markets includes some instruments, through which companies can finance themselves, such as bills of exchange, forfaiting and bank acceptances (Eiteman, Stonehill, & Moffet, 2002; Porfirio, 2003).

Eiteman et al. (2002), state that bills of exchange are a form of short-term financing. On one hand, when paying an invoice through a bill of exchange, a client may lengthen its payment period. On the other hand, the counterpart may cash it at the bank, receiving the money in advance.

Figure 1. The confirmed documentary credit

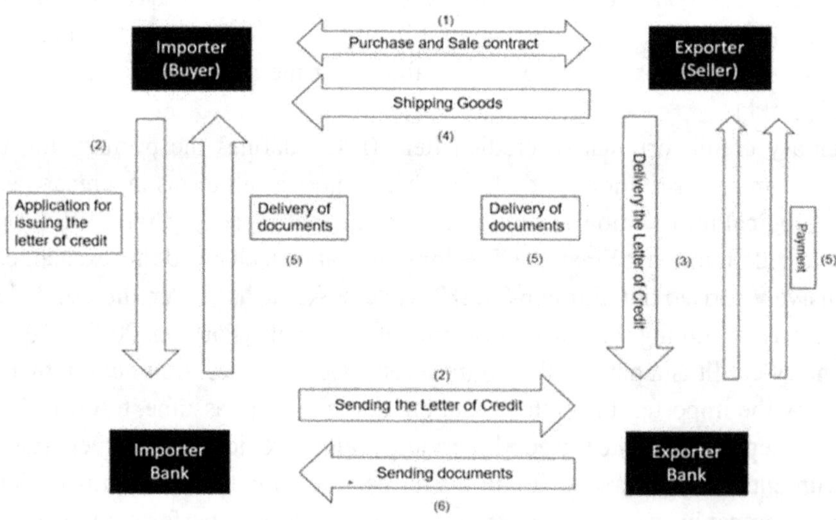

In foreign trade, though, bills of exchange are often bought by banks, in an operation called forfaiting. By doing this, the bill of exchange' seller can eliminate risk exposure (Banco Comercial Português [BCP], 2015).

Thus, forfait financing, or forfaiting, consists in a discount purchase of debt securities by the forfaitor bank, that the exporter cannot undo. Debt securities include letters, promissory notes and other debt recognition instruments. The forfaitor bank, by purchasing without recourse to the exporter, assumes all the international transaction' risk. Hence, these operations may often be subject to a foreign financial institution' guarantee, which, in this case, assumes its client's (the importer) risk. This solution allows the exporter to sell the bank the debt securities, in order to take immediate payment' advantage, rather than waiting for maturity, releasing the credit limits to the extent that the exporter exonerates himself from the operation. The exporter immediately receives the net amount (deducted from interest and expenses), while the importer pays within the agreed timeframe the imported goods, most of the times including, in that payment, bank interest and expenses.

The "(...) use of banks acceptances assumes the existence, in a company's portfolio, of some credit titles accepted by a particular importer of another country and guaranteed by a financial institution of the importer's country" (Porfírio, 2003, p.152). In other words, bank acceptance is used to designate a contract in form of a title, accepted by a bank, for a future payment. These titles will allow the exporter to discount money in the bank account, with recourse chances, at an agreed fee (BCP, 2015).

With regard to funding sources in international trade, companies may resort also to international factoring consisting of the credit transfer to a specialized company that will take care of the later charge the buyer by benefits, at a cost usually between 1% to 5% of the debt (Boczko, 2005).

Finally, can also be performed external financing in foreign currency in order to pay investments, anticipating a concern an export value to be received in the future, or to anticipate the purchase of foreign currency to finance imports at term (Porfírio, 2003). For example, in Portugal the financial institution

Figure 2. Forfaiting

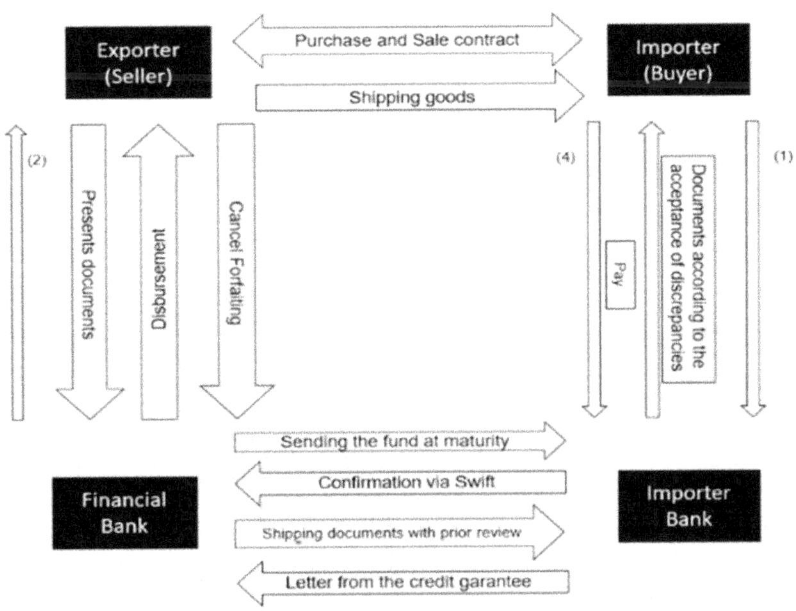

SOFID offers credits up to the amount of EUR 2.5 million for the internationalization of Portuguese companies in several emerging markets, with special emphasis on countries with Portuguese as official language. These operations may have maturities of up to 10 years with a grace period of 3 years (there is only the payment of interest).

In addition to the funding sources mentioned above and available in most financial systems of the major Western economies, there are some financial instruments made available by international institutions, specific to support the entry and consolidation of companies in emerging economies by encouraging their development. The World Bank and the International Bank for Reconstruction and Development (IBRD) offer attractive financing options, hedging instruments of currency risk, interest rate, credit and property. The African Development Bank (ADB) plans to combat poverty and underdevelopment of African countries by offering financing with special conditions, bank guarantees, technical assistance, monitoring and advising on the response to the impacts of financial and technical crisis currency hedging and interest rates. The European Investment Bank, through the Trust Fund EU-Africa Infrastructure provides interest subsidies on loans, the extended deadlines, technical assistance, including feasibility studies and capacity-insurance premiums for country risk coverage for the project baseline.

In conclusion, there are several payment practices and financing systems applicable to activities performed in international markets, which decrease foreign clients' credit risk. Current techniques to be used should consider risk knowledge about the debtors with whom the company does business with, and the activity's financial needs, namely liquidity and receiving deadlines.

CURRENCY RISK MANAGEMENT TECHNIQUES

Companies can use a variety of techniques to manage and hedge the exchange rate risk and interest rates. As per Alves, Teixeira e Rita (2007), the exchange rate risk management techniques can be distinguished between internal and external as shown in table 1.

Table 1. Risk hedging techniques

Internal Techniques	Existing Positions	- Advance payment - Technique of *Leading and Lagging* - Compensation
	Future Positions	- Choice of invoicing currency - Actions on sales prices - Actions on assets and liabilities - Diversification of currencies
External Techniques		- Fixing of Exchange rate (Forward) - Arbitration of futures positions - Matching - Advance payment of foreign currency - Prompt payment discounts - Currency Futures contracts - Currency Swaps - Currency Options contracts - Coverage by official entities

Source: Adapted from Alves, et al., 2007

Internal techniques represent lower costs, because they consist in hedging operations performed without resorting to financial markets. Conversely, external techniques are financial instruments' hedging procedures, where companies must resort to external entities, thus incurring in higher costs.

Internal techniques may be further divided into those which apply to existing positions and those applicable to future positions.

Internal Techniques of Exchange Risk Management

These hedging methods involve the adoption of strategic measures, regarding financing, commercial and investment policy. Typically, this kind of risk management leads to production relocation and financing in the same currency or another with a strong correlation with the billing currency of exports (Porfirio, 2003).

Regarding internal techniques on existing positions, previously referred to, companies may choose prepayment as leading technique as well as lagging and compensation.

Prepayment is the most interesting option from any seller' point of view, who gets paid in advance. The importer assumes the risk of not receiving the goods or receive it in conditions not previously agreed upon. Although the advanced payment is not a usual procedure, it can occur when there is a trust relationship between the companies involved. It is also used amongst companies of the same economic group and, also by importers that seek to avoid future currencies appreciations.

Leading and lagging strategies involves an amendment to payment and receipt dates as a precaution against possible devaluations or expected appreciations of foreign currencies. Abor (2005) defines lead strategy as receivables anticipation when the currencies involved are likely to suffer depreciation, and payments anticipation when a foreign currency appreciation is expected. Regarding lag strategy, it is a balanced combination of performance indicators which aims to delay the recovery of receivable amounts, when an appreciation of the associated currency is expected, as well as payments delay, when the currency is expected to suffer a depreciation. This method requires some leverage and strong trust relationships between business partners, being always easier between companies within an economic group than between practically unknown ones. This technique's accomplishment also depends on the interest rates. It may lead to short-term funding needs or no funds applications, if there is receipt delay, and, it may result in funds' applications, if receipts' anticipation takes place.

Another internal practice on existing positions is compensation. According to Abor (2005), it can be described as the attempt to reconcile payable and receivable amounts under the same currency, with the same partner, and on coinciding dates, to reduce exchange rate risk exposure and funds transferring costs. This sort of practice implies actual treasury management and is widely used in multinational companies.

Concerning future positions' internal techniques, the invoicing choice currency stands out. This technique depends on the company's client's negotiation capacity: if the company can invoice and receive in its domestic currency, it will eliminate currency risk. But, if the company is unable to invoice in its domestic currency, it is critical to be able to invoice and receive the money in currently or potentially strong currencies. When buying, the company must try to negotiate in currencies with a tendency to depreciate.

The euro circulation in most Europe' countries increased companies' stability, because there is usually less interest rate and foreign exchange risks, as well as less transaction and accounting risks in trade relations among companies based in countries that join a single function currency.

According to Peynot (1987), whenever the company envisages a possible foreign exchange loss, it can also take actions on the sales prices as a procedure, and consisting in increasing products or services' price in order to compensate currency depreciation when selling, or the attempt to negotiate a lower price when buying. Two parties may renegotiate prices considering appreciations or devaluations in the invoicing currency. When that happens, the foreign exchange loss of one of the parties compensates the gain on the other party, and vice-versa. Another possibility is indexing prices to the extent that exchange rates compensate one party's gains with the losses of the other.

The author also refers to practices on assets and liabilities, to avoid losses in the accounting records and conversion in the consolidation process, among subsidiaries abroad and the parent company. The purpose is to reduce asset values and boost liabilities in depreciable currencies and do the opposite in the presence of currencies that are expected to appreciate.

At last, currencies' diversification is another management risk technique, that consists in extending the range of conducted currencies, avoiding single currency dependence. Brealey and Myers (1998) referred to a strategic adoption in currencies' diversification as a way of ensuring attractive profitability, that simultaneously decreases risk. The diversification focus is a natural choice for currencies which have little or no correlation, i.e., differing behaviors.

Despite internal techniques being common and present lower costs for companies, usually it is not enough for effective foreign exchange risk management. Hence, sometimes, companies must choose external techniques.

External Techniques of Exchange Risk Management

As mentioned before, external performances consist on financial instruments hedging operations, which are negotiated with other entities.

Within the range of choice of existing Forward contracts, the Exchange Forwards and the Short-term Interest Rates Forwards (FRA - Forward Rate Agreement) are the most commonly derivatives used, that allow the hedging of two sorts of risk – exchange risk and interest rate risk.

Concerning Foreign Exchange Forwards, and using Mota and Custodio (2006) concept, they is a binding agreement amog two entities, for purchase (sale) of a currency A and sale (purchase) of a currency B, at a price (forward rate A/B) at a future date (forward maturity). In these dealings, there are two types of motivation, exchange risk hedging or speculation. In exchange risk hedging, the uncertainty about future value of a certain exchange rate is eliminated by fixing its Forward price, thereby limiting in advance a certain transaction' future value. As regards speculation, the contract can be performed in order to obtain a gain, which comes from a favorable difference between the contracted exchange rate through the Forward, and the maturity exchange rates.

For example, on a dollar import, if the euro depreciates, it means that the US dollar will become more expensive, resulting in a higher payment from the importer. In an export in dollars, if the euro appreciates, when the exporter exchange the dollars received from the customer will get less euros. The forward allows to set the exchange rate to be used now of the monetary flows of operations.

The arbitrage technique of forward positions allows the arbitration between two foreign currencies short or debtor position and long or creditor one. Take, for instance, a situation in which a company has a foreign currency X amount to receive within three months, and a foreign currency Y amount to pay in six months. It may purchase at a three months term the foreign currency Y using the previously explained forward contracts. The company may change the foreign currency X received at the end of

Figure 3. Logic of the forwards

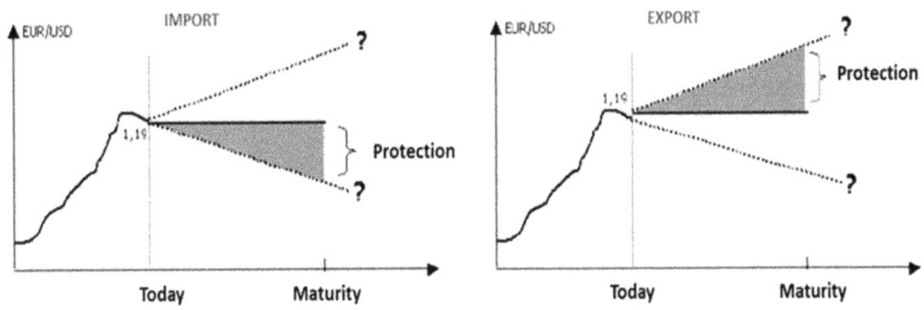

the three months' term, for the foreign currency Y which will need to pay within a 6 months' term and may even benefit from interest from a possible financial investment, until the payment is due. Then, the exchange rate risk would be removed. If the amount received on currency X exceeds currency Y amount, the surplus can be sold over time against the national currency. If the currency X amount is lower than that of Y, it will be necessary (for example) a forward buy of the currency Y on the payable amount. This method allows, in the present, to foresee future foreign currencies transactions, to eliminate or greatly reduce foreign exchange risk of more than one currency.

For example, suppose a company has the following situation:

- Have a three-month debt of 500.000 USD;
- Have a six month receipt of 600.000 GBP;
- The current exchange USD / GBP: 1,2.

The matching consists in compensating entries and withdrawals on a currency, if companies in different countries have coinciding debits and credits. According to Dhanani (2004), companies with more frequent import and export movements have greater ease in finding receivable and payable amounts in the same currency with similar timelines, eliminating currency risk.

The currencies advance, according to Abor (2005), allows an exporting company to receive in advance an amount expressed in a foreign currency, converting it to domestic currency, as soon as the goods

Figure 4. Logic of the Arbitrage technic

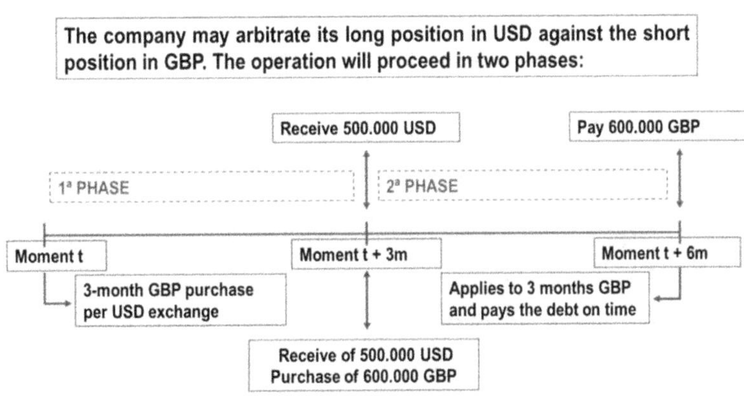

are dispatched and not only on payment date, eliminating much of the currency risk. This technique is based on a short-term financing request in the commercial operation' currency, the amount of which it will be returned, as soon as the client pays. Thus, the received foreign currency amount shall be sent to the bank, which will require interest payment. Interest amount will be the only value subject to currency risk if the sum receivable is inferior.

For example, one company made an export of 10.000 USD, which will be received in 3 months. The information of the markets is as follows:

- Spot Exchange USD / EUR 1,2;
- Future Spot Exchange Expectations USD / EUR 1,1.

Hypothesis 1: The company do not cover the risk

Exchange cost if the expectations are confirmed:

((11.000-12.000) / 12.000) * 100 = - 8,3%

Hypothesis 2: The company cover through Advance Currency

With an annual interest of 7% the company have a quarterly financial cost of 1,75% with the loan obtained. When the company receive the 10.000 USD from the customer will pay to the bank the same amount. In that way will not be subject to eventual USD devaluations

Prompt payment discounts consists in obtaining or granting a discount if goods or services' payment or receipt takes place at the business transaction's date, which makes it attractive to both parties, as it matches both economic and financial flows (Alves et al., 2006). It avoids uncertainty, since the foreign exchange risk occurs between the negotiation date and that of the operations' liquidation.

For example, one company did a import of 100.000 USD to be paid within 6 months, with these conditions:

- 6-month financing cost: 12%
- Spot Exchange USD / EUR: 1,1
- Forward Currency for 6 months USD / EUR: 1,2

At the very least, the discount of prompt payment to be negotiated, must guarantee a cost identical to what would be obtained if the payment deadlines were respected.

- Amount to be paid at the end of the period with forward rate: 100.000 USD * 1,2 EUR = 120.000 EUR
- Discount calculation:
- 100.000 USD * 1,1 EUR * (1 - d) * 1,12 = 120.000 EUR;
- (110.000-110.000 d) * 1,12 = 120.000;
- d = 0,02597 → 2.597% → discount value from which the company will be interested to make the payment in advance.

As Pinho et al. (2011) mentioned, derivatives are primarily used for risk hedging, but can be also used for speculative reasons. Given risks multiplicity that investors mean to transfer, derivatives contracts have multiplied, and there are many to choose from, highlighting, by its greater use, the Futures contracts, Swaps, and Options.

Futures are forward contracts executed in regulated markets (stock exchanges) which enforce a set of rules and functioning mechanisms, that set them apart from the Forwards referred earlier (Mota & Custodio, 2006).

In a Swap, the parties agree to exchange, on a regular basis, until the contract expiration date, flows (fixed interest rate vs. variable interest rate, variation of a stock index vs. the variation of another stock index, et cetera) which are calculated from a theoretical amount (Mota & Custodio, 2006).

Regarding options, the purchase (sell) options provide the buyer, upon premium payment to the seller, the right to buy (sell) a underlying asset given amount, at an initially established price (exercise price) at or up to determined future date - the option expiration (Mota & Custodio, 2006).

According to Pinho et al. (2011), the hedging of risk through derivatives contracts reduces both operational and financial risks, in case of underlying asset prices' adverse movements. So, for the investor to hedge the risk, it is necessary to acquire, in the derivatives market, an equal position, but of opposite direction to that of the holding asset. That is, the hedging strategy is achieved using a position-taking in derivatives contracts, contrary to earlier positions taken on the spot market. This is possible because asset prices of the spot market and the forward market derivatives are correlated.

According to Mota and Custodio (2006), a Future is a contract between two entities for the purchase/sale of a given asset at a future known date. What differentiates Future and Forward is that the first is handled in an organized market (stock exchange), with a set of rules and procedures.

At this contract expiration date, two distinct situations may occur: the physical or the financial liquidation of the contract. The physical liquidation may happen when the underlying asset is materializable. The Future's seller delivers the related assets to the active contract, while the buyer pays the corresponding amount, which is based on the last day's closing quotation. In case of financial settlement, after the last day of transactions, the balance of the margin account is made both available to buyer and seller (Mota & Custodio, 2006).

Despite these conditions, the Future buyer or seller can liquidate its contractual position before the due date. To do so, they must perform a symmetrical transaction to that performed at the beginning of the contract and may then withdraw the margin account's balance (Mota & Custodio, 2006).

When comparing Futures and Forwards, the former presents distinctive characteristics that aim greater liquidity and credit risk minimization. This happens because Futures are more standardized, enforcing a reduced number of due dates, a fixed minimum amount which may only by multiplied. This standardization aims to increase market liquidity, avoiding capital dispersal by a wide range of amounts and maturities, allowing prices optimization. Finally, there is a lower credit risk, because there are daily clearance mechanisms of results and margin, as well as, the business's counterpart presence in the stock exchange (Mota & Custodio, 2006).

With regard to Currency Futures' contracts (or exchange rates), they are an agreement in which the contracting parties compromise to hand over (one party) and to receive (the other party) a certain given currency amount, at a future date, at a price (exchange rate) agreed upon in the present, and all the clauses of that agreement, other than price, are predefined in a standardized way by the markets' managing entity in which this agreement is concluded (Ferreira, 2008a).

As per Eitman et al. (2005), Futures are contracts that, at the beginning of the 19th century, allowed to guarantee prices of agricultural products and some raw materials for a future date, mitigating the impact of markets price fluctuations. At the beginning of the 70's, due to variable foreign exchange quotations development, by fixed exchange rates abandonment, fluctuations required currency derivatives introduction for risk managing (risk on the price of products and raw materials). The most relevant currencies are US dollar, Euro, Japanese yen, Sterling Pound, Canadian dollar, Australian dollar, Swiss franc and Brazil's real. The weight of foreign exchange futures in total futures contracts has been negligible, despites the growing trend. The American market is the most representative, with 90% of the total foreign exchange futures. A foreign exchange futures contract is traded only in organized markets and specifies the price at which a currency can be bought or sold at a future date. The contracts are adjusted every day at its market value, and stakeholders may, at any time, close the positions. The International Money Market (IMM), from Chicago, was the pioneer market and continues to be one of the main markets, along with the Chicago Board of Trade (CBT), the New York Futures Exchange, the London International Financial Futures Exchange (LIFFE), the Singapore Mercantile Exchange (SIMEX), the Marché à Terme d' Instruments Pomegranate (MATIF), from France and the Tokyo Stock Exchange.

For example, one company has an import of 300.000 USD to settle on 20 December, and decided to make the cover with a future contract with the following characteristics:

- Description - Future EUR FX;
- Trading unit - 125.000 USD;
- Tick (minimum variation considered in the contract) – 0,0001;
- Tick value (each 0,0001 variation value) - 12,5 USD;
- Start margin - 5.400 USD.

The company expects the Euro to fall against the Dollar, so it decides to sell 2 contracts at 1,3325 per protect itself from the obligation it will have to meet on 22 December.

On November 24, it takes the position in the market shown in Table 2.

Thus, on November 24, the company guarantees the sale of the euros (USD purchase) at the exchange rate on that date, which means that it can make the purchase on December 22 of 333.125 USD for a counter value of 250.000 EUR.

On the date of settlement of the invoice, 22 December, the EUR/USD exchange rate on the spot market is 1,3000 and the futures contracts sold on November 24 are currently at 1,2988. With coverage, the financial effort will be lower.

Differentials in futures:

1,3325 – 1,2988 = 0,0337

Table 2. Future contracts conditions on November, 24

Day	Exchange rates Bid / Offer	Number of contracts	Value of the operation
November, 24	1,3325 / 1,3327	2	(2 x 125.000€) x 1,3325 = 333.125 USD

Conclusion

As each tick of 0,0001 has an associated value of 12,5 USD, the company will have to receive the tick value of 0,0337 (0,0337 x 12,5 / 0,0001) → 4.212,5 USD, which worth 3.240 EUR on the spot market (4.212,5 USD / 1,3000).

So, the decision about fixing the Euro / Dollar exchange rate of 250.000 euros on 24 November, avoid the loss of 3.240 euros.

According to Ehrhardt and Brigham (2011), a Swap is quite what its name suggests – a two parties' agreement to exchange (swap) something, usually obligations, to make certain payments. Most Swaps involve the payment of interests or currencies, but almost everything can be the goal of a swap.

Swaps can reduce risk by allowing each company to associate its interest payments variability of with the one of its cash-flows. However, there are situations in which Swaps can reduce both the risk and the effective cost of debt (Ehrhardt & Brigham, 2011).

As Pinho et al. (2011) stated, companies can be exposed to certain markets' risk in different currencies or operations, with fixed or variable interest rate, which are not the most appropriate to countries' economic and financial development, to reduce or eliminate those risk exposures. By allowing exposures exchanges, swaps allow an equilibrium improvement in investment portfolios or financing management. For example, interest payments exchange through swaps allows risk separation associated with financing inherent commitments, such as interest rate and foreign exchange risk.

According to Silva, Quadri, Mota and Pereira (2013), swap currency is an agreement in which both parties shall exchange among themselves a currency by another, over an agreed period, in order to ensure currency risk hedging. The negotiated exchange rate for the Swap transaction will tend to reflect the benchmark interest rate of both money markets. In other words, different markets exchange and interest rates, will tend to match up swap operations (interest rates parity theory), promoting a balance among different markets rates. Currency Swap allows cheap dynamic management in obtaining foreign currency financial resources, diversifying funding sources and reducing financial costs.

For example, 2 companies have the financing terms in Euros and British Pounds shown in Table 3.

The amount of financing is 1.000.000 GBP, the maturity of the operation is 4 years and the exchange rate GBP / EUR is 1,32.

The swap operation will be performed as follows:

- **Initial Financing:**
- The English company has an initial financing in EUR;
- The Portuguese company has an initial financing in GBP.
- **Amount of initial financing:**
- English company loan: 1.320.000 EUR (has a lower cost in this currency);
- Portuguese company loan: 1.000.000 GBP (has a lower cost in this currency).

Table 3. Interest rates of both companies

Divisa	Portuguese company (POR)	English company (ING)
GBP	6%	7%
EUR	9%	8%

- **Final Objectives:**
- The English company intends a final financing in GBP;
- The Portuguese company intends a final financing in EUR.

In resume, both companies have a saving of 1% of interests.

Figure 5. Initial cash-flows of the Swap - Year 0 - Initial Capital Exchange

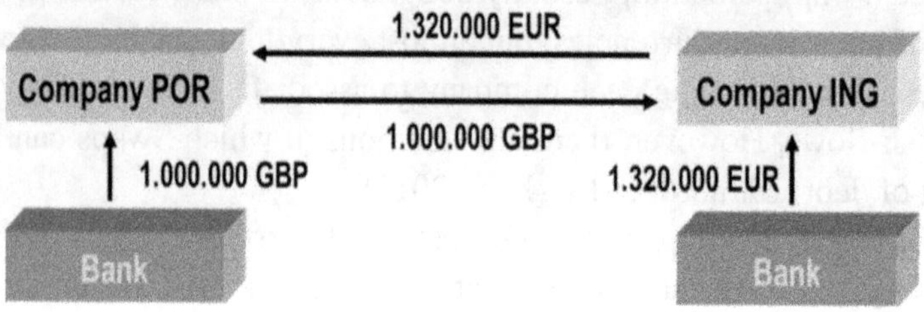

Figure 6. Periodic cash-flows of the Swap - Years 1, 2, 3, 4 - Reciprocal Payment of Interest

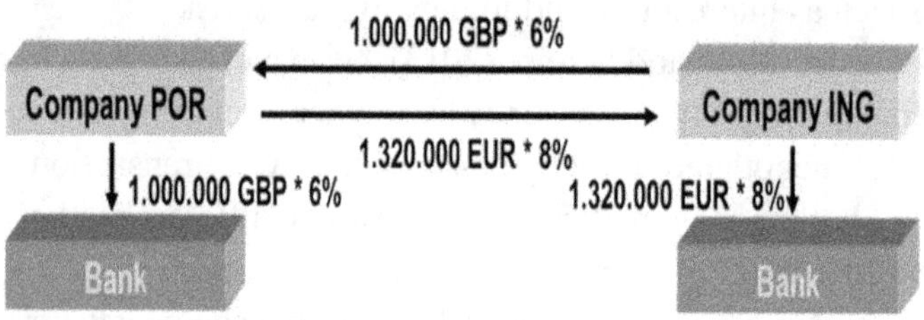

Figure 7. Final cash-flows of the Swap - Year 4 - Final Swap of Capital

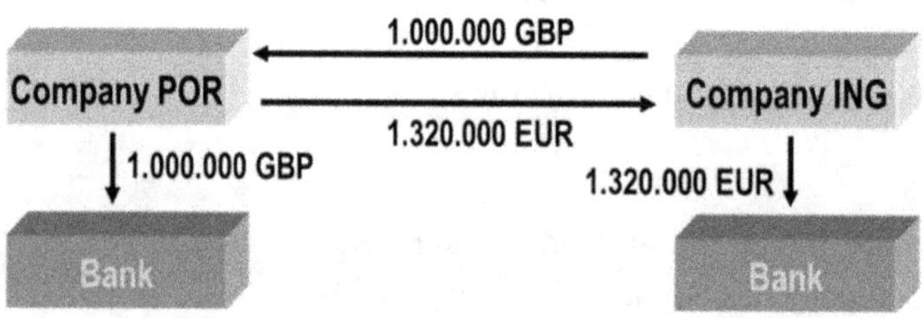

Table 4. Resume of the Swap operation

Items	Portuguese company	English company
Loan	6%	8%
SWAP	Port. pay to Ing.: 8%	Ing. Pay to Port.: 6%
Cost with SWAP	8%	6%
Cost without SWAP	9%	7%
Saving with SWAP	**1%**	**1%**

Currency Options contracts, according to Black and Scholes (1973), allow the negotiation between two parties (buyer and seller) to establish an exchange rate and a financial transaction date.

Eitman et al. (2005), considered them a kind of insurance contract in which the premium payment was made at purchase time. Nonetheless, it differs from an insurance contract in two aspects: those who acquire it are not obliged to exercise it, although they keep the right to do so; in the insurance contract one party wins, while, in an option, it is possible for both parties to win or lose. While the buyer may exercise the right (to buy or sell), the seller cannot, having to stand by the former's decision, getting, in return, an amount equal to the market price of the option and what is known as option prize. If the option' buyer decides to use the right to buy or sell, it is said that he exercised the option and used the exercise price.

Options present several advantages that can be summarized in the fact that it offers complete coverage, in case of market unfavorable development, letting potential gains, in the event of underlying asset favorable development. Finally, it offers total flexibility, which allows the buyer to decide about the option's exercise, considering share price evolution anticipation, volatility and other relevant decision variables (Eitman et al., 2005).

According to Dhanani (2004), these contracts are divided into American options (where the option holder can exercise it at any time, up to the contract maturity date) and European options (where option's holder may exercise it at contract maturity). American options present a higher seller risk, as it may represent significant losses when the buyer has the option of choosing the moment to boost winnings. In this case, the premium to be paid to the seller must be higher.

An option, according to Matos (1992) is called "at the money" when its price equals that of the underlying asset (immediate exercise of the option does not originate losses or gains). In this case, buyer's loss is the premium paid to the seller, and it is indifferent to opt for the fulfillment of the contract or not, given that the exercise price equals the market price on that date (spot price). Whenever exercise price is lower than spot price in a Call Option, or the opposite in a Put Option, the option is called "in the money", i.e., the exercise of the option immediately originates a benefit.

In the reverse situation, namely, when the exercise price of the underlying asset is higher than the market price (the immediate exercise of the option would lead to a loss) the option is called "out of the money", and it should not be drilled. It will be advantageous to negotiate it at the spot market. One can say that a buyer's loss (long position) is limited to the premium paid, and that earnings are unlimited and as big as higher the evolution towards "in-the-money". About the seller (short position), the situation is completely opposite, i.e., gains are limited to received premium, losses are unlimited and as higher as the movement towards "in the money". Therefore, this type of instrument represents a low risk to the buyer, since losses are limited and known since the beginning. On the other hand, the seller's risk is enormous, because it has limited gains to the initially received premium, but it can have unlimited losses, this being the reason why this type of approach (seller of options contracts) is typically used by speculators and not by managers.

For example, one exporter wants to guarantee a maximum exchange rate of EUR / USD for the sale of 1.000.000 USD, in 6 months. In this way, he buys a CALL (because he wants to guarantee the purchase of euros) EUR / USD at 1,20 and pays a premium of 12.500 EUR (1,5% EUR).

At the expiration of the contract, in 6 months, 2 scenarios are possible:

- Exchange EUR / USD> 1,20, customer exercises the option and sells the dollars to 1,20.
- Currency EUR / USD <1,20, does not exercise the option and sells the dollars at the market price.

Figure 8. Logic of options

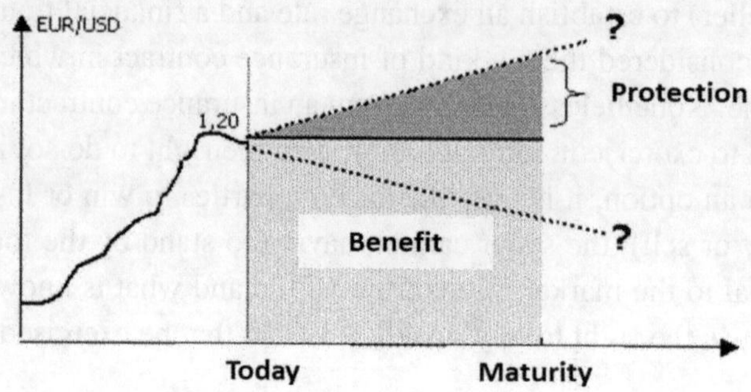

In relation to the traditional options, in the banking market there are available financial instruments with some specific features, such as forward plus which is a derivative of the options contract but which, through a previously established limit, allows to take advantage of favorable evolutions of the currency market. It completely eliminates the risk associated with unfavorable movements of the exchange rate, maintaining a large part of the benefit of a favorable movement. The cylinder is also a derivative of the options but with the particularity of giving the customer a minimum and maximum exchange rate at a future date. It thus protects against unfavorable exchange rate fluctuations and, at the same time, guarantees the benefit of a favorable exchange rate movement.

For example, an importer wants to guarantee a minimum exchange rate in the EUR / USD for the purchase of 1.000.000 USD in 6 months without paying any premium. So, he negotiates a Cylinder contract with these conditions:

- Importer buys EUR / USD PUT at 1,18 (he buys the right to sell euros at 1,18 USD – the maximum price to buy the USD);
- Importer sells a EUR / USD CALL at 1,24 (he has the obligation to sell euros at 1,24 USD – the minimum price to buy the USD);

At the expiration of the contract, in 6 months, 3 scenarios are possible:

- EUR / USD exchange <1,18, importer exercises option and buys USD 1,18
- EUR / USD exchange rate> 1,18 and <1,24, no options are exercised and the importer buys the dollars at the market price;
- Exchange EUR / USD> 1,24, the buyer of CALL (Bank) exercises the option and the importer buys the dollars at 1,24.

In other example, the importer wants to guarantee a minimum exchange in EUR / USD for the purchase of 1.000.000 USD in 6 months without paying any premium. This time, he negotiates a forward plus contract with these conditions:

- The importer buys a Put EUR / USD at 1,19;
- The importer sells a EUR / USD CALL at 1,19 with a barrier at 1,28.

Figure 9. Logic of Cylinder contract

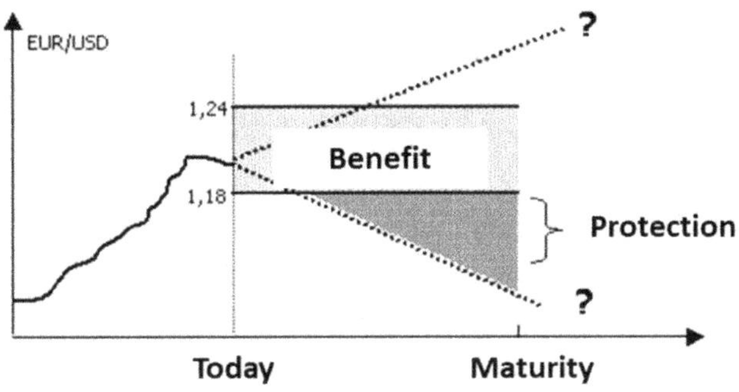

At the expiration of the contract, in 6 months, 3 scenarios are possible:

- EUR / USD exchange <1,19, the importer exercises the option and buys the USD 1,19 (he buys the right to sell euros at 1,19 USD – the maximum price to buy the USD);
- EUR / USD exchange rate> 1,19 and the 1,28 exchange rate was never reached during the life of the contract, no option is exercised and the importer buys the dollars at the market price, having a greater margin of benefit compared to the situation foreseen in the cylinder contract.;
- EUR / USD exchange rate > 1,19 and the 1,28 exchange rate was reached over the life of the contract, the Bank exercises the option and the importer purchases the USD 1,19, losing the benefit of the positive evolution of the currency.

Finally, companies can also opt to insurance through official entities, like COSEC and COFACE, for credit risk hedging and management, collateral and investment in commercial or political high-risk countries. Take an exports situation. The exporting company can negotiate insurance that covers 90% of the guaranteed credit, in exchange for insurance premium payment (AICEP, 2015).

Next, we will address the interest rate risk management techniques.

Figure 10. Logic of Forward Plus

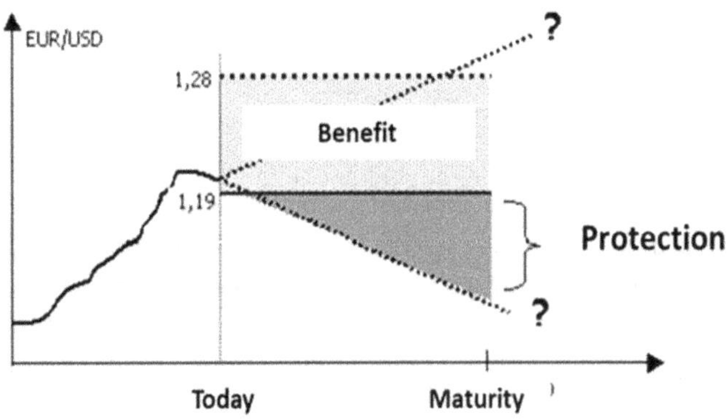

Interest Rate Risk Management Techniques

Concerning interest rate risk management procedures, one of the most used is the long-term interest rates negotiation (fixed or variable). Some contracts that set forward rates do not imply financing or investment, just difference between the interest rate settlement (guaranteed). In this perspective, these are very useful instruments to eliminate the risk.

According to Mota and Custodio (2006) interest rate spinoffs represent a replica of a traditional markets set of operations, that is, they generate a set of identical financial flows to the set of operations on the spot markets that they are replicating, combining them into a single instrument. Within derivative products, one can highlight four groups, which aim to hedge interest rates risk: the Forwards (FRA contracts), Futures, Swaps, and Options.

FRA (Forward Rate Agreement) represents a contract between buyer and seller, of forward fixation, at a certain interest rate.

Like the foreign exchange forwards, this instrument can be used in interest rate risk hedging, concerning the investment income, or the financing cost, at a future date, set in the present. Another motivation that may be present in the FRA use is speculation, and in this case, the claim is to obtain a return with the future variation of a given interest rate. This is possible since FRA purchase does not involve performing any application nor financing (Mota & Custodio, 2006).

In their maturity, the financial settlement is obtained through FRA result's calculation of, in which the party with an unfavorable result, pays the due amount to the other.

The use of the FRA as a mean to establish future interest rate, allows participants to eliminate the uncertainty concerning its future variations. Given this, the investor's position in FRA depends on the type of operation to be developed. If it is financing, the position to assume must be the one of the buyers, setting the rate of future funding. If it is investment, it would be the seller's position, fixing the interest rate that will determine the application's profitability.

For example, a company that intends to protect against rising interest rates (will take the position of money buyer in the contract) and Bank B (seller) agreed on March 16 in an FRA JUN + 6 in the amount of 2.500.000 euros, at the rate of 10%.

Two days before the contract expired (by hypothesis, June 18), the rate in force for 6-month operations was 13%.

When negotiating a FRA JUN + 6, the company and the bank agreed on a 6-month potential loan rate from 18 June (3rd Wednesday) to 18 December. However, this transaction does not necessarily have to be performed and in this case, there is the financial liquidation of the contract FRA, and is calculated the interest differential between the current market rate and the FRA negotiated rate.

$$\text{Result of the FRA} = \frac{(0.13-0.10)\times 2{,}500.00\times 183/365 = {}^{-}35{,}301.83}{1+0.13\times 183/365}$$

The interest differential is calculated on the basis of the following assumptions: the underlying transaction (bank loan) will be carried out at an interest rate of 10% (rate negotiated at FRA contract) for 6 months; as such, there is a saving of 3% interest over 183 days on a capital of 2.500.000 EUR, compared to the rate that is in force on the market at the beginning of that contract - June; however, the interest differential determined up to December should be actualized at the beginning of the agreement (June),

Figure 11. Logic of FRA contract

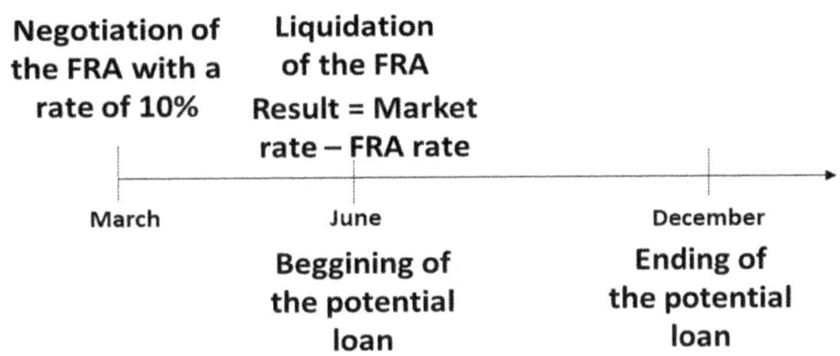

since the payment of this amount is made at the time of the FRA contract (June), which coincides with the possible start of the second operation that may potentially occur (Bank loan).

Therefore, on June 19, the company would receive from Bank the amount of 35.301,83€.

However, if the company wishes to carry out the loan operation, whatever the six-month rate in force in June, it will have guaranteed that the cost of such financing will be 10%, i.e. the rate negotiated in the FRA contract.

Let's simulate two alternative scenarios for the settlement rate that will be effective on June 16: - Scenario A: 13%; - Scenario B: 8%.

Scenario A: TL = 13% - Company (Buyer in FRA contract) Wins

The result of the FRA is equal to 35.301,83 €, being received by the company. As a positive result, the company in June, will only need to contract a financing (with value date of June 18) of:

2.500.000 - 35.301,83 = 2.464.698,17 €

The amount of the repayment of this financing (capital + interest) will be:

2.464.698,17 x (1 + 0,13 x 183/365) = 2.625.342,47€

Which is strictly equal to:

2.500.000 x (1 + 0,1 x 183/365) = 2.625.342,47€

Scenario B: TL = 8% - Bank (Seller in FRA contract) Wins

$$R = \frac{(0.8 - 0.10) \times 2{,}500.000 \times 183/365 = -24{,}101.78}{1 + 0.08 \times 183/365}$$

The amount of the result of the financing to be contracted will be:

2.524.101,78 x (1 + 0,08 x 183/365) = 2.625.342,47€

The final cost of the operation is exactly the same as scenario A (10%).

So, whatever will be the rate in the market at the liquidation date of the FRA contract, the company will always guarantee the FRA rate, 10% on the eventual bank loan to be made.

Interest Rate Swap is an agreement in which the financial institution and the company agree to exchange periodic interest payments, both being financial flows indexed to different interest rates, one at a fixed rate and the other at a variable rate, during the contract (BCP, 2015). The two financial flows of interest payments are in the same currency and calculated on a given nominal amount, which can entirely or partially cover the funding amount (BCP, 2015).

For example, through variable interest rate swap for a fixed one, on each interest payment dates, the following exchange will occur (BCP, 2015):

- The financial institution delivers the company the interest amount, based on the variable rate that was fixed for that interest period, covering the loan operation financial costs that originated the Swap.
- The company delivers to the financial institution the amount of interest calculated on the fixed rate agreed in the Swap, which allows it to become immune to undesirable increases in variable interest rates.

Also, Swap is a product of interest rate hedging, structured according to company's needs, and whose main characteristic is to transform responsibilities, regarding interest rate - fixed to variable - of any given financing. If the company has fixed rate financing, the financial institution can also structure the hedge operation with a fixed interest rate Swap to a variable one (BCP, 2015).

For example, two companies will contract a financing of 500.000 EUR for a term of three years. The final objectives of each entity are as follows:

- Company X intends to finance itself at a variable rate;
- Company Y intends to finance itself at fixed rate.

The financing conditions of each entity are described in Table 5.

They will start the Swap with the opposite finance operation where they have competitive advantage (company X has a better cost on fixed rate and company Y on variable rate). After that they will change the loans between them.

In that way, both companies will have a saving on the interest of the loans, compared to the initial conditions at the finance market.

Concerning contracts options, they are constituted by the contracting of interest rate options, Cap, Floor or a combination of both, known as Collar (BPC, 2015).

Table 5. Interest rates of both companies

Interest rate	Company X	Company Y
Fixed rate	16%	17%
Variable rate	Euribor + 2,5%	Euribor + 2%

Table 9: Resume of the Swap operation

Items	Company X	Company Y
Loan	16%	E + 2%
SWAP	X pay to Y: E + 2%	Y pay to X: 16%
Cost with SWAP	E + 2%	16%
Cost without SWAP	E + 2,5%	17%
Saving with SWAP	**0,5%**	**1%**

Cap is an interest rate risk hedging financial instrument, indexed to a variable interest rate, which allows the buyer, upon payment of a premium to ensure the upper limit of the index fluctuation, fixing maximum cost financing. Simultaneously, Cap buyer company may benefit from reductions that will occur in the reference rate, below the rate guaranteed by the Cap, throughout the operation (BPC, 2015).

For example, a company will contract a financing and want to guarantee a maximum interest rate for the term of the financing. Hire a Cap under the following conditions:

- Amount: 2.000.000 EUR;
- Term: 3 Years;
- Cap Level: 3,5%;
- Periodicity of the cash-flow exchange: Semester.

During the 3 years, in each semester interest period, there are 2 possible scenarios:

- If the fixing of Euribor 6m> 3,5%, the company receives the interest differential;
- If the fixing of Euribor 6m <3,5%, there are no payments resulting from the contracting of Cap.

The Floor is a financial instrument to hedge interest rate risk for indexed applications to a variable interest rate, which allows the buyer, upon premium payment, to ensure the lower limit of coverable index fluctuation, fixing its minimum income. At the same time, Floor buyer can benefit from increases that occur in the reference rate, above guaranteed rate by the Floor, throughout the operation (BCP, 2015).

For example, a company invests in a 5-year financial product worth 1000.000 EUR.

Figure 12. Logic of Cap contract

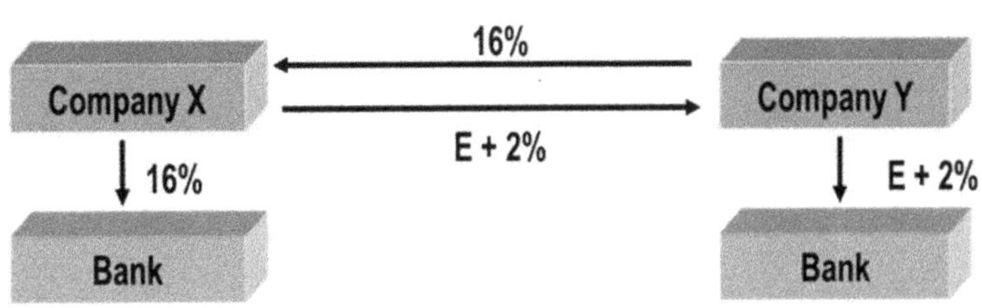

The receipt plan provides for the monthly amortization of capital accompanied by the payment of interest at a variable rate (Euribor-3M) and the company does not want to be subject to any downgrades of the indexer.

It contracts a floor option for the amount in question, with a duration of 5 years, and establishes a minimum for the interest rate (1,3%).

Throughout the duration of the loan, on each amortization date and interest payment:

- If Euribor-3M < 1,3%, interest is paid at the rate of 1.3%, protecting the client from falling;
- If Euribor-3M > 1,3%, interest is paid at the Euribor-3M reference rate and the customer benefits from favorable market developments.

The Collar is the interest rate risk management financial instrument that comes from the combination of two options - Cap and Floor - both with the same characteristics, regarding amount, rate and term, being one of the options bought to the Bank and another sold.

Thus, the Collar is a product that is intended to manage any operation interest rate risk from indexed to variable rate, financing or application, with the periodical roll-over, for equal and successive periods. The company's position in the Cap and Floor purchase or sale, will depend on the underlying operation whose risk is intended to hedge (BCP, 2015).

If the underlying operation is financially indexed to variable interest rate, the company buys a Collar, that is, purchases a Cap and sells a Floor to the Bank, getting protection against rising interest rates above Caps' rate, but benefiting from lowering rates up to Floor level.

If the underlying operation is a variable interest indexed financial application, the company sells a Collar, that is, purchases a Floor and sells a Cap, becoming protected against lowering interest rates, below the Floor rate, but benefiting from rising interest rates only up to the level of the Cap.

For example, a company will contract a financing and want to guarantee a maximum interest rate for the term of the financing without having to pay premium. Hire a Collar under the following conditions:

- Amount: 2.000.000 EUR and Term: 3 Years;
- Maximum Interest Rate: 4,0%;
- Minimum Interest Rate: 2,5%;

Figure 13. Logic of Floor contract

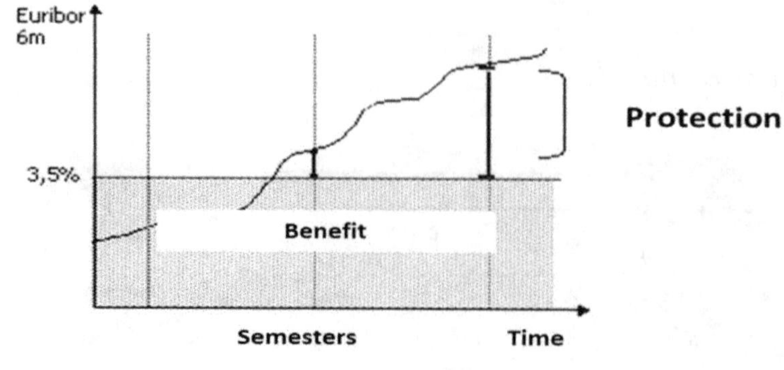

- Periodicity of the cash-flow exchange: Semester.

During the 3 years, in each semester interest period, there are 3 possible scenarios:

- If the fixing of the Euribor 6m> 4%, the company receives the interest differential;
- If the fixing of Euribor 6m> 2,5% and <4%, there are no payments resulting from the contracting of the Collar;
- If the Euribor fixing <2,5%, the company pays the interest differential.

Finally, Futures contracts on interest rate hedging tend to reflect market expectations about interest rates' evolution, thus allowing to fixate an interest rate of an application or financing instrument at a term, beginning at a specific future date, minimizing associated fluctuation interest rates risk.

For example, a company intends to make a bank deposit, but is afraid that interest rates may fall. So, it decides to hedge that eventuality with an interest rate futures contract. The contract has the following characteristics:

- Name - Future EURIBOR 3 months;
- Trading unit: 3 months deposit in the amount of 1.000.000€;
- Method of quotation: 100,00 - Implied interest rate;
- Reference price at maturity: 100,00-EURIBOR at 3 months;
- Tick Size: 0,005;
- Tick value: 12,5€;
- Start margin: 1,025€.

The company expects that the 3-month Euribor will be lesser than 1,71%, for this decides to buy 1 contract at 98,29.

In practice, the company is securing an interest rate to sell money (apply – lend) to a financial institution.

On November 19, according to company expectation, the 3-month Euribor was lower than 1,71%, leading it to sell 1 contract at 98,445 (by assuming the opposite position, the financial settlement of the contract).

Figure 14. Logic of Collar contract

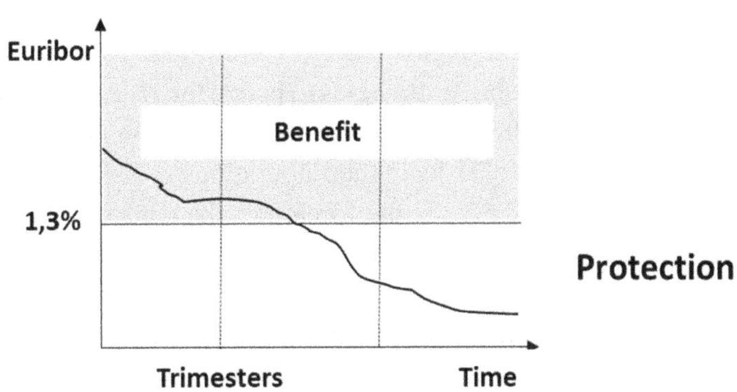

Table 10: Future contracts conditions on August, 18

Day	Exchange rates Bid / Offer	Number of contracts	Implicit rate
August, 18	98,285 / 98,290	1	100 – 98,29 = 1,71%

Table 11: Future contracts conditions on November, 19

Day	Exchange rates Bid / Offer	Number of contracts	Implicit rate
November, 19	98,445 / 98,45	1	100 – 98,29 = 1,555%

Differentials in futures:

98,445 – 98,29 = 0,155

Conclusion

As each tick of 0,005 has an associated value of 12,5 EUR, the company will have to receive the tick value of 387,5 EUR (0,155 x 12,5 / 0,005).

With a differential of 3 months (0,155% x (90/360) = 0,03875%), the gain is € 1.000.000 x 0,03875% = 387,50 €.

The investor's profit was 387,50 €. Due to the fact that the company only had an initial investment of 1,025 €, it managed to achieve a considerable profitability with the business: 387,50 € / 1,025 €= 37,80%

It should be noted that if the company decides to carry out the application, it may do so at the interest rate contracted in futures on August 18 (1,71%).

CONCLUSION

Internationalization of the activity through commercial activities, among others, with partners of different nationalities is a reality that is strongly present in corporate governance. Thus, conducting international trade activities involving the transit of goods / services and capital (settlement of transactions) increases exposure to various types of risks: country, foreign exchange, credit, among others. Thus, corporate leaders need to assess the positions taken and establish strategies to hedge the risks arising from those positions.

First, were discussed the payment techniques and sources of financing in international trade as a way for companies to reduce credit and country risks in their operations.

Besides that, one of the most critical risks is the foreign exchange risk. In this sense, the hedging techniques for currency risk and how the company can use them were addressed. It has been found that companies can use various techniques and instruments to manage their exchange rate risk. Generally, the techniques can be divided between internal and external. Internal ones can be used by companies without negotiation with external entities, such as financial institutions. Therefore, It was suggested that, if possible, the company privileges the use of internal techniques, because these can be used without resorting to financial institutions, leading to lower costs.

Due to the relationship between interest rates and exchange rates, the interest rate risk management techniques were also analyzed.

REFERENCES

Abor, J. (2005). Managing foreign exchange risk among Ghanaian firms. Academic Press.

AICEP - Agência para o Investimento e Comércio Externo de Portugal. (2010). Retrieved August 31, 2018, from http://www.portugalglobal.pt/PT/Internacionalizar/Paginas/bemvindos_internacionalizar.aspx

AICEP - Agência para o Investimento e Comércio Externo de Portugal. (2015). *Portugal Global Angola – Ficha de Mercado.* Retrieved August 31, 2018, from http://www.portugalglobal.pt/PT/Biblioteca/Paginas/Detalhe.aspx?documentId=c394b4f8-db0b-4d6a-b38c-95ed9a940b5d

Alves, M., Teixeira, N., & Rita, R. (2006). *Foreign exchange risk: Management and disclosure of information. The case of PSI20 companies.* Paper presented at XII Encontro AECA, Córdoba.

BCP - MILLENNIUM BCP. (2015). Retrieved September 4, 2015 from http://corp.millenniumbcp.pt/pt/public/solucoesfinanceiras/riscofinanceiro/riscodetaxadejuro/Pages/OpcoesDeTaxaDeJuro.aspx

Black, F., & Scholes, M. (1973). The pricing of options and corporate liabilities. *Journal of Political Economy, 81*(3), 637–654. doi:10.1086/260062

Bolt, W., & Chakravorti, S. (2010). *Digitization of retail payments.* Working Paper, The Nederlandsche Bank.

BPI – Banco Português do Investimento. (2018). Retrieved August 4, 2018, from http://www.bancobpi.pt/empresas/internacional/solucoes-trade-finance/cheques-emitidos-sobre-o-estrangeiro

Cornell, B., & Shapiro, B. C. (1983). Managing foreign exchange risks. *Midland Corporate Finance Journal*, 16-31.

Dhanani, A. (2004). The Management of Foreign Exchange-Rate Risk: A Case from the Manufacturing Industry. *Thunderbird International Business Review, 46*(3), 317–338. doi:10.1002/tie.20011

Ehrhardt, M. C., & Bringham, E. F. (2011). *Financial management: Theory and practice* (13th ed.). South-Western Cengage Learning.

Eitman, D. K., Stonehill, A. I., & Moffett, M. H. (2005). *International Financial Management* (9th ed.; V. Pezerico, Trans.). New York: Bookman.

Ferreira, D. (2008a). *Swaps and Credit Derivatives – Win (and lose) in the OTC markets.* Lisbon: Silabo Editions.

Ferreira, D. (2008b). *Futures and other derivatives.* Lisbon: Silabo Editions.

Gogoski, R. (2012). Payment Systems in Economy - Present End Future Tendencies. *Procedia: Social and Behavioral Sciences*, *44*, 436–445. doi:10.1016/j.sbspro.2012.05.048

IAPMEI. (2011). *Business Assistance - SME Academy*. Retrieved from http://www.iapmei.pt/iapmei-art-03.php?id=2498

Matos, J. (1992). *Finanças Internacionais*. Lisboa: Editorial Presença.

Montepio. (2014). Retrieved from www.montepio.pt/SitePublico/pt_PT/empresas/negociointernacional/tradefinance/creditos-documentarios

Mota, A. G. & Custódio, C. (2006). *The company's finances*. Wall: Booknomics.

Peynot, D. (1987). *Gestion financière internationale des entreprises*. Paris: Montchrestien.

Pinho, C., Valente, R., Madaleno, M., & Vieira, E. (2011). *Financial risk: measurement and management*. London: Walker Editions, Ltd.

Porfírio, J. (2003). *International finance*. Lisbon: King of the Books.

Silva, E. S., Qadri, M., Mota, C. & Pereira A. (2013). *International risk management and finance*. Economic Life.

Chapter 3
Management Control Systems:
A Key Strategic Resource for Business Success

ABSTRACT

In the current business context, characterized by uncertainty and constant innovation, management control systems may have a prominent role in organizations' success because they can contribute to decision making based on more credible and personalized available information on the origins of both value creation and value destruction. This chapter is about the importance of management control systems to achieve business success and intends to give an insight into the potential contribution of management control instruments to a more effective response to the current challenges of the competitive context and, consequently, to business success.

BUSINESS CONTEXT AND ORGANIZATIONS' MANAGEMENT CHALLENGES

We are living times of great changes in the business context, as result of international competitiveness, that puts face to different world regions players, with very differentiated production costs, with direct impact on sales prices and the way companies seek to conquer the markets, more and more through the mastery of unique competences, that provide them with sustainable competitive advantages.

Alongside globalization, technological innovations approximated markets and business partners, transforming speed and the way of conducting the business, as well as monitoring work processes, more effective monitoring chain value of business activities.

So, currently it is unanimously accepted that market information, competition and internal organizations functioning is a key strategic resource for business success.

In this sense, management control instruments increasingly seek to ensure that the facts registration is not limited to complying with the applicable accounting and financial normative, but to produce information on the activity evolution and companies' competitive environment itself.

DOI: 10.4018/978-1-7998-2007-9.ch003

However, management control instruments may also represent a very important tool for disseminating both mission and strategy defined by different hierarchical levels and functional areas, therefore contributing to a greater involvement in establishing objectives and critical actions to the business success. Besides, establishing operational and management performance assessing systems not only enables more effective activity monitoring, but also a performance alignment, in pursuing organization's global objectives, by its various players.

In fact, away are the days where organizations worked only for domestic markets and that competition was national (Bartol & Martin, 1998). World and organizations are changing. We live today in the so- called Knowledge Society, instant communications and global business, where changes occur so quickly that they are imperceptible.

After World War II and until about 1970, there was a high economic growth and a real social progress characterized by populations greater income (Murteira, 1997). At that time, there were five basic principles that guided the management of organizations' management (Drucker, 2001):

- The company owned production means and so it generated wealth;
- Overall, the work tasks were little complex, and people had low qualifications and so it was vulgar to work throughout their lives, only for one company, not having great bargaining power in wages definition and other benefits arising from their collaboration;
- Decision-making was centralized in the managers, being the most efficient way to coordinate both resources and activities;
- Suppliers and brands had a high market power, because competition was limited or non-existent;
- Technology was in possession of a small number of companies and there was no sharing or knowledge dissemination among different industries.

However, the economic slowdown and the oil crises of the 70 decade have completely changed the economic and financial situation of countries and organizations.

The largest companies, in the constant search for efficiencies in their value chains, internationalized their activity to the most diverse points of the globe (Donnelly *et al*, 2000). At the same time, technological innovations and Media development succeeded at an exponential pace liberalizing access to new markets and businesses (Murteira, 2002).

Thus, the globalization phenomenon had an impact at all levels in our societies, including organizations managing itself.

Business environment, previously characterized by high stability, and where managers simply monitored results' evolution, with sporadic activity adjustments and resources use, was now confronted with a reality in permanent mutation, where uncertainty was always present in making decisions (Freire, 1998):

1. Competition is no longer a purely local factor, it became global. In fact, any company in any sector would now have to worry about organizations of many different nationalities, being essential to be able to constantly innovate products or services to be placed on the market (Freire, 2000);
2. Media development, together with higher supply, allowed access to different markets and information, making consumers' choosing criteria more demanding (Freire, 2000);
3. Information technologies' development and scientific techniques has given the opportunity to better monitor the market and the activity (Laudon & Laudon, 2002);

4. Due to internet, that broke trade boundaries, new marketing channels permitted faster business, with less obstacles, in different geographic points (Laudon & Laudon, 2002);
5. Robotics, computer aided design systems, and new working processes such as just in time, master requirements planning and total quality management techniques, allowed bigger resources' efficiency and higher quality levels (Chase & Aquilano, 1997);
6. Skilled, multipurpose and flexible workers have become an invaluable resource for any organization, as knowledge carriers, vital in obtaining competitive advantages through new technologies, working processes and innovation in responding to market changes (Drucker, 2001).

As such, we are now faced with a global market, characterized, on the one hand, by countless companies offering similar or equivalent products and, on the other, by demanding demand that seeks more and more differentiating factors in the products it consumes.

Thus, it is not surprising that price, once upon a time the final choice exclusive variable, is now being complemented by other variables such as certificate quality, ecological label, design, technic assistance specialization, brand, package, etc.

This new competitive reality has demanded an important change in the performance of modern-day organizations. In fact, nowadays, managers must orientate their attention to the market, its intervenient and critical business factors, being the company seen as an open system, constantly interacting with its environment. Nowadays, business success depends on customer value creation, of different relations reinforcement activity upstream and downstream, and both operational and strategical inefficiencies' elimination that matter so much to reduce competitiveness. (Laudon & Laudon, 2002). There is, therefore, an incessant search by conquering competitive advantages, either by offered products and services' differentiation, as by cost leadership trough a bigger operational processes efficiency.

As referred by Freire (1998) if so, strategy became action, as strategic planning began to base itself in managers capacity of recognizing environmental changes and take adequate measures in the shortest notice. This will simplify business players knowledge, the monitoring of their evolution and value creation on offered goods and services.

Nevertheless, as the markets became more competitive and the information became more available, the differentiating factors were also becoming more uniform, forcing organizations to look for new formulas of success formulas. Simultaneously, over time, it came up that companies with less share market presented bigger business profitability, that could not be justified only by scales economies or experience associated with organizations size and considered, up to the decade of 70 of the past century, as the decisive factors for obtaining financial results.

So, in addition to constant environmental monitoring, companies have also begun to focus attention in its organizational structure singularity and how they managed and coordinated their resources and adjusted and optimized them, to obtain unique competitive advantages over competitors (Collis & Montgomery, 1997). In this sense, it was assumed that products, due to their sophistication and permanent innovation, resulted from knowledge, joining, among other factors (Edvisson & Malone, 1997):

- Human Resources competences, such as qualifications, experience and criativity;
- Organizational competences, such as organizational structure, management quality, working processes and techniques, organizational values and culture, information systems, speed of action, investigation, notoriety and upstream / downstream relations.

- The aforementioned competences are closely connected to customers' knowledge, products, technologies, the ways in which the company operates. In this way, although knowledge is not accounted for, its uniqueness in each organization is fundamental to value creation. On the other hand, it turns out that a significant part is centred on Man. (Bueno, 2000).

Organizations are formed by people and, as such, conditioned by their values, motivations and relations within working environment. Therefore, companies must be able to motivate and hold their employees accountable, coordinating different knowledge, linking the different functional areas and hierarchical levels, adjusting the organization to the turbulences of the surrounding environment (Sanchez, 2000). Consequently, losing a worker may drive to stringency in relationships with the company customers and suppliers, losses in the best operational practices and significant gain losses (Amaral & Pedro, 2004).

So, there are several challenges put to companies in the XXIth century:

- Privileged information access, ensuring market needs monitoring, supply personalization, partnership endurance with business main players and controlling organizational purposes realization;
- Constant supply innovation, at the market and structure organization level, guaranteeing a faster and more effective answer to the surroundings changes;
- Processes management, linking different functional areas trough new technologies, more adequate working processes and methods, in order to obtain reduced deadlines and inferior operational costs;
- Knowledge management, leveraging existing synergies from each worker' experience and know-how, making the final product increasingly closer to the client needs.

We face several constraints factors of business success, that make organizations' management harder and harder. On the other hand, this makes obvious that information is one of the business activity main resources. In fact, regardless the organization dimension, or the business nature, it is a fundamental instrument to obtain sustainable competitive advantages, either by a more efficient activity management or by a bigger efficiency on approaching the markets and the critical success factors. (Jordan, *et al.,* 2011).

Bearing this new business context reality in mind, it has been developed, over the last few years, methods for carrying out the registration of the property facts, namely segmented information and activity-based costing, which allow managers to better know the markets where their company operates and internally executed activities.

Segmented information allows to clearly measure companies' performance in several of its dimensions, namely: market segments, geographical areas, products, responsibility centres, projects, etc. On the other hand, activity-based costing identifies the associated cost of performed activities throughout the working process, showing those that create and those that destroy products value. That's why it is so many times used the expression of "accountancy at management service" to designate those systems that allow financial information production about business functioning, and that contribute to decision-making.

Current business context, however, does not only require detailed business information. Due to changes' speed, it is fundamental that it also exists useful response capacity, that is, that allows deviations analysis on the performed activity and eventual threats and opportunities anticipation, without other competitors taking a more comfortable market position.

For this to happen, it is necessary that the company's mission and the organizational purposes are divulgated by all hierarchic levels and functional areas, in a way that there is a behaviour alignment between top management and operational responsibles, who deal with companies' daily problems. In order to do so, it is equally important to have effective authority decentralization, in a way that those in charge by the operations may act upon its problems, being evaluated e reworded on their decisions, according to negotiated and previously accepted success references. Only by doing this nowadays organizations will function as a whole and have an effective resources management, focused on constant adequation to market needs

Thus, alongside the changes in accounting for property facts, several management control instruments have been studied and developed, that try to respond to the new challenges of the business context and are now a reference in the bibliography, and in many successful organizations (Anthony & Govindarajan, 2007).

Management Control Objectives, Principles and Instruments

Management control is a set of instruments that motivate those responsible, decentralised, to achieve the company's strategic goals, pprioritizing action and useful decision-making and encouraging authority delegation and accountability. (Jordan et al., 2011; 21)

Considering the previous definition, it is possible to mention that management control systems are based on instruments that seek to (Teixeira & Teixeira, 2008):

- Involve and align operational managers' behavior in the face of the organizations' global purposes;
- Ensure timely decision-making based on reliable information.

To do that, Jordan *et al.*(2011) report that management control instruments follow a set of principles to achieve its purposes:

- it includes information of diverse nature in order to measure the achievement of critical success factors such as quality, process efficiency and innovation, which are fundamental to the performance of organizations, but which are not included in the financial statements normally used as a benchmark for evaluating business success;
- it is based on decentralisation and authority delegation, in order to disseminate and accept the strategy to be implemented by the operational managers, allowing to act on the resources they have at their disposal, contributing to the achievement of local objectives, but also to the global ones;
- it requires a timely action and response to the market as key to business success, and therefore, the necessary information must be available within due dates, even if this implies some rigorous data estimates that may be available only when there are no longer useful;
- it allows activity results comparison with historical data, but also with the forecasts, giving a complete view of business evolution;

- it assumes that main users are the operational managers, because they are the ones that respond daily to the company's activity and resources, and it is essential that the objectives and performance assessment systems to be implemented are accepted and represent a real contract between managers and company.

At the same time, Anthony and Govindarajan (2007) state that management control instruments enable the Organization's strategy to be operationalized, as they focus especially on the short-term (usually annual periods), Defining programs, budgets and monitoring performance and achieving interim objectives. Thus, strategic planning and management control complement each other and should be properly aligned. This is because, it is only possible to achieve medium and long term strategic objectives with the proper short term activity monitoring; also, it is also not feasible to define objectives and actions for annual periods without knowing the mission and strategic objectives for, for example, three years from now.

In practice, this link between strategic planning and management control systems is extremely important because it is what allows the dissemination of the mission and organizational objectives by the various hierarchical levels, to align the various activities, functional areas and workers, to the path defined by the top management. This is because it is the top management that holds the company global vision and the contexts which condition business, and that, therefore, is in better condition to trace the adequacy of the company to the environment (Chiavenato, 1993).

In this regard, Kaplan and Norton (2004) report that most companies fail, not due to lack of planning, but because of the inability to implement the defined strategy, due to the reduced dissemination of the mission and organizational objectives, or by the lack of behavior alignment among different functional areas or hierarchical levels.

It is therefore intended that management control systems contribute to ensuring true market response uniformity to the different business partners, for an easier achievement of the strategic objectives defined.

Jordan *et al.*(2011), report that the management control systems consist of three types of instruments, covering the different stages of its work methodology:

- Pilotage;
- Behavioral orientation;
- Dialogue.

Pilotage

It represents the management control instruments that allow to initiate the strategy dissemination by the various hierarchical levels and functional areas of the organization. Trough pilotage:

- the objectives of each sector, department, business unit or division are established;
- the necessary activities and resources plans are defined;
- the objectives and action plans are quantified and scheduled in time;
- the performances are evaluated by comparing the forecasts with the achievements and measuring the scope of the objectives defined.

In the pilotage instruments are included:

- Operational plans;
- Budget;
- Budgetary control;
- Strategic control.

The **operational Plan** is usually carried out for annual periods and intends to identify the activities and resources needed to achieve each area goals and the organization hierarchical level. Establishing the operational plan requires the participation of each sector manager, because no one will know better the impact of taken decisions on the specific area activity. In addition, contribution will identify objectives to be attained, involving it and holding it accountable to the organization.

The **budget** main purpose is to quantify and temporally frame, the defined objectives for each company area. Together with the operational plan, they form the preliminary tools for pilotage. Generally, forecasts are also made for annual periods and consider the decisions already made in the action plans. Thus, the budget will represent the financial valuation of the commitments assumed by the manager and defined in the operational plan.

It is also necessary to carry out the proper monitoring of the results, and this is the way of verifying the extent to which the objectives defined are being achieved. This is the role of budgetary and strategic control of the organization's performance.

Budgetary Controlling is characterized by monitoring the evolution of financial data and is supported by Financial and Analytical Accounting. Therefore, it is a tool of heavy analysis and slower availability. However, it is through it that one can have a perfect notion of the scope of the financial forecasts defined and the measurement of the existing deviations.

The instruments of strategic control, notably the ***tableaux de bord*** and the ***Balanced scorecard***, emerged as complements of the previous instrument. In fact, they intend to be flexible, available and fast-acting, based on financial and non-financial indicators. Thus, it is its goal to equip customized information managers according to their desktop, containing data of the most diverse order, since the organizational objectives are not only financial. In addition, it is essential to enable operational leaders to act quickly on existing deviations, and it is vital that they are readily available.

In summary, it can be affirmed that pilotage instruments allow operational managers, to reflect on their work area, to prospect the necessary objectives, activities and resources, as well as to monitor forecasted achievements evolution. To promote its contribution in objectives definition, is to enable its connection in top management strategy development, disseminating company mission and organizational values.

Behavioral Guidance Instruments

One of the major problems of management control is to ensure that the organization functions as a whole, that is, that the objectives and activities of each sector contribute to the company overall success.

In fact, with the pilotage tools, the participation of operational leaders in the strategy to be implemented is encouraged to. However, it is necessary to ensure that the actions and decisions of decentralized managers, aimed at satisfying the company's objectives and not only the achievement of the local objectives (Vancil, 1973). This is the great goal of the behavioral guidance instruments that can be framed in:

- Responsibility Centers;
- Performance assessment criteria for responsibility centers and managers;

- Internal transfer Pricing Systems.

Through the organization in **responsibility centers**, it is intended, precisely, to define each manager operation area, establishing its goals, activities and means at disposal over which there is decision power. The responsibility centers typology varies according to the manager autonomy degree and may have, among others, the following classifications:

- Cost Centers;
- Results Centers;
- Investment Centers.

The **performance evaluation criteria** will be applied based on the classification of the responsibility centers, and it is essential that the manager be held accountable only for the means on which he/she has decision-making power. If this does not happen, the manager will be assessed on an elements basis that are not directly related to his/her decisions. This situation may have as consequence an uprising behavior and demotivation about the implemented management control model, which will lose its usefulness.

Finally, the **internal transfer pricing Systems**, aim to value the exchanges of goods and services carried out internally among different company sectors. Its implementation is crucial in guiding the performance of managers, because it leads them to optimize the resources at their disposal, to become competitive and create value in the activity they perform.

Thus, behavioral guidance instruments emerge to ensure that decentralized managers action will contribute not only to achieve each working area local objectives, but also to the company's global objectives. The use of pilotage instruments should be carried out considering, the various sectors correct framing, the response centers classification and the performance assessment criteria, and the definition more of internal transfer pricing systems, in each specific case.

Dialogue Instruments

The management control success and the effectiveness of its instruments very much depends on the articulation and participation of the various hierarchical levels and working areas, in the dissemination, throughout the organization, of both Mission and ideas defined by the top management.

To this end, it is essential that there are instruments that allow high fluidity of communication and the assiduous and informal dialogue. Assim, tradicionalmente os instrumentos de diálogo são compostos por reuniões periódicas e relatórios de informação. However, another instrument has been prominent: the *intranet*. In fact, the internal electronic network of organizations enables the rapid sharing of information, with several examples of successes in large international business groups with the creation of true communities of exchange of ideas and resolution of problems, making internal processes more efficient and responsiveness to the customer faster (Kluge et al, 2002).

Management control should act as a contract between the company and the manager in relation to its performance given the proposed goals. Therefore, it is essential that all interested parties feel involved and identified with the responsibilities to assume. Only in this way can a uniformity of actuation and a true union be ensured in order to achieve the organizational objectives.

MANAGEMENT CONTROL AND BUSINESS SUCCESS

The new business reality characterized by global competition and technological innovation has brought the constant uncertainty in decision making, leading to the strategic reinvention of the company and the transformation of the way of acting in the markets.

For example, the creation and evolution of *e-business* has boosted the traditional business by complementing it with the new dimension of the Electronic business. In fact, *e-Business* has come to combine two approaches in recent business management (Freire, 2000):

- Through technologies and information systems, companies began to give more attention to optimizing their internal activities;
- Through telecommunications technologies and systems, e-commerce has enabled new ways of penetrating the markets together with both customers and suppliers.

Thus, in addition to accessing new markets, *e-Business* has come to allow business value chain integration online, through information sharing among all stakeholders. Customers and suppliers began to be regarded as true business partners, sharing all the relevant information for the joint activities, obtaining synergies at various levels, from more competitive prices to shorter deadlines and more personalized products (Freire, 2000).

Today, it is imperative that organizations have a clear market orientation and better meet their needs. The price is no longer a variable controlled only by the company and, therefore, revenues are also formed through other factors such as differentiation or processes efficiency, which foster the customer value creation.

This dynamic led to a change on the internal organizations functioning and, currently, all the functional areas are closer to those who enjoy the result of their work. As such, the detection of threats and opportunities and new ideas, can arise from anyone at any time in the organization, making it vital both privileged information access and internal communication fluidity in all directions.

Thus, modern managers more than rigorous planners, experts in technical areas, cautious leaders and rigid controllers must be able to (Mintzberg, 1979):

- Motivate collaborators and create team spirit;
- Disseminate the mission and involve employees in the organizational objectives;
- Fostering creativity in problem solving;
- Monitor the enclosure;
- Ensure fluid and informal communication;
- Make timely useful decisions.

Thus, managers should mainly be drivers of men and teams, involving them in decision-making, always trying to ensure excellence in their way of acting.

Management control instruments may constitute a powerful support to the manager in duties performance and a good vehicle for achieving success, as they can contribute to addressing the previously identified challenges of current business context, i.e. access to detailed and useful information on the business, knowledge management and operational processes and constant supply innovation, in the markets covered and in the internal organizational structure.

The **pilotage instruments**, in addition to defining actual objectives and actions for each sector, allow managers and teams to be involved in the organizational purposes. However, they should also provide accurate information on the market and on the internal functioning of the company.

In this sense, and as previously mentioned, the new methods developed in accounting for property (segment information and activity-based costing), contribute to managers to know better the attractiveness of the actuation markets and the efficiency of the activities carried out internally. The segmentation of information, can highlight the performance achieved in various dimensions, for example, market segments, geographic areas, products, responsibility centers, project s, etc. Activity-based costing, allows to determine the associated cost of operational activities processes, identifying their contribution to the value creation in the offered product (Jordan et al, 2011).

Thus, management control is assumed as an essential tool in obtaining privileged information, which allows, on the one hand, to choose with greater certainty the most profitable segments and those that the company should abandon and, on the other, Optimize its internal functioning by identifying activities to be corrected or not executed, which may destroy value throughout the working process. As such, **pilotage instruments** can contribute to **access to insider information about the business and the management of work processes**.

Regarding **instruments of behavior guidance**, they attempt to ensure symmetry among local objectives and organizations, through the various sectors and levels involvement, autonomy and managers accountability (Jordan et al, 2011). Thus, it is intended to achieve a uniform performance for the outside and that the organization's mission becomes the mission of each of its collaborators.

By fostering authority decentralization and decision-making participation in decision-making, higher levels of motivation, commitment and creativity are obtained in formulating solutions for the most varied types of problems. By feeling a part of the organizational project, people give their best and place their knowledge at the service of the company, permanently seeking excellence in their way of acting (Peters & Waterman, 1995).

Thus, the **instruments of behavior guidance**, when concerned with the alignment of the global and local objectives, allow a greater commitment of the individual towards the organization, which benefits from its creativity, qualifications and experience. In this way, they contribute to **knowledge management** within the organization. Considering that competitive advantages are built on a basis of supply sophistication and customization and process efficiency, ensuring the manifestation, dissemination and maintenance of knowledge within the organization, is an extremely important step for achieving business success.

However, knowledge management largely depends on the company communication capacity, among different operational areas and hierarchical levels. Thus, **dialogue instruments**, are key to fostering informal communication and team spirit, enabling regular contact among different sectors and distinct hierarchical levels. This ongoing negotiation and sharing of information, instills in managers a broader view of the entire organization, both upstream and downstream of their work area. As such, it becomes simpler to align the objectives and actions of each sector, with the whole representing the company.

Thus, the *brainstorming* resulting from these recurrent meetings can create important synergies both in the speed of action and in the effectiveness of the solutions found for most of the challenges that arise. Thus, there is a belief that **dialogue instruments**, through debate and information sharing, are equally essential for the knowledge management to succeed, but also to provide a spirit of change that it clearly contributes to constant market adaptation and **innovation** and to the internal realization of the working processes.

Obviously, the creation of these synergies depends on the opening of the various actors to dialogue and discussion of different points of view. It is up to the management controller and the top organs to encourage a culture of mutual and natural dialogue along the chain of command.

It can be concluded that the role of **management control instruments** is not a follow-up to the activity to verify the extent to which the objectives are achieved and to penalize those who fail. When well applied, **management control** can be a powerful tool in the service of business success, contributing to:

- Market monitoring and approximation to the customer through **information** availability about each segment profitability;
- Sales price flexibility because of the **process's efficiency** through an effective costs knowledge associated with carried out activities;
- The involvement of all employees in the defined strategies implementation and organizational purposes achievement, taking advantage of each one's **knowledge** at techniques level and working processes as well as the market level and business players;
- The development of a culture based on **innovation** and action through dialogue and information sharing.

The **management control** should be regarded as a tool that allows the evaluation of performance, not to penalize those who do not achieve the objectives, but rather, to better guide each one's future decisions (Jordan et al, 2011). Tolerate eventual failures, means (Peters & Waterman, 1995):

- Giving opportunity to creativity and innovation, since it is not possible to make innovations unless you are willing to accept the errors;
- Encouraging action and market response for bureaucracy, because making mistakes, implies that decisions have been made.

CONCLUSION

We made a reflection about the potential contribution of management control instruments to a more effective response to the current challenges of the competitive context and, consequently, to business success.

In current business context, due to changes' speed, it is fundamental that it exists useful response capacity that allows deviations analysis on the performed activity and eventual threats and opportunities anticipation, without other competitors taking a more comfortable market position. For this to happen, it is necessary that the company's mission and the organizational purposes are divulgated by all hierarchic levels and functional areas, in a way that there is a behaviour alignment between top management and operational responsible, who deal with companies' daily problems.

Thus, the management control systems should be based on instruments that involve and align operational managers' behavior in the face of the organizations' global purposes and ensure timely decision-making based on reliable information.

We concluded that the role of management control instruments is not only a follow-up to the activity, to verify the extent to which the objectives are achieved and to penalize those who fail. When well applied, management control instruments can be a powerful tool. It may contribute to mmarket monitoring and approximation to the customer through information availability about each segment profitability, to the involvement of all employees in the defined strategies implementation and organizational purposes achievement, and to the development of a culture based on innovation and action through dialogue and information sharing.

REFERENCES

Amaral, P., & Pedro, J. (2004). *O Capital Conhecimento – Modelos de Avaliação de activos intangíveis*. Lisboa: Universidade Católica Editora.

Anthony, R., & Govindarajan, V. (2007). Management Control Systems (12th ed.). New York: McGraw-Hill.

Bartol, K. & Martin, D. (1998). *Management* (3rd ed.). McGraw-Hill.

Bueno, E. (2000). *De la sociedade de la Information a la del conocimiento y el aprendizaje*. Especial IX Encuentro AECA – Gestion de la Información en la Sociedade del Conocimiento y la Globalización.

Chase, R., & Aquilano, N. (1997). Gestão da Produção e das Operações – Perspectiva do Ciclo de Vida. *Monitor (Charlottetown)*.

Chiavenato, I. (1993). *Introdução à teoria geral da administração* (4th ed.). São Paulo: Makron Books do Brasil.

Collis, D., & Montgomery, C. (1997). *Corporate Strategy – Resources and the Scope of the Firm*. McGraw-Hill.

Donnelly, J., Gibson, J., & Ivancevich, J. (2000). *Administração – Princípios de gestão empresarial* (10th ed.). McGra-Hill.

Drucker, P. (2001, Nov.). The Next Society – A survey of the near future. *The Economist*.

Edvinsson, L., & Malone, M. (1997). *Intellectual Capital: Realizing your Company's true value by finding its hidden roots*. New York: Harper Business.

Freire, A. (1998). *Estratégia – Sucesso em Portugal*. Lisboa: Verbo.

Freire, A. (2000). *Inovação – Novos Produtos, Serviços e Negócios para Portugal*. Lisboa: Verbo.

Jordan, H., Neves, J., & Rodrigues, J. (2011). *O Controlo de Gestão - Ao Serviço da Estratégia e dos Gestores* (10th ed.). Lisboa: Áreas Editora.

Kaplan, R., & Norton, D. (2004). *Mapas Estratégicos* (6th ed.). Rio de Janeiro: Editora Campos.

Kluge, J., Stein, W. & Licht, T. (2002), *Gestão do Conhecimento – Segundo um estudo da McKinsey & Company*. São João do Estoril: Principia.

Laudon, K., & Laudon, J. (2002). *Management Information Systems* (7th ed.). Prentice-Hall, Inc.

Mintzberg, H. (1979). *The Structuring of Organizations*. Prentice-Hall.

Murteira, M. (1997). *Economia do Mercado Global – Ensaio sobre condicionantes Mega e Macro das Estratégias Empresariais*. Editorial Presença.

Murteira, M. (2002). *A Economia em 24 Lições (4th ed.).* Editorial Presença.

Peters, T., & Waterman, B. (1995). *Na Senda da Excelência* (3rd ed.). Publicações Dom Quixote.

Sanchez, P. (2000). *Necesidades de Informacion en la Sociedad del Conhecimento: Especial Referencia al Capital Humano.* Especial IX Encuentro AECA – Gestion de la Información en la Sociedade del Conocimiento y la Globalización.

Teixeira, N. & Teixeira, A. (2008). *Preços de transferência interna e a avaliação do desempenho de centros de responsabilidade.* XVIII Jornadas Luso -Espanholas de Gestão, Porto, Portugal.

Vancil, R. (1973, Mar.). *What Kind of management control do you need? Harvard Business Review.*

Chapter 4
Management Control Instruments' Characterization

ABSTRACT

A number of important themes should be the basis of the definition of management control tools, through the collection and production of the necessary information for monitoring the activity and its competitive context and management control adequacy at different business development stages with very different planning and controlling requirements. In addition to the use of management control instruments for piloting the activities, they can also be instruments conducive to behavior modulation and dialogue. This chapter gives a description of management control instruments and their pilot function, and as guides of behavior and dialogue. The various models of organizational performance evaluation are also described.

PILOTAGE INSTRUMENTS

Operational Planning

Operational planning represents the link of the major strategic orientations to managers of the various hierarchical levels, and of the various functional areas of the organization.

Its result is the creation of action plans (also called operational plans) that act as a script to intermediate managers and define a set of essential information for achieving the strategies defined by the top structures. Thus, each responsibility center must draw up its action plan, and this should contain the following data (Jordan et al, 2011):

- Objectives to be achieved and which have been previously negotiated by the manager and hierarchical superiors;
- Necessary activities to achieve goals, their timing, responsible and expected results;
- Necessary resources for the realization of the defined activities, namely, marketing investments, technologies, personnel and their financing sources;
- Income and expense forecasts according to combined time schedule;

DOI: 10.4018/978-1-7998-2007-9.ch004

- Analysis of the action plan presented.

After its discussion and approval by the top organs, each responsibility center operational plans should be internally disclosed.

In this way, operational planning plays a key role in organizations' management, since, in addition to trying to ensure consistency between medium and long-term strategic planning with short-term achievements, it allows coherence between global and local objectives, and between different responsibility centers, minimizing efforts risk duplication through greater integration of the various functional areas in the working processes, a better definition of each manager operations role and orientation, in the overall company functioning (Lopez et al, 1996).

Lastly, it is noteworthy that communication and negotiation, both in the vertical and horizontal direction, characterize the operational plans elaboration and, also, allow to verify the proposed goals rationality and their congruence with the activities defined by the various responsibility centers (Anthony & Govindarajan, 2007).

This is because, the established objectives should not be very easy to obtain, to avoid the risk of promoting a lower dedication by the operational managers, nor being impossible to achieve, not to provoke frustration feelings at the various hierarchical levels.

For the elaboration of action plans, several authors and institutions associated with quality management recommend the use of the 5W2H system which is based on a questionnaire that seeks to find answers to 7 fundamental questions in the organization operation.

Figure 1. 5W2H System

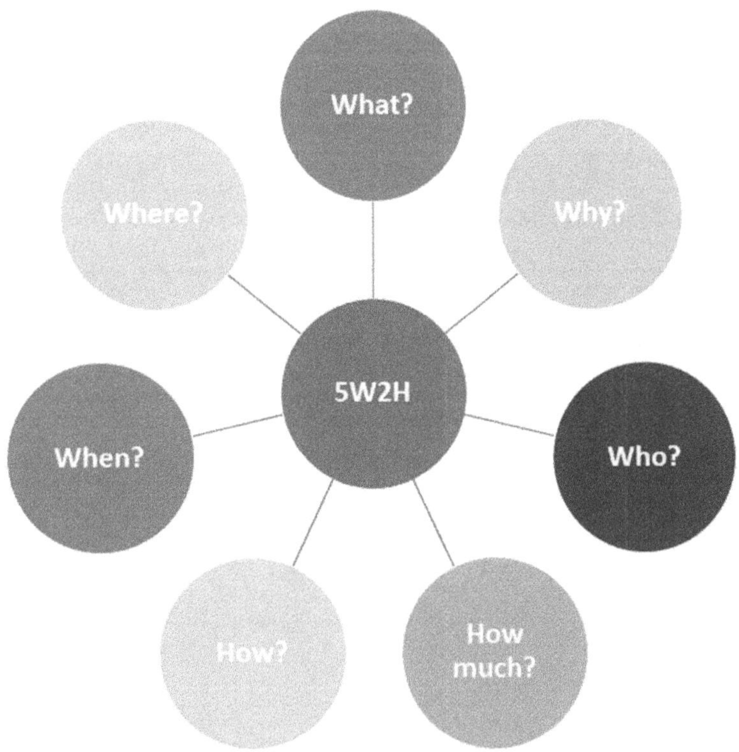

In general terms, bearing in mind the issues that are part of the 5W2H system, the actions to be carried out should be influenced by seven circumstances that an action plan should be able to formally respond:

- **What** should be done? (the action, itself);
- **Why** should this action be performed? (The goal);
- **Who** should perform the action? (those responsible);
- **Where** should the action be performed? (location);
- **When** should the action be performed? (Time or condition);
- **How** should the action be performed? (Necessary procedures);
- **How much** will the carried-out action cost be? (Required resources).

Thus, an action plan should be able to demonstrate the purposes that are intended, as well as the necessary activities to achieve them. In addition, it should clarify which persons responsible for each activity to perform, as well as the place and time where they should be carried out. Finally, it should also identify the procedures to be fulfilled and the financial resources necessary to ensure adequate assets (human and material).

We then present a possible structure for an action plan (Table 1).

In a more entrepreneurial aspect, action plans should also be defined considering the fundamental variables for the business success, bridging the strategic reflection carried out by the top organs and the actions to be undertaken on the "field" by operational managers.

For this reason, it has been developed over the years THE CANVAS model, which intends to ensure that the actions to be carried out are framed in four key areas for the companies to succeed: the support infrastructure, the products and services definition, target market identification and the monitoring of the financial impact of the actions to be carried out.

Thus, the CANVAS business model is a map of the main items that a company should have as reference to the operational planning of its activity, to put the strategy into practice, and is based on the answer to four fundamental questions that comprise the nine blocks to be worked:

Table 1. Example structure of an action plan

Generic Goals:						
Specifics Goals	**Activities (actions)**	**Responsbles**	**Localization**	**Schedule**	**Procedures**	**Human and material resources**
Income to be generated:						
Required expenses:						

Figure 2. Business Model CANVAS

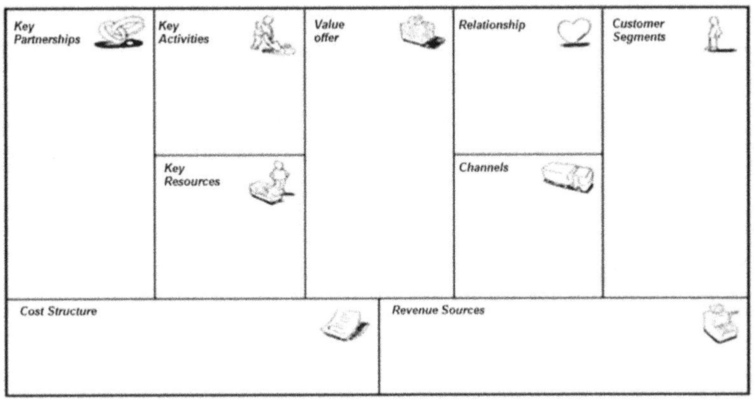

Question 1: How?

To answer this question, the model is based on the internal infrastructure of the company, namely:

- Key activities: These are the most important activities to execute the value proposition of the company and in which it should focus attention, because they are fundamental to ensure the desired quality and the deadlines agreed in the orders made by customers;
- Key resources: They represent the fundamental resources to create value for the client, and are typically associated with the key activities to accomplish. They may be human, financial, material or intangible;
- Partner Network: These are business alliances that allow for greater vertical integration upstream, through raw materials and services access, needed for business development.

Question 2: What?

This issue focuses on clarifying the offer to be developed and the value proposition that the company will suggest to the market. In other words, the answer to this question should be defined as the company differentiates itself from its competitors and the reason why customers will purchase their products and services in favor of its competitors.

Question 3: to whom?

The answer to this question should clearly identify the target market, as well as how the relationship with customers will be developed, in order to achieve that they continually repeat acquisitions over time and publicize the company offer. Note that it is cheaper to get sales replication together from current customers than new sales in potential markets, due to the communication effort that is needed to accomplish. Thus, to answer this question, the model proposes to clearly define the following areas:

- Customer segments: definition of the target audience for the products and services to be developed;

- Marketing channels: definition of the business partners that will allow to get the product to the customer, as well as marketing and communication strategy of the company in each market segment;
- Customer relationship: definition of the actions to be undertaken that will allow more and more strengthening of the relationships with customers and the constant adequacy of the offer to their needs. It is therefore intended to establish real partnerships and to develop the customer relationship management process, usually called *customer Relationship Management* (CRM).

Question 4: How much?

This issue focuses on the financial impact of the envisaged actions in the remaining blocks and seeks to quantify two important areas:

- Cost structure: Identifies the costs necessary for planned actions implementation and to ensure the means that are used in the business model;
- Income to be generated: Identifies the expected business income to be achieved through the actions to be carried out.

With the definition of the objectives and the elaboration of the action plans, the budgetary procedure begins. After establishing a responsibility center for the types of objectives, the activities to be carried out and the necessary resources, it is essential to quantify the strategy and management policies developed. Thus, the budget arises.

The last stage of the budgetary procedure relates to deviations control, in which the abnormal discrepancies between the carried out and the expected, which may be damaging the economic and financial development, are to be verified. In Scheme we get Figure 3.

The Budgetary Procedure

The budget is the financial quantification of the action plans, and its monitoring allows to verify the scope of the previously defined objectives. Therefore, it should not be a mere extrapolation of the previous year values. The budget represents a contract between the manager and the organization. In this sense,

Figure 3. Planning and control process
Source: Adapted from Teixeira and Teixeira, 2008

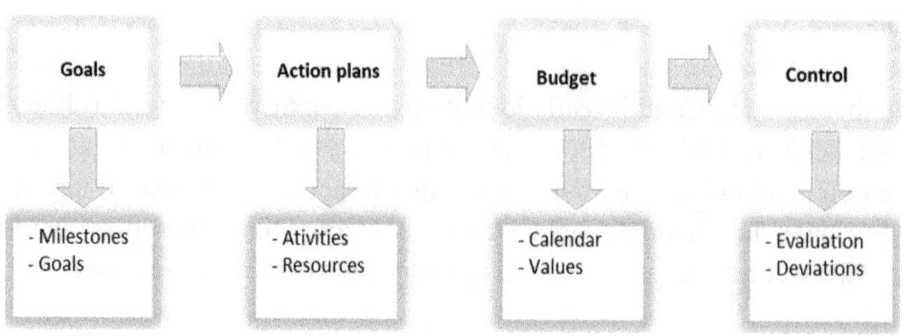

the predictions made should show, in numerical terms, the reflection and negotiation carried out by the various hierarchical organs and functional areas, on the actions to be promoted during the following economic year (Anthony & Govindarajan, 2007).

Thus, the budget should be coherent at three levels (Almeida, 2001):

- Coherence in time: the budget should have a continuous relationship with the company's surroundings. Therefore, it should represent strategy quantification and defined action plans, both in the short and in the long term. It is indispensable to make periodic revisions of the defined hypotheses, being the elaborated plans susceptible to changes throughout the achievements and the events realization, so as to ensure adherence to the environment and markets reality;
- Coherence in space: the elaborate budget, should be the final result of the interactions between different functional areas and various hierarchical levels, in order to describe the essential of the evolution of the various units that constitute the organization;
- External and internal coherence: the prediction of the endogenous variable, turnover, should reflect the constraints of the market (new products or markets, prices to be practiced, etc.), in order to exist coherence between the strategy outlined and the environment where the company develops. However, there should also be the so-called internal coherence by defining the necessary resources to ensure the desired level of activity.

As such, the budget carried out within the described perspective, can be a powerful helper of management, having a very important role to play as a planning tool, but also of decentralization and motivation. This is because it allows everyone to be involved in the objectives definition and actions necessary to develop the developed business strategies. However, its usefulness is also felt as an instrument of coordination and evaluation, because it favors communication and negotiation between different hierarchical levels and functional areas, defining each one's responsibilities and criteria evaluation, by comparing forecasts and achievements (Jordan et al, 2011).

Regarding the elaboration of the budget, regardless of the type of structure that the company presents (departmentalization by functions, by product, by market, by region or matrix), the model of Budgeting should always include the amounts related to turnover, various costs of operational activity, financial impact of deadlines for receipt, payment and rotation of defined inventories, as well as investment amounts, Types of sources of financing to be used and their required capital costs.

After verifying the coherence between the budgets of the various responsibility centers, the consolidation of the values of the income and costs presented, giving rise to the **profit and loss account** of the company.

In order to determine financial developments, the **Treasury and financial budgets** are drawn up, which will be based on the time of receipt, payment, alternative sources of financing and the possibilities of funds applications that may exist.

Lastly, the **forecast balance sheet** will demonstrate the patrimonial situation with the execution of the annual budget.

Financial statements groundwork will allow a clear idea about accounting results evolution, as well as the values invested in the activity and the respective financing sources used. Thus, one can estimate what the future patrimonial situation will be and verify the financial sustainability in the medium and long term. Furthermore, the financial statements preparation will also allow references creation to eco-

Figure 4. Logic of annual budget

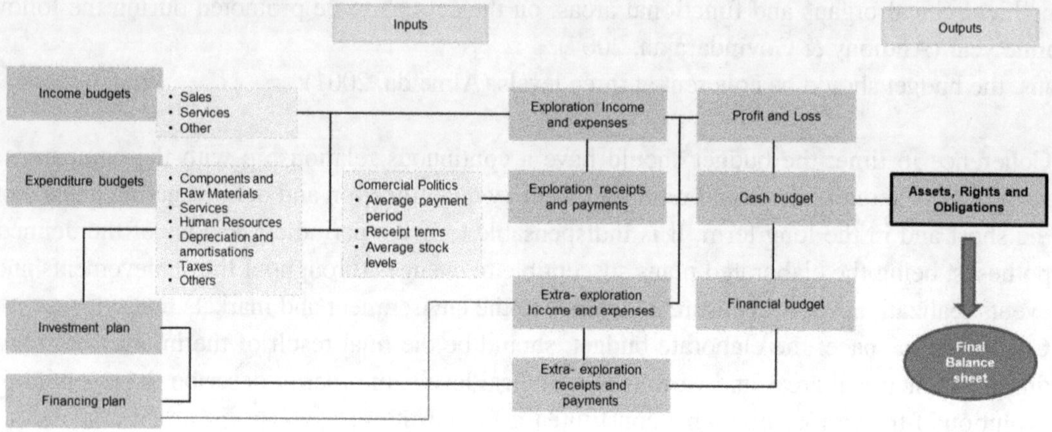

nomic and financial targets to be achieved, making it possible to monitor and control achievements and the possible action when facing periodic activity deviations.

Still in relation to budget preparation, this is traditionally based on financial and analytical Accounting, and its various maps, based on the financial headings (for example, cost of sold goods and consumed raw materials, external supplies and services, etc.) and the functional organization areas (e.g. production, marketing, procurement, administrative, etc.), which makes it difficult to create forecasts associated with the activities level and needed resources to achieve the desired objectives, as well as a comprehensive view of the ability to create value.

In this sense, an effort has been observed in several organizations, in implementing an alternative methodology for the annual budget grounding, which is based on three major cost areas, associated with necessary financial resources consumption for the activity development:

- Costs of products and services to be developed;
- Costs of human resources required;
- Costs of material resources to be used.

Thus, the preparation of sales forecasts, which can be carried out on the basis of the classical methodology of quantities sold multiplied by the sales prices to be practiced, or by defining a global value, for example, the market share that is intended to be achieved, then distributed by different target segments (customers or products), according to their weight in turnover, will give rise to costs of goods consumption budget, raw materials, packaging and services necessary, taking into account the characteristics of the offer to be developed. At the same time, having as reference the level of activity that is intended to be achieved, the budgets for distribution and marketing communication can be drawn up, where all the costs necessary for the placement of the offer with the customer and its disclosure. At this stage, special attention should be paid to the costs related to the establishment of partnerships that not only promote the offer, but also facilitate success with the target market.

Knowing the type of offer to be developed, the level of activity, the necessary consumptions and the commercial policies to be implemented (deadlines for receipt, payment and stock rotation), it is possible to identify the human and material resources that will be necessary to ensure the normal development of the activity and, to which, the vast majority of the business costs will be affected.

For example, people, in addition to the various financial benefits they enjoy, could lead to a series of operating costs such as car purchases, hygiene and safety and health procedures, representation expenses, insurance, mobile phones, furniture, administrative equipment, tools and utensils, among others. At the level of material resources, in addition to the costs related to their use, they have consumption of energy, of materials and may require insurance, conservation and maintenance, cleanliness and hygiene, among others.

Thus, the budget is elaborated considering costs origin, in favor of the simple values attribution to the financial accounting headings, contributing to a greater activity knowledge and ways of optimizing the productivity of carried out operations. In this sense, few will be the estimated costs that will not have a direct explanation and that will have a generic character in the activity (for example, fees from certified accountants and lawyers working with the company, rents of the facilities, etc.)

Then, the budget follows the rationale previously explained, determining the global financial statements, which present the consolidated values for the period.

After knowing the methodology and the sequence of preparation of the various budgets, it is essential to emphasize the importance of the flexible budget concept (Caiado, 2002).

"Budgets can be static or flexible. The first refer to a certain degree of activity and use, when expenditures and incomes can be predetermined with enough safety or approximation. The second is based on several alternative to make their rapid adjustment easier to supervenient facts, that is, the different conditions of those that were considered more probable at the time of their elaboration" (Silva, 1979; 395).

Context business changes succeed at a high speed that does not suffer from the eventual rigidity of an organization's budget. Thus, it has become essential that changes in activity levels may be reflected in the budget. This methodology is particularly important in the control of the necessary resources and the values to estimate costs for the different activity values, as well as to measure operational efficiency. This is because, in the knowledge of the existing deviations, directly related to production levels, it can easily be verified whether the existing differences were or not provided for.

To implement flexible budgets, it is central to identify variable costs and fixed costs depending on the different production levels. Hence, using the information technologies and simulation models, data are obtained that allow verifying the impact of several operational alternatives for different occupancy rates of the company's resources, evidencing the deviations that can be considered normal and that result from the production capacity used, and those resulting from activity fluctuations, that require the company's management accomplishment.

Thus, the preparation and control of the budget should allow an easy review of the assumptions and forecasts made. Consequently, it will be possible to evaluate the objectives, strategies and action plans, favouring decision-making and strategic alternatives adequacy to the circumstances of the markets and surroundings (Taliani, 2001).

As can be seen, the elaboration of the annual budget requires a high coordination and flexibility among the managers of the various areas. Therefore, during the budget preparation process, it is normal to carry out corrections in the action plans, because there are objectives or activities that are not coherent considering the capacities of other responsibility centers. Thus, it is a process where negotiation and organizational communication are very important, obliging the various hierarchical levels and the various functional areas to share information and to coordinate efforts in favor of the company's global purposes.

However, Jordan et al (2011) call attention that the implementation of the planning and budgeting process may face some difficulties.

Sometimes, top organs privilege speed and constant reaction to the market needs, not caring about strategic reflection, nor defining goals or actions to be developed, making budget a mere set of accounting maps, based on data extrapolation from previous years.

In other cases, there are organizations where the top organs, especially when they have stronger competences in finance, want to control in detail the economic and financial evolution of the business. Thus, there is always the danger that the budget has excessive information and is difficult to be consulted and monitored.

On the other hand, the lack of financial knowledge from the top organs, may also lead to the existence of unjustified budgeting cuts in some of the responsibility centers, due to lack of each one's actual needs verification. In response, managers present overvalued budgets so that cuts do not condition their regular activity.

Finally, in more directive leadership styles, where there is less authority delegation, there may be an organizational communication deficit, which causes the lack of managers involvement in budgeting, decreasing their commitment to the defined objectives. The same happens when heavy sanctions are defined to penalize non-achievement, which leads managers to make easy achievable commitments, not contributing to value creation and benefiting from prizes without having a real commitment.

It is concluded, therefore, that the planning and budgeting process can contribute to the organization's success by defining a strategy based on a more complete business internal and external vision, because it is based on the different views of the various hierarchical levels and functional areas, and on the dissemination of this same strategy by all the stakeholders of the company's internal structure, making the alignment of its performance easier towards the established goals. However, this requires everyone's involvement and a permanent dialogue that will enable to respond in the best way to the challenges posed in the activity normal development.

Budgetary Control

Budgetary control is an instrument that accompanies goals achievement and defined means use in planning and budgeting. Without control, the entire budgetary process would lose a great matter of importance, because there would be no such strong concern in fulfilling the objectives outlined and, as such, the diagnoses and previously made forecasts would lose their value.

The deviations analysis has not the purpose of sanctioning managers but rather, to help them in decision making and to reconduct the company in order to carry out the entrepreneurial strategies and the defined ambitions.

Thus, budgetary control represents an important management tool since (Anthony & Govindarajan, 2007):

- It encourages the manager, through constant monitoring, to define objectives aligned with the existing resources and to outline operational plans oriented to obtain them. To this end, it is essential to possess knowledge about the competitive environment and the differentiating competences that can potentially be generated through the company's resources;
- Allows managers to monitor their activity over time, identifying deviations between achievements and forecasts;

Table 2. Deviation types

Deviation Type	Purpose of Calculation	Deviation calculation
Volume Deviation	Measures the difference between outputs and forecasts caused by the change in the overall amount of the budget element analysed.	Flexible Budget nº1 – Initial Budget **= (Vr x Ms x Es x Ps) – (Vs x Ms x Es x Ps)**
Mix Deviation	It shows the impact of not respecting the estimated composition for the element under analysis. For turnover, the mix can be established by weighting the importance of each product or product group.	Flexible Budget nº2 – Flexible Budget nº1 **= (Vr x Mr x Es x Ps) - (Vr x Ms x Es x Ps)**
Efficiency Deviation	Determines the impact on results, resulting from the use of available resources.	Flexible Budget nº3 – Flexible Budget nº2 **= (Vr x Mr x Er x Ps) - (Vr x Mr x Es x Ps)**
Price Deviation	It shows the impact on the results, of the variation of the unit price of the analysed budget element.	Realizations – Flexible Budget nº3 **= (Vr x Mr x Er x Pr) - (Vr x Mr x Er x Ps)**

Legend: V = Volume; M = Mix; E = Efficiency; P = Price; R = real; S = Standard

- Encourages managers decision-making, because the permanent knowledge of the business evolution allows them to outline corrective actions to cope with possible deviations, which may jeopardize goals' achievement.

In this way, budgetary control will focus its usefulness on comparing achievements and budgets. However, in order to succeed, it is essential to demonstrate the causes of deviations at the level of the centers of responsibility, so that corrective actions are taken that directly influence the organization performance.

Thus, a global deviation by itself does not constitute a means of identifying the origin and responsibility of the deviations and does not permit, thus, the corrective measures' application.

The deviations analysis, when conveniently performed, is a powerful organization orientation instrument for the defined strategies and objectives. Therefore, it is presented below the methodology for the clearance of deviations, considering the most frequent changes causes in the budgeted elements, namely, the volume, mix, efficiency and price (Jordan et al, 2011).

A table is then presented with the summary of the deviations referred to in (Table 2).

Regarding the deviations presented in the preceding table, the following features are to be highlighted.

- **Volume Deviation:**

The volume deviation, in addition to highlighting the existing differences concerning the quantities of the analyzed budgetary element, also clarifies managers' responsibility. For example, if sold quantities increase, naturally, production costs will grow due to the greater number of quantities produced. If we analyzed the manufacturing section in isolation, we would say that the costs had increased and were the responsibility of the manager of that section. However, when the volume deviation is carried out, the true responsibility of the existing differences in the achievements is determined.

When applied to turnover, the volume deviation may be due to both endogenous variables and exogenous variables:

- Endogenous variables: They allow to verify whether the increase or decrease in the quantities sold was due to a greater or lesser penetration of the company in the market. The study of these variables gives rise to **market share deviation;**
- Exogenous variables: They allow to ascertain whether the increase or decrease in the quantities sold was due to a widespread growth or slowdown in demand. In turn, the study of these variables determines **industry deviation.**

Thus, the deviation market share deviation, allows verifying whether the evolution of turnover is due to the success or failure of the company to the target market. Its form of calculation is shown in Table 3.

Thus, this deviation clears the difference between estimated and realized values at the level of turnover, considering the expected market share in relation to the actual evolution. In this sense, there may be situations where turnover has grown, due to market growth, even if there is a decrease in market share. These cases should be identified because they could mean a loss of competitiveness, hidden by the positive evolution of the market size.

Industry deviation allows quantifying turnover deviation derived from the target market' growth or slowdown. Its form of calculation is shown in Table 4.

- **Mix Deviation:**

In addition to the weight of the different products in the turnover, mix deviation can be calculated on several headings. For example, in the case of personnel costs the mix can be established by salary, age structure, Professional category, level of qualifications, etc. These are just some of the examples of its application

Mix deviation also helps to assign responsibilities. For example, shipping costs may increase due to the marketing division having opted to serve markets with higher unit transport costs. Thus, the manager of the distribution costs could not be held accountable, since it only ensured the satisfaction of the needs of the marketing division.

Table 3. Calculation of deviation from market share

1. Actual Company Sales - Quantities	
2. Real Industry Sales - Quantities	
3. Expected Market Share - Percentage	
4. Expected Market Penetration (2 x 3)	
5. Deviation in Quantities (1 - 4)	
6. Estimated Price	
7. Deviation in Value (5 x 6)	

Source: Jordan et al, 2011

Table 4. Industry deviation calculation

1. Real Industry Sales - Quantities	
2. Industry Forecast Sales - Quantities	
3. Difference (1 - 2)	
4. Expected Market Share - Percentage	
5. Deviation in Quantities (3 x 4)	
6. Estimated Price	
7. Deviation in Value (5 x 6)	

Source: Jordan et al, 2011

- **Efficiency Deviation:**

This deviation is usually calculated on the production area in order to verify the resources consumption in the normal course of the activity. However, it can also be calculated on other headings, such as turnover. If a company performs various types of services, whose sales price is defined according to the number of hours, it can calculate the volume deviation in accordance with the type of services performed and the deviation of efficiency by comparing the estimated and effective hours carried out.

- **Price deviation:**

This deviation is the least controlled by the company, since most of the time, the price determination does not depend on the managers, but rather on the market and competition (exogenous variables), which is therefore not possible to impute any responsibility.

Thus, it can be concluded that budgetary control is a very important instrument in the activity monitoring in terms of achieving objectives and available means used. However, it has some limitations that the company should consider when implementing its management control system (Jordan et al, 2011).

- It only holds financial data, with several important factors in the success of the manager and the organization, beyond the control of extracted information;
- It has a great dependence on financial and cost Accounting systems, sometimes resulting in delays in access to information and consequently obstacles to decision-making;
- The results are conditioned by several variables, many of which are difficult to predict and beyond the control of managers. Thus, their performance may be impaired without direct responsibility for the deviations occurring;
- The short-term performance assessment may lead managers to seek better results immediately by jeopardizing the medium-and long-term strategy;
- Managers can define objectives and action plans consistent with the company's strategy without considering the correct use of available resources, by creating operational inefficiencies;
- The use of the complete costing (allocation of the company's total costs to the centers of responsibility), blames cost managers for costs that are imputed to them by distribution keys on which they do not have any decision-making power. As such, an environment of revolt and indifference is easily created in the face of the management control system implemented.

Strategic Control

Strategic control aims to complement budgetary control, very focused on financial information, through the monitoring of various variables such as quality, innovation, customer satisfaction, processes efficiency and internal resources development, which, while being key to financial and business success, are not covered by the traditional control tools used by companies. Thus, it intends to observe the extent to which the defined business objectives and strategies are to be achieved during the normal course of activity, in order to obtain a broader view of organizational performance.

The term performance, is normally used in the areas of economics and management when one intends to evaluate the activity of a company, being, in many cases, exclusively used economic and financial indicators (Ribeiro, 2003).

However, already in the years 50 with the development of several theories in the field of business management, several researchers, for example, Argyris (1952) and Ridgway (1956), drew attention to the negative consequences of the measurement of performance Only through financial metrics, given that good performance in financial aspects did not only provide for itself the sustainability of continued development. In this sense, Drucker (1954) reported that a possible solution would be to establish a set of balanced measures in business activity' key areas: market share, productivity, innovation, physical and financial resources, profitability, managers' performance, employee development and social responsibility.

In 1980, after 30 years, Hayes and Abernathy stressed that measuring the performance of companies and managers only with financial measures, drew management to focus on short-term results, damaging the organizations sustainability.

Also, Chandler (1977), state that accounting principles were virtually unchanged since its inception, which made it inadequate to assess performance only through economic indicators and Financial.

For the reasons pointed out, performance should be a comprehensive concept that covers several definitions. For example, Scherer (1980) argues that good performance is achieved when resources are efficiently used, when the goods produced respond to the quality and quantity sought by the market, when taking advantage of the opportunities created by the Scientific and technological advances that allow better levels of productivity and the creation of superior products and, when the company's management policies are integrated with macroeconomic objectives and there is a fair distribution of income.

Associated with this definition, comes efficiency and efficacy. In this regard, Drucker (1967) states that efficiency means "doing things well" and effectiveness "making things right". Thus, efficiency can relate to the working processes and efficacy with the products, that is, the results of an activity (Ribeiro, 2003). However, efficiency and efficacy are not always side by side (Chiavenato, 1993; 238). In fact, a company can better utilize its resources and have worse results than another company that uses its resources worst, because they are better resources. On the other hand, evaluating the performance of an organization requires a reference of values, whether based on the company's history, the competitor metrics or the activity sector itself (Moreira, 1997).

Thus, in the current business context in constant mutation, it was growing the need to measure performance in variables that help explain the financial results and enable a better prediction of future performances (Neely, 2005).

As such, it becomes a challenge to evaluate the performance of an organization, both in the objective and in the choice of indicators to be used, or in the selection of a referential to compare the achievements with a standard accepted by analysts.

The performance of a company is affected by several external and internal factors of its activity. In external factors, there is a highlight of the impact of different contexts (economic, political and legal, social and technological) and the structure and attractiveness of the industry. In the internal factors, the company's strategic orientations are highlighted, in the way it addresses the different businesses and markets and manages to develop and align their distinctive competences through the internal resources.

ORGANIZATIONAL PERFORMANCE EVALUATION MODELS

Several models and instruments for evaluating organizational performance were, meanwhile, developed. The first, developed with the aim of giving a broader view to managers of the various important variables for business success, was the *tableau de bord* created by French researchers and whose origins date back to 1932. This instrument emerged as a response to the U.S. stock Exchange crisis in 1929 that evidenced that accounting data were insufficient for decision-making and is still widely used by companies in France. Later, with the economic crisis of the 70's, this theme gains importance again and Charnes et al (1978) and Banker et al (1984) developed through linear programming, one of the first models that intended to study empirically the relationship between activity *inputs* and *outputs* generated.

However, with the increase of turbulence in the business context and with the progressive development, during the decade of 80, of the theory based on resources, which focused on the importance of internal competences for the creation of competitive advantages, it became increasingly evident that companies did not monitor key variables for financial success. In this sense, Kaplan and Norton (1992) argued that most companies could not achieve the planned objectives, because they failed to implement outlined strategies. This fact was mainly due to three reasons (Jordan et al, 2011):

- Difficulty in disseminating, through the various hierarchical levels and functional areas, their mission and their business strategies, which clearly reduces the possibility of Uniformity of performance to achieve defined objectives;
- Difficulty in monitoring and controlling the activity, because usually the performance analysis is done only on a financial basis, which implies the loss of knowledge about a series of variables that contribute strongly to business success and to the financial results, such as innovation, quality, customer satisfaction, human resources skills, etc.;
- The systems that normally provide information for management, namely general and cost Accounting, are characterized by being thorough, detailed and exhaustive. For these reasons, it is usually quite time-consuming not being available at the necessary moments, losing part of its importance.

In the decade of 90 several models emerged that intended to respond to these problems (Neely et al, 2000; Neely & Adams, 2001):

- The *performance measurement matrix*, developed by Keegan et al (1989);
- The *results and determinants framework*, developed by Fitzgerald et al (1991);
- The performance assessment system for companies competing through rapid response, developed by Azzone et al (1991);
- The *performance pyramid*, developed by Lynch e Cross (1991);
- The Excellence Model, developed by European Foundation for Quality Management (1991);
- The *balanced scorecard* developed by Kaplan e Norton (1992);
- The performance assessment system based on logic inputs – processes – *outputs* – Sales, developed by Brown (1996);
- The *navigator* proposed by the Swedish group Skandia and presented by Edvinsson and Malone (1997),
- The *performance prism* developed by Neely and Adams (2001).

The *performance measurement matrix* corresponds to a decision support framework, which seeks to integrate different types of business performance-financial and non- financial, internal and external.

Figure 5. The performance measurement matrix
Source: Adapted from Keegan et al, 1989

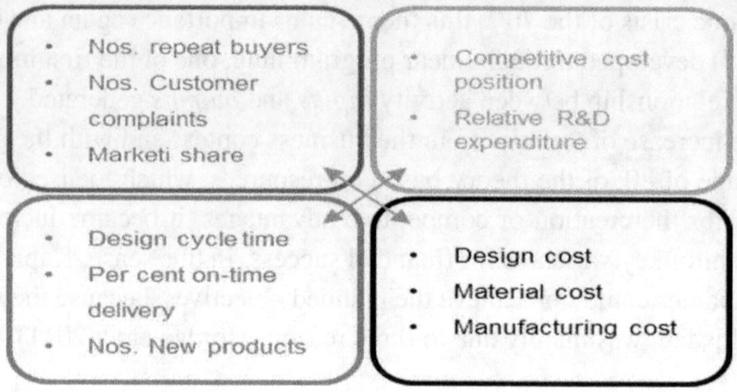

It is a comprehensive model that allows to verify all possible performance measures of an organization and identify omissions or where there is need for greater focus (Felizardo, Félix & Thomaz, 2017). However, its simplicity has been criticized for not considering some perspectives and relationships that are more explicit in other models (Neely et al., 2000; Neely et al., 2005).

The *results and determinants framework* is based on the premise that there are two basic types of performance measurement in any organization: the results (competitiveness, financial performance), and those that focus on the determinants of results (quality, Flexibility, resource utilization and innovation).

It is thus highlighted that the results obtained are a function of the performance of the past business in relation to specific determinants-that is, the results are delayed indicators, while the determinants are the main Indicators (Neely et al, 2000).

Azzone et al. (1991) present the structure shown in the following table, in which, through the efficiency dimensions (internal configuration) and efficacy (external configuration), is sought to identify the most appropriate measures for organizations that have opted to follow a time-based competition strategy.

The model *Performance Pyramid* proposed by Lynch and Cross (1991), links the organizational strategy with the internal processes of the business, translating the objectives of the Organization, with the indicators coming from the base of the organization.

The model provides a comprehensive view of the organization, with four levels of objectives, combining the external effectiveness of the organization (left side) and its internal efficiency (Rodrigues, 2010).

Table 5. Results and Determinants Framework

Results	Financial performance
	Competitiveness
Determinants	Quality
	Flexibility
	Resource utilisation
	Innovation

Source: Fitzgerald et al, 1991

Table 6. Measures for time-based competition

	Internal configuration	External configuration
R&D	Number of changes in projects	Development time for new projects
Engineering time	Δ average time between subsequent innovations	
Operations	Adherence to due dates	Outgoing quality
Throughput time	Incoming quality	Manufacturing cost
	Distanced travelled	
	Value-added time (as a percentage of total time)	
	Schedule attainment	
Sales and marketing	Complexity of procedures	Cycle time
Order processing lead time	Size of batches of information	Bid time

Source: Neely, Gregory and Platts, 2005

Figure 6. Performance pyramid
Source: Adapted from Olve et al, 1999

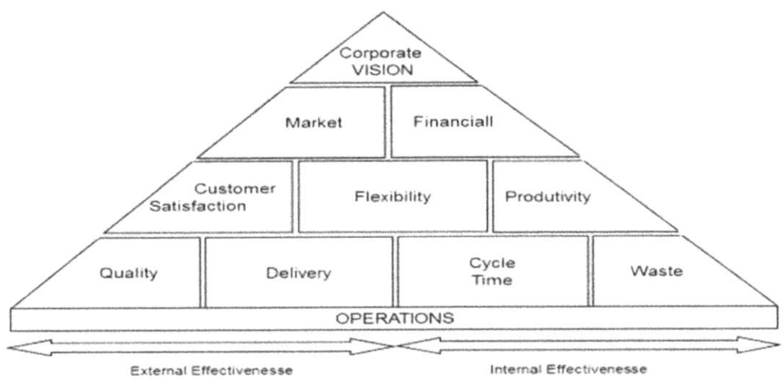

The Excellence model developed by the EFQM (European Foundation for Quality Management), considers 9 criteria, 5 associated with the means and 4 to the results, as shown in figure 7.

The model allows to make the diagnosis and evaluation of the degree of excellence achieved by an organization and stimulate, thereafter, its continuous improvement.

The *Balanced Scorecard* focuses on management in the strategy, translating it into purposes, initiatives and indicators, in the four perspectives (financial, clients, internal processes and innovation and Learning).

Brown's framework considers the different inputs (quality quantities, etc.), processes (design, production and distribution), outputs (products services, financial results) and results (satisfaction, needs), trying to explain the difference between them.

Another very popular model, is the *navigator* proposed by the Swedish group Skandia and presented by Edvinsson and Malone (1997), which aims to evaluate intangible assets. This model determines a financial value for intangible assets, assuming that they are subdivided into five major groups: financial, customer, process, innovation, development and human (Amaral & Pedro, 2004).

Figure 7. Business excellence framework
Source: Adapted from EFQM

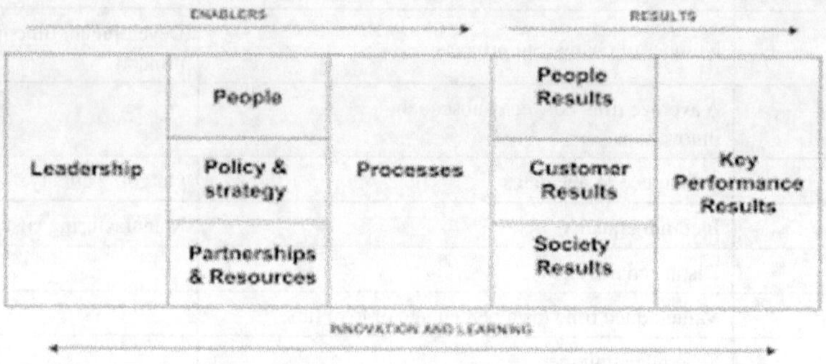

Figure 8. Balanced scorecard
Source: Neely, Gregory and Platts, 2005

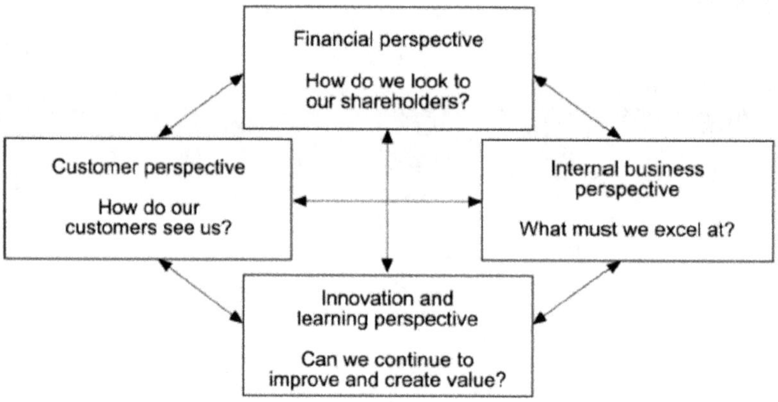

Figure 9. Brown's framework
Source: Neely et al, 2000

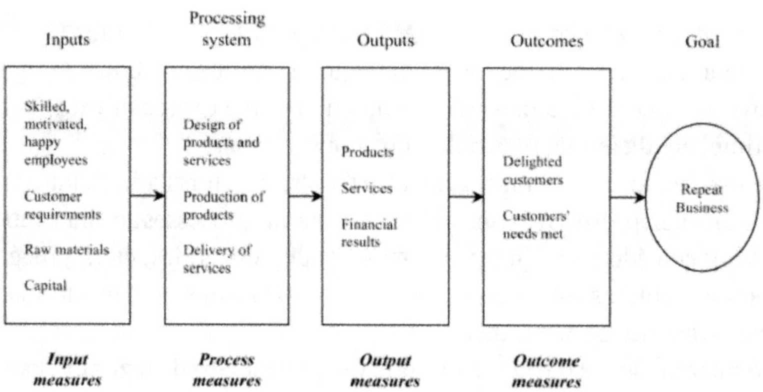

Figure 10. Skandia navigator
Source: Edvinsson and Malone, 1997

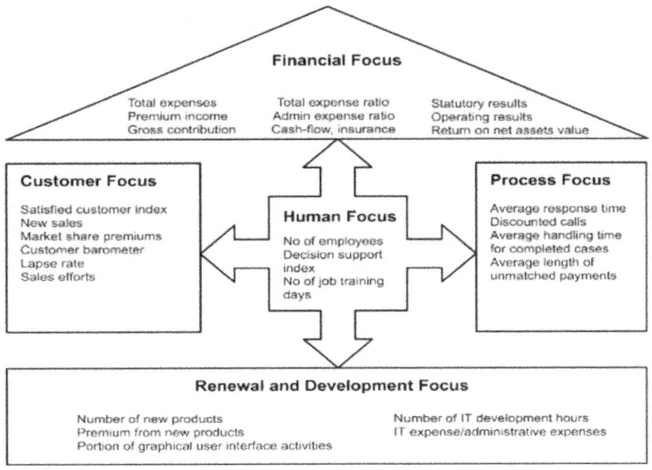

The Performance Prism is a five-sided model that allows to evaluate the organization's performance under five perspectives:

- Stakeholder satisfaction – who are the stakeholders and what are their needs and expectations?
- Strategies – what strategies are required to ensure stakeholders interests?
- Processes – which critical processes are to be implemented for strategies' success?
- Capacities – what skills are required for processes operation?
- Stakeholder contribution – what skills can stakeholders provide to maintain and develop capacities?

In greater detail, the characteristics of the *tableaux de bord*, which, despite its antiquity, continues to be used in the business environment and the *Balanced Scorecard*, which is currently the world's major benchmark in terms of strategic control and evaluation of organizational performance.

Figure 11. Performance prism
Source: www.accaglobal.com

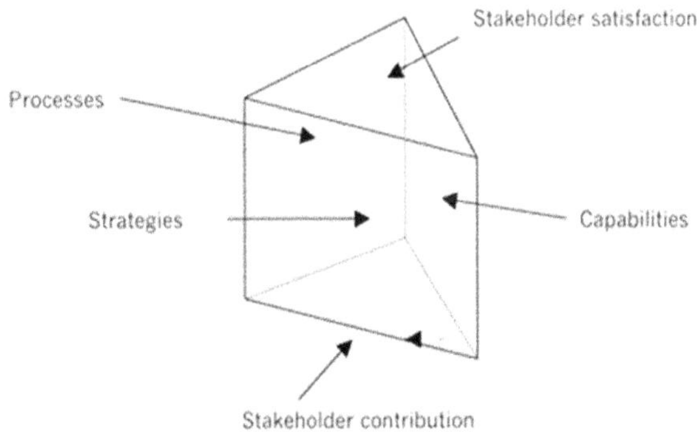

Both instruments (*tableaux de bord* and *Balanced Scorecard*) are complementary to the process of planning and financial control. This is because they intend to give an integrated view of the performance of the organizations, relating the economic and financial indicators, with the results in variables of other nature, which are strategic for the sustained development.

Thus, they intend to provide managers with oriented information to the purposes of the respective work area, containing data on the important activity variables and that condition the local financial performance and, consequently, that of the organization.

Like budgetary control, these instruments should also be readily available, so that operational managers can act on the deviations that occur in the activity, guaranteeing an adequate and timely response to business partners (Kaplan & Norton, 2004).

The *tableaux de bord* present as main requirements (Jordan *et al.*, 2011):

- Be readily available after the completion of the analysis period to which they relate, to facilitate timely decision-making;
- To contemplate historical and foresight data in order to give an integrated view of the activity evolution;
- Include financial and non-financial indicators in order to allow better insight into the origin of value creation;
- Be synthetic, because the excess of information may hinder the analysis and decision-making capacity. Therefore, they should only include indicators that ensure the monitoring of the fundamental variables for the success of the action plans and to achieve defined objectives;
- Be frequent and to contemplate permanently updated information in order to ensure that the manager can decide on a credible data basis.

Thus, *tableau de bord* should be a management tool that favors the actions of managers and, as such, it is important that it is fast, synthetic in terms of information and frequently updated, increasing communication and dialogue between different hierarchical levels and working areas, in order to help the manager in decision-making (Epstein & Manzoni, 1998).

In this sense, the implementation of a *tableaux de bord*, system should associate operational and strategic managers, in order to implement management tools that contemplate an integrated view of the functioning of the organization and the competitive environment, favoring organizational performance and the acceptance of the objectives and actions to be undertaken by all stakeholders.

According to Jordan *et al.*(2011), the implementation of the system of *Tableaux de bord*, is based on five phases:

Phase 1: Definition of the organizational structure and the managers of each work area;
Phase 2: Identification of objectives and key variables of action;
Phase 3: Choice of indicators;
Phase 4: Gathering Information;
Phase 5: Construction and usage rules.

In Phase 1, the aim is to identify responsibility centers and their relations at the hierarchical level and with the other functional areas, determining the resources available to each manager, as well as their authority. As a result of this phase, we intend to obtain a pyramidal scheme of the organizational structure and of the *tableaux de bord* to develop (Teixeira, Teixeira & Mata, 2008).

Phase 2 begins by identifying the key objectives and variables that each manager will be responsible for. To do this, it is important to define the most important types of objectives, that is, the results that are fundamental to be achieved by responsibility centers.

The key variables represent the means on which managers have authority, and that they may condition the achievement of the objectives. After the definition of both, a grid can be built that crosses objectives and key variables and facilitates priorities determination in activity development. Thus, it is possible to verify the impact level of each variable on each objective (Jordan *et al.,* 2011).

After filling in the grid, it would be possible to identify the least data rows and columns. In the case of the former, there are key variables that are not important for achieving the objectives. In the second situation, it means that there are objectives on which no means are being defined to achieve and, as such, either those are not priorities or the key action variables should be reviewed, so that they can be achieved (Teixeira et al, 2008).

In addition, for the types of objectives to be more readily understood and accepted by all, it must be divided into (Jordan et al, 2011):

- Qualitative goals, which discriminates what is intended to be achieved in each type of objective;
- Objectives that quantify the expected results for each purpose type.

Finally, a new matrix should be carried out that identifies which responsibility centres should act on each key variable. Thus, it is ensured that there is always someone hold responsible for the realization of the necessary key variables to achieve proposed goals (Jordan et al, 2011).

From the observation of this new grid several problems can be identified that may jeopardize the defined strategy (Teixeira et al, 2008):

- Several responsible for a single variable, which obligatorily increases the coordination needs, to ensure the alignment of the different managers and the lack of Overlapping activities;
- Variables on which no one acts and which, therefore, may jeopardize the achievement of objectives that depend on their performance;
- Responsibility centers that do not act on key variables. Thus, its importance should be measured, as well as its contribution to the success of the company.

Table 7. Example of a grid objectives/key variables

	Objetive 1	Objetive 2	Objetive 3
Variable A			
Variable B			
Variable C			

Source: Adapted fromTeixeira et al, 2008

Table 8. Example of a grid key variables / responsibility centres

	Centre A	Centre B	Centre C
Variable A			
Variable B			
Variable C			

Source: Adapted fromTeixeira et al, 2008

It is also noteworthy that to ensure the dissemination of the strategy by the various hierarchical levels, the key variables that a responsible delegate, become the objectives of the leaders of the immediately lower level. At the same time, one must also ensure that there is coherence and connection between the different responsibility centers' activities. As such, the definition of a *tableaux de bord* system should be a participated process, where, after negotiation, everyone who is involved must accept objectives and actions to accomplish, and there is a real commitment to the defined strategy (Teixeira et al, 2008).

Phase 3 must establish indicators that will allow performance evaluation in the objectives and key variables defined initially (Jordan et al, 2011).

Thus, in addition to results and resources' use indicators, convergent indicators, which depend on the results of other centers and means, can also be defined, allowing to monitor the evolution of certain characteristics of the competitive environment that can condition the success of the company's strategy (Jordan et al, 2011).

A Phase 4 has as its priority the identification of the information sources that will feed the entire *tableaux de bord* system, so that the indicators can be calculated in the established periodicity. That is, no indicators should be contemned that hinder results determination.

Finally, in phase 5, construction and disclosure rules of *tableau de bord* of each responsibility center should be clearly defined. Bearing in mind that the use of these management control instruments aims to favor decision-making, so that its implementation is efficient, stipulated deadlines must be valued. Thus, the following rules should be considered:

- In calculating the indicators, it is preferable to obtain a coherent estimate, available within the prescribed time limits, than a real value but obtained at a time that does not allow timely action on the deviations;
- They should contain few indicators, as simplicity favors decision-making and excess data increases the complexity of analysis for the manager;
- In order to give an overall view of the evolution of performance, they must contemplate, for each indicator, not only the forecasts, achievements and eventual revisions made in the light of the deviations occurring, but also historical values.

With regard to the *Balanced scorecard*, developed by Kaplan and Norton over the years (1992, 1993, 1996a, 1996b, 2001a, 2001b, 2004), this model that aims to show the relationship of cause and effect among intangible assets (people, systems of Information and organizational resources), working processes, customer satisfaction and financial performance, has become a reference for both researchers and the business environment.

For a better reading of the relations of cause and effect among the various variables analyzed, the researchers created an auxiliary instrument, which they called strategic maps, which intends to clarify the dissemination and implementation of the strategy through the established relationships established in the four areas of analysis of the *Balanced Scorecard* (resources, processes, customers and financial performance).

According to Neely (2005), the Balanced Scorecard is the model for evaluating the organizational performance most cited in international scientific publications and the most widely used by European and American companies. Through it, a grid of objectives, initiatives and indicators is built in the four perspectives, helping managers to identify the different performances in the various stages of value creation.

Although its purpose are similar to those of the *tableaux de bord*, disseminates the information, as already mentioned, in four specific Perspectives (Kaplan & Norton, 1992): financial; market and customers; processes and organizational development.

The methodology of its construction is based on the definition for each perspective, the objectives, the critical factors, the performance indicators, the goals and the initiatives (Jordan et al, 2011).

Thus, the *Balanced scorecard* intends, like *tableau de bord*, to align the activity of the operational responsible to the objectives and long-term strategy, focusing on managers in the so-called critical factors, which correspond to the key variables of the *tableaux de bord*. Thus, it is ensured the monitoring of the business evolution and success in the four mentioned perspectives (Teixeira et al, 2012).

For interconnection between operational activities and strategic objectives, the definition of *Balanced Scorecard* in organizations must go through four processes of strategic management (Kaplan & Norton, 1996):

- Clarification and dissemination of the strategic vision: being delineated considering relations of cause and effect, disseminates the mission and clarifies the actions to accomplish to achieve the desired objectives;
- Communication and strategic alignment: contributes to the communication of the strategy throughout the company, identifying a link between the organizational objectives and each working area. As such, operational objectives are more easily aligned with global strategy;
- Resource allocation: knowing the organization' objectives and identifying the critical factors to achieve them, the resources allocation is more effective and there is better activities management, making the budget more real and aligned with the defined strategy;
- Organizational Feedback and learning: assisting managers better understanding the strategy and critical factors of success of the activity, makes it easier to implement a logic of continuous improvements in business development.

As previously mentioned, according to Kaplan and Norton *(*1992*)*, the philosophy of the *Balanced Scorecard* is based on critical success factors that are grouped into four perspectives, namely, development Internal processes, clients and finances, and which can be characterized as follows:

- Organizational Development Perspective: Includes the most important resources and competences that the company should manage in order to ensure the successful achievement of key working processes and, in sequence, customer satisfaction and financial results;
- Working processes perspective: Stresses the priority activities and processes to ensure customer satisfaction and financial results;
- Customer perspectives: Identifies key factors for customer satisfaction in order to ensure that financial growth is sustained over time;
- Financial Perspective: Evidence whether business development manages to generate a good return for the invested capital.

However, the philosophy of the *Balanced scorecard* is also based on the existence of a relationship of cause and effect between the different perspectives (Kaplan & Norton, 1992):

- For example, if employees are involved and dominate the most important competencies, working processes are better accomplished. Therefore, the appropriate experience, qualification and organizational culture are the basis for the existence of good internal performance;
- If the work processes are better achieved, the quality of the offer will tend to be better, the response deadlines may be reduced, and customers may eventually be more satisfied;
- If customers are more satisfied, they will tend to be more faithful to the company and pass the word to potential customers, so there is a greater probability of increasing turnover;
- If the turnover is higher and, at the same time, there is an improvement in working processes' efficiency, there will probably be greater capacity to create value, which will generate superior results and, consequently, greater availability of Financial resources to continue to optimize the resources and competences needed for the sustained development of the business.

For the establishment of such cause-and-effect relationships, Kaplan and Norton (2004) found that companies regularly resort to another instrument, to which researchers have called strategic maps.

Through them, the *Balanced scorecard* will link indicators associated with the prospects of activity results (customer and financial perspectives) with indicators related to activity and resource management (perspective of the Organizational development and processes), contributing to evidence that it conditions the achievement of the objectives of the different areas and to better explain the creation of financial value through the business. Thus, decisions regarding the actions to be undertaken to ensure success can be taken based on more credible information on the critical factors of business success (Kaplan and Norton, 2004).

In addition, the accumulated experience of researchers with the implementation of strategic maps, allowed them to reach some conclusions that came to enrich the initial model of the four defined perspectives (Kaplan & Norton, 2004):

- Financial Perspective: The long-term value for owners can be created through productivity and turnover growth. As such, the indicators in this perspective will have to be always associated with

Figure 12. Example of Strategic Map
Source: Adapted from Jordan et al., 2011

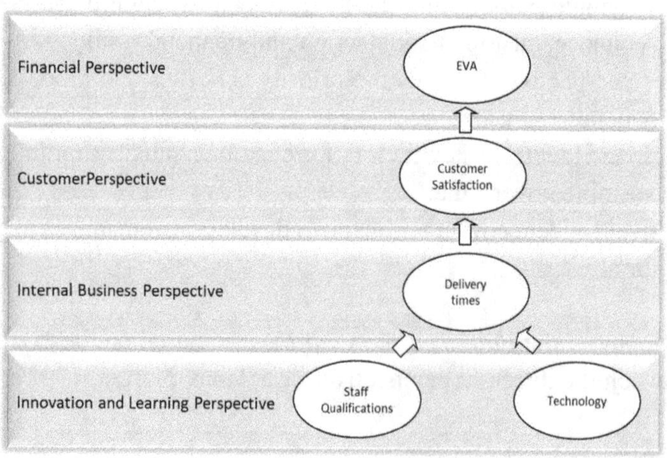

the improvement of the cost structure, the increase in the rotation of assets, the achievement of new customers and the increase in turnover in existing customers;

- Customer perspectives: Value creation is associated with customer satisfaction. The retention of existing customers and the achievement of new, through mouth-to-mouth advertising, increases profitability and market share. As such, the indicators to be defined in this area will have to be able to measure the success of these critical factors;
- Internal processes' perspective: To achieve the goal of customer satisfaction, it is essential that the company develops competencies at the level of 4 internal processes:
    - Operational management processes: represent the working processes with which companies produce products and services with the desired attributes;
    - Customer management processes: Represent the working processes which companies develop in order to select, conquer, restate and increase turnover among customers, focusing on market knowledge, relationships with customers and auxiliary services and in the image to the outside;
    - Innovation processes: represent the working processes related to the development of new products, services and processes that permit the entry into new markets and customer segments;
    - Regulatory and social processes: Represent the working processes that ensure a good relationship within the community, through compliance with environmental laws, hygiene and safety, etc.. Thus, they facilitate access to the best human resources and reduce the burden on work and environmental accidents, reducing operating costs and increasing productivity;
- Organizational Development Perspective: To ensure the intended implementation in internal processes, it is essential to hold the necessary resources properly aligned with the strategy. In this sense, researchers have divided this perspective into 3 intangible assets considered to be the basis of business success:
    - Human capital: *know-how* and skills of the various collaborators;
    - Capital Information: Communication and information systems, which provide the necessary information on the environment and internal processes;
    - Organizational Capital: Culture and types of leadership that foster an organizational climate of innovation, ability to work in teams and share knowledge, etc.

Thus, researchers highlight the role of knowledge management as an essential basis for the business success of any organization. In fact, it is the integration of the *expertise* and skills of the various collaborators with the existence of an organizational climate that favors teamwork and creativity, duly supported with reliable and timely information, which allow an improved performance in the various internal processes and favor the relationship with customers and the Community. Thus, the company manages to create true partnership relationships both upstream and downstream of the activity, guaranteeing the resources needed to obtain operational efficiencies and the loyalty and conquest of the market, through the creation of greater value to its customers. Because of these competitive advantages, it is ensured a better organizational performance.

Finally, the authors verified that the strategies implemented by the companies have a clear consequence in the orientation of the internal processes:

- Differentiation strategy: It has more impact on customer management and innovation processes to more and more customize and optimize the available offer;
- Cost Leadership Strategy: It has mainly an impact on operational management processes, as companies try to optimize production costs and asset occupancy capacity.

Thus, it can be concluded that the Strategic Maps act as a roadmap for the implementation of the strategy and, simultaneously, for the elaboration of the *Balanced scorecard* and the action plans.

However, the *balanced scorecards* associated with strategic maps, in addition to reaching the objectives and actions defined, also allow to quantify dynamic relationships between the different variables of the 4 perspectives mentioned. As such, it becomes possible to measure the impact in different perspectives, if there are changes in a given variable, fostering the philosophy of continuous improvements over time and a dynamic system of evaluation of organizational performance that will enable the decision-making based on deeper knowledge of the company's functioning, its resources and working processes. For example, you may want to know the impact on sales of an increase of x% in the quality of the service, but also on the level of resources needed, evidencing the contribution of this decision to the creation of Financial value.

Thus, through strategic maps, objectives and relations between the various work processes are defined in order to ensure the implementation of the strategy outlined. Thus, it facilitates the establishment of goals and indicators to incorporate in the *Balanced scorecard*, as well as the actions to implement and the necessary resources.

Although there is no exact number of indicators that should be included in the *Balanced scorecard*, Salas (2001) refers to some examples of what are commonly used by Spanish companies in each of the perspectives mentioned:

- Organizational Development Perspective: Motivation Index, number of improvements' suggestions, carried out training, productivity and employees' seniority;
- Processes' Perspective: Percentage of new product sales, time required to develop new products, production deadline, order response deadline, defective product turnover rate and stock rotation;

Figure 13. Example of dynamic system
Source: Adapted from Fernandes and Calôba (2006).

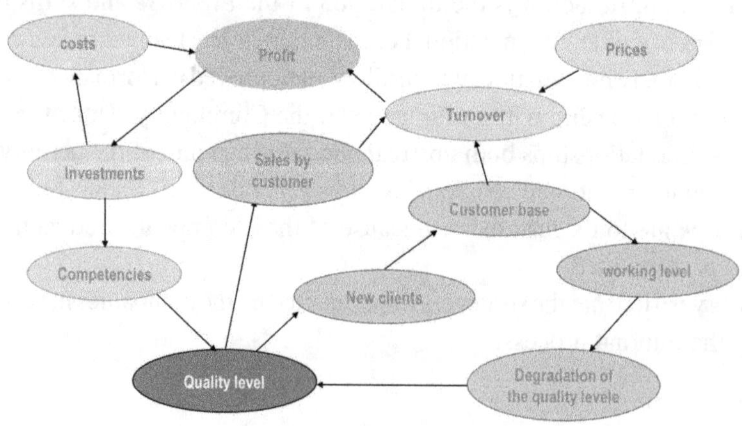

- Customer perspectives: Market share, increased number of customers, level of customer satisfaction and profitability per client;
- Financial Perspective: Capital profitability, *economic value added* (EVA), assets' profitability, Turnover growth, cost reduction and products' profitability.

In conclusion, pilotage instruments allow operational managers to reflect on their working area, defining objectives and identifying necessary activities and resources. In addition, they allow the monitoring of the evolution of the business, framing the achievements against made forecasts.

Thus, the pilotage instruments contribute to a greater dissemination of the mission and strategic objectives by the various hierarchical levels and various areas of work, involving the operational managers in the definition of the company's strategy, Making them the main actors of the company's success.

BEHAVIORAL GUIDANCE INSTRUMENTS

Responsibility Centers

According to Jordan et al (2011), a center of responsibility is the entire unit of the company that:

- Have a responsible;
- Have its own goals, for which it guides business;
- The person responsible can decide on the resources needed to achieve the objectives of the working area.

Company organization structure in responsibility centers, aims to identify the area of operation of each manager, defining objectives, activities and resources that it can use and over which it has decision power (Teixeira, 2007).

Thus, there is always someone who responds to the degree of achievement of the planned objectives and of the use of the means available. Thus, the creation of responsibility centers is associated with management by objectives, decentralized structures and authority delegation. Therefore, its success depends on the ability of the top management to be able to disclose the mission and the defined strategy, but also to align the performance of the different operational managers (Jordan et al, 2011).

Regarding the classification of the responsibility centers, it is made in accordance with the responsible' degree of authority over production and resources management. We have thus three types of classifications (Anthony & Govindarajan, 2007):

- Cost centers;
- Results centers;
- Investment centers.

In cost centers, the person responsible has the power to decide only on the costs generated using resources at their disposal. Thus, the manager only controls the costs associated with the plant. In this way, the necessary resources (*inputs*) and their use (costs) are considered, not measuring the generated *outputs* (Anthony & Govindarajan, 2007). In this sense, the responsibility centers that are normally classified in this way, relate to those in which it is very difficult to measure their achievements. The following examples are as follows:

- Administrative and financial centers;
- Research and development centers;
- Marketing and logistics centers.

In the case of results centers, the manager has power to decide on income from products and services generated by the activity of its center and on expenses, i.e. the acquisition of goods and services consumed in income formation. Thus, managers ' decisions aim to maximize the result and not only achieve greater cost efficiency.

Therefore, the results centers are fundamentally distinguished from the cost centers, because within the scope of their activity, the necessary *inputs* with the *outputs* generated are to be compared in financial terms. This possibility is also associated with a greater advantage, in terms of management, of the results centers compared to the cost centers. This is because, in cost centers, the main objective is expenditures' reduction, and this does not necessarily imply an increase in the results of the company, because it may, for example, lead to the selection of less qualified collaborators, the acquisition of less productive technologies or low-quality raw materials (Teixeira, 2007). In this sense, sometimes companies try to transform cost centers into result centers.

Considering the types of decentralization that organizational structures can represent, the results centers can be based on the following forms (Jordan et al, 2011):

- Functional decentralisation: The structure is organized according to the management functions, namely, finance, marketing, production, procurement, among others, with one responsible for each functional area;
- Decentralisation by Product: The main functions of the company are aggregated, for example, production and sales by product or families of products;
- Decentralisation by geographic area: It is commonly used in companies with facilities in various regions;
- Decentralisation by Project: It is usually used in companies that work on demand in large projects (such as civil construction and shipbuilding) or in-service delivery companies where you can easily allocate the income and expenses generated for each held project;
- Decentralization by activity: It is used in companies with differentiated activities. This is the case with consulting firms that have a diversified supply of services, in which each type of consultancy can be organized in a results center, having a responsible person who will respond to the results achieved.

As far as investment centers are concerned, they are classified in this way when the manager can decide on resources that generate expenses and income, but also, assets and liabilities (Jordan et al, 2011).

Thus, the results to be achieved will not only be the difference between income and spending but should also include the cost of capital of investment associated with the assets and liabilities generated. Therefore, the manager in his decisions aims to maximize result and, at the same time, the adequacy of the value of the assets and liabilities over which he has responsibility (Teixeira, 2007). In this way, for example, it is avoided that managers increase sales volume based on a higher average time of receipt, creating a negative impact on the Treasury situation, which will have to be suppressed with the possible negotiation of loans with financial expenditures.

In conclusion, the investment centers differ from the results centers because the manager can decide on assets and liabilities, conditioning the amount of capital invested in the activity.

Therefore, responsibility centers should be carefully defined, because a wrong classification, can induce an assessment with inadequate criteria and a demotivation by the operational managers, and may cause the achievement of overall objectives.

Performance Assessment Criteria for Responsibility Centres

In relation to the performance evaluation criteria, these should be used in view of the classification of the responsibility centers, so that the manager is responsible only for the resources on which decisions can be made. Otherwise, operational managers might develop disapproval and demotivation behaviors regard the implemented performance assessment system not identifying themselves.

Any manager should be evaluated according to three strands (Jordan et al, 2011):

1. Value of the result obtained in relation to the predicted values;
2. The effectiveness in achieving the objectives, comparing the established standards and the values of the achievements;
3. The efficiency in resource management for achieving the results.

Cost centers' evaluation should be carried out considering the actual costs compared to the estimated ones, and the standard costs that were initially established should be referenced in order to observe the efficiency levels obtained in resources' use (Teixeira, 2007). In addition, direct costing should be used and only costs over which the manager has the power to decide should be attributed to. As such, those that the manager has no influence on should be excluded. Thus, cost centers have a positive performance assessment if their activity' expenses do not exceed those initially foreseen.

The results centers shall be assessed by the contribution margin which is constituted by the difference between the income and the direct costs necessary to produce goods and services. Therefore, only the income and expenses on which the manager has authority are considered, avoiding the distribution of expenses and distrust of managers, because they are evaluated by the performance in variables by which they have no Responsibility.

However, there are several indicators that can be used to evaluate the performance of results centers (Jordan et al, 2011):

- Gross margin: The difference between income and variable expenditures. This indicator is considered when the manager does not have the power to decide on fixed costs, which normally does not happen;
- Centre result: It contemplates the difference between income and the direct and indirect expenditures attributed by distribution keys, which can associate expenditures to the center unduly, making it difficult to assess its performance;
- Contribution margin: Only considers the expenses allocated directly to the generated turnover, i.e., it includes the difference between the income and the direct costs of turnover, avoiding expenses' division. This logic assumes that there are no indirect costs, because they all originate in

some center of responsibility and, as such, there is always a manager with decision-making power over them.

In the case of investment centers, because the managers have the power to decide on the investments made in the activity, the performance assessment, in addition to the accounting results, must also take into account the cost of the capital invested in the business (Neves, 2012).

Thus, it is essential to determine the center associated investment volume, usually referred to as economic assets, because it includes only headings related to the business development on which the manager has decision power.

Thus, the concept of economic asset includes the assets' amount deducted from liabilities originated in, or affected to the center, since it decreases the real investment level of the business (Jordan et al, 2011). Its form of calculation is as follows (Neves, 2012):

Economic Asset = Fixed Assets+ Working Capital needs

Being that:

- Fixed assets are represented by assets with a low degree of liquidity (their transformation into net financial means is more than 1 year)
- The working capital needs include the fixed cyclical assets less cyclical liabilities, and both headings are the result of the normal business exploration cycle;
- Cyclical assets include inventories, customer debts, advances to suppliers, debit balances from Government and other public bodies (e.g. VAT to be recovered), debts of other debtors and accruals and deferrals associated with normal business exploration;
- Cyclic liabilities include debts to suppliers, advances from customer, credit balances before Government and other public bodies (e.g., Social Security contributions and income tax retained) debts of other creditors and accruals and deferrals associated with the normal exploitation of the business.

Thus, this concept of economic asset, allows the manager to verify the amount of capital investment that the activity is demanding to the company. Its value will be fundamental in the performance analysis, because the investment center must be able to generate results that ensure the return of the investment realized.

As such, indicators are normally used that try to measure the capacity of the activity to create value against the cost of capital needed to finance each plant investment.

The value creation evaluation can be made by dividing the indicators into three distinct groups, which are indicators of results, profitability and cash flows (Teixeira et al, 2012).

Starting with the results indicators, consider the results created in the activity against the cost associated with the required investment. The *Economic Value Added* (EVA), the Residual contribution margin and the *Cash Value Added* (CVA) are part of these indicators, which try to measure the capacity of the responsibility centers to generate sup abnormal profits.

EVA is a measure of financial performance assessment, which seeks to measure the value created by the management. This value is created whenever the business manages to generate a result that exceeds the cost of the capital. It is determined by the difference between taxes net operating income (NOI and the amount of results required by the owners and creditors. In this way, it corresponds to the surplus of the business results, in relation to the result required by those who financed the activity (Neves, 2012).

EVA = NOI – Economic Asset x cost of capital

Thus, EVA represents the value created in relation to the cost of opportunity of the capital invested in a center, including in its calculation all remuneration (of debt and equity) intended by the financiers (Silva & Queirós, 2010).

Residual Contribution Margin - RCI distinguishes itself from the EVA because it does not consider the tax effect on the results of the investment centers, since the income tax payable is a legal obligation on which the manager has no authority. Thus, the operational incomes (OI) are used as a reference to measure the ability to create value (Jordan et al., 2011).

RCM = OI – Economic Asset x cost of capital

The CVA is an indicator that allows evaluating the financial performance of an organization, trying to combine the advantages of measures based on the profits with the concept of cash flows (Young & O'Byrne, 2001).

According to Neves (2012) The calculation formula of the CVA is identical to that of the EVA, the difference lies in the substitution of net operating income tax (NOI) by the net operating means (NOM– Net operating results plus non-disbursable costs). It should be noted that this indicator includes non-disbursable costs (for example, imparities, provisions and amortizations and annual depreciation) as period results, since they represent costs, but do not require any monetary output, which means that it is income that contributes to self-financing creation, that should be considered in the capacity to release business surplus (Teixeira, 2008a). In addition, in doing so, the results are not conditioned by the different accounting policies adopted by the companies in respect of amortization and depreciation, the imparities and the provisions of the financial year (Teixeira & Amaro, 2013).

CVA = NOM – Economic asset x Cost of capital

or

CVA = EVA + Undisbursable costs – Economic asset x Cost of capital

As similar indicators in the logic and calculation formula, Young and O'Byrne (2001) draw attention to the fact that o EVA and RCM have the advantage of show business ability to cover all costs arising from the activity.

With regard to indicators of value, creation based on profitability, different bibliography highlights, and the supra-abnormal profitability (SAP) and the *Cash Flow Return On Investment* (CFROI).

The SAP It is based on the comparison of the profitability generated with the cost of the investment capital made, the same principles as EVA (Teixeira, 2008a). The profitability generated is represented by the ROI, as it observes the relationship between the results created by the activity with the necessary investment. As for the cost of capital will be discussed later its calculation.

SAP = (ROI – Cost of capital) x Economic asset

Thus, through the analysis of the formula, we can conclude that there is value creation if the profitability created exceeds the cost of capital. This margin, multiplied by the amount of the investment (economic asset), shows us the ability to create value in monetary units, and should have a result identical to the EVA (Teixeira, 2013).

As for the CFROI, emerged as an alternative to ROI and was created by CSFB-Holt Value Associates (Neves, 2011). However, it is the most difficult indicator to operationalize and aims to determine an internal rate of return (IRR) that takes into account the current value of the investment (non-current assets and existing management fund needs, associated with the Business), its useful life and the net operating means generated in the year, which are considered as a reference for the following financial years. In addition to these procedures, the values should be calculated at current prices and, in the last year, the residual value of existing assets is considered to determine the IRR of the analyzed time period (Neves, 2012). In practice, the calculation formula is as follows:

$$CFROI = - EACP + NOMCP / (1+IRR) + NOMCP / (1 + IRR)^n + RV / (1 + IRR)^n$$

Legend: EACP – Economic assets at current prices; NOMCP – Net operating free means at current prices; RV – Residual value

Thus, due to the way it is calculated, several criticisms are pointed at this indicator (Neves, 2011):

- The way inflation has an impact on each type of asset is very subjective, being very difficult to operationalize its effect for the determination of created value;
- The fact that they consider the net free means always equal over the years, is a utopia that does not represent the true capacity of the responsibility centers to create surpluses during analyzed period;
- The investment in the Management fund is not considered in the previsional years, because it is assumed that it also does not change its value against the amount it presents in the year considered as investment, which is also not correct;
- Thus, a IRR on potential results and not on cash flows is being determined, which is not going to meet the defense of the financial theory.

In practice, the CFROI is calculated through procedures similar to the valuation of investment projects, with the main difference being that it does not work with cash flows, but rather with free means. In this way, it intends to verify the profitability that investments could provide, taking into account the current capacity of the activity to generate financial surpluses over the expected life of existing assets.

As far as cash flows are concerned, they are a powerful instrument of financial planning and control, as they allow investors to observe the real business ability to create *cash-flows* in the periods and are not influenced By criteria of accounting records, such as amortization and depreciation and imparity, which influence the level of surplus created, when they are measured through the results or the means released (Esperança & Matias, 2009).

Thus, they allow a clear view on the Treasury situation of companies, representing the actual monetary flows of an investment and are calculated by the difference between all funds' inputs and outputs (Silva & Queirós, 2010).

The operational cash Flow (OCF) illustrates the surplus generated by the business of an organization after covering investments in non-current assets and the needs of the working capital, necessary for its operation, without considering the selected financing form (Neves, 2012). Therefore, the OCF is determined as follows:

$$OCF = OI \times (1 - t) + D + P - \Delta WCN - I$$

Legend: OI – Operational Income; t – Tax rate; D – Depreciation and amortization; P – Provisions and Impairment; ΔWCN – Working Capital Needs variation; I – Fixed capital investment (Exploration)

Finally, in order to measure the capacity to create value, it is essential to consider the cost of invested capital, that is, the remuneration required by investors. Thus, Neves (2011) recommends the use of the indicators economic value created (EVC) and internal rate of effective return (IRRE), which are based on historical cash flows. Its calculation is based on the capitalization of the various operational cash flows (OCF) for the end of the last year in analysis, verifying the profitability generated throughout the implementation of the investments that were previously projected.

The EVC and IRRE can be calculated as follows:

$$EVC = OCF_1 \times (1 + \text{cost of capital})^{(n-1)} + OCF_2 \times (1 + \text{cost of capital})^{(n-2)} + \ldots + OCF_n$$

$$0 = OCF_1 \times (1 + IRRE)^{(n-1)} + OCF_2 \times (1 + IRRE)^{(n-2)} + \ldots + OCF_n$$

In conclusion, it is verified that all indicators of value creation, although starting from different bases (results, profitability and cash flows), always have the objective of verifying whether the business was able to generate a remuneration higher than the cost of capital required by different investors, owners and financial institutions.

In this sense, the concept of the cost of capital will be discussed.

The "cost of capital" is usually associated with the return that a given investment should provide, being defined as the remuneration rate required by investors, considering the risk of the business. In particular, at business level, the concept of capital cost relates to investor decisions about the assets in which to invest and how to finance them, bearing in mind the maximization of the organization's value (Neves, 2002).

Business activity can be essentially financed through foreign and equity capital, being associated with both a specific cost, which varies depending on the risk incurred by the different investors (usually the owners require a higher remuneration, because, in addition to having a greater concern with business management, in the event of bankruptcy of the company, they can only access the existing assets after the obligations with third parties have been fulfilled). It is based on this idea that there are different costs for the various sources of financing, which emerged the concept of weighted average cost of capital, the WACC- *weight Average cost of capital* (Teixeira, 2008a). Your calculation formula is as follows (Teixeira & Alves, 2003):

$$WACC = (E / A) \times Ke + (L / A) \times Kd \times (1 - t)$$

Legend: E- Equity; A- Net Asset; Ke- Equity Cost; L- Liabilities; Kd- Capital Cost; t- Income Tax effective rate.

Having as reference the presented formula, the optimum capital structure (or optimum indebtedness level) is the one that minimizes WACC, and consequently maximizes the value of the company.

The WACC consists of the sum of the capital costs and liabilities, duly weighted by their weight in the financing of the net asset. Thus, it is intended that managers take into consideration the cheaper financing sources, making the cost of the capital necessary to finance the activity lower. Thus, by decreasing the value of WACC they also contribute to value creation, because they reduce the cost of investment and, at the same time, increase the value of the financial surplus created (Teixeira et al, 2012).

As for the cost of the sources of financing, it is often determined by the interest rates contracted with the financial institutions, or through the relationship between the financial expenses of the period and the remunerated liabilities at the end of the previous year (Neves, 2012).

As regards the cost of equity, in the case of listed companies, is represented by the expected profitability, determined by the *capital Asset Price Model* (CAPM) which measures the remuneration to be required by the owners with Market profitability and the risk associated with securities; In other cases, it may be calculated by reference to the average profitability of the equity of the activity sector or, by the addition of a risk premium to the cost of bank financing of the company (Neves, 2012). In this regard, Damodaran (2007) and specialized organizations, such as COFACE, suggest risk premiums to be used as a benchmark in companies, according to the risk of the countries where they operate.

In conclusion, the adoption of the logic of value creation leads to the penalisation of the most demanding centres in terms of investment volume and consequent financing. In addition, it makes decisions more coherent according to the cost of capital of the company, as managers act to cover all the costs of the activity, including the opportunity cost of equity, creating value for the Owners (Basso & Lima, 2002). In this way, there is greater convergence between local and global decisions.

Managers' Performance Assessment

Until recently, managers were only evaluated on obtaining financial goals. However, the so-called knowledge society and globalization have increased the competitive level and the need to make faster decisions about the various variables that condition the business (Bartol & Martin, 1998). This new reality has come to recognize that companies should define and monitor objectives of diverse nature such as quality, process efficiency and innovation, which condition customer satisfaction and consequently financial activity results themselves (Kaplan & Norton, 2004).

Thus, it has become imperative to create information systems that simultaneously integrate financial and non-financial indicators into performance analysis. However, more than evaluating the consolidated activity of organizations, it is important that one can analyze the contribution of each working area and each manager to companies' results. Only in this way will it be possible to identify the causes and those responsible for the existing deviations and to act in a timely manner (Jordan et al, 2011).

In this sense, and as previously mentioned, were developed over the years, instruments that intend to respond to this need, such as *tableau de bord* and the *Balanced scorecard*. These instruments aim to be more focused on the dissemination of the strategy to be implemented and for an adequate monitoring of personal and organizational performance, favoring the action and decision-making by managers, integrating the local and organizational objects' evaluation.

Regarding the performance assessment of managers and incentive systems to be practiced, Anthony and Govindarajan (2007) refer to a set of ideas that should be followed by companies in the implementation of this type of systems:

- Individuals tend to have a greater motivation for achieving the objectives, if there are possibilities to be rewarded for their effort;
- The financial reward is an important form of satisfying the needs, being, however, deprecated in favor of non-financial incentives (travel, cars, etc.) at higher hierarchical levels;
- Workers have a greater tendency to follow the procedures and to worry about achieving the objectives, when the example comes from their hierarchical superiors;
- Employees feel more motivated when there are instruments that provide them with *feedback* on the performance of their activity;
- There is a greater commitment of managers to the objectives, when they are called to intervene in their definition;
- The objectives can't be neither easy nor impossible to achieve, or the risk of causing demotivation and revolt can be real.

Thus, it is evident the importance of evaluating the performance of employees to achieve the organizational objectives, as well as the importance of the definition of incentive policies or Penalization to ensure effective levels of motivation and involvement of individuals (Teixeira & Carreira, 2008).

As for the incentive system, and considering the deadlines for achieving the objectives, there may be two types of prizes in a company (Anthony & Govindarajan, 2007):

- Short-term incentives: they refer to the annual performance of managers and are usually associated with the financial results;
- Medium and long-term incentives: they are generally 3 and 5 years of time frame and usually assume the *stock-options* figure (during a pre-arranged period, the manager may acquire shares of the company at a lower value compared to the stock market price, gaining more for the sale of the securities in that time horizon), monetary premiums according to the financial results achieved, or rights over lots of company' stocks.

In this sense, in order to ensure the involvement of managers in the immediate and Long-term objectives, companies generally opt to create incentive schemes linking the two modalities of premiums (Teixeira & Carreira, 2008).

Finally, Anthony and Govindarajan (2007) also refer to several challenges that should be considered when establishing a system for assessing performance and awarding prizes:

- Choose between financial and non-financial incentives, with the option related to the status of managers and the wage level they hold. The higher the incomes, the greater the tendency for the valuation of non-financial incentives;
- Option between paying high wages and low wages, betting more on variable remuneration complements depending on the achievement of the objectives. Of course, extra remunerations may motivate managers to run in pursuit of the objectives defined when drafting budgets;
- Define whether the calculation of the incentive to be granted must be carried out with reference to company result or only that of the responsibility center that the manager coordinates. In companies whose business diversification is not high, the center's success is interconnected. As such, in order to ensure greater organizational cohesion, it is believed that the premium should result from a combination of the two indicators;

- Deciding whether the incentive to allocate should be calculated only with reference to financial indicators or also include indicators of other nature. As previously mentioned, the success of a company is not only dependent on financial variables, but rather a set of factors that properly combined create excellence in performance. Therefore, non-financial indicators should be considered in the incentive plan to be granted. This situation is especially important in centers where performance cannot be easily measured through financially quantifiable data;
- Determine the basis of comparison to assign the incentives. Typically, choices fall on budgeted data, similar centers, or direct competitors.

Management control is based on authority decentralization, as a way for the company to become more competitive in the market, through a greater speed of action and a greater capacity to constantly adapt to the business partners' needs. This is achieved through an effective participation of the various functional areas and hierarchical levels in the objectives definition and actions to be accomplished, taking advantage of the knowledge of the existing activity in the internal structure, and the alignment of the vision of top organs with the operations of operational managers who know deeply the work processes and the business players, which allows a better responsiveness to the challenges of the competitive environment.

Thus, in addition to the planning phase, it is essential that there is effective control of the achievements, so as not only to give constant *feedback* on the development of the activity, but also to reward the managers who contribute most to the creating value, making them behavior references in the organization.

In this sense, in addition to the definition of the form and the amounts that the premiums should have, the evaluation systems of managers should be able to reward according to the performance obtained by responsibility centers in the key variables to company's success. As such, they should include monitoring of financial and non-financial indicators that allow obtaining a clear picture on the actions and objectives achieving. At the same time, to reduce the possible internal competition and the lower collaboration between centers, caused by the concern of each manager only with the local objectives in favor of the strategic objectives of the company, the evaluation systems should also frame the incentives to be granted, depending on the contribution of each center to the overall results achieved.

As such, the establishment of cause and effect relations between objectives and actions, using instruments to evaluate organizational performance, such as the *tableaux de bord* or the *Balanced Scorecard*, allows managers a clearer picture of their performance in the different areas of activity. However, derived from the high number of indicators to be monitored in these instruments, the incentive and performance assessment systems become more complex.

Therefore, the performance assessment systems have progressed, in order not only to make it possible to monitor the evolution of activity in financial and non-financial variables, but also to create a single *SCORE* that measures the performance of company and each working area and its contribution to achieving global objectives. The **Integrated systems for evaluating organizational performance – ISEOP** are thus emerging.

Thus, managers should be evaluated according to the objectives of the responsibility centers that coordinate, but also, for their contribution to achieving the organizational objectives. Thus, an effective performance evaluation model should be able to monitor the activity of managers in key financial and non-financial variables, which are fundamental to the sustained success of organizations.

To clarify this idea, an example of an integrated organizational performance assessment system is presented below.

Suppose a company whose strategic objectives are quality, profitability and dimension. In its organizational structure, there is a responsibility center called the Business Support unit – quality, whose activity focuses primarily on quality control and monitoring in the various existing centers.

According to the criteria defined by the management, the strategic quality objective has an importance of 20% for the success of the outlined business strategy and its acquisition depends on the activities of the quality units (40%) and production (60%).

The activity of the Business Support unit – Quality focuses on 2 objectives, whose performance is fundamental to its success:

- Audit of the units (objective A) that has a weight of 50% in achieving its operational objectives;
- Analysis to Customer satisfaction (objective B) that also has a weight of 50% in achieving the objectives of its activity.

To analyze the performance in each of the objectives, there are a set of actions of the unit that should be monitored:

A1: Audits of processes (40% of weight in objective A);
A2: Audits of finished products (30% of objective weight A);
A3: Procurement audits (30% of objective weight A);
B1: Surveys (50% of objective weight B);
B2: Information Processing (50% of objective weight B).

In short, we have the situation depicted in Figure 14.

Let us now assume that the degree of achievement of the objectives and actions defined for the quality unit were those indicated in tables 9 and 10.

Figure 14. Integrated model of performance evaluation

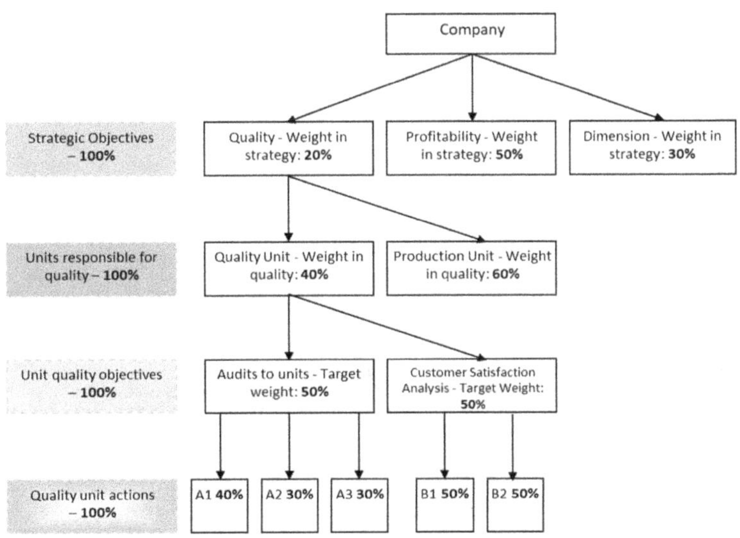

Table 9. Performance in the activities performed in the quality unit

Evaluation criteria	Weighting	Degree of Compliance	Contribution to the objective of the Unit
A1: Process Audits	40%	75%	**30%**
A2: Audits of finished products	30%	50%	**15%**
A3: Audits to purchases	30%	50%	**15%**
A: Audit of the units			**60%**
B1: Surveys	50%	100%	**50%**
B2: Information processing	50%	75%	**37,5%**
B: Customer Satisfaction Analysis			**87,5%**

Table 10. Performance on objectives in Quality Unit

Evaluation criteria	Weighting	Degree of Compliance	Degree of achievement of the objective
A: Audit of the units	50%	60%	30%
B: Customer Satisfaction Analysis	50%	87,5%	43,8%
Degree of achievement of the objective of the quality unit			73,8%

If the production unit had reached its goal in 90%, we would have the degree of achievement of the strategic quality objective shown in Table 11.

Thus, it became evident that the objective in terms of quality had only been reached by about 84% and that there were corrections to be made, especially in the quality unit, since it was in this activity that major deviations occurred.

At the same time, the managers are evaluated according to the objectives of their responsibilities center and their contribution to achieving the strategic objectives of the organization, leading to the existence of greater cohesion between different working areas.

In this example, it was natural for managers to gather together to realize what synergies could create in order to promote performance in each center and also to contribute to improving the common results.

Thus, through the use of an integrated performance evaluation system, it becomes easier for managers to realize where they should focus their attention to improve their performance, to achieve the local and organizational objectives.

Table 11. Performance in the strategic goal quality

Evaluation criteria	Weighting	Degree of Compliance	Degree of achievement of the objective
Quality Unit Performance	40%	73,8%	29,5%
Production Unit Performance	60%	90%	54%
Degree of achievement of the objective of the quality unit			83,5%

However, the implementation of a ISEOP requires a strong commitment of all hierarchical levels and functional areas, and it is essential to perform various activities that ensure the necessary acceptance of the system:

- Clear identification of responsibilities and negotiation between top management and managers of the working areas on the objectives to be achieved and the necessary actions;
- Definition of the degree of importance of each organizational objective for the organization's business success;
- Definition of the contribution level of each working area to obtain each organizational objective;
- Definition of the contribution level of each action to obtain each organizational objective.

To this end, the hierarchical analytical process is normally used, based on the opinion of the collaborators of the various working areas and different hierarchical levels, obtaining priorities averages and weighting the model to be implemented. There are even software that treats data from surveys and identifies the different weighing that has to be attributed to the objectives, actions to be undertaken and the various areas of work. Thus, it intends to ensure the participation and involvement of all in achieving the organizational objectives, favoring the implementation of the formulated strategy.

Internal Transfer Pricing

In organizations based on results and investment centers, it is necessary to define a way of valuing transfers of products and services between suppliers and customers. The internal transfer price is an instrument to value these flows, that is, value the products or services provided by a profit or investment center to other responsibility centers (Anthony & Govindarajan, 2007).

Internal transfer prices are also a way of converging local objectives with the company's global as well as to bring managers to meet the budget (Jordan et al, 2011). For example, if top management wants to reduce capital needs, it can establish a higher cost of equity to finance them, making these internal operations more expensive. As such, managers will tend to be more careful in negotiating the average deadlines for receiving, paying and rotating inventories (Teixeira, 2008b). At the same time, if the top management wants the budget to be respected, it may stipulate higher prices for internal transfers exceeding the predicted values. Thus, it tries to ensure that the defined strategy is a priority for each responsibility center and that there is an alignment between the interests of the organization and that of the managers. In this way, managers will only exceed the budget when important incomes are at stake for the centers and for the company.

In addition, by monetarily valuing transactions between the different centers of responsibility, internal transfer prices contribute to the existence of great autonomy in decisions, equating them to companies Independent. In this sense, managers should have the authority to select the supplier that best suits their needs, regardless of whether they are internal or external to the activity (Jordan et al, 2011).

Horngren et al. (2002), report that the most used domestic transfer prices in the business context are standard cost, Standard cost with margin and market prices. However, researchers draw attention that, irrespective of the valuation used, the internal transfer prices defined should result from negotiation with the managers involved and their acceptance of the defined criteria. Jordan et al (2011) also highlight several ways of determining internal transfer prices.

Through the actual cost of the activity, the price is determined depending on the costs actually incurred to create the product or the service. However, the authors do not advise the use of this method, because the client centers, which acquire products or services to others, will always have their performance conditioned by the best or worst efficiency of the centers that provide them the service or that sell them the product needed for their activity. At the same time, the supplier centers will not tend to improve their performance because their goals are always fulfilled.

Another way to determine internal transfer prices is by default cost, based on pre-determined and stable costs during the established time period. Thus, the suppliers' centres already have their performance affected by the good or malfunctioning of the activity, aiming to have actual costs lower than the defined standard costs. At the same time, the customer centers know in advance the costs they can hire the internal suppliers (usually at lower costs to the market to generate greater internal efficiency) and will not have their performance conditioned by the way as the other center carries out its activity.

Jordan et al (2011) also refer to the use of standard costs which may be added to a marketing margin when the market price of transacted services or products is known. However, in this case, there may be a risk that, if these operations occur in various centers of the internal structure, the price will be more expensive to the customers, which clearly conditions the competitive position of the company. In addition, they also refer to the possibility of a margin partition. In this modality, the production transfers to the commercial area the products at standard cost and, after their sale, the obtained result is divided into two components: one that will cover the supported commercial costs and another, representative of the gross margin, which will be between production and commercial areas. Thus, the production area will also feel motivated to achieve its goals

However, the authors argue that whenever the sales prices in the market are known, the best method to define the prices of internal transfer, are the market prices themselves. When using this modality, it can, for example, compare the profitability of the centres with that of direct competitors. Therefore, the centers of responsibility will have to be competitive, because they run the risk of the client centers choosing external competitors that ensure better conditions.

Finally, Teixeira (2008b) also mentions that the definition of domestic transfer prices should always be negotiated and accepted by the parties involved in the operations carried out within the companies. In this sense, it is essential to look at the prospects of the sellers and the purchasing centers, in order to create synergies in the activity through prices to practice and to promote internal transfers in favor of use of services and goods of other competitors.

In conclusion, it can be inferred that the instruments of behavior guidance have as an end, to ensure that the activity of the operational managers meets the objectives of the centers of responsibility that lead, but also, of the goals the organization's strategic. In this sense, the definition of the pilotage instruments should also be in reference to the existing responsibility centers in the structure, as well as the performance evaluation criteria and the internal transfer pricing systems to be used in various situations of internal service benefits.

DIALOGUE INSTRUMENTS

Nowadays, the success of an organization depends largely on the effective coordination capacity of an increasingly diversified workforce. As we have already mentioned, people are perhaps the company's most precious internal resource. They provide the knowledge, skills and create a dynamic that advances the organization.

However, several changes occurred in the current workforce (Donnelly et al, 2000):

- Great cultural Diversity: the development of communication pathways, globalization and market opening have encouraged the circulation and migration of the population to levels never seen. As such, today any organization has collaborators of the most diverse ethnicities and cultures, making the processes of communication and organizational negotiation difficult;
- Women's emancipation: Currently, females represent about 50% of the workforce. Therefore, family habits and company's organization were changed due to the childcare, traditionally of the mothers ' responsibility;
- Less fidelity of the individual to the organization: In the last decades, the result of the greatest uncertainty always present in the business context, organizations have greatly lost their structures leading to mass redundancies that had as a direct consequence, a lower loyalty from the employee to the company. Even because of the importance of knowledge as resources for organizations, the individual has taken control of his destiny;
- Aging of the population: economic development and the best conditions of hygiene and health have greatly increased the average hope of human life, leading to a significant part of the population today being constituted by elderly workers. Obviously, this alteration has also been felt in the workforce and the number of individuals with age of retirement, who work with organizations, being an inexhaustible source of knowledge.

In view of the cultural diversity and values increasingly present in companies and the immensity of interpersonal relationships that can be formed in a company, due to the various hierarchical levels and existing functional areas, it is easy to see how complex the organizational communication process may be.

Thus, effectively managing people in modern organizations, becomes a real challenge, highlighting the capacity of communication as one of the main skills of the of nowadays managers.

At the same time, and as previously mentioned, one of the main objectives of management control is to involve operational managers in the company's strategy and mission functioning as a contract between both parties. Thus, the circulation of information and negotiation are always present in the implementation of a management control system. For example:

- The mission, business strategies and organizational objectives are defined by the top management. However, the various hierarchical levels and the various functional areas should be aware and actively participate in their dissemination. Otherwise, there is a risk that there are actions and behaviors that jeopardize the sustained growth of the organization;
- The success of the budgetary process, consisting of the definition of objectives, the elaboration of action plans and budgets and budgetary control, is largely dependent on constant negotiation and coordination of efforts between different hierarchical levels and functional areas;
- The definition of performance evaluation criteria also requires the participation of all those involved with the risk, that the managers do not consider the criteria elaborated and there are behaviors of revolt and indifference in the face of the system of management control and the success of the organization itself.

Therefore, management control dialogue instruments are key to fostering communication and negotiation within the organization. Thus, the dialogue instruments should be based on meetings and events that provide friendliness and information sharing between people from different areas of the internal structure of the company, but also in documents and mechanisms that allow access to existing knowledge in the organization. In this sense, and as previously mentioned, the intranet has been facilitating the processes of knowledge management in companies.

It is essential that periodic meetings are defined where employees can monitor the results obtained, compare them with the budget, decide on corrective actions and share information in order to reduce duplication of efforts and create synergies in troubleshooting.

In addition, the meetings should be viewed with the utmost seriousness by the administration and top organs. As such, there should be no delays or postponements of the meetings. Otherwise, there is a risk for employees to feel that the meetings are just a bureaucratic procedure rather than a useful event to determine solutions and discuss ideas.

Finally, the instruments of dialogue should allow information to circulate in a fluid way within the internal structure. That is, the parties involved should have the opportunity to expose their views by finding negotiated and unenforced responses. By engaging employees in the objectives to achieve and by fostering the sharing of information and exchanging opinions, the company manages to be responsible for the quality of the performance. Thus, it benefits, the execution of internal processes and the realization of products to be offered abroad, through a philosophy based on continuous improvements and service excellence.

In conclusion, the success of management control systems is very dependent on the decentralization capacity of the authority and the alignment of the action of the different hierarchical levels and functional areas.

This requires communication and negotiation between the various parties, and therefore the instruments of dialogue are a fundamental basis for the operation of the management control system which is intended to implement.

However, the function of the instruments of dialogue goes far beyond the simple organizational communication. In fact, by allowing everyone to be involved in the definition of objectives, action plans, budgets and control and evaluation systems, they are contributing to the sharing of knowledge in the people and structure of the company, which in turn, potentializes the application of this strategic resource in other areas of work and in the development of new knowledge that favors the creation of innovative solutions in the market.

CONCLUSION

We made a characterization of management control tools, through using a diverse reference bibliography on the subject and we developed some important themes that should be the basis of the definition of management control tools, in particularly, a description of management control instruments and their pilot function and as guides behavior and dialogue.

The pilotage instruments allow operational managers to reflect on their working area, defining objectives and identifying necessary activities and resources and contribute to a greater dissemination of the mission and strategic objectives by the various hierarchical levels and various areas of work.

The management control instruments as behavior guidance ensure that the activity of the operational managers meets the objectives of the centers of responsibility that lead, but also, of the goals the organization's strategic. In this sense, the definition of the pilotage instruments should also be in reference to the existing responsibility centers in the structure, as well as the performance evaluation criteria and the internal transfer pricing systems to be used in various situations of internal service benefits.

Considering that the success of management control systems is very dependent on the decentralization capacity of the authority and the alignment of the action of the different hierarchical levels and functional areas, this requires communication and negotiation between the various parties, and therefore the instruments of dialogue are a fundamental basis for the operation of the management control system which is intended to implement.

After describing some of the models developed in the meantime, it appears that there are several with diverse characteristics and areas of intervention.

REFERENCES

Almeida, J. (2001, Apr.). *Os Instrumentos de Gestão Previsional e a sua Auditoria: O Caso Português. OROC – Revisores & Empresas.*

Anthony, R., & Govindarajan, V. (2007). Management Control Systems (12th ed.). New York: McGraw-Hill.

Argyris, C. (1952). *The impact of budgets on people.* Nre York: Controllership Foundation.

Azzone, G., Masella, C., & Bertelé, U. (1991). Design of performance measures for time-based companies. *International Journal of Operations & Production Management, 11*(3), 77–85. doi:10.1108/01443579110143412

Banker, R., Charnes, A., & Cooper, W. (1984). Some models for estimating technical and scale inefficiencies in data envelopment analysis. *Management Science, 30*(9), 1078–1092. doi:10.1287/mnsc.30.9.1078

Bartol, K. & Martin, D. (1998). *Management* (3rd ed.). McGraw-Hill.

Basso, L., & Lima, A. (2002). *Análise de Processos de Gestão Voltados à Criação de valor para o Accionista – Um Estudo de Caso do GVA- FGV/SP. In 3º Encontro Ibero-Americano de Finanças e Sistemas de Informação – A Empresa do Século XXI.* Setúbal: ESCE.

Brown, M. (1996). *Keeping score: using the right metrics to drive world class performance.* New York: Quality Resources.

Caiado, A. (2002). *Contabilidade de Gestão* (2nd ed.). Áreas Editora.

Chandler, A. (1977). *The visible hand – Managerial revolution in American business.* Boston: Harvard University Press.

Charnes, A., Cooper, W., & Rhodes, E. (1978). Measuring efficiency of decision-making units. *European Journal of Operational Research, 2*(6), 429–444. doi:10.1016/0377-2217(78)90138-8

Chiavenato, I. (1993). *Introdução à teoria geral da administração* (4th ed.). São Paulo: Makron Books do Brasil.

Damodaran, A. (2007). *Return on Capital (ROC), Return on Invested Capital (ROIC) and Return on Equity (ROE): Measurement and implications*. SSRN Electronic Journal.

Donnelly, J., Gibson, J., & Ivancevich, J. (2000). *Administração – Princípios de gestão empresarial* (10th ed.). McGraw-Hill.

Drucker, P. (1954). *The practice of management*. New York: Harper.

Drucker, P. (1967). *The effective executive*. New York: Harper & Row.

Edvinsson, L., & Malone, M. (1997). *Intellectual Capital: Realizing your Company's true value by finding its hidden roots*. New York: Harper Business.

Epstein, M., & Manzoni, J. (1998). Implementing Corporate Strategy: From Tableaux de Bord to Balanced Scorecards. *European Management Journal, 16*(2).

Esperança, J., & Matias, F. (2009). *Finanças Empresariais* (2nd ed.). Texto Editora, Alfragide.

Felizardo, A., Félix, E., & Thomaz, J. (2017). *Organizational Performance Measurement and Evaluation Systems in SMES: The Case ofThe Transforming Industry in Portugal*. CEFAGE Working Paper 2017/05.

Fitzgerald, L., Johnston, R., Brignall, S., Silvestro, R., & Voss, C. (1991). *Performance measurement in service business*. London: CIMA.

Jordan, H., Neves, J., & Rodrigues, J. (2011). *O Controlo de Gestão - Ao Serviço da Estratégia e dos Gestores* (10th ed.). Lisboa: Áreas Editora.

Kaplan, R., & Norton, D. (1992, Jan.). The balanced scorecard – measures that drive performance. *Harvard Business Review*, 71–79. PMID:10119714

Kaplan, R., & Norton, D. (1993, Sept.). Putting the balanced scorecard to work. *Harvard Business Review*, 134–147.

Kaplan, R., & Norton, D. (1996a, Jan.). Using the balanced scorecard as a strategic management system. *Harvard Business Review*, 75–85.

Kaplan, R., & Norton, D. (1996b). Linking the balanced scorecard to strategy. *California Management Review, 39*(1), 53–79. doi:10.2307/41165876

Kaplan, R., & Norton, D. (2001a). Transforming the balanced scorecard from performance measurement to strategic management: Part I. *American Accounting Association, 15*(1), 87–104.

Kaplan, R., & Norton, D. (2001b). Transforming the balanced scorecard from performance measurement to strategic management: Part II. *American Accounting Association, 15*(2), 147–160.

Kaplan, R., & Norton, D. (2004). *Mapas Estratégicos* (6th ed.). Rio de Janeiro: Editora Campos.

Keegan, D., Eiler, R., & Jones, C. (1989). Are your performance measures obsolete? *Management Accounting, 70*(12), 45–50.

Lynch, R., & Cross, K. (1991). *Measure up – the essential guide to measuring business performance*. London: Mandarin.

Moreira, J. (1997). *Análise de empresas – da teoria à prática*. Porto: Associação da Bolsa de Derivados do Porto.

Neely, A. (2005). The evolution of performance measurement research – developments in the last decade and a research agenda for the next. *International Journal of Operations & Production Management, 25*(12), 1264–1277. doi:10.1108/01443570510633648

Neely, A., & Adams, C. (2001). *Perspectives on performance: the performance prism*. Cranfield School of Management. Retrieved from www.crandield.ac.co.uk/som/cbp

Neely, A., Gregory, M., & Platts, K. (2005). Performance measurement system design A literature review and research agenda. *International Journal of Operations & Production Management, 25*(12).

Neely, A., Mills, J., Platts, K., Richards, H., Gregory, M., Bourne, M., & Kennerley, M. (2000). Performance measurement system design: Developing and testing a process-based approach. *International Journal of Operations & Production Management, 20*(10), 1119–1145. doi:10.1108/01443570010343708

Neves, J. (2002). *Avaliação de Empresas e Negócios*. Lisboa: McGrawhill.

Neves, J. (2011). *Avaliação e Gestão da Performance Estratégica da Empresa*. Academic Press.

Neves, J. (2012). *Análise e Relato Financeiro – Uma visão integrada de gestão (5th ed.)*. Lisboa: Texto Editora.

Olve, N., Roy, J., & Wetter, M. (1999). *Performance Drivers: a practical guide to using the balanced scorecard*. Chichester, UK: Wiley.

Ribeiro, J. (2003). *Modelo de identificação de grupos estratégicos para a indústria metalomecânica de produção, por encomenda, de bens de equipamento* (Unpublished doctoral dissertation). ISCTE, Lisboa, Portugal.

Ridgway, V. (1956). Dysfunctional consequences of performance measurements. *Administrative Science Quarterly, 1*(2), 240–247. doi:10.2307/2390989

Rodrigues, J. (2010). *Avaliação do desempenho das organizações*. Escolar Editora.

Salas, O. (2001). *El Cuadro de Mando Integral*. XI Congreso AECA – Empresa, euro y Nueva Economia, Madrid, Spain.

Scherer, F. (1980). *Industrial market structure and economics performance (2nd ed.)*. Boston: Houghton Mifflin Company.

Silva, E., & Queirós, M. (2010). *Gestão Financeira - Análise de Investimentos*. Porto: Vida Económica.

Silva, F. (1979). *Contabilidade Industrial* (8th ed.). Livraria Sá da Costa.

Taliani, E. (2001). *La Actual Concepcion de los Processos Presupuestários – Evolucion o Revolution*. XI Congresso AECA – Empresa, Euro e Nova Economia.

Teixeira, A., & Alves, T. (2003). *A Contabilidade e o Valor, na Perspectiva dos Utilizadores da Informação Financeira. In XV Encontro nacional da ADCES: Contabilidade e Valor: Novos Contextos*. Setúbal: ESCE.

Teixeira, A., Teixeira, N., & Mata, C. (2008). *Implementação do Tableau de Bord – Estudo de caso no sector das Rochas Ornamentais.* IV Congresso de Custos do Mercosul – Montevideu.

Teixeira, N. (2007). A avaliação do desempenho de centros de responsabilidade – Estudo de caso. *XIV Congresso da AECA.*

Teixeira, N. (2008a). *A Rendibilidade e a Criação de Valor. In XIII Encuentro AECA*. Aveiro: Universidade Aveiro.

Teixeira, N. (2008b). *A caracterização da estrutura financeira do sector das tecnologias de informação.* Estudo apresentado no âmbito do Concurso de provas públicas para Professor Adjunto na ESCE na área científica de Finanças (edital nº 682/2008).

Teixeira, N. (2013). A avaliação do risco e da criação de valor no contexto empresarial. In *Empreendedorismo, Coesão Social e Dinâmicas Empresariais. Caderno da Sociedade e Trabalho nº17.* GEP/MSESS.

Teixeira, N., & Amaro, A. (2013). Avaliação do desempenho financeiro e da criação de valor - um estudo de caso. *Revista Universo Contábil, 6*(4), 157–178. doi:10.4270/ruc.2013436

Teixeira, N., & Carreira, F. (2008). Implementação de um sistema de avaliação do desempenho - Estudo de caso no sector português das Rochas Ornamentais. *XV Congresso Brasileiro de Custos* – Curitiba.

Teixeira, N., Mata, C., Pardal, P., & Teixeira, A. (2012). *A aplicação da rendibilidade supranormal para a avaliação da criação de valor*. XXIII Jornadas Hispano Lusas de Gestão Cientifica, Málaga.

Young, S., & O'Byrne, S. (2001). *EVA® and Value Based Management*. New York: MacGraw-Hill.

Chapter 5
Management Control Instruments:
Support Topics

ABSTRACT

The definition of the dialogue instruments is closely linked to the management of the knowledge that companies want to implement and should contribute to the proper functioning of the management control tools and to the sharing, application, and knowledge creation within the organization. In this chapter, some knowledge management techniques will be presented, which should be defined, taking also into consideration the management control systems to be implemented. In view of the constant changes in the business environment, the company must be market-oriented, and adequate information by segments will be highlighted for decision making. Being important to obtain efficiencies in the realization of internal work processes, the authors also describe some topics of the activity-based costing and activity-based management. As organizations are becoming more complex and decentralized, the information system should also adapt. In this sense, the authors describe organizational types and the adaptation of the management control instruments.

KNOWLEDGE MANAGEMENT

The Importance of Knowledge

As mentioned, the offer developed by most companies is currently based on the sophistication and permanent innovation or the efficiency of the work processes, therefore, the competitive advantages very associated with the result of knowledge, which encompasses, among other factors (Hislop, 2013):

- Human Resources skills: qualifications, experience and creativity;
- Organization Competencies: organizational structure, quality of management, work processes and techniques, organizational values and culture, information systems, speed of action, research, notoriety and upstream and downstream relations.

DOI: 10.4018/978-1-7998-2007-9.ch005

As it can be seen, all the factors enunciated are intimately related to the knowledge of customers, products, technologies, company's working methods. In addition, it can be inferred that there are two types of knowledge:

- Tacitus: It is the one that is incorporated into individuals and that is why it is not easily transmissible. As examples we have: life experiences, organizational values and culture;
- Explicit: It is articulated and coded knowledge, which is described in rules and procedures known and accepted by everyone in the organization, so it is easily transmissible.

However, they are in such a way interconnected, that it is very difficult to analyze them separately. For example, the interpretation of a document (explicit knowledge) often depends on the experiences of each one (tacit knowledge). In this sequence of ideas, it is fundamental to interconnect the two types of knowledge, align them with the company's strategy, share them and act on them (Hislop, 2013).

In this regard, Edvinsson and Malone (1997), two of the main investigators in this area, defined knowledge (for these authors, the term intellectual capital assumes the same meaning), using an analogy: comparing the company to a Tree. The visible part constituted by the trunk, branches and leaves is constituted by the explicit knowledge composed of documents and reports. The hidden roots are in fact the largest part of the tree, hence the fruit quality, flavor and color (tacit knowledge). Therefore, they propose the separation of knowledge (or intellectual capital) in two perspectives based on the criterion of possession:

- Human Capital: It is the combination of the experience, skills, innovation and individual capacities of employees in the performance of their tasks, including the company' values and culture;
- Structural Capital: *Hardware*, *software*, databases, organizational structure, patents, customer and supplier panoply, brands and all other assets that support employee productivity.

Thus, the company can transact structural capital, but cannot own human capital. Despite this, human capital expands other knowledge capacities. The company must consider a process that ensures its creation, sharing and application in the organization, in order to awaken a culture of innovation and entrepreneurship in the internal structure, contributing to greater flexibility and adequate response to the market constant surroundings changes (Amaral & Pedro, 2004).

Knowledge and management can be defined as follows (Kluge et al, 2002):

- Knowledge consists in understanding relationships and causalities, so it is fundamental to make operations effective, elaborate business processes or predict business models' results;
- Management is a conscious and systematic decision on how best to use scarce resources in an environment of uncertainty to achieve lasting improvements in the performance of an organization.

Combining these definitions, one can infer that knowledge management consists in understanding the relationships within the organization and in its surroundings, to coordinate the available resources, in order to improve products, processes and customer relations, creating value for activity stakeholders and obtaining competitive advantages that allow sustained growth. Thus, knowledge management should be properly aligned with the organization's business strategy and accepted by all hierarchical levels and functional areas assuming the risk, being, otherwise, ineffective.

Considering the challenges of the business context, figure 1 is presented with a suggestion of a model of business success that will contribute greatly to the management of knowledge.

Knowledge Management Tasks

Knowledge management must develop three fundamental tasks in order to foster an organizational culture that awakens to knowledge (Kluge et al, 2002): generation, distribution and application of knowledge by all hierarchical levels and functional areas.

However, it is noteworthy that knowledge management does not succeed in stages, and all tasks should be performed simultaneously, since knowledge is created, shared and applied at anytime and anywhere in the organization. However, companies live on results and therefore, if a priority order is to be established to implement knowledge management, the task of the application should be favored, because it is the one that is more quickly reflected in the operation and results, making the effects of knowledge more readily visible in organizational success (Hislop, 2013).

Then, according to the same logic, the distribution arises and, ultimately, the generation (Kluge et al, 2002). This sequence is justified, because on the one hand, in any organization there is available knowledge that is only waiting for it to be applied, and on the other, quick results help to integrate everyone into the project and generate the enthusiasm needed to that knowledge becomes an organizational priority (Valente & Lourenço, 2019).

Now, in more detail, each of the tasks of knowledge management:

Figure 1. Business success model

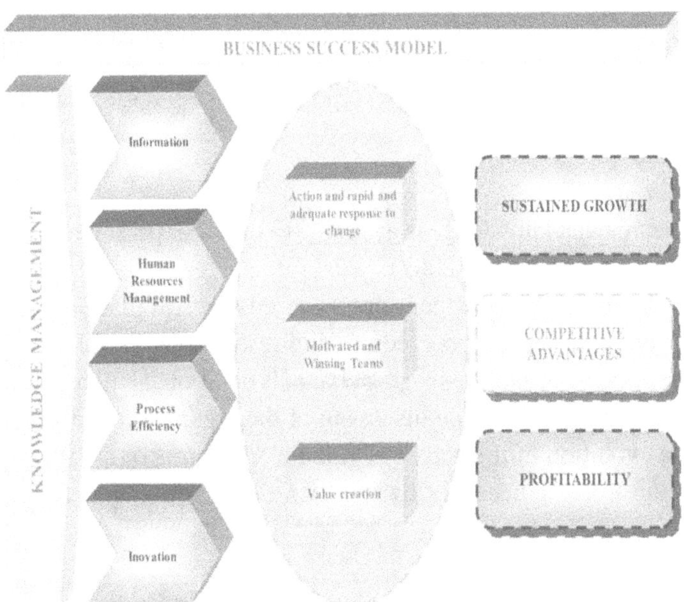

Figure 2. Knowledge management process

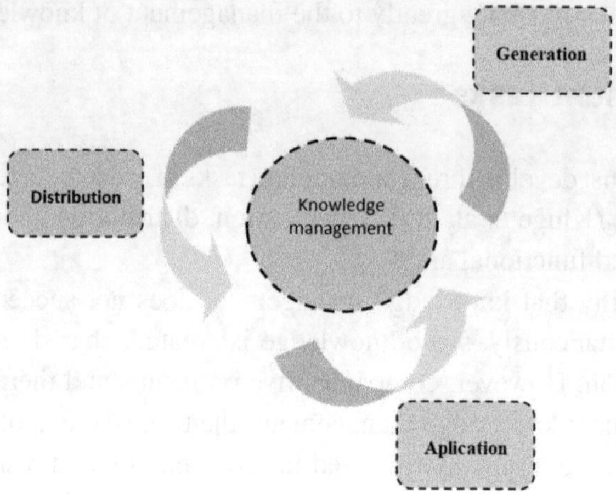

Knowledge Application

Knowledge happens spontaneously within the organization, whether in discussing ideas in a meeting or in the use of certain machinery. However, the concern of knowledge management should focus on techniques that allow the application of available and still unused knowledge, which can contribute to obtaining better results (Kluge et al, 2002; Gupta & Pepetu, 2007).

Without an effective application, the distribution and knowledge generation tasks lose relevance. This is because it is not logical to create or share knowledge when it cannot be put into practice (Valente & Lourenço, 2019).

This is one of the errors that is detected in organizations, since it is not uncommon for companies to make substantial investments in the development of ideas to improve work processes or products, but which are not applied for lack of due involvement in the project by increasing the archive of documentation. The same is the case with information technologies, with the use of high sums to acquire *software* or databases, which are never used for lack of training of human resources or adapting to company needs (Hislop, 2013).

Knowledge Distribution

The distribution task ensures that knowledge is available to the right person in the right place at the right time (Kluge et al, 2002; Gupta & Pepetu, 2007).

The company must ensure that knowledge is not imposed, but still made available to those who have the need to access it, avoiding information excesses and restrictions. In addition, complex procedures should be avoided, instigating information-sharing channels creation, at all hierarchical levels and by the various functional areas, as well as from the inside out of the organization, allowing the involvement of the various actors in the evolution of the activity (Valente & Lourenço, 2019).

Within an organization, communication flows in four distinct directions (Donnelly et al, 2000; Hislop, 2013):

- Ascending: Flows from people from a lower hierarchical level to people of higher levels;
- Descending: Flows from people from a higher hierarchical level to people of lower levels;
- Horizontal: Flows from people of the same hierarchical level but from different functional areas;
- Diagonal: Flows from people of different hierarchical level and from different functional areas.

As such, it is easy to see the immensity of interpersonal relationships that can be formed in a company and how complex the organizational communication process can be. Good ideas do not have the right time to occur, can succeed from anyone, anywhere and at any time. Therefore, knowledge management should ensure the existence of communication channels that provide the easy sharing of information within the organization (Hislop, 2013).

In addition, information technologies have completely changed the role of the various players in the business world. Today, the *Internet* represents an open door for previously inaccessible markets, as well as a vehicle to further strengthen customer-supplier relationships. Through the so-called network, the contact is very intense facilitating communication and speed in trade. On the other hand, the client becomes a participant in the entire operational process, from the conception phase to the delivery of the final service and can insert new *inputs* at any time (Eiglier & Langeard, 1999).

Obviously, this new way of being in business can also bring clear benefits in terms of process efficiency, as several steps can be eliminated, overcoming the traditional bureaucracy. In addition, information technologies have also come to acquire a very important role in supporting management and decision-making. In fact, through the personalized information systems created, companies can now more easily control business and know their customers, and can have real time information available (Eiglier & Langeard, 1999).

In this way, it is in the distribution that investment should be greater at the infrastructure level, through the information systems implementation, the *intranet* and the *internet*, fostering a knowledge-oriented culture.

Finally, it will be important for companies to create dialogue instruments that ensure personal interaction, in particular, meetings and conviviality with collaborators of different hierarchical levels and functional areas, which allow for greater involvement and that information, circulates in a fluid way in the various directions within the organizational structure. That is, the parties involved should have the opportunity to expose their views by finding negotiated and non-imposed responses, favoring the excellence of the internal processes and the products offered, as well as the constant adequacy to business partners ' needs.

Knowledge Generation

The task of generating knowledge is one that can make you feel in the company's success only in a relatively long-time frame. This is because, until there are projects that create real innovations at the level of processes or products, it is normal for several attempts to fail and only to create small improvements in short-term results (Kluge et al, 2002; Gupta & Pepetu, 2007).

Thus, in order to avoid demotivation, unambitious objectives must be established that, over time, can give rise to great achievements that act directly on the competitive advantages of the company (Hislop, 2013).

In addition, the generation task should identify areas where knowledge should develop more rapidly. Therefore, it is very important to align knowledge management with business strategy and organizational objectives, so that knowledge creation is adequate to the company's needs. This factor is even more important in the industries with shorter products life cycles, where the need for innovation in supply, working processes and markets to cover becomes more important (Valente & Lourenço, 2019).

Finally, the task of generating knowledge must ensure its permanent updating, so that eventual outputs of employees do not jeopardize company's competitiveness.

Knowledge' Characteristics

As previously mentioned, knowledge presents some characteristics that clearly distinguish it from the remaining resources of an organization and that condition the definition of the most appropriate techniques for carrying out the tasks of the of knowledge management (Kluge et al, 2002; Gupta & Pepetu, 2007; Hislop, 2013; Valente & Lourenço, 2019):

Subjectivity

The interpretation of documents or attitudes in various situations depends on the experiences and values of each individual. Therefore, being the knowledge largely in the possession of the employees who form the company, it is characterized by the subjectivity inherent to each person, it is not possible to treat it identically to the remaining resources much easier to measure and quantify.

Transferability

Knowledge can be transferred to different realities. For example, successful work processes and techniques in a factory can be transferred to another, in order to obtain operational efficiencies or innovations in the manufactured products.

Sedimentation

Knowledge is present in the normal functioning of an organization. However, it may not be easily available. This is because it is often not shared between different functional areas or only found in a worker's mind. How often does a business unit fails to quickly respond to a customer because it is confronted with some new situation, having already been another unit to solve a similar situation earlier? The simple sharing of information could eliminate these operational inefficiencies, which affect the organizations competitiveness.

Self-Worth

Knowledge increases in value by simple sharing throughout the organization's functioning. For example, innovations in certain processes or products in a given business unit or functional area, when shared, can also optimize other business units or functional areas, increasing value creation and company global profitability.

Perishability

The value of knowledge is very unstable, being much interconnected, with the exclusivity of its detention or the opportunity of its application. For example, if a company has a patent that grants it the opportunity to be the sole supplier of a given market segment, it will have a very valuable knowledge. On the contrary, a company that is developing a new product and that is surpassed by a competitor who puts a similar product faster on the market will have a knowledge that will easily devaluate.

Spontaneity

Knowledge is unpredictable. It does not have an appointment or a right time to take place. It can appear through any employee, anytime, anywhere.

The understanding of these characteristics is essential for the convenient realization of the tasks of knowledge management. This is because any of the characteristics enunciated greatly influences its success.

For example, **subjectivity** greatly conditions the **application** of knowledge, because if there is no uniformity in the way of working in different functional areas and several hierarchical levels, it becomes very difficult to put knowledge into action and align the local objectives of each sector with those of the organization.

As for the **transferability,** it is closely linked to any of the tasks of knowledge management. It can be directly related with **distribution,** but also with **application,** because knowledge transfer fosters its performance in new areas of the organization. However, **generation** is also conditioned by new knowledge that can be created with information sharing from different stakeholders.

Sedimentation and **self-worth** are interconnected with **distribution,** because it is essential that knowledge is shared, in order to optimize the value chain of the activity and to provide the creating competitive advantages for the company.

Regarding **perishability**, it is also related to any of the tasks of knowledge management, because the faster the **generation**, **distribution** and **application, the** greater the hypotheses of knowledge to bring added value to the company, against its competitors.

Finally, **spontaneity** is entirely linked to the **generation,** because the company will have to know how to cope with the unpredictable character of knowledge. In summary, we have the Table 1.

Considering the intrinsic characteristics of knowledge, several techniques that can be used by knowledge management will be discussed in order to create real competitive advantages that allow the sustainable success of Medium-and long-term organization.

Table 1. Interconnection between the characteristics and tasks of knowledge management

Characteristic of Knowledge	Conditional Tasks
– Subjectivity	– Application
– Transferability	– Generation, Distribution and Application
– Sedimentation	– Distribution
– Self Appreciation	– Distribution
– Perishability	– Generation, Distribution and Application
– Spontaneity	– Generation

Knowledge Management Techniques

The approach followed, intends to highlight in relation to each characteristic of knowledge that techniques should be applied, as well as what objectives are intended to achieve, so that knowledge management can contribute to the business success of the organization (Kluge et al, 2002; Gupta & Pepetu, 2007; Hislop, 2013; Valente & Lourenço, 2019).

Subjectivity

"It's rare for managers to work directly with things they worked before, with information about it." (Donnelly et al, 2000; 373). This sentence shows the importance of communication skills. In most organizations, statements such as the following are regularly heard: "The invoice did not follow, because no one said it was urgent; When the administrator says as soon as possible, it means now "(Donnelly et al, 2000; 374). In these situations, what is underlying, is a failure of communication between functional areas and hierarchical levels or different perceptions of reality according to each worker professional experiences.

Thus, the message often suffers distortions along the chain of command, arising inefficiencies in the working processes and ineffective consequences regarding the clients. Hence, the techniques that allow filling subjectivity, assume a strategic role in the design of a knowledge system. Communication and information sharing between the various hierarchical levels and different functional areas are the fundamental basis.

Thus, in order to cope with subjectivity, knowledge management should establish as purpose:

To promote the organizational, in order to involve the various hierarchical levels and functional areas in strategic company's mission, working as a contract between the parties. Thus, there will be the involvement of all in the decisions taken, the linking of the local objectives with the organizational and, finally, a standardization of acting in various situations, favoring the company in favor of individual or departmental interests.

To achieve this goal, the appropriate techniques may be (Kluge et al, 2002; Gupta & Pepetu, 2007; Hislop, 2013; Valente & Lourenço, 2019):

- *Rotation of functions: the realization of different roles, gives a broader idea of the organizational functioning and the different problems of each functional area or working process;*
- *Flexible organizational structure with few hierarchical levels: provides lower possibilities of distortions in messages and favors a more informal climate, fostering the sharing of ideas;*
- *Multidisciplinary team training: Allows the sharing of information from different specialists generating greater knowledge of the value chain of the activity and, consequently, greater efficiency in the working processes;*
- *Implementation of systems such as the tableauxs de bord or Balanced scorecard: Allows the alignment of objectives between hierarchical levels and functional areas, as well as finding objective indicators for evaluating the employees;*
- *Employee performance analysis based on individual and collective assessment indicators: in order to ensure greater organizational cohesion, evaluation should be done according to a combination of indicators that measure the achievement of the company's objectives and of the individual;*

- *Realization of meetings and informal events: the conviviality among the collaborators of the different hierarchical levels and functional areas fosters the sharing of information and the creation of a true organizational culture.*

Transferability

Knowledge transferability allows its application in different contexts, permitting the working processes improvement or of the products themselves. However, it may ultimately favor the emergence of new business opportunities. For example, a company that has a high specialization on a more efficient manufacturing process in an industry can provide consultancy in the implementation of this process in other companies of the same branch.

Thus, at the level of transferability, companies should aim to:

Create information channels, which allow to know more and better the value chain of the activity as well as to monitor market trends and innovations and suggestions from the various business players.

To this end, the following techniques are preponderant (Kluge et al, 2002; Gupta & Pepetu, 2007; Hislop, 2013; Valente & Lourenço, 2019):

- *Internal Benchmarking: Allows the comparison of the way internal processes are carried out and which are the best solutions to be applied within the organization;*
- *Implementation of the intranet: it ensures the existence of a space where experiences, doubts, cases of success, etc., constitute a true center of knowledge sharing;*
- *Conducting alliances and partnerships with the various business stakeholders: it allows the exchange of information on different perspectives of the business to be at the market's needs, access to marketing channels or innovations at the level of products' processes;*
- *Formalizing protocols with research centers, schools or specialists: the relationship with institutions dedicated to research, can guarantee the company the timely monitoring of trends in relation to techniques and working processes, as well as to products and services to offer;*
- *Conducting market studies: allow to better know the needs of the client, being this a very important factor in the current business context characterized by the high competitiveness.*

Sedimentation

Each collaboration holds a significant amount of knowledge that it puts into practice in the daily performance of its tasks and does not share with the rest of the organization. Therefore, the loss of an employee also represents an effective loss of knowledge.

As such, the great goal of knowledge management to deal with the sedimentation characteristic should be:

Extract the knowledge provisioned in each employee and intervener of the activity, so that the good ideals and success cases can be shared and that best practices are repeated, as well as avoiding the loss of knowledge with the natural rotation of Human Resources.

In order to achieve this goal, the following techniques are applied (Kluge et al, 2002; Gupta & Pepetu, 2007; Hislop, 2013; Valente & Lourenço, 2019):

- *Databases with the identification of employees of the company: must contain the name, functional structure to which they belong, as well as the area of specialization. Thus, true libraries of knowledge are generated within the organization;*
- *Training on the job: personal contact should be favored because it allows to more effectively transfer the knowledge of the teacher to the learner, generating the copies of the best practices;*
- *Participation of customers and suppliers in the operations: meetings must be held periodically, with the various business players being fundamental, as they are part of the working process, from the research phase and development to the post-sale service itself, and they certainly have a perspective of the business different from the company, generating new ideas.*

Self Appreciation

Unlike other resources, knowledge can be valued through its transfer to other areas or company' workers. Thus, the objective of knowledge management in this characteristic may be the following:

Select information receivers to avoid the excesses or restrictions of data and to ensure that the knowledge arrives to the employees who can potentiate their value by creating competitive advantages for the company.

The techniques suggested are as follows (Kluge et al, 2002; Gupta & Pepetu, 2007; Hislop, 2013; Valente & Lourenço, 2019):

- *Management based on activities: All processes are monitored, analyzed and evaluated, obtaining a greater fluidity in the exchange of outputs and information between the various areas of work, knowing better the cost generators and developing more and more competencies in activities that create value for the customer;*
- *Implementation of information systems (ERP's) that enable the stakeholders of each process to follow all stages from development to after-sales assistance, guaranteeing the cohesion of performance at the level of the various functional areas;*
- *Introduction of Supply Chain and Customer Relationship Management systems in order to allow business players both upstream and downstream to actively participate in work processes, contributing to optimize the final offer;*
- *Training by internal or external specialists: it intends to provide specialized knowledge to workers in functional areas and working processes. In addition to in-person training, e-learning is gaining importance because it manages to overcome the problems related to the availability' scarcity. However, it is advisable to combine the two methodologies, because personal contact fosters a greater transfer of knowledge, while e-learning may be more practical to share opinions or to solve fewer complex doubts.*

Perishability

The value of knowledge is very variable, being dependent on the exclusivity of its ownership and the degree of opportunity of its application. Therefore, the goal of knowledge management in this area can be:

Ensure the organizational speed of performance to allow knowledge to be generated, distributed and applied in good time, providing competitive advantages by the systematic adequacy to the environment and market needs.

Regarding the following techniques are suggested (Kluge et al, 2002; Gupta & Pepetu, 2007; Hislop, 2013; Valente & Lourenço, 2019):

- *Strategic planning: Monitoring of the environment, market and competition is essential. In this way, the trends and state of the art of the industry are verified, and that areas of knowledge should be developed and those that lack competences should be abandoned;*
- *Authority decentralization: it is very important that those who deal with everyday problems, who have the possibility of making decisions, do not create bottle necks in the working processes, increasing the speed of action;*
- *Total Quality Management: The certification of the company, its products and services, as well as its work processes allows the standardization of procedures and make the quality a concern of the entire organization. Thus, the definition of responsibilities, tasks and objectives aims to facilitate the exchange of inputs and outputs between functional areas, freeing employees for the development of organizational competencies and decreasing the cycle of innovation;*
- *Quality control: Although quality should be a concern of the whole organization, there should be an agency responsible for verifying compliance with the procedures defined, in order to check for possible operational difficulties and to optimize the Implementation of the various work processes.*

Spontaneity

As a resource that emerges unpredictably, knowledge management should have as a concern to deal with spontaneity:

Create an organizational culture of innovation, stimulating the debate of ideas and access to different internal and external opinions on the various organizational themes.

In this sense, the following techniques are identified (Kluge et al, 2002; Gupta & Pepetu, 2007; Hislop, 2013; Valente & Lourenço, 2019):

- *Personal contact with various business players: The post-sales assistance service, as well as attendance at fairs and visits to customer, supplier and business partner facilities, may be important vehicles for access to information on the activity and products made available;*
- *Access to the Internet and specialized discussion groups: Allows employees to consult different proposals for the organization's problems and, if possible, find better solutions;*

- *Workshops and brainstorming: The realization of events where opinions can be debated, can be a great technique to foster greater organizational cohesion and to create better solutions to be applied in different functional areas;*
- *Rewarding the good ideas: the success of organizations, comes largely from the so-called champions, that is, from the collaborators who for their dedication to the projects and the company itself, develop solutions that create value and competitive advantages that sustain the Medium-and long-term growth. Therefore, it is essential to create myths and models of excellence showing that individual and organizational development are closely related. In addition to the financial prizes, there should be public recognition of who contributes to the success of the company;*
- *Encouraging entrepreneurship: Each employee should represent a potential entrepreneur. Whoever creates an idea that can add value to the organization should be able to present and follow a development project, defining objectives, actions, deadlines, resources to be used and financing plan.*

Next, we present figure 3 that summarizes the integration of the various characteristics with the objectives, techniques and tasks of knowledge management.

The development of knowledge management emerged as an attempt to highlight knowledge as a strategic resource, in organizations that intend to be competitive in the current business context, contributing to a greater sharing and knowledge application, as well as, for a greater action alignment for the different sectors and intermediate company managers.

At the same time, the explanation of this working point also allowed for further important conclusions:

- It is the top organs that should encourage a management that favors the generation, distribution and application of knowledge, since they have a broader view of the business and the environment,

Figure 3. Integration of knowledge management characteristics, tasks and techniques

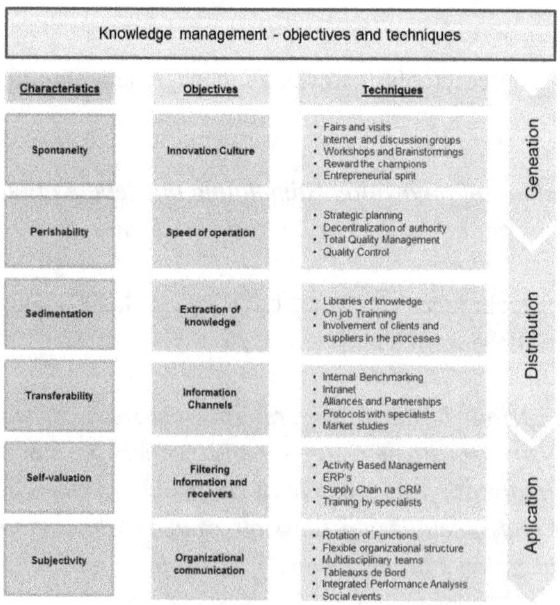

can define the priority areas of innovation and align the action to organizational structure with the outlined corporate strategy;

- Knowledge management should be an organizational concern, stimulating the existence of a culture of innovation and entrepreneurship and rewarding good ideas and good models;
- Knowledge management is based on organizational communication and dialogue tools that allow information sharing, contributing to more efficient internal processes and better market responsiveness;
- Information technologies are a great vehicle for knowledge access and companies must invest in it, according to their needs, in instruments such as *internet*, *intranet*, *ERP*, *Supply Chain* and *CRM*.

SEGMENT INFORMATION MANAGEMENT

As previously mentioned, globalization, market opening, and constant technological innovations have caused profound changes in economic activity. Nowadays, business is very fast, there are several opportunities associated with different levels of risk, and the manager has multiple options and needs to choose the one that guarantees a more sustained growth of the business.

In this way, and in view of the constant changes in the business environment and demand, the modern company must be market-oriented, demanding a rigorous and adequate information system that allows it to monitor its activity properly, as well as its surroundings.

Thus, concerns such as the profitability of customers, the value generated by project, activity or distribution channel, are fundamental for the managers of our days and the accounting systems should adapt to this new reality, with the aim of become true instruments of decision support. In this sense, financial information by segments has been highlighted in the collection and organization of financial information for decision-making.

Segment Information' Goals

Due to the uncertainty always present in the business context, access to information and speed of action have become critical factors of success in companies.

As such, accounting systems have sought instruments to verify where value is created and destroyed in the business. Thus, the registration of property facts ceased to focus only on the optimization of costs, to prioritize the analysis of company segments' profitability, being the segment an organizational unit, whose information is important to disclose, as support for the evaluation of performance and decision-making (Lourenço, 2001).

It is increasingly common to see that companies' operational planning and budgetary process tends to disaggregate information by markets, products or services, by business units or responsibility centers, etc. This is because the organisational structure and the circulation of information should be increasingly flexible to allow a quicker and more appropriate response.

Today, the company intends to know the value generated and not only the levels of consumption of resources, because low costs are not synonymous with good results, as well as high costs do not necessarily cause bad results. Thus, what is intended to be known is the contribution margin of each segment to the company's results (Jordan et al, 2011).

Thus, disaggregating the information, it seeks to determine which segments generate value and which ones destroy value, consuming resources, decreasing the margin and the overall result.

Defining and Identifying Segments

The bases and structure of internal reporting by segments must be adapted according to the characteristics of each company, seeking to respond efficiently to the needs of the management, namely, to hold timely and relevant information for its decision. Segment's typology to be adopted may be of different order and must be the managers to define the most appropriate.

However, it is currently possible to find guidelines in the international accounting standards that enable companies to define and identify their segment structure, namely the International Financial Reporting Standards-IFRS 8. Although this standard intends to regulate the presentation of information by segments in the financial statements of listed companies in the stock exchange, it has a set of concepts and rules that can be adopted internally by companies as a reference, essentially in relation to segments materiality measurement and identification.

Thus, companies may define their segmentation typology by reference to the normative suggestions (although IFRS 8 states that if the financial information system and the internal organization have another focus, such as the existence of business units, the company is free to define the segmentation bases that it understands) namely:

- By Business Area, by identifying individualized products or services, or related groups of products or services.
- By Geographic Area, considering the possibility of segmenting by customers or assets location

Thus, the internal segment reporting structure should begin by identifying the segmentation basis. The elaboration process is based on three major phases:

- Selection of the segmentation base and identification of the segments to report taking into consideration their materiality and relevance;
- Determination of segments costing methodology to apply;
- Definition of the format and content of the information to be disclosed.

Materiality and Relevance of the Segmentation Base

IFRS 8 defines specific rules to assess the materiality of the segments and their identification as reportable. The standard establishes that most of the income of a segment to report should be obtained from sales to external customers or belonging to the same business group, and cumulatively, Exceed at least one of the following quantitative limits:

- Income shall be equal to or greater than 10% of the total income;
- The results must be equal to or greater than 10% of the highest absolute value of the following:
- Total profit from segments with profit;
- Total loss of segments with loss.
- The asset must represent 10% or more of the total assets of the segments.

Segments that do not meet any of the criteria do not have material relevance and their financial information may be presented in aggregate form. It is recalled, however, that in an internal reporting logic, managers should undertake an analysis of relevance to the segments not identified as relatable by the requirements of the standard. For example, the identification in the internal reporting structure, of segments whose revenues derive mainly from operations with other segments, is generally extremely important information for analysts and internal decision-makers, due to represent operational units of the company or group of companies, with autonomous power of decision on resources, with a view to conducting sales or services "internally".

Other management criteria may condition the identification of reportable segments beyond that established by the standard. For example, segments with exceptional results in the criteria presented, but which will not be of any importance in future terms, should not be presented, since their information will not be relevant. On the other hand, segments with reduced current values that will have weight in the future, should have duly identified financial information, so that managers can follow their evolution. It can be given as an example, the case of a product in the launching phase.

Another important requirement of the standard is the materiality of the set of segments selected as relatable and which should represent a significant part of the exploitation of the company.

To this end, the standard establishes that the value of the income belonging to the segments identified for reporting, must constitute at least 75% of the total consolidated income or the individual income of the company. If this limit is not fulfilled, other segments must be identified for reporting, even if they have not satisfied the minimum limit of 10% in the aforementioned tests, until 75% of the total yields are made.

Presentation of Segmented Financial Information

The clearance of results by segments should be made in a logic of contribution, based on the principle that the company operates in segments that contribute to its results. Thus, the value generated in each of them is evidenced. To do this, direct costing should be used, assigning to each of the segments only the income and expenses that concerns it.

Another precaution in the presentation of financial information by segments is the clear identification of controllable and non-controllable expenses, and this should not be assessed on headings in which there is no decision-making power. Thus, there are two essential rules to be respected in financial information by segments:

- They must be assigned to each segment, only expenses directly related to its activity;
- The expenditure on which managers should be held accountable should be clearly identified.

Next, a profitability analysis model is presented to be applied in segment information (seen in Table 2).

Figure 4.

$$\frac{\text{Generated Revenues}}{\text{Total consolidated revenues or total company revenues}} >= 75\%$$

Table 2. Income statement information by segment

Items	Total	Segment A	Segment B	Segment C
Turnover				
Variable costs				
Contribution Margin for Fixed Costs				
Scheduled Fixed Costs				
Operating Contribution Margin				
Other Costs Attributable But Not Controllable				
Contribution Margin by Segment				
Company Common Fixed Costs				
Net Income before Taxes		-	-	-

From the observation of the table presented, comes the following classification of expenditures:

- Variables;
- Fixed, directly attributable to segments or programmed;
- Fixed, directly attributable to segments, but not controllable in the segment;
- Fixed, common to different segments.

At the level of performance evaluation in the different segments, the following contribution of this type of income statement is evidenced:

- The classification between variable and fixed costs, allows to easily carry out the analysis of the economic risk of each segment, analyzing the critical point, the safety margin and the behavior of the different types of expenditures in relation to the turnover evolution;
- The contribution of action, allows us to identify the surplus created that directly results from the manager's action, since it only includes controllable expenses;
- The contribution per segment also includes non-controllable fixed costs in the segment, but which are directly attributable to each of them. Thus, we know the contribution per segment to the total result, because we calculate turnover minus the various related costs.

Performance Assessment in Segment Information

In relation to the assessment of financial performance, where possible, in addition to the results, the assets and liabilities directly related to their exploitation should be determined by segment, which was previously designated as economic asset.

Thus, it is calculated not only the contribution of each segment to the overall result, but also the amount of investment required for the company's activity in this specific area of the business. Thus, it evaluates not only its capacity to cover the costs directly related to its exploitation, but also, if the surplus created is sufficient to finance undistributed common expenditures and investments made.

In this sequence of ideas, the indicator that should be used in the evaluation of performance in information by segments is the **Residual Contribution margin (RCM)** presented in the point regarding the evaluation of the centers of responsibility, since measures the creation of value without taking into account the fiscal effect that is not directly associated with segment's evolution.

It is important that top organs define the cost of capital, according to sector's profitability and its financing sources. To do this, the calculation of the RCM should be carried out as follows:

RCM = Contribution Margin by Segment – (Economic Asset x Cost of Capital)

The product of the cost of capital by the economic asset identifies us the minimum value that the segment should generate to remunerate the sources of financing used. Thus, through the MCR, it is verified whether the segment creates value against the amount of investment required for its existence.

When the MCR is difficult to determine, because it is not able to identify the economic asset associated with each segment, the **contribution margin per segment** containing all the income and expenses related to the business area shall be used for analysis.

In view of the above, the importance of disseminating information by segments is evident. Decision-making must have genuine support, and it is essential that the operational planning and budget elaboration, as well monitoring and controlling, are carried out based on the information needs of the company at the level of its performance in the market, and simultaneously, at the level of the development of its internal processes, in order to increasingly yield its activity.

PROCESS-BASED MANAGEMENT

In view of the competitiveness of the current Business context, where companies are facing a global competition, often with cheaper production factors, the price of the offer developed is no longer a Variable exclusively managed by the organizations.

Thus, it is increasingly important to obtain efficiencies in the realization of internal work processes, to optimize the utilization of resources and increase the margin between sales prices and operating costs, making the first more flexible to face competitors in the market.

Next are the topics of the activity-based costing and activity-based management, which can contribute to a better creation of value through better organizational performance, through efficiency in working processes.

Activity-Based Costing

Traditional cost-clearance systems have not always been presented to managers as the best alternative, due to the distortion caused by the cost absorption criteria of support activities, usually referred to as indirect costs. In addition, several changes occurred in the economic context leading to the faster obsolescence of traditional information systems (Jordan et al, 2011):

- Companies are market-oriented and not product-oriented. More than evaluating the product, it is important to evaluate its contribution margins in the markets in which it operates;

- The price is no longer determined as a function of the cost. Therefore, companies must invest in value creation in their own value chain, since the market tends to reject the payment of the producer inefficiencies;
- There is a large diversification of business and an increasing weight of support areas, such as marketing and information systems, making it increasingly more difficult to allocate indirect costs;
- Products' life cycles are increasingly reduced, making it more difficult to correctly count the imputation criteria;
- There is a greater market demand leading to more urgent profitability analysis per customer;
- Constant technological innovations allow for the emergence of very effective management support tools.

It is in this context that a new costing system is emerging, based on the activities, normally designated by ABC. Its great advantage is to prioritize indirect activities, seeking to respond more realistically to the indirect costs' breakdown.

The motto of the activity-based costing is "the activities consume resources and the products result from the activities" (Rodrigues, 1992).

Thus, ABC intends to guide the managers ' attention to support activities, which represent very important cost-generating facts. Within them are the activities of marketing, design, conservation and maintenance, planning and control, quality, supply, distribution and administrative services. As such, it intends to determine to what extent products or customers use the resources associated with these activities.

Its implementation goes through the following steps (Jordan et al, 2011):

- Define the activities by organizing them between primary (business-critical) and support (business support);
- Identify the resources associated with it;
- Determine the cost generators for each activity;
- Identify units of measure to determine unit costs for cost generators;
- Create Activity Centers;
- Determine the levels of utilization by the segments of these activities, obtaining the approximate cost for each of the segments defined.

Thus, it is possible to assign indirect costs to segments according to the resources consumed, minimizing the risk of decisions based on these costs. On the other hand, it is possible to monitor activities' cost, providing the opportunity to rationalize internal services and achieve greater process efficiency through reduced operating costs.

As such, for ABC, all costs are variable, since they are the result of some cost generator, that is, an activity resulting from the decisions of managers (Moreno, 1993).

The Importance of Activity-Based Management

The activity-based management is fundamental, because it allows to evidence the organization's functioning, as well as to identify the needed resources for the desired service levels, and the working processes' inefficiencies. At the same time, based on the principle that the defined objectives are obtained through the realization of activities, the knowledge of its costs, allows management to more easily check the evolution of the actions developed and measure the achievement of the organization's success with more reliability. This is because the extracted information relates exactly to what is done and what it consumes resources, and there is a great confidence in the attribution of values to the defined segments, be it products, customers, markets, etc. (Brimson & Antos, 1994).

To make proper identification of activities in an organization, some fundamental concepts should be considered that guide us in the definition of an information system centered on ABC (Brimson & Antos, 1994):

- **Activities:** They consist of a set of tasks that consume resources to produce certain *outputs*;
- **Functions:** represent a set of activities that relate due to a common purpose. As examples we have marketing, finance, human resources, production and procurement;
- **Processes:** They consist of a set of related and interdependent activities, due to the *outputs* exchanged among themselves. A given act initiates the first activity that triggers the exchange of *outputs* and information between the other activities, directly related to the respective working process;
- **Tasks:** These operations perform the combination of working factors and ensure the execution of the activities.

Thus, two different levels of analysis are obtained:

- When the aggregation of activities in functions or work processes is carried out, the areas that may be contributing with higher levels of costs and impairing the economic viability of the organization are verified.;
- When the activities are decomposed in tasks, it is visualized in detail how the work is done, and this is the appropriate level to make changes that optimize the efficiency of the processes.

It is equally important to identify the primary activities and secondary activities of the organization. This is because the primary activities are those that are directly related to the company's business, and in these, we should develop the necessary competencies to acquire competitive advantages; Secondary activities, are intended to support the first.

Figure 5. Scheme of the interconnection between functions, activities, tasks and processes

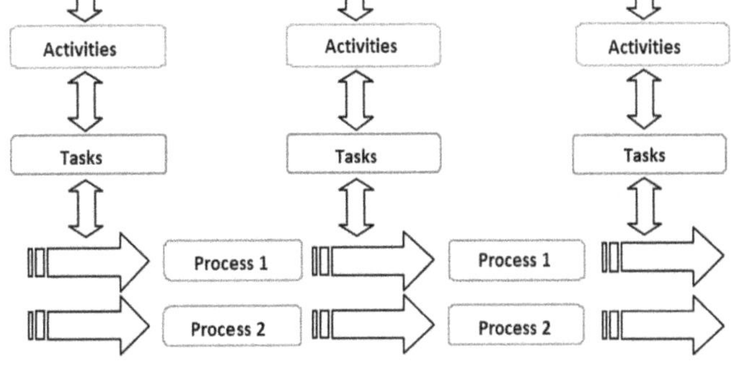

Not being vital to the organization, it should be properly monitored, verifying the associated cost levels and the benefits of being internally, in favor of a potential subcontracting. For the identification of the main business activities, Porter (1985) suggests the study of the internal value chain of organizations, which can be described generically in Figure 6.

Thus, the importance of activity-based management focuses on the following points:

- Clarifies the consumption of resources by each segment, avoiding the use of indirect cost allocation rates and unreliable information production;
- It allows more efficient management of resources, because planning, actions developed and control, meet the reality of functioning of each area and working process;
- Identifies activities that create and destroy value, contributing to the philosophy of continuous improvement and greater process efficiency.

Activity-Based Management on Activities and Processes' Efficiency

In most companies, the organizational structure is oriented to functional separation, leading to the existence of several phenomena that greatly condition service excellence and, consequently, the organization's competitive advantages (Chase & Aquilano, 1997):

- Planning does not reflect real needs: plans and budgets are based on data from previous years, since the activities to be developed and the essential resources to ensure the desired level of service are not reasonably known. Thus, obtained instruments only represent numbers with little adherence to the organization's reality;
- There is task's specialization: workers only relate to other individuals of the same working area, with a very limited view of the importance of their functions in the whole organizational;
- There is a lack of dialogue between the users of the *outputs* developed: The clear separation of the work areas, does not allow the exchange of information between different sectors of the activity. As such, there is no *feedback* on the quality of the work developed, since customers do not have the opportunity to discuss any inefficiencies recorded;
- There is little autonomy and accountability of employees: workers dedicate themselves only to the execution of a specific task, without immediate control over the work done. Thus, inefficien-

Figure 6. Value chain

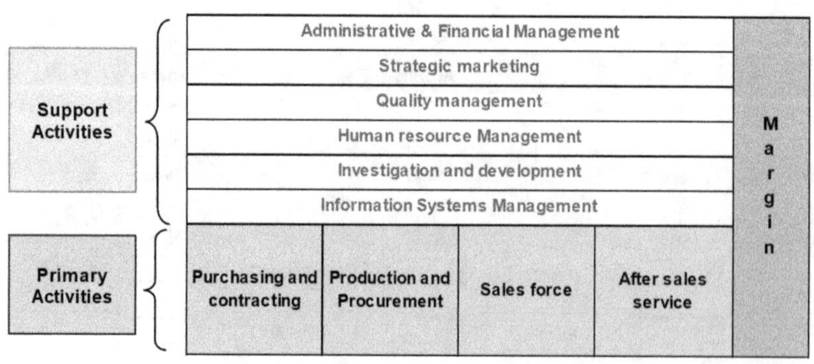

cies and errors are detected *a posteriori*, there being waste and increased costs that condition the optimization of the resources used.

In the current competitive scenario, optimizing resource utilization and process efficiency have become key factors in achieving business success. In fact, the market is increasingly less available to pay for organizational inefficiencies. Therefore, the company should operate considering the customer's needs at the level of the valued quality, the cost that it is willing to pay and the intended deadline. Today, successful organizations are those that create value for their business partners.

Thus, activity-based management became essential in organizations, because it focused decision makers' attention in what is really done in companies and in the real cost generators: activities. There are several advantages of this new vision of management:

- It obliges the dialogue between the collaborators of different working areas, with constant *feedback* about the *outputs* developed;
- Eliminates waste and inefficiencies by executing *best practices* and eliminating unnecessary activities that destroy value;
- There is more effective management of resources, identifying the sub-capacity used;
- There is more rigorous control over the work done, through the autonomy and accountability of employees;
- It contributes to more efficient processes and lower costs, reflecting a greater responsiveness in terms of deadlines and sales prices' flexibility and, consequently, competitive advantages over competitors.

Pretends to obtain a greater fluidity in the exchange of *outputs* and in the exchange of information between the various working areas, as well as a better knowledge about cost generators, to develop more and more competencies in activities that create value for the customer. Thus, all processes and sub processes are monitored, analyzed and evaluated, and managers can make decisions with greater reliability (Brimson & Antos, 1994).

For example, let us look at the case of the process of satisfying an order:

- The following functional areas are involved: commercial, finance, acquisitions, production and distribution;
- The following activities are developed: negotiation, credit analysis, invoicing, acquisition and hiring of the necessary production factors, product preparation and customer delivery.

As it can be seen, there is some complexity, because there are several functional areas involved, having to perform several activities sequentially. In scheme, we get Figure 7.

Thus, it becomes evident the advantage of managing based on the activities and processes. In fact, for the company to pursue excellence, it is essential that there is a real interconnection between the various functional areas, so that the logical sequence of activities can occur without disruption. Thus, analyzing each functional area without considering upstream and downstream activities strongly increases the possibility of inefficient processes and activities that destroy value.

For the implementation of activity-based management, three instruments can be used:

Figure 7. Order fulfillment process
Fonte: Laudon and Laudon (2002)

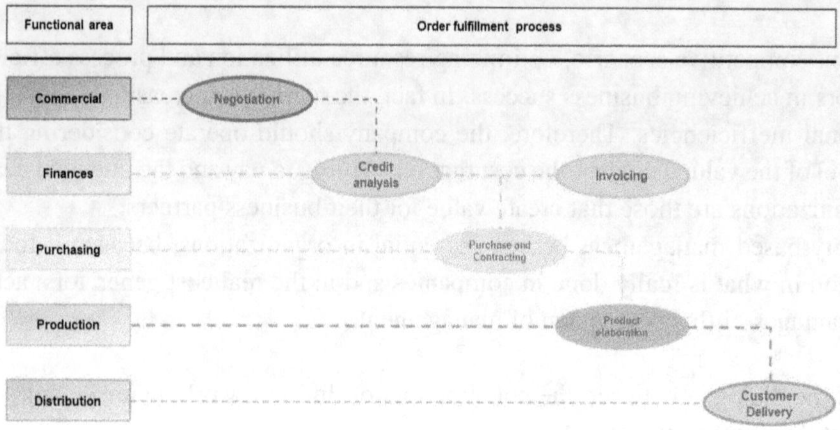

- **Quality circles:** They are periodic meetings between collaborators from different areas to debate existing problems or work on suggestions that enable work processes with higher quality, and faster;
- **Philosophy *Total Quality Management*:** quality is no longer just a concern of the quality control department to become a problem for all members of the organization. Quality values are underpinning all leadership, *design*, planning and improvement initiatives. It is a form of management adopted by the entire company to exceed what is important to the customer in all dimensions of the products or services;
- **Activity-based costing:** Values the cost of activities, allowing monitoring organizational performance at the level of the various working areas.

These three instruments privilege operational links in favor of the functional hierarchy, which facilitates the communication and connection between the various units of the organizational structure.

The implementation of an organizational culture seats on the philosophy of continuous improvements:

Figure 8. Process interconnection and organizational structure

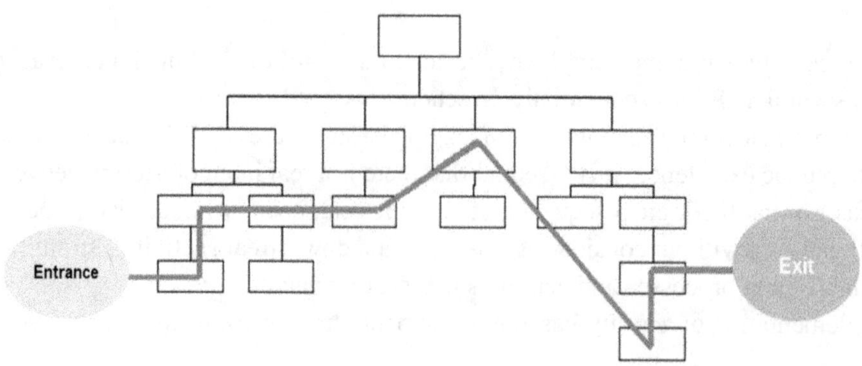

- Customer focus whether it is internal or external;
- Everyone is responsible for quality;
- It is always possible to do better.

Thus, it can be concluded that the management based on activities intends to optimize the utilization of resources and the efficiency of processes, decreasing deadlines and operating costs.

ABC is one of its fundamental instruments and is a new perspective in the allocation of indirect costs, affecting them to activities, and these to the decisions of managers. As such, this method allows the clear identification of the main cost generators and the activities that truly contribute to the creation of value in the company.

It is to be stressed that the implementation of the activity centers should not jeopardize the traditional responsibility centers. In this way, it is intended to identify in parallel that departments and activities create value and generate costs.

COMPANY DEVELOPMENT AND MANAGEMENT CONTROL SYSTEMS

As organizations grow, their organizational structure changes, moving from simple structures to business units or conglomerates, due to the larger dimension and consequent need for power decentralization, in order to ensure the constant flexibility in responding market. In this sequence of ideas, organizations become increasingly complex, with more hierarchical levels and a greater number of operational leaders, leading to an inevitable internal structure and information systems' adaptation, so that planning, budgeting and monitoring and performance evaluation can be carried out in the various working areas that constitute the organizational structure (Donnelly et al., 2000).

Organizational Types and Structures

The normal organization's development and its progressive growth increases specialized work. It comes to a point where a single manager can no longer effectively coordinate it. Thus, there is a need to create a number of workable jobs, to be gathered in small groups, and a new working function – the group manager, who is usually designated as the operational manager of a particular sector of the company (Donnelly et al, 2000). Specialized works are separate but interconnected parts of the global task. In turn, this implies the realization of each of the works. However, they must be executed in the specific form and sequence that the managers have designed at the time of their definition.

In this way, departments are essential to identify the bases for grouping the work. The departmentalization bases are grouped essentially in two major axes (Donnelly et al, 2000):

- Bases centered on internal activity: Division of the Company by functions or by working processes;
- Bases centered on the environment and the market: Division of the company by products, consumers' types or geographic area.

In addition, organizational structures vary according to three characteristics (Bartol & Martin, 1998):

- Formalization: Refers to the degree to which expectations on means and ends of work are specified and written. In this sense, an organizational structure is said to be highly formalized when the rules and procedures are clearly explained by saying what each one should do;
- Centralization: Refers to the location of the authority to make decisions in the hierarchy of the organization, identifying the existing level of delegation of authority inside the organization;
- Complexity: consists of measuring the number of completely different occupations and departments. The higher the number of hierarchical and departmental levels, the greater the problems of aligning the action of the various workers and working areas.

Taking into account the characteristics inherent to the organizational structures and the orientation that the top organs intend to ensure in the employees' action (focus on the environment or focus on task efficiency), the following organizational structures can be defined:

- Simple structure: It is characteristic of young and small companies, where the owner is the manager. The authority is centered on the owner and there are no hierarchical levels. Formalization is non-existent and is valued above all the response to the market, requiring a great deal of flexibility and versatility for the various collaborators;
- Structure by functions: The work is structured according to the functions of the Organization, that is, the activities that are performed in its operation, as are the cases of production, marketing, acquisitions and procurement, finance, Personnel, accounting and research and development. These are characteristics of small organizations and with a specialized offer. Its main advantage is efficiency, because it gathers specialists in their area of expertise, thus achieving better execution of tasks. As disadvantages, excessive orientation to internal activity and lack of alignment between different functional areas may cause inefficiencies in the working processes;
- Divisionary structure: The organization is based on the division of tasks based on working processes, products, customers or geographic areas. Each division has its own specialists in the various functional areas, in order to hold part or even the entire value chain associated with its responsibility. As regards the divisionary structures, the most advanced forms are:
  - Business units: are responsible for their own products and markets, having specialists from each functional area. In practice, they represent mini and are frequent in organizations that intend to achieve a high level of diversification in related businesses, creating synergies in the market supply. They have as a great advantage the fact that they focus on the work of employees in the constant adequacy to the characteristics of the surrounding. On the other hand, they have the great disadvantage of progressively creating a closed spirit, leading to internal competition for resources and the smallest sharing of information between different units;
  - Conglomerates: They are equally responsible for the entire value chain of a business within the organization, but they have greater decision-making autonomy in relation to the business units. However, they are characteristics of companies that operate in different industries without common aspects. They have as main advantage the dispersion of business risks;
- Matrix structure: It is characteristic in companies that have to manage projects with high complexity, which require different knowledge of the various areas of the organizational structure and therefore include people from different functional areas and working processes. It has as great advantages, the sharing of knowledge and the increase of the design capacity, but, on the other hand,

it presents the disadvantages of decreasing the definition of responsibilities and slowing down the decision-making process, due to the constant *Brainstorming* among team members;

- Network structure: Represents the most recent type of organizational structure and consists of the existence of a top organ that buys and sells to the other units that constitute the company, each being autonomous in the performance of its responsibilities. Thus, each unit is free to act according to its interests, eliminating the services and activities less efficient and at the same time, to give preference to the acquisition of services abroad in favor of the internal benefits of other units with higher costs.

Taking into account the normal functioning of the companies, the types of organizational structure and the management style adopted, Larry E. Greiner, presented in 1972 (revised later in 1998), a model that intended to highlight the development phases of the organizations and which has been a reference in the diverse bibliography and research work in management.

In this model, the author defined five phases of natural development of the organizations, each of them associated with moments of rupture in the internal structure and the style of management adopted, derived from the level of growth of the activity. Moreover, it also defined the conditioning variables of the different evolutionary stages of the companies.

Thus, each stage of the development of organizations involves an adequacy of the internal structure and management style and, consequently, the management control tools to be adopted.

The Organizational Structure Development Phases

Throughout its research work, Greiner defined five key variables that conditioned the behavior of companies in their various stages of development, as well as the length of stay in each evolutionary stage.

1. Company age

The older a company, the greater the difficulties of organizational changes, because there are norms and procedures that are fulfilled and accepted by all over several years. As such, the resistance to change is extremely large.

2. Company dimension

The larger the size of the company, the more complex the transformations are to be performed. This is because, more easily, problems of coordination, clearance of responsibilities, delegation of functions and communication arise. In other words, the management techniques to be applied in companies with thousands of employees, several hierarchical levels and located in different regions, will be quite different from those used in small-scale organizations.

3. State of evolution

The evolution analysis on the level of activity growth allows us to situate the company. Each phase has specific characteristics. Periods between four to eight years of stable growth are limited by troubled moments and it is necessary to perform changes to surpass the evolutionary state.

4. State of Revolution

As it is intended to define growth periods, also the time intervals of disputes can be predicted. In general, difficult movements are the result of the development of the activity, imposing the need for a new internal organization more suited to the current business dimension, with innovations in the rules and procedures to establish.

5. Industry growth rate

Companies that are embedded in industries with high growth rates are usually more subject to rapid and radical changes. For example, the recruitment of new jobs may imply a new internal organization appropriate to the new number of human resources. However, in very profitable markets, evolution may be prolonged, and the revolution phase delayed. As long as the activity pays the investments, the manager will have no need to make changes in the organization and management techniques to be adopted.

Thus, considering the key variables defined, according to Greiner, the evolutionary framework of an organization has five phases. Each one is characterized by the level of growth of the company, due to crises resulting from the need to adapt the internal organization to the new business dimension and, finally, the management style developed by the top organs to reach the desired changes.

As such, the various evolutionary moments are composed of periods of stability, followed by crises that originate changes in the organizational structure, as shown in the following figure, and which will be summarily explained.

The first phase is called **creativity**. This period corresponds to organizations' start-up, the company and its products implementation in the market. This moment fosters management through creativity, based on a very informal and flexible structure, able to respond quickly to market signals. As such, efforts are centered on the commercial and production aspects, referring to the background of the concerns related to the control of the activity and the optimization of the resources.

However, as the company grows and an increase in activities occurs, the degree of complexity of processes increases radically. New needs arise at the level of internal communication, the attribution of responsibilities, the definition of new procedures and norms in the organization, which cause conflicts

Figure 9. Business growth phases
Source: Adapted from Greiner (1972)

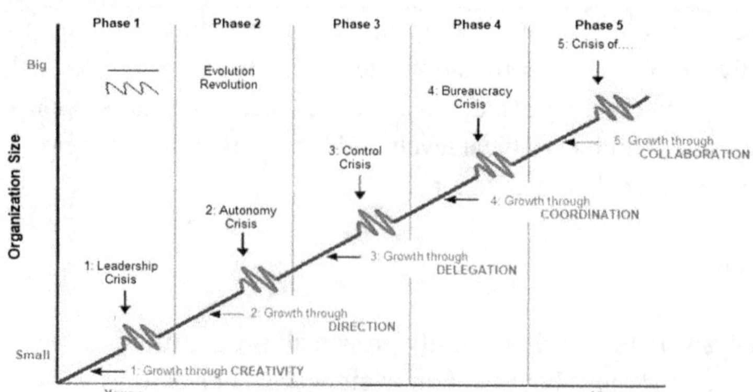

throughout the organization trying previous solutions for new problems. The adaptation to this new reality creates a period called of **leadership crisis**, being most often found the answer in new managers with experience and strong leadership capacity, in which the founders delegate authority to decide on operational activity.

The second phase arises during the resolution of the leadership conflict, through the adoption of a management that prints **direction** and cohesion. The main concern in this phase is the specialization of the functions separating the responsibilities of each one and usually creating departments. In this way, the hierarchical structure is clearly defined.

Consequently, the directors (managers) of intermediate hierarchical level are entrusted with the functional issues. However, the decision-making power continues to center in the top frameworks.

Thus, the intermediate frameworks despite the *expertise* of the activity, do not participate actively in decision making provoking this situation, a general demotivation. As such, the **crisis of Autonomy** is initiated, which is characterized by the difficulty of the top leaders in decreasing the degree of self-responsibility and the small capacity of initiative of the intermediate frameworks which, however, do not have developed the habit of deciding.

To overcome the problems arising in the previous phase, a separate structure is adopted, in which there is decentralization of authority and an increase in the participation of intermediate managers in the decision on the activity. An increase in delegation is implemented through autonomous units based on managers with decision-making power and incentive systems to reward the achievement of objectives.

The delegation of decision-making powers at the various hierarchical levels seeks to be an instrument of motivation. However, the new division of powers promotes an initially beneficial spirit of competition between the divisions, which gradually transforms into a fifth spirit, making the objectives of each unit overlap with those of the company.

When problems occur in the control of activities at intermediate levels, a new troubled period, called the **control crisis**, originates.

In view of the need to overcome the crisis, which normally leads to the delegation phase, the use of a set of formal systems is established, with a view to greater **coordination** and assumption of responsibilities on the part of the top bodies.

The organization focuses on products, each product group being treated as an investment center, which leads to a more efficient distribution of resources, with the responsibility centers being able to cover the cost of capital. Participation in global profits encourages greater identification with the company as a whole.

The tables maintain a high decision-making capacity, but there is greater control on the part of the administration, forcing them to carefully justify their options in periodic meetings.

However, the adoption of formal and rigid systems, as a consequence, is the installation and development of bureaucracy, and there is less time to solve the concrete and important problems for procedures that are not always suitable for Current issues of the Organization. The **bureaucracy crisis** emerges.

To overcome the bureaucracy crisis, dynamic participation and interpersonal **collaboration** give wide to spontaneity and creativity, through multidisciplinary teams, aiming at solving problems and innovation.

The teams are often framed in a matrix structure. Formal control is replaced by social control and self-discipline. The managers have behavioral training, with the aim of improving teamwork and resolving conflicts. The teams participate in the definition of the objectives and the prizes are attributed according to their reach, at the level of the team and their contribution to the success of the organization.

This phase seems to lead to the saturation of employees due to the fatigue caused by the pressure of teamwork, motivated by the systematic search for the best results and innovative solutions. Hence the possibility of a sixth phase triggered by a **psychological saturation crisis.**

The way to overcome this crisis could be through the creation of systems for the revitalization of employees and the organization or the search for more ambitious projects with external partners, through integration into a *holding company* or the creation of a networked organization.

Thus, as companies grow, they adopt different leadership and management styles; adapt their organizations, control and evaluation systems. It then presents a framework with the summary of the basic ideas of each phase of business development.

Table 3. Basic ideas of the business development model

<table>
<tr><th>Phases</th><th>Growth Factors</th><th>Management focus</th><th>Organizational Structure</th><th>Control System</th><th>Awards System</th></tr>
<tr><td rowspan="2">Phase 1: Creative</td><td>– Entrepreneurial spirit
– Creativity</td><td>– Product. function
– Commercial function</td><td>– Simple and informal</td><td>– Type of market response</td><td>– Low Remuneration
– Promises of higher yields</td></tr>
<tr><td colspan="5">– Signs of the crisis:
– Informal communication becomes inadequate as staff numbers increase
– Inefficiency of production, control and supply operations
– Founders face new demands but resist their recognition
– There is a leadership crisis due to conflicts between those responsible, how to resolve them</td></tr>
<tr><td rowspan="2">Phase 2: Directive</td><td>– Efficiency
– Organizational cohesion</td><td>– Organization and control
– Standardization</td><td>– Functional and centralized</td><td>– Budget-Information</td><td>– Budget Incentives</td></tr>
<tr><td colspan="5">– Signs of the crisis:
– Procedures are beginning to be inadequate in the light of the knowledge gained by operating staff, whose opinions are not considered, each tending to do their own thing.
– Demotivation by excessive centralization, even in relation to current decisions</td></tr>
<tr><td rowspan="2">Phase 3: Delegation</td><td>– Market Focus
– New Products</td><td>– Expansion
– New production units</td><td>– Decentralized
– Business units</td><td>– Regular follow-up reports</td><td>– Results Centres and associated awards</td></tr>
<tr><td colspan="5">– Signs of the crisis:
– Business units each act according to their criteria regarding investments, technologies and human resources, without adequate consideration for the overall objectives and results.
– Freedom and the spirit of competition degenerate into a fifth spirit
– Top management is beginning to have difficulty aligning the performance of the various units in accordance with the company's overall objectives.</td></tr>
<tr><td rowspan="2">Phase 4: Coordination</td><td>– Greater efficiency in resources allocation</td><td>– Planning
– Resource optimization</td><td>– Greater importance of support areas</td><td>– Centralization of control and supervision</td><td>– Share in global profits and stock options</td></tr>
<tr><td colspan="5">– Signs of the crisis:
– Operational managers resent the rigidity and outdated procedures, given the specific experience and conditions of each business area.
– With the formalities to overlap to the problem solving and innovation being blocked, there is a need to reduce bureaucracy</td></tr>
<tr><td rowspan="2">Phase 5: Collaboration</td><td>– Teamwork
– Innovation</td><td>– Promotion of participation
– Behavioural training of managers</td><td>– Metrical
– Multidisciplinary teams to solve problems</td><td>– Self-discipline
– Social control
– Real-time decision. Sup. information</td><td>– Participation in defining global goals
– Team Awards</td></tr>
<tr><td colspan="5">– Signs of the crisis:
– Employee saturation due to tiredness caused by the pressure of teamwork, motivated by the systematic search for better results and innovative solutions.</td></tr>
</table>

Business Development and the Adaptation to the Management Control Instruments

The business development model created and worked by Greiner, takes into account that several changes occur in the internal functioning of the organizations, caused by the different stages of growth of Activity:

- Hierarchical levels and departments are increasing due to the greater delegation of authority, which makes organizations more complex and more difficult to manage;
- There is a focus on the market but also on the efficiency of processes, trying to maximize profitability both by increasing turnover, as well as by the efficiency in the use of internal resources;
- The control and evaluation systems are no longer focused solely on the objectives and overall results of the companies, to devote much attention to the performance of the various areas that constitute the internal organization of the company.

At the level of management control instruments, it appears that each phase of business development has quite diversified requirements for planning and controlling the activity.

In the first phase, called growth through creativity, the focus is the response to the market and is to give visibility to the company and its products with target customers. In this sense, the planning and control of the activity is very informal and verbally done, in order to facilitate internal communication and ensure the speed of action. On the other hand, due to the reduced size of the company, decision-making is centered on the founders, actively participating in all operational areas. Thus, management control instruments are usually based on the planning carried out during the preparation of the business plan to create the company and the control is, above all, financial, periodically measuring the overall results achieved in the face of previously elaborated forecasts.

In the second phase, called growth through the direction, intermediate levels of management are established with several functional areas where there is a greater specialization of tasks. Thus, although the decision-making process remains very focused on the founders, planning and control already cover the financial evolution of the different sectors of the organization and the communication becomes more formal, through the establishment of dates and rules of monitoring activities. However, in view of the lack of delegation of authority, the performance assessment and incentive systems for managers are residual or non-existent.

In the third phase, called growth through delegation, in order to strengthen market competitiveness there is an effort to decentralize decision making to intermediate managers, because they are the holders of knowledge Appropriate for responding to the needs of business partners. Thus, centers of responsibility are formed, and financial planning and control are made according to the evolution of each center. In addition, the first systems for evaluating performance and incentives for managers are established, usually based on obtaining the local financial objectives. At the same time, it is also at this stage that the first internal transfer prices are usually developed, aimed at valuing the operations performed between different responsibility centers and areas of business support (e.g., services marketing, financial, etc.). As for the instruments of dialogue, there is a greater concern with the formalization of meetings and the production of monitoring reports of the activity.

The fourth phase, called growth through coordination, provides an effort to reduce the spirit in the previous phase. In addition to financial information by responsibility center, there is a strategic control development of instruments (e.g. *tableaux de bord and balanced scorecards*). This ensures performance monitoring of various non-financial variables that are key to the business, and motivates systems to cover diverse objectives (financial and non-financial). It also compensates each center contribution to reach overall objectives. Finally, at the level of the instruments of dialogue there is a greater care with the regular monitoring of the activity, passing the reports of each center to contemplate a greater wealth of information about the business. Thus, in this phase the information by segments gains a greater importance, since there is a concern with the origin of the creation of value (for example, which customers or regions more favorable to financial performance).

Finally, in the last phase called growth through collaboration, where the aim is to achieve greater organizational cohesion through the creation of multidisciplinary teams of different business units that participate in the development of Common projects, management control instruments have to be able to control the contribution of each business unit to the success of projects. Thus, information systems should be able to produce financial data not only on the responsibility centers, but also on the activities that they undertake for the realization of each project. Therefore, in this phase it becomes imperative to implement the management based on activities and the costing method based on activities, usually called ABC. Thus, as for dialogue instruments, there is a greater realization of meetings and events that allow knowledge sharing between different areas and reports producing with information from the responsibility centers and undertaken projects.

Thus, major challenges are now being made to business management control systems, in order to produce credible and timely information for decision-making. Changes in the internal functioning of companies may corroborate that the accounting information systems and traditional financial instruments are not suited to the new competitive reality.

Planning and budgeting should be able to meet the financial information needs that the different stages of business development require, notably at the level of the different departments or units of business, allowing a better understanding of the contribution of each area to the creation of value and to the sustainable success of the organization. For example, it is essential that the information system is able to present the financial statements by a defined responsibility center.

In this sense, as organizations are becoming more complex and decentralized, the information system should also adapt, making it possible to carry out the planning, budget and periodic control of the various areas of business and support companies that comprise the organizational structure.

However, in addition to involving managers in objectives' definition, plans, budgets and financial control of the activity, management control instruments should also ensure the proper alignment between each responsibility center' attitude. Organizations grow and the complexity of monitoring internal functioning increases. The overall objectives of the company and performance assessment systems should be flexible in order to enable effective monitoring of Origins of Value creation (which are most often associated with non-financial variables such as quality and innovation) and to reward those who contribute more to the company's sustained success.

Only in this way is that management control can continue to have its key role of compromise between the manager and the company, and function as a real instrument of planning, decentralization and motivation.

CONCLUSION

Knowledge management, segment information and process-based management are fundamental for the implementation of management control systems that allow the monitoring of the environment in which the company operates and the internal functioning of the different hierarchical levels and functional areas.

In addition, it was concluded that management control systems should be flexible and able to adapt to the different growth stages of organizations.

REFERENCES

Amaral, P., & Pedro, J. (2004). *O Capital Conhecimento – Modelos de Avaliação de activos intangíveis*. Lisboa: Universidade Católica Editora.

Bartol, K. & Martin, D. (1998). *Management* (3rd ed.). McGraw-Hill.

Brimson, J., & Antos, J. (1994). *Activity – Based Management – for Service Industries, Government Entities and Nonprofit Organizations*. John Willey & Sons, Inc.

Chase, R., & Aquilano, N. (1997). Gestão da Produção e das Operações – Perspectiva do Ciclo de Vida. *Monitor (Charlottetown)*.

Donnelly, J., Gibson, J., & Ivancevich, J. (2000). *Administração – Princípios de gestão empresarial* (10th ed.). McGrawhill.

Edvinsson, L., & Malone, M. (1997). *Intellectual Capital: Realizing your Company's true value by finding its hidden roots*. New York: Harper Business.

Eiglier, P., & Langeard, E. (1999). *Servuction – A Gestão Marketing de Empresas de Serviços*. Lisboa: McGrawhill.

Greiner, L. (1972). *Evolution and revolution as organizations grow*. Harvard Business Review, July – August.

Gupta, V., & Perepu, I. (2007). *McKinsey's Knowledge Management Practices*. IBS Center for Management Research.

Hislop, D. (2013). *Knowledge Management in Organizations: A Critical Introduction*. OUP.

Jordan, H., Neves, J., & Rodrigues, J. (2011). *O Controlo de Gestão - Ao Serviço da Estratégia e dos Gestores* (10th ed.). Lisboa: Áreas Editora.

Kluge, J., Stein, W. & Licht, T. (2002). *Gestão do Conhecimento – Segundo um estudo da McKinsey & Company*. São João do Estoril: Principia.

Laudon, K., & Laudon, J. (2002). *Management Information Systems* (7th ed.). Prentice-Hall, Inc.

Lourenço, I. (2001). *A informação Financeira por Segmentos*. ISCTE.

Moreno, C. (1993). *Cambio Tecnológico y Contabilidad de Gestion*. Ministerio de Hacienda y Administraciones Públicas-Secretaría General Técnica- SGIDP.

Porter, M. (1985). *Competitive advantage*. New York: Free Press.

Rodrigues, J. (1992). *Custeio Baseado na Actividade*. Revista Portuguesa de Gestão.

Valente, F., & Lourenço, R. (2019). Academic Entrepreneurship, Knowledge Transfer and Academic Spin-off. In N. Teixeira, T. Costa, & I. Lisboa (Eds.), *Handbook of Research on Entrepreneurship, Innovation and Internationalization* (pp. 178–206). Hershey, PA: IGI Global. doi:10.4018/978-1-5225-8479-7.ch007

Chapter 6
Characterization of the Information Technology Industry

ABSTRACT

In this book, we present a case study of a Portuguese company of the information technologies industry that has traveled through an internationalization process and has implemented a management control system with a very interesting complexity level. Thus, this chapter will begin with the definition of the scope of the industry and the supply typology, and then the situation is analyzed both globally, regionally, and at Portugal's level (the company's nationality) in order to enable the understanding of the competitive environment. It seeks to develop the analysis of the sector's attractiveness level, showing how competitive conditions can be felt in company performance. Finally, the main trends, challenges, and management variables that need to be implemented to ensure a good performance in the industry are presented.

SCOPE OF THE INFORMATION TECHNOLOGY INDUSTRY

The information technology sector has a great diversity, both in the panoply of products that constitute the supply, as in the typology of customers that it serves. Therefore, there is frequent non-stabilization and inaccuracies in concepts, when comparing different empirical studies or statistical publications.

The European Information Technology Observatory (EITO, 2000; 40) considers "*...information technology (...) the combination of hardware Industries for office equipment, data processing equipment and data software and service communication equipment.* "

The Portuguese company INSAT from consulting services, in the context of the Portuguese market studies of systems, solutions and information technologies, computers and computer technology considers "*information technologies, the set of products and services for processing, storing and communicating data using computers. It includes hardware, systems software, applications, training, consulting and related services. It does not include products and services strictly connected with telecommunications*"(Insat, 2000; 10).

DOI: 10.4018/978-1-7998-2007-9.ch006

Nordhaus (2002) refers to the sector as the "*New Economy*" and involves acquisition, processing, transformation and distribution of information. The three main components are hardware, communications systems that acquire and distribute information and software that, with the help of human resources, manages the entire system.

Analyzing the above described definitions, it can be noted that the second has as reference the typology of products and services and the rest the scope of developed activities.

In addition to the aforementioned definitions, it is also noteworthy that the various studies conducted by the International Data Corporation (IDC), the world's leading market intelligence Company for the Markets for technology Information, always include the analysis of the business hardware, software and different associated services, and also the communication technologies and the New ICT (IoT-Internet of Things, robotics, AIR/VR- Augmented and virtual reality, AI-Artificial Intelligence and 3D printing).

The present work will only consider the areas of hardware, software and related consultancy services, on which IDC considers:

- Hardware, which can be subdivided into systems (workstations, laptops and optional equipment), peripherals (magnetic disks, magnetic strips, printers, etc.) and data communication equipment (local network and external network equipment);
- Software can be divided into software development (tools to support the development and use of other software), application (software for use in the various areas of organizations) and systems infrastructure (software management systems, networks, security. etc.);
- Services, being these constituted by consulting segments (from diagnosis and assessment needs to suppliers selection), implementation (system or prototype development), operations management (network management, helpdesk, remote monitoring of systems and networks, information storage, security and recovery services, etc.), support (services that ensure that the systems work seamlessly) and raining (includes education and training in products or technologies).

The table 1 shows the various classifications of economic activities used in this area.

It should be noted that there are companies engaged in activities of the information technology sector, but which are classified with different codes, and there are also companies with the code of information technology but who do not exercise such activity, what should happen, possibly and in some cases, due to the activity's conversion.

SUPPLY TYPOLOGY

The technology information sector's supply can be characterized by considering the following perspectives:

- The sector business' types;
- Integrated products and services solutions;
- The impact on the value chain of organizations.

However, given the existing complementarity among the three businesses that constitute the sector (hardware, software and services), part of the companies presents an offer based on integrated solutions, which include equipment, software, networks and services of the most diverse natures.

Table 1. Classifications of ICT Economic Activities

Standard	Hardware	software	Services
ISIC	2620 - Manufacture of computers and peripheral equipment	6201 - Computer programming activities	6202 - Computer consultancy and computer facilities management activities 6209 - Other information technology and computer service activities
SIC	3572 - Computer Storage Devices 3575 - Computer Terminals 3577 - Computer Peripheral Equipment, Not Elsewhere Classified	7371 - Computer Programming Services	737 - Computer Programming, Data Processing, And Other Computer Related Services
NAICS	332510 Hardware Manufacturing 3341 Computer and Peripheral Equipment Manufacturing	511210 - Software Publishers	518210 - Data Processing, Hosting, and Related Services
NACE	26.20 - Manufacture of computers and peripheral equipment	62.01 Computer programming activities	62.02 - Computer consultancy 62.09 - Other information technology and computer service activities

Legend:
ISIC - International Standard Industrial Classification of All Economic Activities
SIC - Standard Industrial Classification
NAICS - North American Industry Classification System
NACE - Statistical classification of economic activities in the European Union

Thus, considering the type of integrated solutions defined by IDC (2007), the sector's supply may also be characterized in various ways, including, among other designations, business Performance Management & Business Intelligence, Contact Centers, System and Network Management, Customer Relationship Management, Enterprise Resources Planning, Wireless & Mobile, etc..

Considering the third perspective, in a study developed for the National Association of Information Technology and Electronics companies (*Associação Nacional das Empresas das Tecnologias de Informação e Electrónica)* – ANETIE (Católica, 2001), the supply of the information technology sector was segmented, Considering its impact on the value chain of organizations, and its representation translates itself into the figure 1.

It can therefore be concluded that the products and services offered by the information technology sector, irrespective of its characterization according to the type of business, integrated solutions or impact on the value chain of organizations, they cover a wide range of applications, ranging from the aid in strategic decision-making to simple use as an operational tool, through solutions that intend to achieve greater integration with the main business partners (Alajaasko, 2006a).

WORLD-WIDE INFORMATION TECHNOLOGY SEARCH

According to IDC (2019), the global expenditure on ICT grew less than 5% each year since the financial crisis in 2009, representing the traditional markets of IT and telecommunications an increasingly mature sector of the economy.

The global demand for information technologies was, according to IDC (2019), mainly located in the USA and Asia.

Figure 1. Information technology sector supply
Source: Universidade Católica, 2001

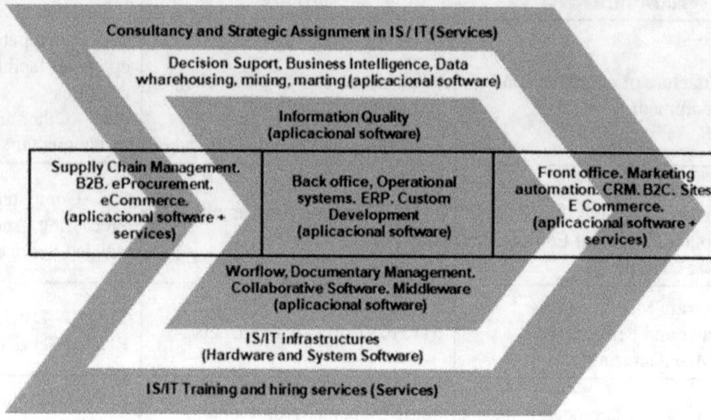

Figure 2. Worldwide ICT spending
Source: IDC, 2019

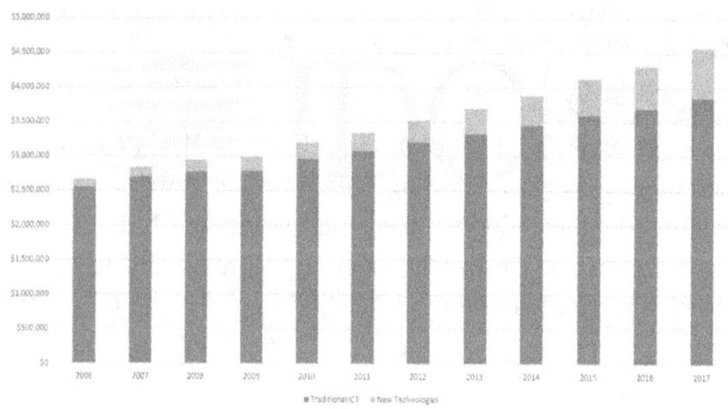

Figure 3. Demand for information technologies by region in 2017
Source: IDC, 2019

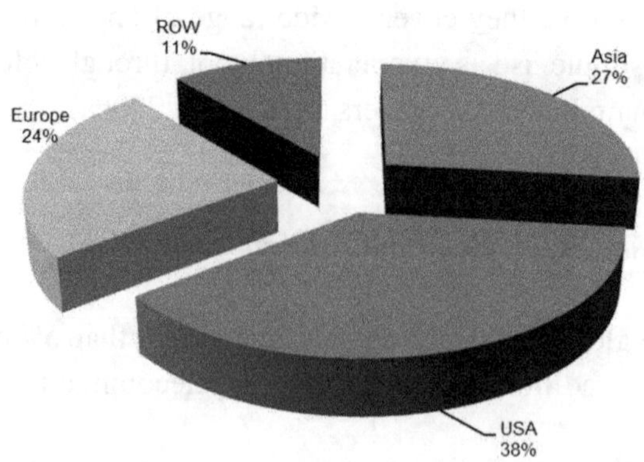

The figure 4 presents the sales in $M Dollars, in 2017, corresponding to hardware, software and services, by region.

According to IDC (2019), the hardware market is dominated by smartphones in terms of volume and revenue, which projected Asia as the largest region in terms of general spending with traditional hardware.

In the U.S. and Europe, cloud growth generates demand for server/storage hardware, software solutions, and professional services related to cloud deployments.

In all regions, a growing proportion of hardware, software, and service expenditures are linked to the cloud and mobile devices, while traditional technologies such as desktop PC, local storage systems, and fixed telecommunications services, are stable or declining.

Asia Pacific is, today, the largest traditional hardware market, after the explosion of mobile proliferation in recent years. Led by China, Japan and India, this region now accounts for more than 40% of traditional spending on hardware (PC, tablets, telephone, peripherals, server/storage and network infrastructure).

However, Asia still represents a small portion of software and service revenues, as companies in the region continue to spend a small proportion of the average ICT budgets on applications, tools, and professional services that can leverage traditional ICT in broader economic benefits. North American companies still lead the way in adopting cutting-edge software, with Europe not far behind.

As for the evolution of the sector, according to IDC (2019), it is anticipated that traditional ICT spending would largely follow GDP growth over the next decade, with the general industry catapulted to a growth of more than two times GDP as new technologies start to represent a larger market share, in particular, IoT, Robotics and AIR/VR.

It is anticipated that over the next five years, all the growth of traditional technology spending will be driven by only four platforms: cloud, mobile, social and big data/analytics. Meanwhile, the cost savings generated by cloud and automation will result in more expenses diverted to new technologies such as IA, robotics and AR/VR

Figure 4. Demand for hardware, software and services in 2017
Source: IDC, 2019

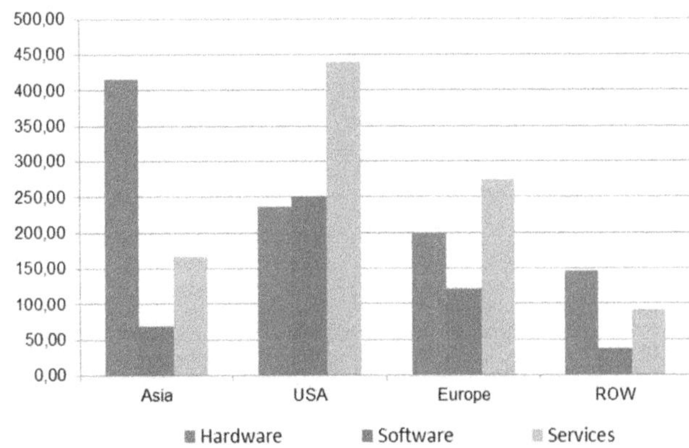

Figure 5. Worldwide ICT Spending 2016-2022 ($Millions)
Source: IDC, 2019

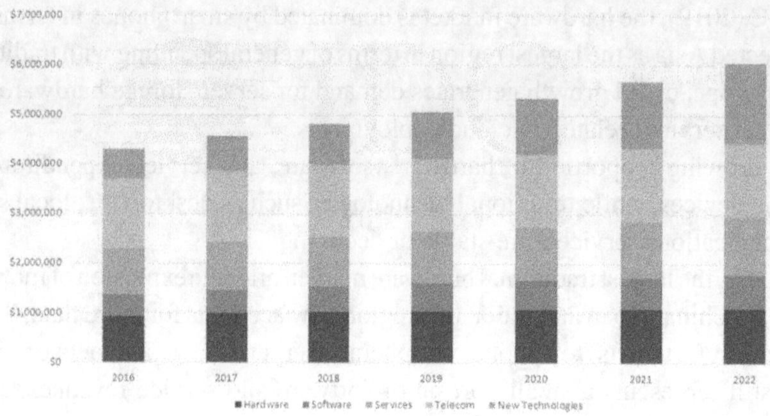

THE WORLD OFFER

According to Fortune Global 500 magazine, the world's largest companies in the sector, sorted according to turnover in the area of information technologies (including hardware, software, electronics, semiconductors, Internet, telecommunications equipment, e-commerce and computer Services) were explained in Table 2.

It is thus noted that six U.S. companies are among the first ten.

Table 2. The world's largest companies in the sector

Rank	Company	Revenue ($B) USD	FY	Country
1	Apple Inc.	$229.2	2017	US
2	Samsung Electronics	$223.4	2017	South Korea
3	Amazon.com	$177.8	2017	US
4	Foxconn	$154.7	2017	Taiwan
5	Alphabet Inc.	$110.8	2017	US
6	Microsoft	$110.4	2018	US
7	Huawei	$89.3	2017	China
8	Hitachi	$84.5	2017	Japan
9	IBM	$79.1	2017	US
10	Dell Technologies	$78.6	2017	US
11	Sony	$77.1	2017	Japan
12	Panasonic	$72,0	2017	Japan
13	Intel	$62.7	2017	US
14	LG Electronics	$54.3	2017	Korea
15	JD.com	$53.9	2017	China

Table 3. World's largest software companies

Rank	Company	Sales (B$)	FY	Country
1	Alphabet	110.86	2018	US
2	Microsoft	110.36	2018	US
3	IBM	79.9	2018	US
4	Accenture	41.1	2018	Rep. of Ireland
5	Facebook	40.65	2018	US
6	Oracle	39.83	2018	US
7	SAP	26.7	2018	Germany
8	Tencent	22.8	2018	China
9	TCS	19.08	2018	India
10	Baidu	110.86	2018	China

According to Forbes magazine 2017, the largest 10 companies worldwide under the "Software & Programming" were explained in Table 3.

At the level of the business dimension, the sector is characterized by a strong predominance of micro and small enterprises.

For example, the percentages of companies in the sector, in the USA and in France, are presented in the following tables.

According to IT Market Statistics and Trends (2016), of the approximately 375 000 companies in the U.S. sector, in 2015, the percentage of Small and medium-sized enterprises in the sector, accounted for about 99.7%.

According to the Insee – *Institut national de la statistique et des études économiques*, from France, the percentage of micro-enterprises in the sector, represented, in 2016, about 95.3%.

Based on the previously presented indicators, it can be concluded that the information technology sector, in general, has a fragmented structure, however, presenting in the activity of hardware production, a more concentrated structure.

Table 4. Size of US ICT companies

	%
Micro companies (<10 people)	82,6%
Small Businesses (10 a 99 people)	15,1%
Medium-sized Enterprises (100 a 499 people)	2,0%
Big companies (>500 people)	0,3%

Source: IT Market Statistics and Trends, 2016

Table 5. Size of ICT companies in France

	%
Micro companies (<10 people)	95,3%
Small Businesses (10 a 249 people)	4,3%
Big companies (>250 people)	0,2%

Source: Insee, 2019

SITUATION IN PORTUGAL

The activities of consulting and computer programming and activities related to information technologies, have recorded gradual increases in invoicing volume, going from about 3.5 to about 4.5 billion of US $, between 2012 and 2017.

The information technology sector consists of many companies. According to the database of the National Institute of Statistics *Instituto Nacional de Estatística* – INE of Portugal, in 2017 there were more than 10.800 companies (an increase of about 28% compared to 2012), of which 4.719 are related to computer programming activities, 4.231 to computer consulting activities and 1.856 to other activities related to information technology and informatics.

It must be stated that there are currently no Hardware production companies in Portugal.

According to the INE, the companies in the sector are located in the main national urban centers, highlighting the regions of Lisbon and Oporto, which, as a whole, represent about 80%, and can be considered various reasons for the effect:

Figure 6. Sales evolution of computer programming and consulting activities in Portugal?
Source: INE, 2019

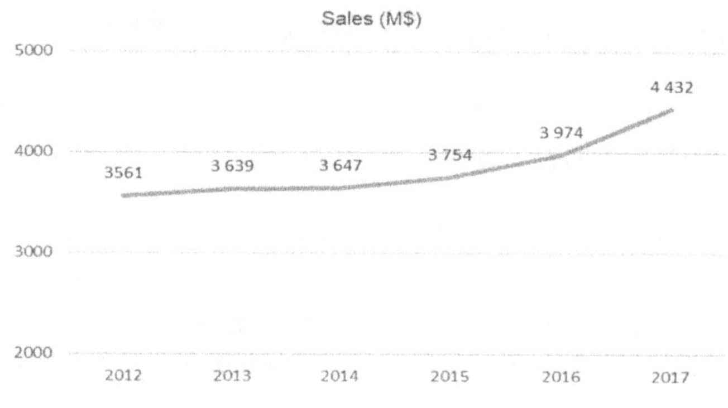

Figure 7. Evolution of the number of ICT companies in Portugal
Source: INE, 2019

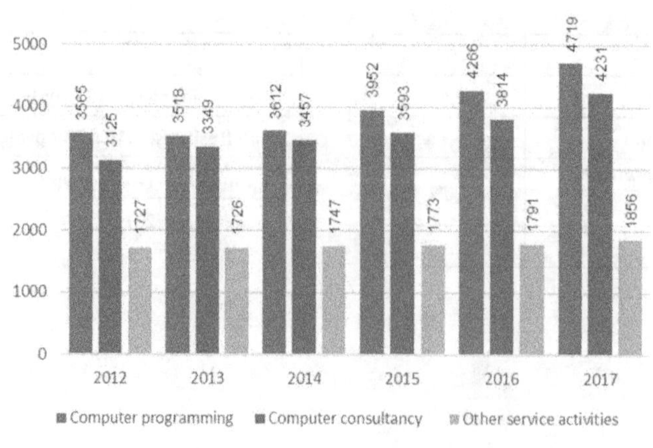

- Large customers' proximity, making it easier to monitor potential opportunities and follow up on the running projects;
- Qualified human resources represent the main source of value creation in this sector and, therefore, it is essential that there is an approximation to higher education institutions that are also located in large cities.
- Existence of technological parks that create synergies.

The corporate structure, in 2017, is characterized by a strong predominance of micro enterprises, representing small and medium-sized enterprises about 6% and large companies less than 1%.

As a prediction of the development of the sector, it should be noted that, at national level, policies in the scientific and technological context have acknowledged the need to qualify the Portuguese and stimulate innovation and technological modernization by accelerating the current changing process of specialization standard of the Portuguese economy and thus create the necessary conditions for the production of differentiated goods and services, supported by research and development activities and increasingly focused to the External markets.

Regarding forecasts up to 2020, IDC expects the industry to grow on average 4,8% per year, with investments in technologies related to the third platform (e.g. cloud computing, social business and big-data) and innovation accelerators (e.g. IoT, 3D printing or robotics), the major responsible for boosting the market (they are expected to represent 52% of the total ICT spending in Portugal).

It can therefore be considered the existence of a technological environment at national level which, in addition to being at a fairly reasonable level, tends to develop in several areas, in particular with regard to new technologies of Information and communication (ICT) as instruments of modernization, innovation, efficiency, effectiveness and quality, services, as well as providing better coordination and simplification of procedures and functioning.

STRUCTURAL CHARACTERISTICS AND ATTRACTIVENESS

In order to identify the structural characteristics and the competitive context of the industry to assess its profitability potential, the well-known Porter Model (1980) will be used.

Thus, the analysis will focus on the five competitive forces: rivalry between existing companies, negotiating power of suppliers, negotiating power of customers, threat of entry of new companies and threat of substitute products or services.

Table 6. Size of ICT companies in Portugal

	Nº	%
Micro companies (<10 people)	10 075	93,2%
Small Businesses (10 a 49 people)	577	5,3%
Medium-sized Enterprises (50 a 249 people)	123	1,1%
Big companies (>249 people)	31	0,3%
Total	10 806	

Source: INE, 2019

Figure 8. Porter's Five Forces Model
Source: Adapted from Porter, 1980

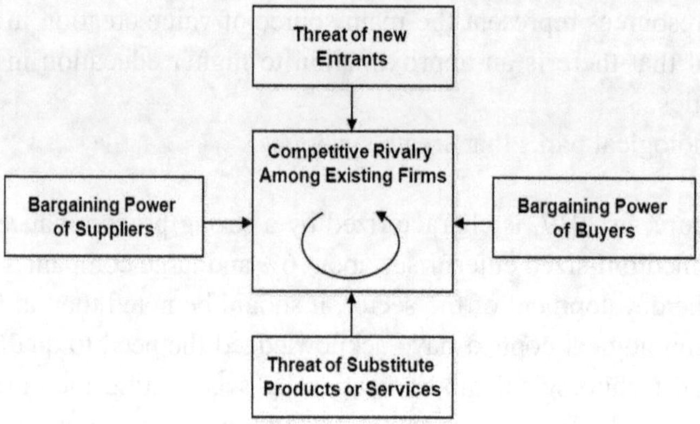

Competitive Rivalry Among Existing Firms

When rivalry between current competitors is high, it usually leads to price wars, comparative advertising campaigns, extensions of product warranties deadlines and, consequently, to losses in the potential profitability of the industry.

The rivalry between existing companies of an industry is influenced according to the characteristics of the following described factors, using a methodology developed by Santos (1992), which is based on the model presented by Porter (1980).

Industry growth: Industries with high growths, tend to have less rivalry, since companies are more concerned about responding to demand and reaching quotas in potential markets. On the other hand, reduced growth causes greater rivalry among companies, due to the utilization of the installed capacity of the various competitors.

According to the values presented, in the analysis of demand and supply, it can be concluded that growth rates are still expected, although more reduced in traditional IT.

Fixed operating costs: The higher the fixed costs, the greater the operational risk, forcing companies to guarantee a higher workload to at least reach the critical point of the activity.

This factor is more relevant in companies with a higher component of development or service delivery, due to the high weight of staff costs, with emphasis on hardware and software, being, however, smaller for commercial activities.

Overcapacity: When the increase in capacity is carried out in large increments, this situation acts on the rivalry, since it obliges aggressive pricing policies to ensure the flow of production in the phases of less demand.

Developments in the sector relate to the economic growth rates of countries and, therefore, capacity may affect rivalry. Thus, periods of lower growth or recession may have a high impact on the performance of information technology firms, as investments in these areas do not normally represent expenditure on the other current activity sectors. Although it is expected that the next few years, as previously mentioned, there isn't great growth in traditional IT, it is admitted, however, that, in global terms, this factor has little influence on the rivalry between companies in the sector.

Product differentiation: When there are several sources of differentiation of the products, the rivalry tends to be inferior, since the competitors present technically different or even complementary offerings, not competing directly with each other, with so much intensity.

In view of the multiplicity of needs at the level of information systems, integration with communication technologies and opportunities arising from the mobility and transmission of voice, data and image, the rivalry among companies with greater focus on Development of solutions is greatly attenuated. Still, in the production of hardware, software and the provision of more standardized services, rivalry tends to be superior, because competition is mainly done through efficiency and price wars.

Irreversible investments: The requirement for irreversible investments requires greater returns over time, increasing the rates of rivalry.

While the hardware production activity is required to invest in specific physical assets for the other activities (software and services) the largest investment relates to the recruitment of qualified human resources and their training and certification in the companies' priority activity areas.

However, in a biased way, these investments can be rewarded, since the acquired competences allow a broad range of action at both the technological level of supply and the level of markets covered. Therefore, most of the time, companies are organized through business units that manage the qualification of their human resources according to the priorities in terms of supply and target customers.

Concentration and balance: When there is a fair distribution of market shares by a small number of firms (balance and concentration), rivalry tends to be higher by the ongoing struggle for market share, especially when none of the competitors present competitive advantages over the remaining.

The information technology sector, with the exception of hardware producers, is characterized as a fragmented industry, where there is a great diversity of companies with multiplicity of sources of advantages competitive advantages, thus not concentrating, a rivalry generator factor.

Barriers to exit: When disinvestment, derived from the specificity of assets, hinders business abandonment by companies, even if their profitability is negative, it can lead to increased rivalry.

With regard to the activity of hardware production, which requires specific physical assets that may hinder the activity's exit, for the other activities (software if services) the type of assets is essentially at the level of the intangible (human resources, organizational and information systems), not becoming difficult to be disposable, being frequent Small and Medium Sized Companies' integration of into larger structure' companies, complementing their supply.

Working Capital Requirements / Management Fund needs: Industries with lower financial exploitation needs, can more easily increase turnover through more attractive prices and promotions, also increasing the level of rivalry.

In the information technology sector, the working capital needs have a reasonable weight against total assets, not only by the inventories and credits to be granted. Nevertheless, if this analysis is integrated with the weight of the fixed costs of human resources, it is considered that no conditions are established for companies to easily opt for price wars that increase rivalry in the industry.

In the table 7 and based on the above, a summary of the impact level of each factor in the rivalry among existing companies in the information technology sector is presented.

It is therefore considered that the information technology sector is generally characterized by a reduced rivalry among existing companies and a little more pronounced in standardized products or services, and Influenced, above all, with regard to the impact of the level of fixed costs very much associated with access to qualified human resources, which do not exist in sufficient numbers in the face of the needs caused by the growth of companies.

Table 7. Impact of factors on rivalry among existing firms

Factors	Characteristics	Impact on degree of rivalry	
Industry Growth	high	Low	↘
Fixed Costs			
.Hardware/Software	high	Strong	↗
.Services	Reduced	Low	↘
Overcapacity	Reduced	Low	↘
Product Differentiation			
. Standardized Products/Services	Reduced	Strong	↗
. Custom Development	high	Low	↘
Irreversible investments	Medium	Low	↘
Concentration and balance			
.Hardware	high	Strong	↗
.Software/Services	Reduced	Low	↘
Exit Barriers	Reduzidas	Low	
.Hardware	high	Strong	↗
.Software/Serviçes	Reduced	Low	↘
Operating funds needs	Medium	Medium	⇒

Table 8. Impact of rivalry among existing firms on attractiveness

Force	Characteristics	Impact on attractiveness	
Rivalry Among Existing Firms	Medium/Low	Positive	↗

Suppliers' Bargaining Power

Suppliers influence the potential profitability of an industry through sales price policies, payment deadlines, delivery times and product quality.

About the information technology sector, the main suppliers of this sector can be subdivided into technologies, human resources and financial means.

At the level of technologies, they are an important input for the sector and, in many cases, correspond to specific products, acquired from internationally renowned suppliers. Although with increasingly affordable prices, because of their generalization, they have little flexible conditions that penalize companies considerably, thus being an unfavorable factor to the sector' attractiveness.

Regarding human resources, understood as one of the main knowledge providers in the sector, they hold strong negotiating power, in view of their qualifications and the availability of fewer in relation to the needs of companies. Therefore, its cost is usually higher, absorbing a good part of the added value produced.

Another strong restriction of the sector relates to providers of financial means, since in the case of small businesses it will, in principle, have greater difficulties in accessing the financing needed to sustain growth rhythms.

In that respect, Arias et al (2000) ran an empirical study that companies with a higher level of innovation and research and development had longer pay-backs, increasing the risk of the business and decreasing the capacity of indebtedness' capacity.

It can therefore be concluded that, in global terms, suppliers have some negotiating power that adversely affects the information technology sector.

Buyers' Bargaining Power

Customers may affect the potential attractiveness of an industry through acquisitions, pricing policies, payment deadlines and requirements at the level of products' quality and adequacy.

The types of customer users of information technology are quite heterogeneous about the activity sector to which they belong to, but it is considered that the most important ones are in banks and insurers, major manufacturing industries, telecommunications, trade and public administration.

These larger sized customers, through the financial volume of their projects and the possibility of cross-selling, have a high negotiating power. In addition, in greater size and complexity projects, it is common to be required specific certifications that prove the supplier's development capacity (IQF, 2005).

For the most standardized products and services, given change costs' non-existence, customers will be able to exercise purchasing price policies and more aggressive payment deadlines (IGF, 2005).

In the case of software development companies and integrated solutions (which include equipment, software, networks and services of the most diverse natures) in addition to the price, the product quality and the design capacity of the company are also valued, from the diagnostic phase to the implementation and maintenance of the systems (Sousa, 2006). However, in view of the greater complexity of standardized products or services, these companies have more facility to negotiate greater margins with customers.

The table 10 and on the basis of the above, presents a summary of the impact level of customers' negotiating power in the technology sector.

Table 9. Impact of Bargaining Power of Suppliers on attractiveness

Force	Characteristics	Impact on attractiveness
Bargaining power of suppliers	High	Negative

Table 10. Impact of Bargaining Power of Buyers on attractiveness

Force	Characteristics	Impact on attractiveness	
Bargaining Power of Buyers			
. Standardized Product /Services	Strong	Negative	↘
. Custom Development	Medium	Medium	⇒

New Entrants' Threat

The entry of new competitors has an impact on the attractiveness of the industry, due to its increased supply capacity, a decrease in the demand available to the companies installed, increasing the level of rivalry.

The threat of entry of new competitors depends essentially on the entry barriers, which can be identified in six types that are described next, using the methodology developed by Santos (1992), based on the model presented by Porter (1980).

Scale' economies: High operations' volume or functional synergies' use allow to lower the unit cost of installed companies. Therefore, any entries will have to be made through high investments that allow a similar size and capacity regard industry' already existing companies, in order to guarantee prices at least identical.

Regarding the supply of standardized products or services, the scale effect may have some weight, because the competition is mainly through prices and efficiency (lower operating costs and faster delivery times).

However, in the other products or services consisting of integrated solutions, usually tailored to each client' needs, the competition is made mainly through quality levels, adequacy and supply innovation (Meneses, 2003), not being scale factor very important.

Investment needs: the need to invest high financial resources in assets, management fund needs, advertising, research and development and qualification of human resources, may have a very dissuasive effect on potential competitors.

As previously mentioned, hardware production activity requires investment in specific fixed assets and, for the other activities (software and services), the largest investment relates to the recruitment of qualified human resources and their training and certification in companies' priority areas, and these are representative factors of a strong barrier to the entry of new competitors.

To consider, however, that, in relation to international groups, this has not been a variable that has prevented them from entering in several marked, as is evidenced by the proliferation of subsidiaries or representatives of foreign companies.

Access to distribution channels: Extensive coverage of marketing channels may create difficulties in the penetration of new competitors ' products or services.

In companies with the greatest focus on standardized products or services, access to distribution channels is critical to their success, since many customers allow them to ensure the volume needed to present competitive prices. Searching the loyalty of the respective network, they assiduously perform several different actions to boost the dynamics of the partners (e.g. access to sales of the latest product or brand novelties, quantity discounts, promotions, etc.).

As for companies that are more dedicated to products or services consisting of integrated solutions, only in cases where their activity results in the development of a software that is susceptible to widespread use, will they provide the use of partners as marketing channels for their products. Therefore, only in the case of standardized products or services, access to distribution channels may be an impediment to new competitors' entry.

Product differentiation: The uniqueness of the products, their quality or the notoriety of the brands, can contribute to greater by customers' loyalty to already installed companies and demand greater communication investments to the new competitors.

In the case of standardized products or services, this situation does not represent an impediment to the entry of new competitors, given that the costs of change are not significant.

In the case of products or services consisting of integrated solutions, usually developed by companies with greater design capacity and technological leadership, the degree of differentiation is higher, and it can constitute a strong barrier to the entry of new competitors.

Government policy: Government policies (legislation, permits, licensing, etc.) may limit or condition the entry of new competitors.

In general, there are no competition limitations in relation to the information technology sector. Even the political – legal environment considers companies and investments in information and communication technologies as a strategic priority for a country.

Extra-scale costs: Advantages of high costs in areas unrelated to scale economies, such as the mastery of innovative technology, preferential access to raw materials or scarce resources, resulting from business experience, may represent strong barriers to the entry of new competitors.

In activities based on qualified knowledge that is reflected in the unique degree of innovation and complexity of the offer they provide, they do not only create barriers to the entry of new competitors, as they create conditions of internationalizing its know-how.

Thus, the greater the capacity of design and technological leadership, the more barriers are faced to new competitors.

Based on the above. the following table presents a summary of the threat of entry of new competitors' degree, in the information technology sector.

The activities of the information technology sector, based on qualified knowledge, which require high initial investments (hardware production, in addition to human resources, fixed assets are required), presents difficulties in the entry of new competitors. In the remaining activities, there's no major difficulty in entering new competitors.

Threat of Substitute Products or Services

The threat of substitute products or services may condition the attractiveness of the industry *by limiting the maximum sales price to be charged to the customer.*

As a result of production relocation of electronic components and hardware for China, and software for India (it is in this country that there are some of the world's best programmers), technology' price has fallen greatly, over the last few years.

Therefore, for the most standardized products, the trend is for the emergence of new products, more efficient and at lower costs. Thus, once again, companies with the greatest focus on providing stan-

Table 11. Impact of factors on Threat of new Entrants

Factors	Characteristics	Impact on Threat of new Entrants	
Scale economy			
. Standardized Products/Services	High	Strong	↘
. Custom Development	Reduced	Low	↗
Investment needs	High	Strong	↘
Access to distribution channels	Medium	Medium	⇨
Product Differentiation			
. Standardized Products/Services	Reduced	Strong	↘
. Custom Development	High	Low	↗
Government policy	Favorable	Low	↗
Extra-Scale Costs			
.Hardware/Software	High	Strong	↘
.Services	Reduced	Low	↗

Table 12. Impact of Threat of new Entrants on attractiveness

Force	Characteristics	Impact on attractiveness	
Threat of new Entrants			
.Hardware/Software	Low	Positive	↗
.Services	Medium	Medium	⇨

dardized services are more prone to competition for new products. Moreover, one of the great efforts of the various types of competitors in the information technology sector focuses on the formalization of partnerships with the main international brands, in order to obtain commercial advantages, or their exclusive representation (less frequent), in the territory in which they operate.

However, the new products and systems developed are also integrated within the information technology sector, and therefore cannot be regarded as substitute products, concluding by a reduced threat Products from other industries.

Conclusion on the Attractiveness of the Information Technology Industry

A table is then presented, where one intends to summarize the effect of each of the five forces of Porter's model in the attractiveness of the information technology sector.

Table 13. Impact of Threat of Substitute Products or Services on attractiveness

Force	Characteristics	Impact on attractiveness	
Threat of Substitute Products or Services	Low	Positive	

On a comparative basis, the following table presents some indicators relating to the EBITDA margin for each of the subsectors, based on information obtained from the CSI Market, BACH – Bank for the Accounts of Companies Harmonized from the European Committee of Central Balance sheets and Bank of Portugal (BP).

CRITICAL SUCCESS FACTORS

Besides the sector's dependence in relation to the respective contexts, companies' success will also be very dependent on some management variables. Designated critical success factors must ensure a good performance, because, according to Freire (1998), it has its origin on the combination of customer characteristics – key purchasing factors, with the nature of competition – competition factors.

Considering customers' characterization and the sector's competitive environment, the following table presents the critical success factors, in relation to the generic types of previously considered companies (products or Standardized services and software development and integrated Solutions).

Two of the critical success factors of the companies with the most standardized offer, namely scale economies and operational efficiency, derive fundamentally from the need to reduce the products' unit costs and, thus, more attractive selling prices.

Scale economies are mainly dependent on access to marketing channels, to ensure a high number of customers that allow for the optimization of the binomial quantity – price.

In addition, a good logistics capacity, based on stock management, on transport costs' control and on a location close to the partners, reduces operating costs (Meneses, 2003).

At the same time, in order to maintain the loyalty of business partners, it is important that these companies present an appropriate technological diversification, which ensures access to the various models and benchmarks of the sector, allowing the customer to have a variety of choice and can implement the one stop shop philosophy, where the purchase act consists of acquiring several complementary technology products.

In addition, these companies are still able to differentiate themselves from the competition, through a good level of customer service, measured by the response time and the capacity of problem-solving.

In this sense, through the analysis of the institutional sites, it is easy to verify that almost all companies have areas reserved to the commercial partners where they can place orders and ask for problem solving.

Regarding software development companies and integrated solutions' companies, in addition to operational efficiency, critical success factors, namely, technological mastery, innovation, communication and marketing are based, mainly, on the degree of supply differentiation.

Figure 9. Attractiveness of the information technology sector

	Hardware	Software	Services
Competitive Rivalry Among Existing Firms	Reduced rivalry between existing companies and slightly higher in standardized products or services. This is mainly influenced by the impact of the level of fixed costs associated with qualified human resources. *Conclusion: Low*		
Bargaining Power of Suppliers	Technology providers, have inflexible conditions that greatly penalize companies and is an unfavorable factor for the attractiveness of the sector. Human resources have a strong bargaining power, as they are fewer in number than companies require. Small businesses generally have greater difficulties in accessing the finance needed to sustain growth rates. *Conclusion: High*		
Bargaining Power of Buyers	For more standardized products, since there are no switching costs, customers have some bargaining power. *Conclusion: Medium/High*	Software development and integrated solutions companies are better able to negotiate higher margins with customers *Conclusion: Medium*	
Threat of new Entrants	Activities that require high initial investments (physical and human) present difficulties in entering new competitors. *Conclusion: Low*	Activities that require high skilled human resources present some difficulties to entry for new competitors. *Conclusion: Medium/Low*	Activities with lower initial investments present less difficulties in entering new competitors. *Conclusion: Medium*
Threat of Substitute Products or Services	New products and systems developed are also integrated within the information technology sector and cannot be considered as substitute products. *Conclusion: Low*		
Attractiveness	**Medium/High**	**Medium/High**	**Medium/Low**

Legend: Impact on Attractiveness

Table 14. EBITDA Margin of IT sectors

	2014	2015	2016	2017
Computer Hardware				
EUA	20,1%	12,4%	25,0%	25,2%
Europe				
France	1,80%	2,80%	4,30%	n/d
Austria	10,4%	11,4%	12,5%	n/d
Software programming				
USA	29,9%	21,4%	25,7%	23,9%
Portugal	12,00%	10,50%	13,90%	15,20%
Software programming and services				
Europe				
France	6,7%	7,9%	7,8%	n/d
Austria	9,8%	9,9%	12,9%	n/d
Computer consultancy				
Portugal	10,40%	4,60%	10,60%	10,20%
Other IT service activities				
Portugal	7,20%	7,50%	7,60%	10,50%

Source: CSI Market, BACH and BP, 2019

Table 15. Critical success factors

	Purchasing Key Factors	Competition factors	Critical success factors
Standardized products or services	▪ Prices and credit ▪ Product diversity ▪ Lead times ▪ Assistance services	▪ Costs and distribution channels ▪ Technological partnerships ▪ Location and Logistics ▪ E-Business and service centers	▪ Scale economies ▪ Technological Diversification ▪ Operational efficiency ▪ Service level
Software and integrated Solutions Development	▪ Offer quality ▪ Suitability capacity ▪ Notoriety ▪ Assistance services ▪ Prices and credit	▪ Know-How HR/Technology Partners ▪ Research and development ▪ Company and brand Disclosure ▪ E-Business and service centers ▪ Process efficiency	▪ Technological Mastery ▪ Innovation ▪ Communication and marketing

With regard to the technological domain, as a support to the quality of the company's implementation, which is one of the most important factors in the purchasing decision, the notoriety of the certifications obtained, the technologies used and the experience in previous work are important references for customers.

In this way, the strategic partnerships with the main international brands of information technology, as well as the recruitment of consecrated consultants or good students of the major universities, have become fundamental for customer satisfaction and for company success, in the medium and long term.

With regard to the capacity for innovation, both in terms of supply and work processes, it is very important, because it intends, on the one hand, to develop services tailored to the needs of each client, making it a true business partner and, on the other hand, get faster turnaround times and activities with lower costs from non-conformities.

Companies with the greatest capacity for technological leadership will, over time, be the successful competitors of the near future, since their offer will have unique characteristics in the face of the remaining competition.

Multinationals have excellence skills' centers, located in certain countries with highly skilled human resources in information and communication technologies and, therefore, ensure the production of worldwide reference solutions, used by most of the other companies.

For this reason, companies nationwide, whose activity focuses on developing software in packages or tailored to the needs of customers, are increasingly betting on the establishment of own research and development and access to knowledge through the realization of national or even international innovation standards, with institutions of the national scientific and technological system and with other companies of information technologies possessing complementary competences.

Thus, the capacity for innovation over time, will be increasingly fundamental for the guarantee of sustainable competitive advantages (IQF, 2005).

As for communication and marketing, the promotion of companies' image is very important for creating a high market' notoriety, and to decrease the weight of the price factor in the purchase decision.

It can take several forms: good performance on important customers, which generates word-of-mouth and helps build the entity' reputation over time; participation in events with recognized market partners, allowing the company some visibility; partnerships with renowned collaborators or with prestigious schools and business associations, reinforcing the organization's credibility; conducting works and advertising campaigns in the media, to acquire new customers and retain the old ones through greater confidence in the company's competencies (Freire, 1996).

CONCLUSION

There are companies engaged in activities of the information technology sector, but which are classified with different codes, and there are also companies with the code of information technology but who do not exercise such activity, what should happen, possibly and in some cases, due to the activity's conversion.

The products and services offered by the information technology sector cover a wide range of applications, ranging from the aid in strategic decision-making to simple use as an operational tool, through solutions that intend to achieve greater integration with the main business partners.

The global expenditure on ICT grew less than 5% each year since the financial crisis in 2009, representing the traditional markets of IT and telecommunications an increasingly mature sector of the economy.

In all regions, a growing proportion of hardware, software, and service expenditures are linked to the cloud and mobile devices, while traditional technologies such as desktop PC, local storage systems, and fixed telecommunications services, are stable or declining.

As for the evolution of the sector, it is anticipated that traditional ICT spending would largely follow GDP growth over the next decade, with the general industry catapulted to a growth of more than two times GDP as new technologies start to represent a larger market share, in particular, IoT, Robotics and AIR/VR.

At the level of the business dimension, the sector Software & Programming is characterized by a strong predominance of micro and small enterprises. It can be concluded that the information technology sector, in general, has a fragmented structure, however, presenting in the activity of hardware production, a more concentrated structure.

In Portugal is expects the industry to grow on average 4,8% per year, with investments in technologies related to the third platform (e.g. cloud computing, social business and bigdata) and innovation accelerators (e.g. IoT, 3D printing or robotics).

In order to identify the structural characteristics and the competitive context of the industry to assess its profitability potential, the well-known Porter's Five Forces Model will be used and is conclude that the hardware and software activities, are Medium/High attractiveness and services activity are Medium/Low attractiveness.

Considering customers' characterization and the sector's competitive environment, the critical success factors in relation to products or standardized services are scale economies, technological diversification, operational efficiency and service level. Relatively to software development and integrated solutions, the critical success factors are technological mastery, innovation, communication and marketing.

REFERENCES

Alajaasko, P. (2006). *The demand for services: external but local provision*. EUROSTAT.

Arias, C., Martinez, A., & Gracia, J. (2000). Enfoques Emergentes en Torno en la Estrucutura de Capital: El caso de la Pyme. VIII Foro de Finanzas, Madrid: Asociación Española de Finanzas (AEFIN).

BACH. (2019). *Statistics from NACE code 62*. European Central Bank. Retrieved from https://www.bach.banque-france.fr/?lang=en

Freire, A. (1998). *Estratégia – Sucesso em Portugal*. Lisboa: Verbo.

IDC. (2019). *ICT forecasts*. Retrieved from https://www.idc.com/promo/global-ict-spending/forecast

INE. (2019). *Estatísticas do código de atividade 62*. Retrieved from https://www.ine.pt/xportal/xmain?xpgid=ine_tema&xpid=INE&tema_cod=1313

Insee - Institut national de la statistique et des études économiques. (2019). *IT statistiques*. Retrieved from https://insee.fr/fr/accueil

IQF. (2005). *O Sector dos Serviços de Informação e Comunicação. Estudos Sectoriais*. IQF.

IT Market Statistics and Trends. (2016), retrieved from https://www.ironpaper.com/webintel/articles/it-market-statistics-and-trends/

Meneses, A. (2003). *Posicionamento Estratégico: Criar Valor para vencer no Mercado de Tecnologias de Informação*. Lisboa: INSAT.

Nordhaus, W. (2002). Productivity Growth and the New Economy. *Brookings Papers on Economic Activity*, *2002*(2), 211–244. doi:10.1353/eca.2003.0006

Porter, M. (1980). *Competitive Strategy*. New York: Free Press.

Santos, F. (2004). *Estratégia passo a passo*. Edições Centro Atlântico.

Sousa, A. (2006). As 100 Maiores Empresas de TI em Portugal. *Suplemento do Jornal Semana Informática, 809*.

Universidade Católica – Centro de Estudos Aplicados. (2001). *O Sector das Tecnologias de Informação em Portugal*. ANETIE.

Chapter 7
The Company:
The Process of Internationalization and Management Control Systems

ABSTRACT

This chapter presents a Portuguese company of the information technologies industry that did an internationalization process and has implemented a management control system with a very interesting complexity level and that, in reality, crosses the theory present in the different bibliographical references on the subject, with the experience and business practice of its management. Such management practices were so helpful that, in a short period, the company could internationalize its activity and turnover went from 10 million euros to 60 million euros, becoming a reference of its industry in Portugal. It should be noted that the case study was developed through the triangulation of different information sources, such as interviews and meetings, direct observations of management control practices, as well as consultation of documents and internal reports. The authors characterize the company and its evolution, national and international, as well as the management control system implemented with reference to the instruments developed in the previous chapters.

COMPANY CHARACTERIZATION

History and Decisive Moments

"*Technological*" began in 1990, by with two small and medium-sized Portuguese companies, by a set of promoters and management frameworks, which were integrated into the structure Shareholder.[1]

However, in 1999, with the growth of the business and the greater involvement of the work team, it was verified the realization of a "management by Out" (MBO) having the managers acquired the actions belonging to the two companies, becoming the main Shareholders, alongside individual initial investors.

DOI: 10.4018/978-1-7998-2007-9.ch007

The company was born as a software house, having as initial project the development of an integrated management system (currently called ERP), destined to the segment of the Portuguese medium-sized companies. Today, because of this initial investment, it already presents in its curriculum the implementation of thousands of ERP in different organizations.

Since 1992, *"Technological"* developed a set of technological partnerships and strategic distribution agreements, aiming at acquiring specialized knowledge in information technologies, to cease being a mono company Product. This diversification effort was accompanied by a change in the organizational structure, developed from the establishment of SBU-strategic business units.

From 1996 onwards, it opts for a greater focus on its services' provision, aiming, on the one hand, to mitigate the degree of exposure and dependence in relation to its technological partners and, on the other hand, to improve its benefit per worker.

Because of the recorded evolution, *"Technological"* has been positioned, since 1998, in the first quartile of the information technology market in Portugal (using indicators of business volume or productivity).

It is, therefore, a successful company that has continuously been gaining market share, consolidating its competitive position in the Portuguese business context of the information and communication technologies (ICT) industry, as one of the most sustainable dynamic players.

After previous local contacts and respective markets' analysis, *"Technological"* constituted, in 2001, a company in Angola, following the entry into Mozambique in 2004 and in Brazil, in 2011.

Products and Services

As previously mentioned, the company's offer has evolved over time, initially through the development of its own brand software, then by the resale of several reference software's in the market and then by the Integration of different software and information systems according each client's needs.

Thus, the supply logic is based on the development of projects tailored to each client, providing the tools, the implementation and integration models of these tools and the necessary services for their implementation, testing and monitoring the projects' execution.

In terms of tools, *"Technological"* develops its business based on content and software tools in three areas:

- Software and services for asset management and horizontal processes' management, for companies from almost all sectors of activity (ERP/CRM/SCM/BI) – (Value chain management systems, physical and intellectual processes and assets);
- Tools, production management systems and software testing and services provided to software development departments of large companies and software houses – programming languages, modelling systems, production and test team management software, version control, software development services, consulting, etc.;
- Technology infrastructure management Software and services.

In relation to the products and Services integrated by the company in the solutions to customers, main lines offered are listed in the table 1.

In addition, within the integrated supply logic, the company carries out a high technological innovation effort through the creation of its own brands in the form of vertical georeferencing products,

Figure 1. Organizational processes that "Technological" tools integrate

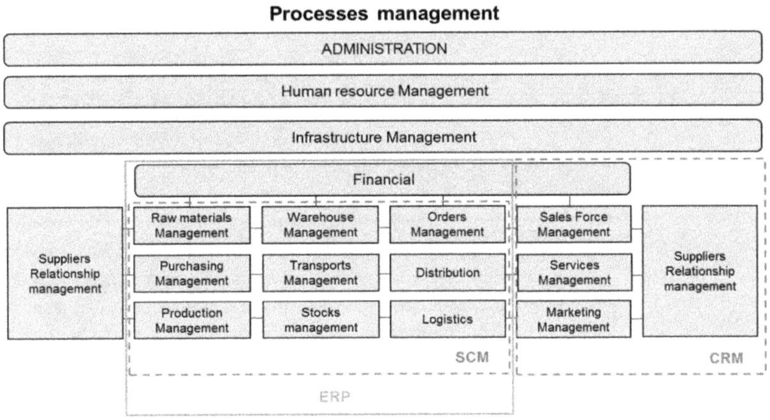

Table 1. Company Products and Services Offer

Product/Service	Description
Outsourcing Services	Management of a service, process or activity on an outsourcing basis
On-site Software development services	It consists in assisting the client in the effort of software development, by strengthening its production team with specialized technicians, to work in its facilities according to the methodologies adopted by customers
Information Technology Tools	Resale or distribution of products from strategic partnerships
Information Technology Consultancy	Technical advisory services to support the use of software development tools
Business Intelligence Solutions	Design and placement of decision support systems
CRM/ERP Solutions Implementation Services	Design and implementation of systems (GIS-Integrated management systems) to support the operational activities of companies.
Services of security management and quality of technological infrastructures	Services that ensure the management of the levels of safety and quality of technological infrastructures
Training & Development	Training and training management services in various technical fields
Consulting and systems development services in accordance with the methodological framework RUP – Rational Unified Process	Services that enable the customer to accelerate and reduce the inherent risk of their learning curve using the RUP and simultaneously broaden their internal responsiveness and can subcontract or work as a team with experienced technicians.
Consulting services and development of solutions for e-commerce	E-Business Solutions development services

biometrics, asset and liability management and telecommunications, among others, representing the markets of Angola, Brazil and Mozambique important business references.

From 2007 onwards, in order to guide the strategic business units to offer solutions tailored to customers and to ensure greater collaboration among the company's different sectors, strategic guidance axes were created that encompass different Competencies of the Organization.

The creation of the strategic axes was aimed at making known to the market the company's ability to develop large transversal projects through agglutination to measure resources with close competences, thus creating the conditions capable of encourage the products' development and innovation and solutions targeted at specific markets.

Figure 2. Milestones in the development of "Technological"

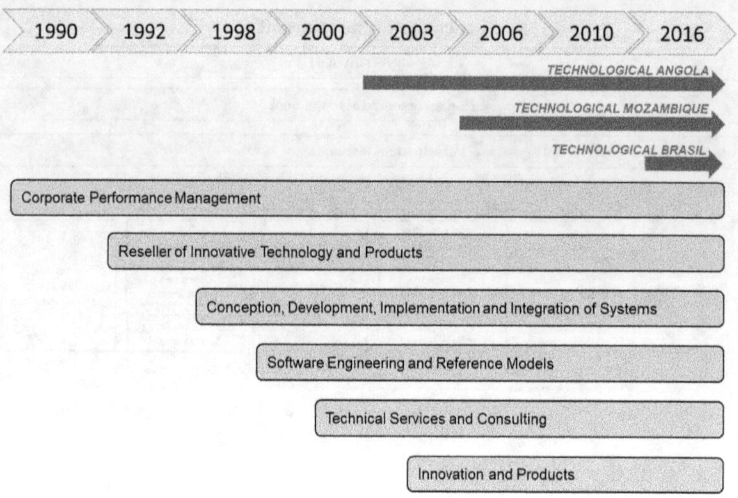

Example of this orientation to the specific needs requested by the market was the realization of the projects of the electoral register of Citizens of the Republic of Angola and the realization of several electoral processes that took place in this country over the Last few years.

Technological Strategic Axes

Technological offer is currently structured around the strategic business axes depicted in Figure 3.

Figure 3. Supply strategic axes

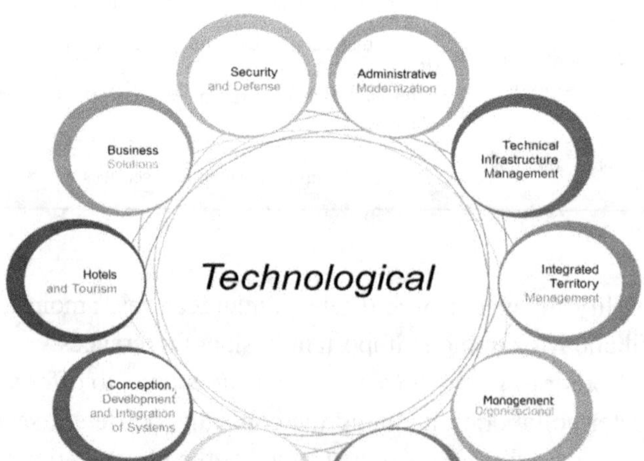

Integrated Territory Management

The company makes available to the market a complete supply of services, instruments and systems of strategic formulation, planning and management, duly articulated with each other and representative of the actors involved in the service of Sustainable development policies and poverty eradication. Works in the areas of Topography; Cartography Geographic information systems; Spatial Planning and Development; Environment and Georesources; Architecture Studies and projects; and Technical Projects' Supervision.

Business Solutions

The company offers structuring solutions in multiple domains, to ensure business' competitiveness, in an increasingly globalized and competitive market. This includes Integrated Management Systems (ERP); Business portals; E-commerce solutions; Capture, Recognition and Document Management solutions; Decision Support Solutions, Mobility solutions; Customer Service Management Solutions.

Administrative Modernization

The company's solutions in this area offer a complete and reasoned view of what should be the administrative modernization in the Central and Local Public Administration. Thus, the solutions in this area complement the design and implementation of quality management systems with the design, design, integration and implementation of information systems and technologies. As such, these projects allow an integrated supply of services and process-oriented management systems.

Security and Defense

Its objective is to develop products and solutions to meet the security and defense challenges of the 21th century in areas such as security, identification and citizens authentication; registration, authentication and events monitoring; strategic infrastructures' security, intelligent border surveillance and security perimeters; reinstatement of order and security in the event of a crisis or catastrophe; integration, connectivity and interoperability of security and defense systems; and traditional areas such as video surveillance and access management and control.

Technical infrastructures' Management

Corporate solutions are available in the area of information technologies, providing and integrating high quality professional products and services in the continuous search for a positive differential in the service and conduction of operational processes. The offer in this area includes the ICT services management, Contact Centers with qualified and multidisciplinary technical teams, technical laboratory and repair center, logistics services, integrated energy solutions in any context. A full range of professional services that includes asset management, logistics, change management and replacement operations (maintenance).

Hospitality and Tourism

"Technological" is the corporate industry partner member of HTNG (Hotel Technology Next Generation), an international association that defines the technological management standards for the hospitality industry and to which belong almost all major hotel chains in the world, as well as the leading technology providers for this industry. The technological solutions that are proposed for this industry respond to the totality of the needs of the operators of this market and consider a future perspective. It intends to ensure the appropriate conditions for management at the highest level and for maximising business profitability. *"Technological"* presents a range of products that encompasses, from the technical management of the building, to the entertainment systems, security systems and billing systems (front office and back-office), as well as the commercial management systems with Agents and reserve centers.

Organizational Management

This is one of the most comprehensive strategic axes of *"Technological"*, providing services and solutions in areas such as information services' strategies, change management, risk management; organizational policies, roles, competencies; process and service platforms; Balanced Scorecard; quality management, information security; recruitment, performance, talent compensation; Real-time monitoring of ICT and operations. The line of professional services and solutions ensures the follow-up, since the strategy design, to the design of the process management models (aligned with the industry reference models), quality management and improvement, passing through monitoring of operations and risks (in real time).

Design, Development and Systems' Integration

The *"Technological"*, since its foundation, dedicates special importance to the value chain of design and development of software systems. It distributes and supports various tools and frameworks that enable, together with the company's qualified human resources, support to practices and processes, such as defining procedures to be established. *"Technological"* is an ISO 9001:2008 certified company in all processes (CDIS) and has also obtained recognition of the maturity level three for the systems development processes (according to the CMMI Reference model). In this sense, the company manages to guarantee an integrated offer, regarding the risk management and the quality of its systems development processes, so that they can constitute a source of competitive differentiation.

Energy and Axis: Transport Solutions

The Axis – Energy and transport solutions develop integrated solutions for the entire value chain of these industries and for the various working processes of these organizations, based on best management and processes engineering practices.

Trademarks Registered by "Technological"

Over the years, *"Technological"* has made a consistent effort to build a portfolio of products/systems aligned with its strategic axes, presenting more and more a logic of complete response capability for its customers, providing them with tailor-made solutions, having registered more than thirty registered trademarks of integrated Information Technology solutions, on the various strategic axes previously described.

To make this global and integrated offer available, the company has a set of technology partners and business alliances, which enable it to provide worldwide reference technologies and to hold unique competences in several major Market demand valences.

Technology Partnerships and Business Alliances

Technological Partnerships

In the technological partnerships, the company has developed a set of long-lasting relationships with several reference multinationals in the industry, for example: INFORMIX, CENTURA/GUPTA, ORACLE, MICROSOFT, IBM, COGNOS, SAP, HP, CA-LOGIC WORKS, RATIONAL, CAPTIVA and CAST.

These partnerships have allowed the company to undertake a continuous effort of improvement and technological innovation in order to ensure a high capacity for execution and value creation for the organizations it serves, and to ensure a strong competitive position.

Business Alliances

At the commercial level, *"Technological"* maintains privileged relationships with countless partners (software-houses and solution integrators) that resell the products and technologies it distributes in Portugal and in international markets. The trade agreements established with partners include also several SW-Houses for resale software.

In addition, and according to the logic one-stop shop, *"Technological"* presents a panoply of business partners belonging to the same group of shareholders, which guarantee a global and diversified offer in the most diverse markets and activity sector (see Figure 5).

- ***Innovation*** **Company:** Ensures competence within the public administration market and administrative modernization;
- ***Biometrics*** **Company:** Ensures wider competences in the area of biometrics, to reinforce the strategic axis of security and defense;
- **GEOGRAPHY Company:** Provides expertise in the area of geographic information and cartography systems;

Figure 4. Examples of Technology Partnerships

Figure 5. Technological" business group

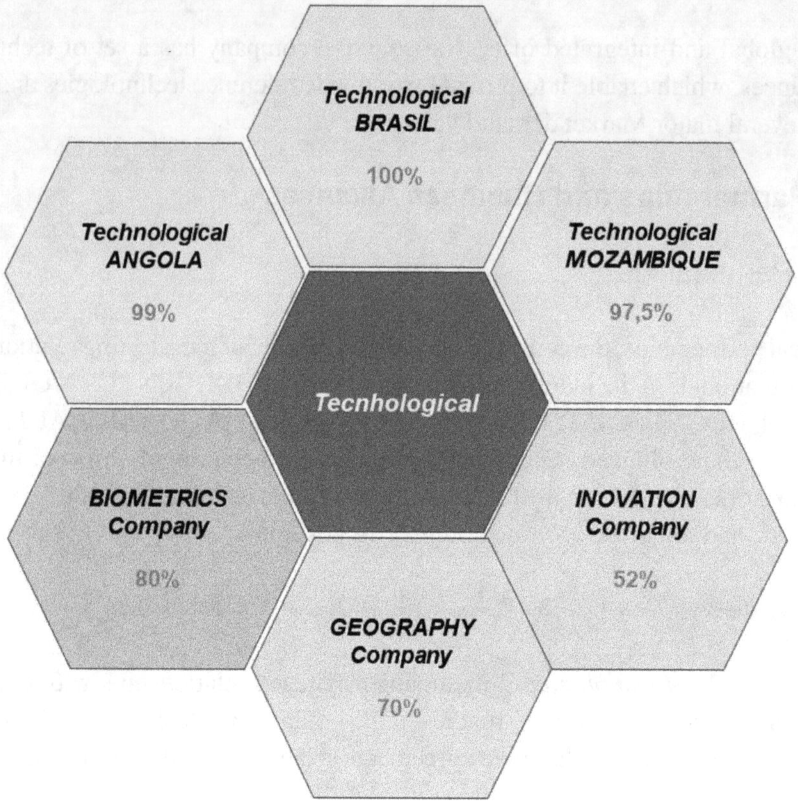

- ***TECHNOLOGICAL ANGOLA*** **Company**: Ensures presence in all provinces of Angola;
- ***TECHNOLOGICAL Mozambique*** **Company:** Ensures presence in all provinces of Mozambique;
- ***TECHNOLOGICAL BRASIL*** **Company:** Ensures the presence throughout Brazil.

Target Markets and Main Customer References

Target Markets

A first analysis of the target markets of *"Technological"*, leads us to conclude that the company has its activity strongly dedicated to the external markets where it has subsidiaries, namely Angola, Brazil and Mozambique, which in its whole, accounted for, in 2014, about 78% of the turnover.

At the level of the Portuguese market, the activity focuses mainly on two types of markets, based on the supply of products and services:

- Specialized services in the area of integration of systems: banking, insurance, telecommunications, public administration, health and distribution and trade;
- Horizontal products and solutions for small and medium sized companies.

Figure 6. Weight of countries in turnover

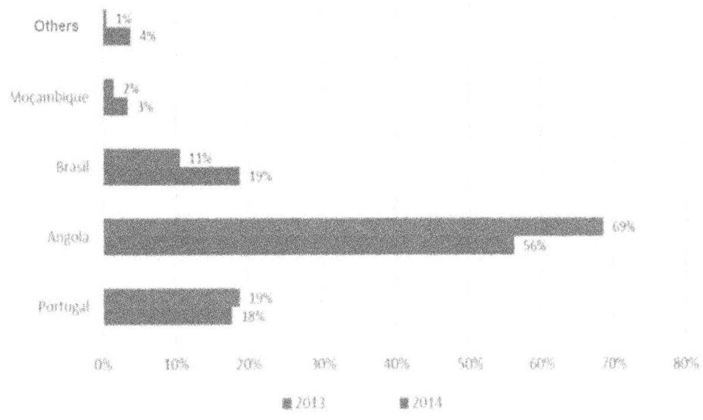

About external markets, the company has been developing an integrated set of support solutions for strategies to combat poverty, notably in information systems in the areas of people management, property, territory and property. As such, the company has managed to penetrate sustainably in the markets of Angola, Brazil and Mozambique, with today's prospects of success in the medium and long term in these countries.

Thus, the current geostrategic positioning of *"Technological"* covers the territories of Portugal, Brazil, Angola and Mozambique, currently serving thirty cities in the four countries referred.

Customers in Portugal

In Portugal, the customers of information technology are very heterogeneous, both in size and in relation to the sector of activity to which they belong. At the level of the sectors, the most important ones are banking and insurers, telecommunications, public administration and large manufacturing industries (IDC, 2016).

Figure 7.

4 Countries:
Angola,
Brasil
Moçambique,
Portugal
30 Cities:
Lisboa, Porto, Aveiro,
Marinha Grande, Águeda, Castelo Branco, Coimbra,
Ponte de Lima, Pombal, Faro, Setúbal, Vila da Feira, Loulé, Leiria, Alcobaça,
Casal de Cambra, Porto Alto, Funchal, Luanda, Lobito, Benguela, Huila,
Ondigiva, Grandola, Kahama, Xangongo, Maputo, Florianápolis, Santa
Catarina e São Paulo

The needs of customers of this type of industry are related to the use of computer technology and processes to:

- Increase the organization's security;
- Increase productivity and innovation;
- Increase the organization's memory;
- Increase individual and collective knowledge;
- Improve internal and external communications;
- Guiding behavior and managing operations;
- Incorporate in the processes the best practices of the industry;
- Manage change;
- Managing and enriching staff skills.

Regarding the value-generating factors and which condition your purchasing decision are:

- Price Related factors:
- Sales prices practiced;
- Credit granted.
- Product-related factors:
- Quality of technologies and services performed;
- Technology functionality;
- Capacity to assist and follow-up in after-sales services.
- Other factors:
- Notoriety and experience in previous works;
- Partnerships with recognized suppliers;
- Ability to execute.

In relation to *"Technological"*, a table is presented with the number of its main customers per activity sector.

Table 2. Main customers in Portugal

Sectors	Nº
Banking	14
Insurance	2
Transport	11
Industries	25
Trade and distribution	3
Business services	5
Government and public administration	11

Strategy, Management Model and Organizational Objectives

Strategy: Competitive Positioning

"Technological" presents as a vision for the development of the business:

Being in the information technology market, a benchmark of excellence, a partner of trust, credible, competent and competitive (C4)

The company's mission specifies the global ideals and orientations for the future and generally represents the written explanation of the vision. In addition, it is very important to disseminate the spirit of the company by all its members and to ensure a joint action for achieving the general objectives.

In this sense, the mission of *"Technological"* is as follows:

To put the information, management and quality technologies to the service and to strengthen the competitiveness and flexibility of the organizations.

In order to ensure an alignment of behavior on the part of different hierarchical levels and business units, *"Technological"* promotes daily a set of values that aim to develop and consolidate a culture Based on innovation and responsiveness to the market, which is considered one of its strategic vectors.

According to the internal documents written and disclosed by the company, the main values promoted and shared are:

- Be ethical and have civic spirit;
- To be supportive at risk;
- Act quickly;
- Institutionalize change;
- Develop equity;
- Promote autonomy;
- Sharing knowledge;
- Encouraging the spirit of initiative;
- Be understanding and cooperative;
- Learn more from the future than with the past;
- Insist on the ludic quality of work.

It is thus intended to value flexibility and change, but at the same time, focus attention on the organization's adaptation to the requirements of the environment. As dominant concerns, there are growth, creativity and adaptive capacity of resources. Motivation is based on individual challenge and initiative, the possibility of innovating, the variety of tasks and the growth.

In fact, it takes only a few moments in the company, in order to realize that the dominant concern of its various workers is the action and timely response to the commitments with the various business players, while there is a constant demand for improve the quality of carried out work.

At the level of its performance in the market, *"Technological"* has been oriented towards two key axes of action:

- Product Strategy – Markets: The company chose to focus its offer on the activity of services in information technologies, at the national territory global level, because it is one of the subsectors with higher growth rates, in which the Portuguese companies and institutions reveal greater needs, namely in the integration of systems and the adequacy of technologies of each business' specificities;
- Strategy for creating competitive advantages: The definition of the panoply of services has undergone the creation of competencies in areas of high benefit, for example, software engineering, where competitive advantages have been obtained through innovation and constant supply adequacy to market needs.

Thus, *"Technological"* has favored growth by betting on high value-added markets, where resource competences are increasingly important to ensure sustained competitive positioning. Thus, it is not surprising that in 2014, it presents a higher VAB in 50% compared to turnover (68%) Moreover, at the same time, a ratio of services with turnover of 73%. This reality reflects the effort made to increase own production, resulting from unique accumulated expertise, in favor of the pure commercialization of software and hardware.

This positioning also highlights the focus on the elaboration of solutions tailored to the customers' needs, which, in addition to increasing the weight of services in the activity, allows the creation of a market offer with value-added and a greater degree of uniqueness.

Management Model: Strategic Business Units

The organizational model of *"Technological"* is based on the vision of intellectual capital advocated by Karl-Erik Sveiby (see Figure 9).

Thus, the organizational model of the company, intends to align the competencies of human resources and develop organizational competencies (for example, capacity of teamwork, knowledge sharing, innovation, information systems), in order to adapt the tailored offer to the customers' needs, making them authentic business partners.

Figure 8. Competitive positioning of "Technological"

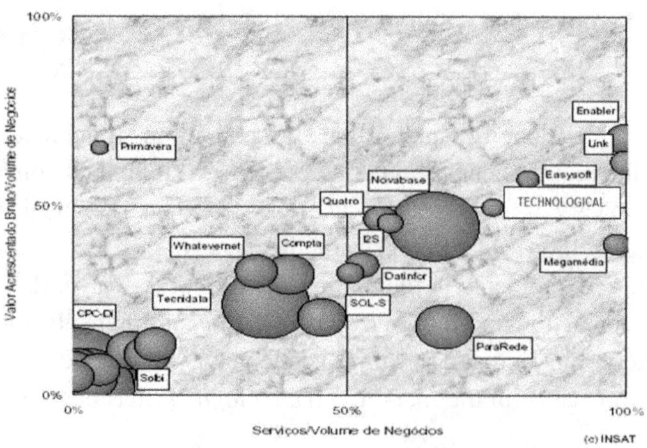

Figure 9. Vision of intellectual capital that underpins the organizational model of the company

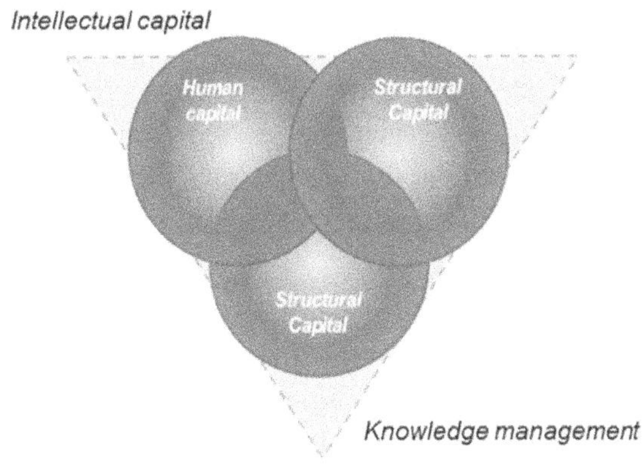

As such, the permanent pursuit of the alignment between the competencies of technical resources and the strategies of information and communication technologies of customers led to *"Technological"* to be structured in strategic units of business and units of business Support (see Figure 10).

The current organizational model is one of the key features of the company, since the existence of strategic business units provides high levels of creativity and motivation, derived from greater autonomy and authority decentralization.

This type of structure emerged as a way to combat the disadvantages of the functional organization, i.e., bureaucratic relations between different departments, greater number of hierarchical levels delaying decision-making, greater procedures' formalization and power centralization, making inflexible organizations and, finally, little attention to market and consumers, because there is clear guidance for internal functioning, rules compliance and chain of command.

Business units, also known as divisional structure, include all functions relating to certain products or markets, thus intending to have a faster response to consumer and competition. They are responsible

Figure 10. Organizational model

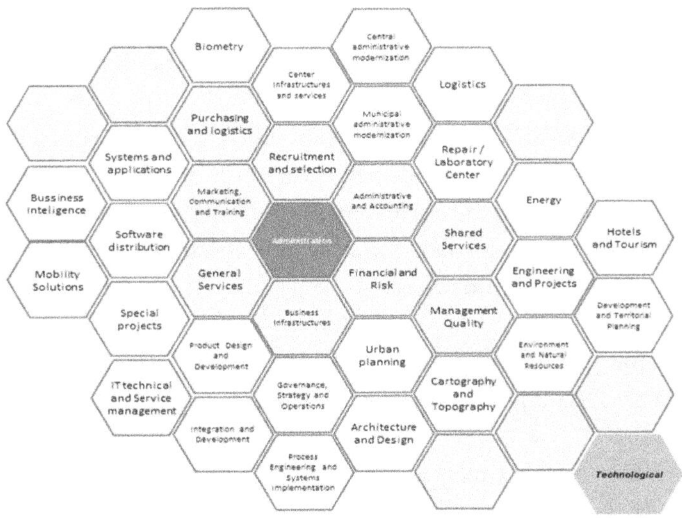

for the planning and coordination of all functions related to the segments they serve, from research to after-sales assistance itself. In this way, there is a constant focus on the environment and consumers, ensuring greater monitoring and control over the external changes.

This characteristic of the organizational structure of *"Technological"* is very important, because an industry with a wide range of products and services offer allows the company to diversify more easily its business, without losing quality indexes at the service level provided.

In fact, real specialized mini companies are created within the organizational structure with some characteristics that we highlight:

- Each manages a set of products and services, with which it has the freedom of action to serve the market segments that judges to be more convenient;
- Define the most appropriate marketing-mix policies for its customers (products and services, prices, marketing channels, promotions and other forms of direct marketing communication);
- They are responsible for the exploration cycle of their activity, from negotiation with customers, acquisitions, production and development, sales and distribution, to service and maintenance services;
- Its objectives and activities are disclosed to the organization through operational plans, being quantified in annual budgets, duly approved by the administration.

Thus, each business unit is centered on a core of technological skills and business solutions that guarantees its customers the competitiveness and quality of services rendered, either through unique offer features, whether through reduced response deadlines.

Developed Certifications and Competencies

The continuous improvement effort has also been carried out at the level of the development of individual and organizational competencies.

In this sense, the company has the quality certification under the ISO 9001:2000 Standard and the level three certification according to the CMMI World Reference Model in the context of information technologies. Level three certification is enabling the company to compete in highly demanding markets, with special focus on external markets and in particular for the public administration, defense, health and tourism sectors – for example, serves as a reference to NATO and the U.S. Department of Defense, in the hiring of ICT suppliers.

In addition, the effort in the certification of employees is constant, with a strong initiative to motivate human resources in their continuous training in specific areas of information technologies, as well as in generic areas of Management, through the achievement of master's and doctoral degrees.

Then, we present some of the various national and international frameworks in which the company is based, in the realization of its work processes:

- SM3-Methodology for the development of the works;
- NP EN ISO 19011:2003-Guidelines for audits of quality management systems and/or environmental management;
- NP EN ISO 9001:2000 – Quality management systems;
- NP EN ISO 9004:2000-quality management systems. Guidelines for performance improvement;

- EFQM – European Foundation for Quality Management;
- CAF – Common Assessment Framework: 2002 – Common Assessment Structure – Portuguese edition;
- COSO – Risk Management;
- COBIT – IT Governance;
- CMMI – Capability Maturity Model;
- PMI – Project Management Institute;
- PMBOK – Project Management Book of Knowledge;
- MORE – Methodology for assessing investments in IT/IT in the public administration;
- BS ISO/IEC 17799:2005 – Information Technology - Security techniques – Code of practice for information security management;
- BS ISO/IEC 27001:2005 – Information Technology - Security techniques – Information security management systems – Requirements;
- BS ISO 20000-1:2005 – IT Service Management – Specification for service management;
- BS ISO 20000-2:2005 - IT Service Management – Code of practice for service management;
- BS 7858:2004 – Security Screening of Individuals employed in a security environment - Code of practice;
- NP 4397:2001 – Occupational Safety and health management systems – specifications.

In addition to the internal development of competences, "*Technological*" has concluded cooperation protocols with various institutions of higher education, to carry out joint research projects in the field of Information Systems Engineering.

Still regarding intellectual capital and if skilled employees are the basis of the organizations' success, that are intended to assume competitive through the development of unique competences, the strategic management of human resources has become vital. Therefore, there are several initiatives aimed at guaranteeing access to the best professionals and their consequent development in the organization. We have as examples:

- Professionalization of the areas of recruitment and selection, also leading to increased reflection on the critical competencies associated with the development of each business. At the same time, there has also been a growing practice in the establishment of candidate grants with the desired profile, which are being recruited to the extent of the company's growth;
- Agreements between "Technological" and higher education schools aimed at guaranteeing access to qualified human resources and aligned with the needs of the company. To this end, they organize several joint actions: progressive placement of students through professional internships that conclude with definitive recruitment; Elaboration of programmatic contents of curricular units and courses, with the participation of the company's professionals, increasingly approaching teaching to business practice; Teaching of curricular units by *"Technological"* professionals, ensuring knowledge transmission and students' competencies alignment to the company's needs;
- To assume that continuous training is a pillar for the success of companies in the medium and long term. Therefore, the ability to obtain certifications from the company and collaborators, as are the cases of CMMi (Capability Maturity Model integration) and the ITIL (Information Technology Infrastructure Library), which represent some of the *best practices* in software and services development, they guarantee to customers that the company has the necessary competencies for the

realization of the most complex projects, contributing to increase its global levels of differentiation and access to higher value markets;

- Change in the remuneration logic, making variable a part of the costs with personnel, depending on employees' contribution to the strategic objectives. Thus, remunerations are articulated with careers' development, which are supposedly in tune with the organization's growth. Therefore, in addition to the fixed component of the salary, there are incentives that are paid according to the achievement of objectives in several strategic areas: fulfillment of business or profitability objectives, ability to do team work and contribution to the value of the company's global projects, innovation capacity and customer satisfaction, etc.

The Corporate Image

The *"Technological"* promotion plan is implemented at the global level (of the company) and at the level of each of the strategic business units or by product line or manufacturers.

In general, the promotion in *"Technological"* is made using the website, direct sales force, demonstrations' realization, advertising inserts, telemarketing actions, new partners' fundraising and commercial partners' relationship reinforcement.

Institutional marketing is responsible for the defense and development of the brand of *"Technological"* – confidence, credibility, competence and competitiveness – C4, and the values' communication and company's global positioning.

For example, here is the list of some of the marketing actions considered to be of priority:

1. Weekly publication of a newsletter that always contains a reference from a client, or a case of success, a technological dossier and the presentation of a business unit;
2. Program of workshops "Wednesdays or Thursdays at the place of the custom" – small events that are held every week and are devoted to topics that UEN consider relevant/differentiators;
3. The use of the training catalogue as an instrument for communication and the consubstantiation of specialized competences;
4. Weekly publication in specialty journals;
5. Periodical publications in expert journals in software development;
6. Conducting events (seminars and conferences) with the participation of experts and opinion leaders;
7. Publication of content on management and information systems, in management journals in the various markets where it is present;
8. Regular presence in fairs on management and information systems in the various markets where it is present.

Organizational Objectives

The objectives to be attained referenced in the *"Technological"* quality system would be summarized in the table 3, aligned with the company's Quality policy.

It is known that organizational goals are closely linked to the positioning that the management intends to guarantee for the company, in the medium and long term.

Table 3. Organizational goals

Goals	Policy
- Customer Satisfaction Index exceeding 85% - 20% of tenders awarded - Grow 10% against the previous year	**CUSTOMER SATISFACTION**
- Minimum 20% result on sunk costs - Average delivery time of 90 days - VAB per worker 75 K €	**RESULT ORIENTATION**
- A certification for every three years per employee - 1000 new subscribers per year for the Newsletters universe - Employee Satisfaction Index exceeding 80%	**DEVELOPMENT OF COMPETENCIES AND CONTENT**
- Zero Customer Complaints - Effectiveness in 80% of the improvement initiatives - CMMi level 3 in all processes until end of 2014	**QUALITY AND CONTINUOUS IMPROVEMENT**
- 20% of sales in new products/services - 20% of sales in new customers - 3 intellectual property records per year	**BUSINESS INNOVATION**
- Monthly Compliance Report - Monthly Management Report - Fortnightly Treasury Report - Implement an Individual Score Card management system, per team and per project	**PERFORMANCE AND RISK ASSESSMENT**

Therefore, in addition to the financial results' analysis (result orientation), the company intends to control a set of factors that have a cause and effect relationship with business success:

- If customers are satisfied, they will tend to be more faithful to the company and improve the propensity to increase turnover. Thus, the "Customer Satisfaction" dimension aims to highlight the company's results with its commercial partners;
- If the internal processes work better, the quality of the products will be better, the response deadlines will be shorter, and the customers will be more satisfied. As such, the dimension "Quality and continuous improvement" aims to show the performance in the working processes against the needs of the market;
- If employees are motivated and dominate the necessary competencies, internal processes work better. Thus, training and motivation are the basis of good internal performance, and the dimension "Development of competences and content" aims to demonstrate the alignment level of human resources in relation to the working processes' development;
- At the same time, the company should have the ability to renew the competences of its human resources cyclically, in order to avoid imitation by competitors. Therefore, the "Business Innovation" dimension aims to highlight the dynamics of creating new competences;
- Finally, the "Performance and risk assessment" dimension aims to monitor the set of critical key variables regarding business success, which have a strong relationship with the working processes' performance and resources optimization, in order to give a more transparent image about the overall organizational performance, and per unit of the *"Technological"*.

THE COMPANY INTERNATIONALIZATION

The Process of Internationalization

The internationalization effort of *"Technological"* took its first steps during the first half of the 90s.

Through contacts with the institutional decision-makers of Angola government, many business development opportunities were identified in the country, related to the incorporation of information and communication technologies (ICT).

This first stage aimed to highlight the importance of ICT in population registering and locating, as well as in infrastructures' creation, which would allow the property registration implementation (Integrated Management, Development and Territorial Planning).

At the same time, with this decision makers' awareness, *"Technological"* sought trading partners that could represent the company more assiduously and continuously along the Angolan market.

Over the years, and especially after the civil war, due to the increased penetration in the Angola market, the company faced the need of a stronger presence in the territory, through technical and human resources. This would allow a real bond between the skills developed in Portugal, business quality offered to costumers in Angola, including initial negotiation process, sales, implementation and post-sales support.

It is in this context that, in 2001, *"Technological" created* the Angolan company *"Technological Angola"*.

The business value chain regarding the internationalization of the business to Angola was split, in responsibility terms, between the two companies:

1. *"Technological"* - was responsible for the strategic activity planning activity, as well as for the technologies and skills' acquisition, necessary for the development of both products and contracted projects with customers in Angola; and
2. *"Technological Angola"* - was responsible, in the Angolan market, for the dissemination of the business group's brands and products, and at the same time, for obtaining new customers. Technical assistance and maintenance of implemented information systems was mostly carried out using national employees trained by *"Technological"*, due to the high level of projects' complexity and taking into account the lower competencies of human resources in Angola.

Figure 11. Chain value of business in Angola

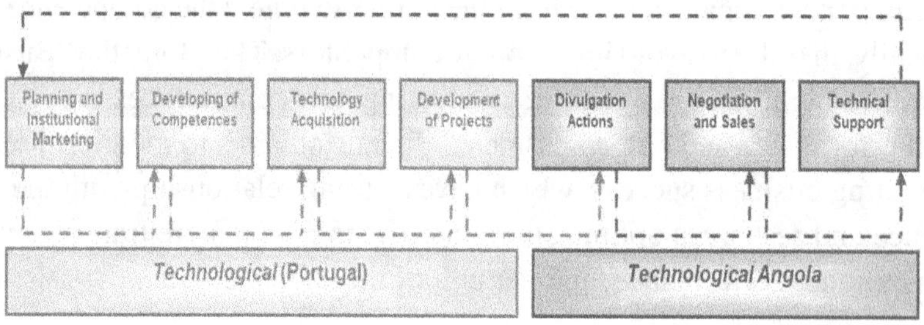

Thus, the activity of planning, research and development and manufacturing was in Portugal. As for *"Technological Angola"*, it focused on commercial activity, doing all the customers contacts. However, as the business in Angola increased, there was a gradual knowledge transfer and a successive focus on the recruitment and ongoing training of local human resources.

This chronological sequence prepared, in 2004, the effective internationalization investment. At that time became widespread in Portugal, the understanding that the company's expansion, based on domestic demand would be economically unsustainable, especially because of private consumption, given the high public external debt and the public finances' condition. Only a strengthening of exports, supported by an external competitiveness recovery and tradable sectors' investment with high benefit, would allow the gradual economic recovery and the regaining of the real convergence process in relation to EU average.

Since Portugal competitiveness was low, when compared with most developed European economies, it was only natural that national companies tried to develop their capacity for competing in global markets, and in particular in the so-called emerging economies, where eventually our players could build sustainable competitive advantages.

In this sense, the internationalization plan of *"Technological"* has obviously gone through analyzing business opportunities in developing economies, particularly in Portuguese-speaking countries, with special emphasis to Angolan economy whose growth indicators had successively exceeded expectations.

Therefore, on that year (2004), *"Technological"* made the natural strategic choice through a strong effort on internationalization in the Angolan market and subsequently in Mozambique, which is a geographically near country with cultural affinity and possessing a large potential market. Thus, in addition to the branch in Angola, *"Technological"* also created a new company in Mozambique that we designate as *"Technological Mozambique"*.

In addition, in 2010, the company makes the decision to internationalize the activity, equally, to Brazil, one of the largest countries in territorial and population dimensions. This decision resulted from several important factors. Portuguese language favours cultural proximity and business practices; there were solutions for products and services already developed for emerging countries in the world economy; there were an accumulated know-how in Africa and in countries with business and governmental practices similar to Brazilian context, which could facilitate the market entry.

Thus, *"Technological Brazil"* appears in 2011. As discussed, the process of internationalization for *"Technological"* across the different markets has generally passed through several stages, that usually started with specific projects or sporadic exportations, and which then gave rise to the establishment of partnerships with local economic agents, who had better access to local key decision-makers and potential customers.

Finally, the consolidation of these partnerships has led to the creation of new subsidiaries in the target markets and new local investments, as a way to more easily disseminate the organizational culture and strategy of those new business structures and to ensure the services' high quality levels, as well.

This option was fundamental in the ability to gain market share and a strong competitive position, because the role of these new companies ensured close monitoring of projects development and contributed to a trustful relationship with the various local business partners.

So far, this option exceeded the most optimistic expectations. The main reference markets are currently in Portugal, Angola and Brazil, but the company also has a branch in Mozambique and develops projects in Sao Tome and Principe, Guinea-Bissau, Gabon and the Democratic Republic of Congo.

The Defined Strategy for The Developing Countries

One of the important characteristics of developing countries is the concentration of millions of people in urban areas, looking for opportunities to improve the life quality through, among other things, obtaining employment and easier access to public services. People moving massively to urban centers originate cities of gigantic proportions, often referred to as mega cities with populations exceeding 10 million.

However, most of these cities do not have facilities suitable for such large amounts of people, and, as consequence, we saw the growth of urban slums in recent decades. It is estimated that, currently, in developing countries, already 43% of urban inhabitants live in such neighborhoods, that experience serious problems in terms of urban organization, basic sanitation, hygiene conditions, transport services, health care, education access, among other difficulties, clearly reducing these populations' life quality and increasing, for example, the illiteracy level and infant mortality. In this scenario, most population has not proper documents, and its characteristics and heritage are unknown. In most cases, they simply do not officially exist.

This reality has a high impact on these countries' economy, since the fact that citizens are not registered, unable them to legalize their property. Even if they manage to buy a house or a car, they have no opportunity to submit them as guarantees for financial institutions, in order to obtain loans. In sequence, without access to financing, they cannot promote entrepreneurship and turn into business their creativity, which is a characteristic developed by most of these people in response to their surviving difficulties. As such, the private sector is insipient and the economy works around services and public companies. Furthermore, without property registration and without private companies, the level of revenue arising from taxes is very low.

Considering that *"Technological"*, at the beginning of its internationalization process, took over as priority markets developing countries, including Angola, Brazil and Mozambique, it produced a strategy for adjusting its offer and skills to the populations' specific needs.

In this sense, the purpose of the developed solutions, at strategic level and of new products, services and businesses' design, was to meet the population pyramid base's needs, in order to generate an economic and human sustainable development.

The approach of *"Technological"* is not focused on charity-based solutions, but in the use of latent entrepreneurial spirit of these populations, combined with public financial support and the vigor of private investment.

Figure 12. "Technological" competitive positioning in developing countries

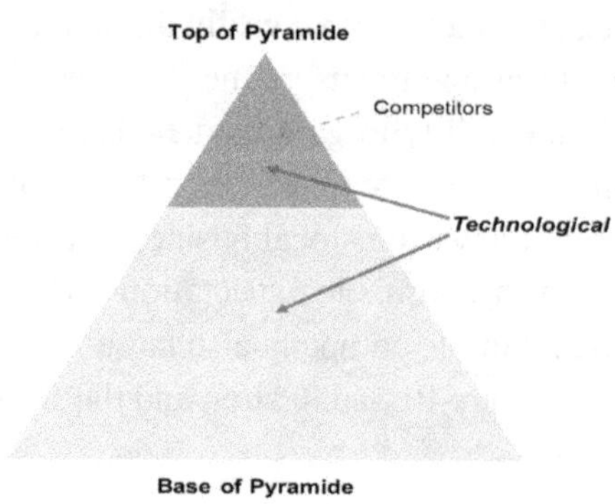

Then, the main products and services offered by *"Technological"* to deal with these markets related to:

- People registration;
- Property registration;
- Tracking systems;
- Territorial planning and management systems;
- Water management systems;
- E-learning systems;
- Etc.

In this sense, the developed products included, among others:

Biometric systems:
  - People Identification;
  - Transactions' certification.

Geographic information systems:
  - Place of Residence;
  - Assets localization;
  - Property Register.

Systems that make use of specific and mobile peripherals:
  - Scanner for documents identification;
  - Bar code identification devices;

Models of imprinted numerical codes:
  - 2D bar codes.

After creating *"Technological Angola"*, more specifically since 2005, when the first higher value investments were performed by Angola and Mozambique partners (*"Technological Angola"* and *"Technological Mozambique"*), there was a need to develop the necessary measures to increase group's activity for these two markets, clearly trying to benefit from the following factors:

1. Core competencies' exploration in new markets, due to being one of the few information technology companies working in these territories, which allowed taking advantages of a growing market without much direct competition at that time;
2. Increased scale economies with upstream commercial partnerships with resident companies (*"Technological Angola"* and *"Technological Mozambique"*), which turned easier the entrance in the market and the use of infrastructure and resources already installed.

From a tactical point of view, this decision required another, which consisted in adapting the communication means to the type of lobbyist that would be addressed in these countries, beginning to develop of a new form of market presentation. First, it was essential to clarify the company's offer, in order to make the offered products' identification easier and improve the ability to meet the needs of new types of potential customers.

It was in this context that the Strategic Orientation Axes were created, aiming to provide the organization with a new structure, more appropriate to the new markets increasing challenges' scale, but maintaining the company's flexibility of adapting to the specific customer needs.

Considering new African markets' characteristics and needs, the company's image, the company's offer and the company's corporate competences began to be organized around the following Strategic Orientation Axes:

1. Integrated Territorial Management, which includes solutions associated with cartography and topography, architecture and urban planning, development and management of the territory and with environment and natural resources;
2. Security and Defense, which includes citizens' identification and authentication, registration, events' authentication and monitoring, strategic infrastructures' security, intelligent border surveillance and security perimeters, order and safety restoration in case of crisis or disaster, and integration, connectivity and interoperability of security and defense' systems;
3. Administrative Modernization, which aims to provide public authorities quality processes and policies, and integrated management systems for procedures that better ensures an activities' control and a continuous organization improvement, as well as the establishment of improved quality services to citizens (e.g., through the implementation of e-government practices);
4. Business Solutions through structuring solutions in many areas, to ensure the business competitiveness in an increasingly globalized and competitive market (attendance service management, enterprise portals, integrated management systems, mobility solutions, decision support solutions, document management, e-commerce);
5. Education, through enhancing lifelong learning, qualification based on professional experience, easier access to quality education, regardless residence (e.g., e-learning solutions can be important for spreading education in these countries, either by enabling people to access educational resources without having to travel long distances to main urban centers, or by allowing access to excellence trainers from other countries).

As regards the internationalization process, in 2011, for Brazil, also based its development offering solutions previously developed for Africa, namely the Geographic Information Systems.

In a country whose number of vehicles increased by 13 million between 2009 and 2017, currently meeting in the 43 million, controlling the fleet, more than a necessity, is a real challenge. It is noteworthy that about 20% of the car park consists of commercial vehicles.

The state of Santa Catarina (SC) has the third largest number of cargo road carriers in Brazil, with 12%, being only surpassed by the state of Paraná (PR), also in the southern region of the country, with 13%, and São Paulo (SP), with 49%.

To join these statistics there are car thefts, which in 2016 amounted to 557,000, according to the Brazilian Public Security forum. Such values represent a high social problem, but also a serious economic problem, considering the costs incurred by the insurers associated with vehicles and the enhancement of the value of the insurance policies payable by citizens.

Thus, the company decided to start its internationalization process to Brazil through the development of a technological solution for vehicle tracking, initiating operations in the south of the country, with the aim of expanding the activity to the remaining states in the following years, and eventually for the various South American countries.

In this sense, the mission of *"Technological"* in Brazil has been to design and offer intelligent geo-localization systems and services that retake innovation, competitiveness and the ability to manage and control the customers' resources/assets.

The company established a central office (headquarters) and a network of sales management points and after-sale services to the customer.

All employees with corporate responsibilities has been in the central offices, being responsible for the operation of all necessary services to support the points of management sales and after-sales services (real or virtual), namely the technological infrastructure that has been managing the entire geographic location system associated with each client.

The expansion of management points' network has been based on a territorial logic occupation or occupation of market segments, which presupposes an activity zone and a set of markets/customers for each management point (physical or virtual).

Management points can have varying size and capacity, depending on the market/community it serves. They may be structures operating on an exclusive basis with the brand or network, or in partnership regime and complementarity with the brand.

Thus, management points can take the following forms:

- Franchising service points and management: in these cases, the expansion happens by developing a business concept for which it will be necessary to attract entrepreneurs. These management/ expansion points will be geographic, but can be segments or communities, such as firefighters, or members of an association;
- Network of franchises agents/representatives that will be included in the equally franchises management points: The model of management points is complemented by the raising of a partners' network, idealized as business owners or individual entrepreneurs, with the ability to represent/ sell in communities or geographic areas. These entrepreneurs will have access to a set of information and work tools that are idealized in a tablet, thus enabling each agent/franchisor to have access to the front office, but also to the back-office and after-sales services. In this way, agents have access to demonstration means of issuing sales contracts, marking services; being also possible to complement the after-sales services through assets' monitoring and geo-localization, as well as alerts and services' parameterization and availability, including support for vehicle recovery. These agents provide commercial (sales and contract raising) services that are debited to the management point to which they report to;
- Network of service providers partners (workshops, installers, resellers, etc.): This service network comprises the recruitment and selection of a partners' network of after - sales service providers for installing and uninstalling crawlers, sensors, or alarms parameterization. This network can also be complemented with partners responsible for providing specialized services such as security firms, service brokers, etc.

In the figure 13, a summary of the expansion plan to be implemented.

It has been intended, therefore, to build a high flexibility commercial network of communities' proximity in the business development geographic areas.

Figure 13. Process of expansion of activity in the Brazilian Market

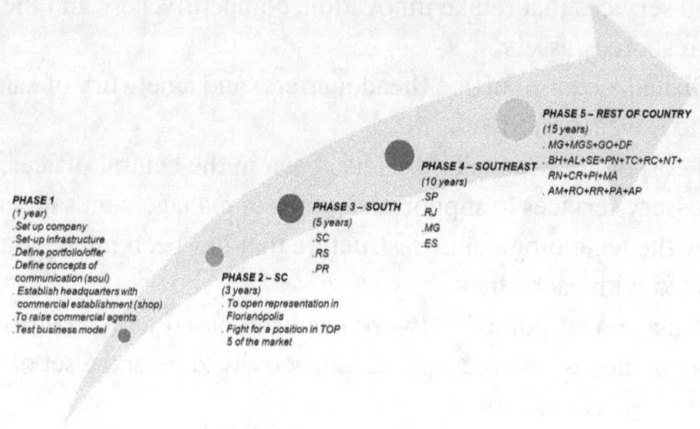

THE COMPANY AND THE INTERNATIONALIZATION RISK

Characterization of International and Foreign Currency Activities

International operations include imports, exports and financing.

For imports carried out in Portugal, there is a volume of purchases of goods and external services in foreign currency, which represents 10% of the total volume of purchases. The currencies concerned are USD and GBP, the average payment deadlines being 60 days. The remaining volume of purchases is in EUR.

The company's sales are expressed in EUR and USD and have a very long average-receiving deadline due to late payment by the Angolan market, representing about 70% of turnover. Salaries are fully expressed in EUR.

As for financial transactions, the company holds long and short-term loans in EUR. The company also contracts short-term loans in USD, through a current account, with a quarterly interest payment at an indexed rate.

Regarding financial applications, they are usually in EUR, and there are also operations carried out in USD (the decision on the currency to be used in financial applications is associated with the evolution of the interest rates of EUR and USD).

In relation to commercial operations in the Angolan subsidiary, there are external service contracts in both USD and the national currency AOA (Kwanza).

Purchases of raw materials and goods in Angolan territory are normally carried out in AOA, whereas imports CAN be IN EUR or ZAR (South African Rand). The average payment deadlines are 60 days, against a period exceeding one year in receipts due to delays of the Angolan Government.

Regarding the sales of the company, it invoices and receives in AOA, and sometimes the receipts happen in USD (about 5%). In the case of large projects carried out for the state of Angola, the value of the proposals is Express in USD but contracted and received in AOA. There is a clause limiting losses and gains resulting from variations in the USD/AOA exchange rate exceeding 3%. However, as they are very high values, losses in absolute values may be relevant.

Salaries are fixed in USD and paid in AOA. Maximum and minimum limits for the USD/AOA exchange rate to be applied at the end of each month are also agreed, thus limiting the losses of the company or the employee in the event of higher fluctuations in the exchange rate. In the case of Portuguese workers with a contract with the Angolan subsidiary, they receive the salary in EUR.

As for financial transactions, there are external loans contracted in USD in the amount 2.5 million USD, which expire within a period of less than 5 years, the variable rate, with quarterly periodicity, representing about 80% of the total amount of financing. As for applications, it only exists in AOA.

For Mozambique, operations are carried out essentially in local currency and the activity is still not materially relevant, and therefore, the international risk is not significant.

Finally, regarding the company in the Brazilian market, its commercial and financial activity is in the local currency, not being directly subject to the foreign exchange risk. However, the evolution of the Brazilian economy negatively affected the increase in turnover and payment deadlines practiced in the country, generating treasury difficulties to the company.

When analyzing the commercial and financial operations of the companies in the different markets where it operates, we can check some complexity in its management, since there are transactions in several currencies, it can be concluded that the business group is exposed to currency risk (Eitman et al, 2005).

Credit Risk Exposure

One of the main constraints that internationalization provoked in the *"Technological"* activity relates to credit risk, due to the main markets to which the company became internationalized (Angola and Brazil), that have been conditioned, either by the global economic and financial crisis, as by the oil price breaks in international markets (Porfírio, 2001).

In this way, economic activity in both markets has slowed and financial entities have begun to have less available currency, conditioning the flows of payments between economic agents and countries' foreign exchange outputs. Thus, payment deadlines widened for several months, damaging the company's treasury in Portugal and its financial health.

Foreign Exchange Risk Exposure

According to the types of exchange risk covered, the company may be subject to three risks: risk of conversion, risk of transaction and economic risk. The risk of conversion is present in the exchange transactions recorded in the accounting, derived from the commercial operations carried out, as well as in the consolidation of the accounts of the Angolan and Brazilian subsidiaries in the Portuguese parent company. Despite the excellent results obtained, if the price of the currency of these countries has suffered a strong devaluation from the European currency used in Portugal, the consolidated value of the group could be severely affected (Alves et al, 2007).

The transaction risk is present in these companies in cash flows, whether positive or negative. Whenever there is a time lag between a purchase and its payment, or a sale and its receipt, in foreign currency, the company is subject to this type of risk, it is a currency mismatch. Regarding receipts in foreign currency, if USD devalues, the parent company will effectively receive fewer euros. In USD or GBP purchases, there is also an associated risk, since on the invoice expiration date there may be a valuation of the currencies, increasing the amount paid for the goods (Alves et al, 2007).

This risk is much more present in the Angolan subsidiary, since there two currencies, which currently are simultaneously, used (AOA and USD). About wages, every month there are oscillations between the USD/AOA exchange that change the payable amount, since the payment is made in a different currency than the previously assumed or contracted. As for goods or services' payment obligations contracted in USD, due to the currency lack of liquidity, are usually made in AOA, incurring once again the company in an exchange risk. Most imports are made in EUR, implying a huge risk due to the substantial amounts. In the case of large projects with the Angolan state, the calculations for the proposals are made in USD. However, the financial flows are in AOA, being again the company subject to the foreign exchange risk. In view of the high values of the projects, such as the Angolan electoral Register or the African Nations Championships, 50 and 23 million USD, respectively, a slight oscillation in the exchange between the two currencies can lead to high losses, compromising the company.

Regarding Mozambique, as previously mentioned, operations are essentially carried out in local currency, with no relevant exchange risk.

In Brazil, and as previously mentioned, operations are carried out in the local currency and thus the company is not directly subject to the foreign exchange risk. However, as the financial statements of the Brazilian subsidiary are presented in BRL, if this currency devaluate on the accounts' consolidation date, the Portuguese business Group's assets value may be adversely affected. In addition, the ability to monetize the investment also decreases, since the results distributed in BRL will also generate lower flows in Euros, diluting the effective profitability of the investment carried out by *"Technological "*.

Consequently, in the medium and long term, these events, alongside with receiving delays, can lead to a reduction in the company's competitive capacity, exposing it to the economic risk (Alves et al, 2007). Economic risk has an impact, essentially, by the influence of variations in currency quotes on medium and long-term cash flows, reducing the competitive capacity of the business group. Currencies mismatch can lead to a decrease in the profit margins of the company, through the practiced prices' reduction or the enhancement of the production factors. In this particular case, the business group is also penalized through its main client receiving delays, leading it to search for paid financing sources, pressuring treasury and results because of the higher financial costs, which may, in the medium term, affect the group's financial capacity.

Currently, in the activity in Portugal, the exchange rate differences' impact in the results have been negative, due to the devaluations of USD against EUR, which has jeopardized sales' commercial margins in that currency. In recent years have represented between 5% and 10% of the company's net results.

In the Angolan company, the recorded exchange rate differences have been positive, since the contracts with the Angolan Government are denominated in USD, which has valued in relation to AOA. This fact has allowed effective receipts in AOA to be higher, increasing business' commercial margin. Its weight in net results has fluctuated between 30% and 40%.

Techniques Used to Cover the Risk

Generally, the Portuguese company maintains a relationship of trust with its partners, using the current account method, rarely requiring payment in advance. Thus, the commonly used payment techniques are bank transfers on settled dates, both with customers and suppliers. Simple shipping, Documentary Remittance and Documentary credit, have also been used in imports, when exceptionally requested by foreign suppliers, with whom there is still no trust relationship.

In Angola current account is also commonly used, and, sometimes, the Documentary credit. The latter is sometimes imposed on the Angolan company, as a solution to make payments to Portuguese *"Technological"*, since it is difficult to transfer funds out of Angola.

About techniques for hedging exchange risk, in particular, the internal techniques, the company practices advance payment on imports, when they have treasury availability, in view of any expectations of foreign currencies' valuation. It also practices the compensation technique, if there are receivables and amounts to be paid in the same currency. As for external techniques, it was never used, due to lack of knowledge of the financial managers regarding their functioning.

As for Brazil and Mozambique, since the operations are carried out essentially in local currency, the instruments of exchange risk hedging are not applicable. In addition, the company does not use any credit risk coverage techniques.

MANAGEMENT CONTROL SYSTEM IMPLEMENTED

As previously mentioned, the management control systems consist of three types of instruments, namely (Anthony & Govindarajan, 2007; Jordan *et al,* 2011):

- Pilotage (Plans, budgets, budgetary control and strategic control);
- Behavioural Orientation (Responsibility Centers, Centers and Managers' evaluation criteria and Internal Transfer prices);
- Dialogue (rules and procedures of the management control system, meetings' periodicity and format and information systems used).

In this sense, a characterization of the "*Technological*" management control system will be carried out, based on these three types of instruments.

The Pilotage Instruments

The budgetary planning and control process have been adapting, over time, to changes in the company's organizational structure.

Each year, during the month of November, a meeting called kick-off is held, where the administration presents the company's strategic plan and the operational managers exhibit their business plan and annual budget for the activity of the unit under their responsibility. The internal transfer prices to be used in services between units are also discussed, as well as the system for evaluating the performance of the various managers.

Business plans include information on the surroundings' impact, competitors' characteristics, offer to develop and trade policies to implement, target markets and key business partners.

About the budget, it presents several singularities, namely:

- The company's budget results from the different financial plans carried out by each unit, and the various assumptions used (e.g. average time of receipt and payment and stock policy) are also explained;

- The units' budgets include the internal income from other units, and the external ones obtained from customers;
- Operating expenses are classified into five categories:
    - Variables: related to turnover's level and representing the inherent expenses to the performed services (for example, hardware and software acquired to develop a certain solution);
    - Fixed: associated with resources used in the activity, which are fundamental for services' performance (for example, human resources and materials). As such, this type of expenditure is budgeted considering the employees and the assets belonging to each unit;
    - Institutional marketing: incorporate the expenses incurred by the company at the level of its image and not of a specific unit;
    - Internal transfers: resulting from the use of services performed by other units;
    - Of structure: They relate to the general expenses of the activity, usually associated with the facilities (e.g. energy, water, hygiene and safety), which are attributed considering distribution criteria such as the number of people and the physical space occupied by each unit;
- The monthly periodicity serves as a reference for the preparation of the budget, and the annual financial statements are also considered;
- The budget is a compromise between the managers and the company, and the achievement of the objectives assumed as reference for the definition of the prizes to be attributed to managers for performance on the economic year.

As regards budgetary control, the implemented system of Accounting and financial information ensures the monthly financial monitoring of the evolution of each unit's activity. By the end of the first week of the following month, financial statements of the different units are made available, on the format laid out in Tables 4 and 5.

At the economic level, through the generated monthly income statement, the results of each unit are monitored, observing the margin obtained by each manager (the unit's contribution margin), in addition to the net result after the allocation of the costs of institutional marketing and facilities. In addition, the classification of variable and fixed costs allows managers to analyze the business risk of their units, by monitoring the indicators critical point and safety margin.

Table 4. Unit income statement format

Headings	January			...	December			Forecast
	Real	Budget	Deviation		Real	Budget	Deviation	
Turnover								
Variable costs								
Gross margin								
Unit fixed costs								
Costs of internal services								
Contribution margin Unit								
Global marketing costs								
Structure costs								
Unit result								

Table 5. Balance per unit

Headings	January			...	December			Forecast
	Real	Budget	Deviation		Real	Budget	Deviation	
Fixed Assets								
Inventories								
Third-party debts								
NET financial resources								
Accruals and Active Deferrals								
Total Asset								
Monthly NET Results								
Monthly results transited								
Total Equity								
Debt to third-party ML term								
Short-term third-party debts								
Accruals and deferred liabilities								
Total Liabilities								
Total Equity and liabilities								

As to the financial situation, through the monthly the balance sheet, each unit's level of investment and sources of financing is clearly observed, in particular, self-financing generated and debts to suppliers because of the negotiation of payment deadlines. It should be noted that, if the period cash flows are negative, the balances of the net financial means may be even negative, which means the unit is generating financial needs to the company.

Thus, the manager is able to follow up business financial evolution against the forecasts initially made.

In conclusion, segmented information contributes to monitoring each unit's economic and financial evolution. However, it does not allow attending several fundamental factors of managers' activity, nor each unit's contribution to larger projects, where several teams collaborate, as well as to the achievement of organizational goals.

Thus, although the company's strategic plan, as well as each unit's business plans present several non-financial goals, fundamental to the sustainable success of the organization, there is no systematic control of its achievement.

Behavioural Orientation Instruments

The company currently has dozens of strategic business units and eight support units, being its most important functions as the follows:

- Strategic business Units (SBU): organized according to a set of technological competencies, representing the company core business, developing integrated solutions of hardware and software tailored to customers. They contemplate the functions associated with the commercial, production and research and development areas associated with the offer within the market;

- Business Support Unit (SBU) – Administrative and accounting: includes the functions associated with administrative, accounting, legal and financial services, namely treasury management and the financing sources' negotiation with financial institutions and other financiers;
- Business Support Unit – Marketing and communication: contemplates the functions related to the operationalization of the institutional marketing policy and the each unit's advertising actions;
- Business Support Unit – Recruitment and selection: ensures recruitment and selection of human resources, as well as training and career development plans within the company;
- Business Support Unit – Quality: ensures all activities related to the quality management system;
- Business Support Unit – Mobile computing: Creates Android applications for the various strategic business units;
- Business Support unit – Editing and Content management: its mission is to give body to the identity of products placed on the market, adapting them to the various countries where they will be sold;
- Business Support Unit – technological infrastructure: it is responsible for the management of the company's work platforms, performing the maintenance of internal and external systems, when duly requested by the business units;
- Business Support Unit – Financial efficiency: it has no physical reality and represents the internal bank that responds to the financial needs of the different units that constitute the company. Thus, "provides non-current assets and capital" to suppress any cash problems, in exchange for a remuneration equivalent to the interest figure.

In addition to the units already mentioned, the organizational structure still contemplates the Administration, who coordinates the activity of the different units, interconnects the local objectives with those of the organization and ensures the financial sustainability of the company over time.

Considering the previous description and the managers' decision-making power, the following typologies of responsibility centers can be identified in the organizational structure of "*Technological*" (Teixeira & Teixeira, 2008) (see Table 6).

Regarding the classification of the different units in responsibility centers, it is important to highlight some specificities:

- Business units can be considered investment centers, because managers control the income and expenses of their activity, and have authority over assets and liabilities, namely, on the payment/receiving policies and stock rotation policies;
- Support units, although it can be considered as results centers, because they have authority over the inputs and outputs of their activity that reflect income and expenses, indeed are treated as cost centers, with the only concern to manage activity's expenditures;
- The financial efficiency unit was defined as a result center, although it could also be identified as an investment center, since it contemplates the company's non-current assets. The acquisition costs of non-current assets are reflected in the activity as opportunity costs, if it comes from the owners' capital, or interest, if the financing was made through foreign capital.

Table 6. Types of responsibility centers in the "Technological"

Units	Control	Explanation	Responsibility Center
SU	– Income – Costs – Working capital needs	– Income comes from internal and external services' provision – Costs come from regular activity and internal services' provision – Working capital needs are associated to payment and receiving' deadline negotiations, and to defined stock rotation policy	**Investment Center**
BU	– Income – Costs	– Income comes from internal and external services' provision – Costs come from regular activity and internal services' provision	**Results Centers**
Financial efficiency	– Non-current assets – Interest-bearing liabilities – Income – Costs	– It has non-current assets, which rents to the units – Income comes from assets rental and interest from units' transferred capital – Costs come from assets' acquisition and interest paid to negotiated financial sources	**Results Centers**

As mentioned above, the financial efficiency unit is regarded as a result center. However, it contemplates asset management and, in this sense, it could also be regarded as an investment center. However, the costs of the controlled assets are accepted by itself, valued as costs arising from its activity, and may take the form of opportunity or interest costs, in accordance with the example in Table 7 (Teixeira, 2007).

Thus, in order to determine the contribution of a responsibility center that has its own financing sources, it is indifferent to classify it as an investment center or a result one.

Regarding the units' performance evaluation, only the strategic business units' activity is periodically monitored, based on the evolution of the monthly financial statements.

Table 7. Example of the value creation of financial efficiency unit

Financing Efficiency's balance (millions of euros)			
Investments		**Financing Sources**	
- Fixed Assets	50	Annual Result	53,6
-Applications	33,6	Capital	20
-Availabilities	10	Bank loan	20
Total Investment	**93,6**	Total Financing	**93,6**
Calculation of the Financial Efficiency Center margin (million euros)			
Option: Treat as Results Center		**Option: Treat as investment center**	
-Operating Results	62,56	Operating income	62,56
- Financial loan C-8%	1,6	Active	93,6
-Capital opportunity cost-10%	7,36	Cost of assets – 9,572% (WACC) *	8,96
Contribution margin	**53,6**	Residual contribution margin	**53,6**

* Weighted average of financial cost and opportunity cost considered

Thus, the business units' financial performance evaluation is made based on the following formula:

Unit result
- Income from non-current assets used in the activity
- Cost of capital calculated on the balances of negative financial means
= Value created by the unit

Thus, it intends to verify whether the business units' activity is able to cover the costs arising from its operation, institutional marketing and structure (unit result determined in the income statement), but also if it has the capacity to guarantee assets' cost return and capital use, to suppress generated period treasury needs.

The evaluation of the managers of the business units is based on the financial results of their units and, if they achieve the goals, are entitled to receive a percentage of the created value, after being covered the amounts relating to assets' income and cost of capital used, which are transferred to the unit financial efficiency. Thus, there is no assessment of its contribution to achieving global purposes and on its performance in non-financial factors, critical to the sustained success of the company (Teixeira & Carreira, 2008)..

The internal activity of "*Technological*" encompasses several types of services, which we now describe.

Strategic and Financial Coordination Services:

- Management Coordination Services, provided to business units and support units;
- Financial services of capital lending and rental of non-current assets provided by financial efficiency unit to the various units.

Services Between Business and Support Units:

- Services performed by business units to support units, for the development of applications to be used in normal activity;
- Services provided by support units in support of business unit activity.

Services Among Business Units and Among Support Units:

- Services among business units are usually related to collaboration in conducting projects with external customers, or support in research and development or after-sales assistance;
- The services among support units are associated with the support provided in the normal course of activity (e.g. accounting services, quality management, recruitment of persons, etc.).

Here comes, in a scheme, the internal relations logic in the "Technological", SA (refer to Figure 14. At the level of the valuation of internal services, its recovery is carried out as follows:

- The services performed by the strategic business units are valued at market prices;
- Although there are some negotiated prices, as is the case of the Marketing Support Unit' services, most internal services are valued through cost-sharing rates, depending on criteria such as turnover or units' customer balances;
- The coordination services performed by the Administration are valued at negotiated prices at the beginning of each year, directly associated with the intervention of the administrators in obtaining business for the units;

Figure 14. Internal Services provided

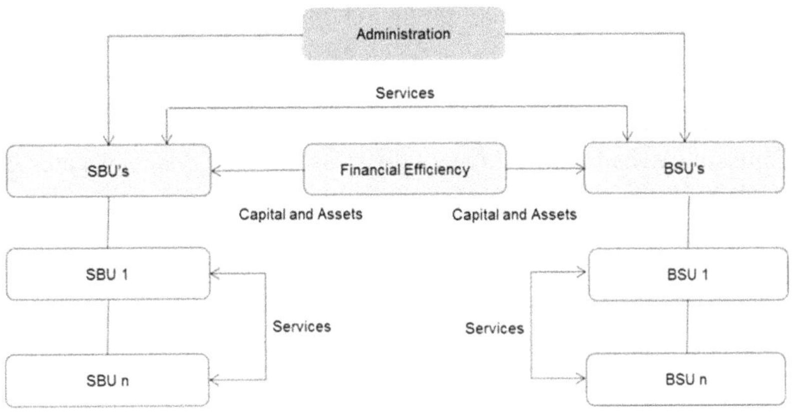

- Financial services provided by the financial efficiency unit, referring to non-current rental assets and capital transfer to suppress treasury deficits, are valued at a cost of capital defined by the administration, which is usually considerably higher than the financing cost of financial institutions and the average profitability of companies in the sector.

By defining the current internal transfer prices, the management intends to ensure that the strategic business units are able to generate a profitability greater than the cost of the capital of the successive investments related to the reduced life cycle of the information and communication technologies sector' products.

In addition, it intends to decentralize the authority, constantly focus the managers on market opportunities and value Creation, compromising them with the company's global objectives.

Dialogue Instruments

Considering the observation and interviews conducted during the visits to the company, there is a clear concern in the dissemination of the strategy by the various working areas and different hierarchical levels. In addition, it is also noticeable that the management control system was designed to ensure an adequate alignment of strategic business units' managers with the company's overall objectives (at the very least the financial goals, related to profitability and growth).

Thus, as mentioned, the planning phase of each economic year starts at the annual meeting that normally takes place during the month of November, called the kick-off. In this meeting, which lasts three days, in everyone's presence, the Administration presents the vision and the strategic plan of the company, and the managers expose the various business plans and budgets for each unit. The way to the company to go in following years is defined, such as the role to be played by each unit for the sustainable success of the Organization.

This Annual Meeting also serves to convey the values and culture of the Organization by the generations of younger employees. In this sense, to stand out the organization' "champions" of the organization and highlight the example of successful employees, everybody wears a company shirt, colored according to each one's antiquity in *"Technological"*, SA. The most recent workers look at the "older" as examples to follow and begin to aspire to the right to wear the shirts with those "antiquity" colors.

As regards budgetary control, it is carried out through monthly meetings held, with rules and procedures known to all, both for the elaboration of progress reports, as for the meetings' format.

The rules currently established are:

Progress report' preparation:

- The Administrative and accounting unit draws up monthly financial statements for the different strategic business units;
- In the preceding week of holding the control meetings, the financial statements are presented to each business unit manager, who can identify and report any errors or incongruences to the Administrative and accounting unit controller, at a meeting between the two, which normally may have a maximum duration of one hour.

Meetings:

- The meetings are held monthly and in a single day;
- The meeting includes the administration, the managers of the various strategic units and the responsible for the administrative and accounting area;
- The overall result of the company and all units is evaluated, bearing in mind the monthly forecasts and the accumulated results' evolution;
- Managers adjust their business plans and budgets;
- The MBU forum (managers of business units) is carried out, with discussion and sharing of information among the various managers;
- The administration summarizes the achieved results and the main business trends and concludes the meeting.

In view of the dynamics of the sector and the reduced lifecycle of products associated with information technologies, the administration has sought to increase the sharing of ideas and knowledge among different units, to provide greater responsiveness to the organizational structure, in its constant adequacy to the challenges posed by the competitive environment. In this sense, three instruments of archive and dissemination of organizational knowledge have been used:

- Company Newsletter, where monthly different managers and collaborators publish articles about experiences in the organization;
- Creation of a projects' repository, with free access to all units, to enable finding solutions based on accumulated knowledge;
- Organized training, conducted by strategic business units, on projects developed with enormous success.

Thereby, the implemented dialogue instruments aim to ensure a more transparent and accepted performance assessment by all, and the sharing of knowledge between the various areas of work seeks to create Synergies in responding to the daily challenges of the activity Teixeira et al, 2008).

THE IMPACT OF INTERNATIONALIZATION ON FINANCIAL PERFORMANCE'

The focus on internationalization to the Angolan and Mozambican markets had a very positive immediate response. In the four years preceding internationalization, the company had an average turnover of between 6 and 7 million euros, while in the following three years, after internationalization, the company showed an increase over 110%, corresponding to total turnover rounding the 14.5 million euros, with exports representing a weight of 70%.

On the economic level, the pace of growth had also an impact on the number of necessary human resources, as the company moved from 124 employees, at the beginning of the internationalization process, to the current 250 employees.

As for the obtained results, they also experienced a strong increase. Within three years, the accumulated net profit reached the remarkable value of 5.141.929 euros against the 940.541 euros obtained in the previous four years.

Table 8 shows the evolution of the company's main indicators from 2008 to 2014, highlighting the stabilization of turnover in the 10 million euros in the most recent years. However, one can also observe

Figure 15. Turnover evolution

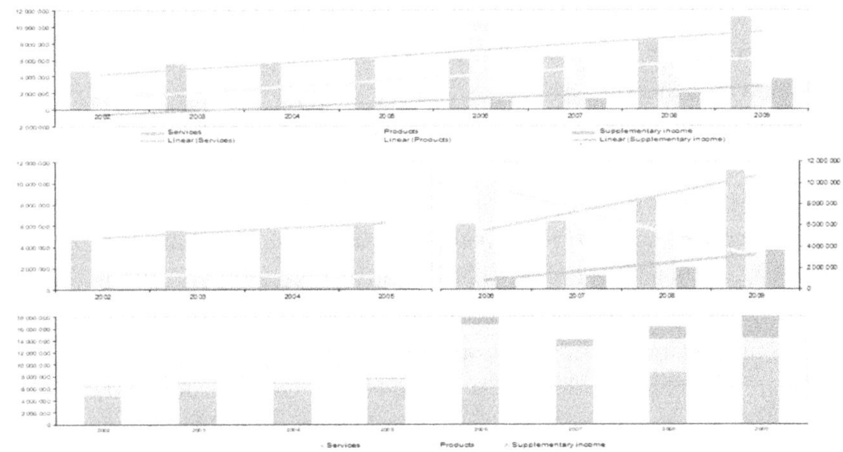

Figure 16. Exports evolution

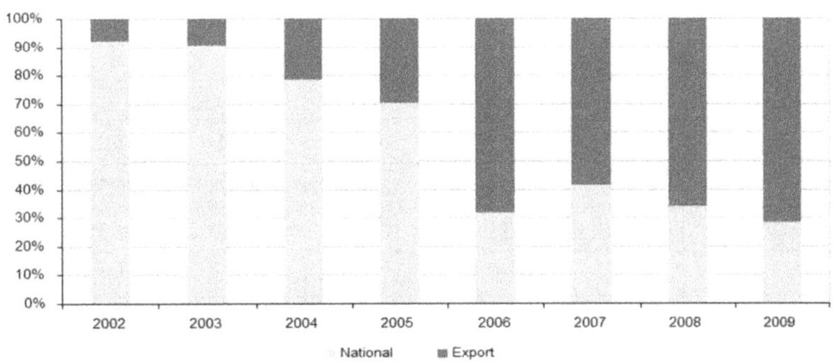

Table 8. Economic Evolution of "Technological" (thousand euros)

Indicators	2008	2009	2010	2011	2012	2013	2014
Turnover	14.230	14.308	10.438	9.132	10.161	12.281	9.359
Operating Profit	1.096	1.262	1.988	2.272	3.261	1.170	-41
Net Profit	1.018	1.250	1.431	1.546	2.593	526	-1.010
Gross Value Added	7.889	9.374	9.213	7.635	9.200	7.832	6.405
Return On Investment	11%	5%	7%	9,72%	12%	3,63%	-0,12%
Return On Equity	22%	14%	13%	13%	17%	3,30%	-7,70%

that the stabilization of the activity favored the creation of results and improved the profitability indices of the company and for the owners until 2012. The results of 2013 and 2014 show the impact of the economic slowdown in Angola and Brazil.

At the financial level, the effect of internationalization is also remarkable, with an increase, during that period, of almost 400% in company's total assets.

To support this increase in its assets, the company needed to finance conveniently. Thus, *"Technological"* increased its equity through new entries from shareholders and by retained earnings, and through using external financing. In that regard, it is noted that investment volume directly related to internationalization was financed through a loan, contracted with several financial institutions. This allowed the company to obtain higher amounts and a debt maturity of 10-year (with a 3-year grace period), reducing the pressure on its treasury.

Thus, there is a significant increase on total liabilities compared to 2008, which is natural, due to the level of growth-associated investments, leading to a decline in the financial expenses coverage ratio (which reveals a lower capacity to cover financing costs, but still high values, when compared to Portuguese industry average). However, the year 2014 shows the company's greater cash-flow difficulties due to the economic slowdown in Angola and Brazil. This has led to an increase in receiving time required and in contracting short-term financial instruments to support the treasury, increasing the activity' financial costs.

In conclusion, although the internationalization represented a significant activity increase in the early years (2009 included), the recent developments in *"Technological"*, were characterized by turnover stabilization of about 10 million euros, which is also a reflection of world economic and financial crisis during those years (2010, 2011, 2012 and 2013).

However, if we analyze the evolution of the *"Technological"* group, the scenario is completely different. For example, the Angolan subsidiary has surpassed in a large-scale the Portuguese parent company.

Table 9. Financial Evolution of "Technological" (thousand euros)

Indicators	2008	2009	2010	2011	2012	2013	2014
Assets	9.868	26.819	28.086	23.376	26.512	32.275	34.826
Equity	4.556	9.136	10.859	12.187	15.354	16.049	13.152
Liabilities	5.313	17.683	17.227	11.190	11.158	16.226	21.676
Financial Autonomy	44%	34%	39%	52%	58%	50%	38%
Financial Expenses Coverage	11,46	11,88	3,94	4,19	7,32	3,22	0,31

In the fifth year after group's internationalization, the Angolan company already had 370 employees, and its turnover exceeded 52 million USD, which is equivalent to about 47 million EUR in current values.

The last years of the Angolan company have proven the success of internationalization. As the turnover, profitability indicators also show a positive evolution. However, financial autonomy is still limited, due to company's recent past and to the fact that retained earnings are still low.

As mentioned, the activity in Brazil began to develop in 2011, with the evolution up to 2014 being quite positive, contributing to the creation of return on investment and to a sustained financial health.

After these last years of more intense international experience, *"Technological"* is nowadays considered as a reference in the Portuguese industry of information technologies and as a reliable player among diverse business stakeholders. The following are examples of company's credibility:

Table 10. Economic and Financial Evolution – "Technological Angola" (USD)

Indicators		2010	2011	2012	2013	2014
Economic Evolution	Turnover	37.000.000	53.000.000	42.000.000	41.000.000	43.000.000
	Operating Profit	1.100.000	2.300.000	3.400.000	3.900.000	3.700.000
	Net Profit	700.000	800.000	1.600.000	2.300.000	1.900.000
	Gross Added Value	6.770.000	12.900.000	13.700.000	13.700.000	14.000.000
	Return on Investment	3,07%	4,29%	8,12%	5,03%	5,28%
	Return on Equity	36,8%	12,1%	20,0%	4,01%	4,04%
Financial Evolution	Assets	40.000.000	55.000.000	70.000.000	78.000.000	70.000.000
	Equity	1.800.000	6.700.000	8.000.000	10.000.000	12.000.000
	Liabilities	38.200.000	48.300.000	62.000.000	68.000.000	58.000.000
	Financial Autonomy	4,59%	12,02%	11,27%	13,48%	17,61%
	Financial Expenses Coverage	3,56	1,99	3,24	6,25	4,11

Table 11. Economic and Financial Evolution – "Technological Brasil" (USD)

Indicators		2011	2012	2013	2014
Economic Evolution	Turnover	30.005	1.037.870	2.757.350	4.967.410
	Operating Profit	-18.080	-138.243	148.112	674.401
	Net Profit	-18.080	-159.633	111.955	635.997
	Gross Added Value	-3.661	318.981	1.106.290	2.044.960
	Return on Investment	-15%	-27%	12%	39%
	Return on Equity	-16%	-71%	24%	56%
Financial Evolution	Assets	116.931	508.790	944.386	1.721.400
	Equity	115.680	223.350	468.992	1.104.990
	Liabilities	1.251	285.440	475.394	616.410
	Financial Autonomy	99%	44%	50%	64%
	Financial Expenses Coverage	--	--	6,25	20,18

- The project of electoral registration in Angola, is considered a world example of excellence in the biometrics area (one of the largest, if not the largest, biometric database of Africa);
- The company, being one of the largest 25 national companies in the information technology sector:
- It is considered an SME leader by IAPMEI (Portuguese Agency to Competitiveness and Innovation), benefiting from financing at lower cost;
- It is a member of the innovation network, formed by the SMEs considered as innovative by COTEC (Portuguese Business Association for Innovation).

Furthermore, it should be highlighted that the consolidated turnover of the companies within the group already amounts to 50 million euros, which means that this is a Portuguese-owned company that has managed to take the national and international market by creating sustainable competitive advantages, based on intellectual capital and on cyclical capacity (Teixeira & Amaro, 2013).

CONCLUSION

The Portuguese company of the information technologies industry (Technological, SA), developed a process of internationalization by stages, according to the knowledge that was being acquired of the markets where the company was present. The process of internationalization always ended up on direct investments through the creation of companies with own resources, which could be associated with the specificity of their culture and of their offer (such as the theory of transaction costs suggests).

In less than a decade, the company managed to increase the turnover of 10 million to 60 million euros, making it one of the largest Portuguese groups in its industry and a worldwide success. Such growth was due to the degree of innovation of its offer, but above all, to the ability of its resources to put the existing expertise for development of solutions that would meet the specific needs of target markets. Thus, the performed projects, not only enriched the company financially, but also contributed to the sustainable development of these countries, making the company an authentic reference of quality, innovation and confidence in those markets.

Regarding the management control system implemented, the company developed an organizational structure supported by strategic business units and business support units, which aimed to ensure greater decentralization of decision making and thus obtain greater flexibility to respond to one market that change constantly.

The piloting instruments were found to be well developed with budgets and monthly monitoring of the economic and financial results obtained. However, such instruments were only assiduously applied to strategic business units, which caused discontent in the managers of the business support units. In addition, there was also an effort to set prices for internal services, but as they were mostly based on cost-sharing rates, they were not well accepted by managers.

However, the control of the units 'activity and the managers' incentive system did not include criteria on non-financial variables that are critical to business success, which led to a focus on short-term performance rather than business sustainability.

Finally, regarding management control system, there was also a concern in the development of dialogue tools that would contribute to greater involvement and alignment of middle managers.

However, the last point of the chapter is about the impact of internationalization process on the financial performance of the company. It shows some financial difficulties.

Developing countries have specific characteristics that increase business risks and, as such, the last years of the study show some financial difficulties result from the economic slowdown in that markets (as was the case of Angola and Brazil), which had a negative impact on the average terms of receipt of customers from that countries.

REFERENCES

Alves, M., Teixeira, N., & Rita, R. (2007). *A gestão do risco cambial, as fontes de risco e as técnicas de pagamento: um estudo de caso*. Paper presented at XXI Congresso Anual AEDEM, Universidad Rey Juan Carlos, Madrid, Spain.

Anthony, R., & Govindarajan, V. (2007). Management Control Systems (12th ed.). New York: McGraw-Hill.

Eitman, D. K., Stonehill, A. I., & Moffett, M. H. (2005). *International Financial Management* (9th ed.; V. Pezerico, Trans.). New York: Bookman.

Jordan, H., Neves, J., & Rodrigues, J. (2011). *O Controlo de Gestão - Ao Serviço da Estratégia e dos Gestores* (10th ed.). Lisboa: Áreas Editora.

Porfírio, J. (2001). *Finanças Internacionais*. Lisboa: Universidade Aberta.

Teixeira, A., Teixeira, N., & Mata, C. (2008). *Implementação do Tableau de Bord – Estudo de caso no sector das Rochas Ornamentais*. IV Congresso de Custos do Mercosul – Montevideu.

Teixeira, N. (2007). A avaliação do desempenho de centros de responsabilidade – Estudo de caso. *XIV Congresso da AECA*.

Teixeira, N., & Amaro, A. (2013). Avaliação do desempenho financeiro e da criação de valor - um estudo de caso. *Revista Universo Contábil*, *6*(4), 157–178. doi:10.4270/ruc.2013436

Teixeira, N., & Carreira, F. (2008). Implementação de um sistema de avaliação do desempenho - Estudo de caso no sector português das Rochas Ornamentais. *XV Congresso Brasileiro de Custos* – Curitiba.

Teixeira, N. & Teixeira, A. (2008). *Preços de transferência interna e a avaliação do desempenho de centros de responsabilidade*. XVIII Jornadas Luso –Espanholas de Gestão, Porto, Portugal.

ENDNOTE

1 For confidentiality reasons, the company's and its associates' designations are fictitious.

Chapter 8
Critical Analysis

ABSTRACT

Given the specific challenges of the internationalization process for emerging markets, which require a constant adaptation of the organizational structure and of management control systems, this chapter aims to analyze the evolution of activity over the years studied, taking into account three key aspects: the assessment of the financial performance, focusing on the analysis of the value creation capacity and on the comparison with the values of the Portuguese industry; the assessment of the internationalization process, where several proposals are made in order to reduce business risk, both in terms of approach to the markets and in terms of the use of credit and exchange risk hedging techniques; the assessment of the management control systems implemented, with a reflection on the various types of instruments used (piloting, behavioral orientation, and dialogue) and elaboration of system optimization proposals, aiming a greater involvement and alignment of managers to organizational goals and business sustainability.

FINANCIAL PERFORMANCE ASSESSMENT

The internationalization process allowed the activity's expansion to countries with much higher growth rates' economies than the European ones, which provided an important turnover increase (Teixeira, Pardal & Rafael, 2017).

This increased activity put the company in contact with management practices and national cultures quite different from the Portuguese reality, which led to the gradual adjustment of the organizational structure and the development of important and singular competencies to achieve strong competitive positions in these markets (Teixeira et al, 2017).

Growth had a direct impact on investment levels and financial needs, which also conditioned the ability to generate profitability.

In order to carry out the assessment of financial performance and to demonstrate a detailed picture of the impact of the internationalization process on the economic and financial situation of the company, two evolutionary studies will be presented:

DOI: 10.4018/978-1-7998-2007-9.ch008

- Evaluation of the capacity to create value from the most serious start of the internationalization process, which took place in the year 2006, until the last period under review, 2014;
- Comparison of the company's evolution throughout the period in review with the economic and financial evolution of the activity sector, notably with the companies included in the activity code NACE 62.0 - Computer programming, consultancy and related activities, which are considered more similar to "*Technological*" in terms of supply and organizational strategies.

Regarding the Financial Concepts considered, in order to assess the capacity of value creation in the analyzed period, the concepts of sup abnormal profitability and weighted average cost of capital were used, as previously presented (Teixeira & Amaro, 2013).

Due to its importance, the calculation of the following headings will be detailed: invested capital, financial liabilities and cost of financing the activity, including the weighted average cost of capital, the cost of equity and the cost of foreign capital.

To calculate the invested capital, it is necessary to construct a functional balance sheet, which allows the conclusion of how the organization obtains and invests its financial resources. Table 1 presents the typical structure of a functional balance sheet (Teixeira & Jorge, 2016).

In view of the accounting balance, the functional balance sheet has a more adequate structure for the analysis of value creation. The structure of the functional balance sheet allows isolating the invested capital, in relation to the capital and the paid foreign capital, giving two complementary views on the company's activity. Namely, the necessary investment value for business unwinding (capital invested corrected by non-financial liabilities that decrease activity investment) and weight of used financing sources, a fundamental information to measure the profitability demanded by investors (Teixeira et al, 2013).

Regarding the sup abnormal profitability, to assess the activity' overall capacity in creating enough surplus to monetize the total investment, the traditional method of calculating the ROI should be adjusted, obtaining as a result of this adjustment the indicator designated by return on invested capital – ROIC investors (Teixeira et al, 2013).

Table 1. Structure of Functional Balance

Headings	Year n
Fixed Assets Set	
NFM Exploration	
-Cyclical needs	
-Cyclical Resources	
NFM extra exploration	
-Active Treasury	
-Passive Treasury	
Total Investment	
Equity	
Financial liabilities	
Total Financing	

In the numerator, in addition to the operating results, the income resulting from capital applications should be considered, as these are usually the result of treasury surpluses usually arising from the operational activity. It is also essential to reflect in the results the so-called fiscal effect, because part of the results obtained reverses, in practice, to the Government. It should be noted that the financial expenses and their tax savings should not be considered, as it intends to measure the capacity of the activity to generate surpluses, and these headings are the result of funding decisions. Thus, the net results without financial leverage (NRWFL) are calculated which could be obtained through the following formula investors (Teixeira et al, 2013):

NRWFL = (OR + Financial income) x (1 - t)

Legend: NRWFL - net results without financial leverage; OR – operational results; t – effective rate tax

In the denominator, the net asset is replaced by the total investment, determined under the functional balance sheet, because in the operating cycle the credits obtained from suppliers and other creditors finance part of its value, decreasing financial needs. Therefore, the total investment item contemplates the values of the assets and rights in which the capital is invested, corrected by the unpaid liabilities, negotiated by the company in the course of its activity investors (Teixeira et al, 2013).

Thus, the total investment includes non-current assets, working capital exploitation needs and Extra-exploitation working capital needs, excluding only remunerated liabilities, such as bank loans and leases, which are claims relating to the financing decision, also not considered in the results determined in the numerator. As such, the ROIC, is calculated by the following formula investors (Teixeira et al, 2013):

ROIC = NRWFL / Investment Total

Legend: ROIC - return on invested capital; NRWFL - net results without financial leverage

In relation to the cost of the invested capital (own and foreign), it shall be calculated, as previously stated, by the weighted average capital cost (WACC). To calculate the WACC we must know the value of the following headings: effective tax rate (t), Cost of foreign capital (KD), cost of equity (KE), invested capital, financial liabilities and equity (Teixeira & Jorge, 2016).

The effective tax rate is calculated considering the relationship between corporate income tax – IRC, reflected in the year Income Statement of each period, and the value of results before taxes – RBT (Neves, 2011).

The cost of foreign capital will be determined with reference to the relationship between the financial expenses recorded in the income statement at the end of the period and the value of the financial liabilities in each economic year that originated it (Neves, 2011).

The cost of equity was calculated according to the profitability of the average equity of the sector in Portugal in each of the studied exercises. To this end, the base was the information made available by Banco de Portugal (Central balance sheet) on the considered period (Neves, 2011).

As regards the values of invested capital, equity and financial liabilities are those in the annual functional Balance Sheet.

The table 2 details the various plots used in calculating the weighted average cost of capital (WACC), and their calculated values, in the period under analysis.

Table 2. Weighted average cost of capital

	2006	2007	2008	2009	2010	2011	2012	2013	2014
Cost of equity	5,30%	14,80%	18,00%	13,40%	12,00%	7,90%	6,60%	9,10%	10,80%
Weight of equity	51,25%	63,20%	79,17%	77,84%	45,78%	50,60%	63,21%	75,79%	64,13%
Cost of foreign capital	31,07%	20,81%	43,25%	16,79%	4,56%	5,12%	6,30%	10,42%	9,39%
Weight of foreign capital	48,75%	36,80%	20,83%	22,16%	54,22%	49,40%	36,79%	24,21%	35,87%
Income tax Rate	31,17%	3,83%	5,59%	5,68%	5,17%	10,89%	8,15%	20,48%	-15,17%
Cost of Capital	13,14%	16,72%	22,76%	13,94%	7,84%	6,25%	6,30%	8,90%	10,81%

In this calculation of the weighted average cost of capital (WACC) We clearly notice the substantial decrease in the cost of foreign capital (associated with the company's greater capacity to obtain bank credits). At the cost of equity level, it is observed that it has declined over the years (although with a slight rise from 2013) which evidences the impact of the financial crisis in Portugal. Thus, WACC decreases from 2009 to 2013, where it starts to increase, derived from the combined effect of increasing the cost of foreign capital and equity.

Next, the evolution of the sup-abnormal profitability from 2006 to 2009 is presented, being the period of great expansion of the international activity. It should be noted that, for the purposes of the study of the capacity to create value of the "*Technological*", the investment value of the functional balance sheet considered as initial investment was that of 2005, since these assets will provide for 2006 results.

By observing the evolution of the sup abnormal profitability between 2006 to 2009 one verifies that, except for the year 2008, value creation was increasing over the years, ending at about 200,000 euros above the first analyzed. However, it is noteworthy that in 2009 generated profitability (ROI) decreased to values close to 2006 (24%), which shows that value creation in that year was also based on a high reduction in the cost of the capital used (from 22% to 14%).

Next (Table 4) the evolution for the years 2010 to 2014, *inclusive*.

Between 2010 and 2014 it appears that, although the activity continues to create value during the first three years, there is a very high increase in the activity investment (it goes from about 6 million in 2008 to 21 million in 2010), which shows greater difficulty in receiving from international customers, which is reflected in high balances of third-party debts. Thus, value creation over these first three years was based, above all, on the decrease in capital cost that stood at values below 7%, that is, half of the 14% registered in 2009.

Table 3. Supernormal profitability from 2006 to 2009 (values in euros)

	2005	2006	2007	2008	2009
The NRWFL	--	977 236	1 200 591	1 397 665	1 455 592
Total Investment	4 086 567	4 186 379	4 469 056	5 852 194	19 954 652
ROI	--	23,91%	28,68%	31,27%	24,87%
Cost of Capital	--	13,14%	16,72%	22,76%	13,94%
Supra normal Profitability	**--**	**10,77%**	**11,96%**	**8,52%**	**10,93%**
Value created	**--**	**440 197**	**500 686**	**380 665**	**639 764**

Table 4. Supernormal Profitability 2010-2014 (values in euros)

	2010	2011	2012	2013	2014
The NRWFL	1 898 517	2 029 849	3 003 581	934 337	-39 156
Total Investment	21 461 000	19 279 000	20 258 000	25 025 000	24 306 000
ROI	9,51%	9,46%	15,58%	4,61%	-0,16%
Cost of Capital	7,84%	6,25%	6,30%	8,90%	10,81%
Supra normal Profitability	1,68%	3,21%	9,28%	-4,29%	-10,96%
Value created	334 690	688 139	1 788 658	-869 214	-2 743 292

In view of the higher investment values, which are even increasing over the analyzed years, from 2013 onwards the profitability created is no longer sufficient to remunerate investors at the cost of capital required, becoming a situation of value destruction.

Finally, in order to verify the accumulation of value creation over the period between 2006 and 2014, the capitalization is carried out at the cost of the capital considered (WACC for each year), of the various created value flows to the end of the last analyzed year, measuring the generated profitability in the various exercises. In the last year, in addition to created value, the existing values residual value (net assets of obligations towards third parties) is also considered, as this may be as well reversed in favor of investors (Teixeira et al, 2013).

When observing the previous tables, it is verified that the value created up to 2012, is almost absorbed by the negative values of 2013 and 2014, since the large portion of the accumulated value is formed by the residual value of the existing assets at the end of 2014. However, it can be stated that, according to the cost of capital required, the company was able to create about 28 million euros of accumulated financial value since 2006, at the highest intensity of its internationalization process, up to 2014, the last analyzed year.

About the company's framework in its activity, from an economic point of view, it has a higher dimension in both turnover, results and gross value added. At the level of profitability, it is observed that, although up to 2012 the company improves its capacity to return the owners in relation to assets' profit-

Table 5. Cumulative created value from 2006 to 2010 (values in euros)

	2006	2007	2008	2009	2010
Value created	440 197	500 686	380 665	639 764	334 690
Value created capitalized on 2014	1 056 225	1 029 283	637 481	940 299	456 165

Table 6. Cumulative created value from 2006 to 2014 (values in euros)

	2011	2012	2013	2014	Residual value	Accumulated value Created
Value created	688 139	1 788 658	-869 214	-2 743 292	24 306 000	
Value created capitalized on 2014	882 711	2 158 386	-963 139	-2 743 292	24 306 000	27 760 119

ability (ROI), the sector values were systematically better, which highlights the substantial investment required by the internationalization process (especially at the level of customer debts), which progressively also influenced the company's financial sustainability.

Next, tables 7 and 8 are presented with the economic values of the company and the sector, during the period 2008 up to 2014.

As far as the financial evolution of the company is concerned, it is confirmed that the value of the asset (which represents the investment level) was not only always higher than that of the activity sector, but also had a high raise over the analyzed years. At the same time, it appears that these values had influenced the financial autonomy degradation and the capacity to cover financial burdens.

In conclusion, it is a fact that the internationalization process provided an important increase in the activity. However, the challenges associated with this decision have also influenced an increase in the investment level and financial degradation in recent analyzed years.

It is therefore important to assess the undertaken internationalization process and the implemented management control systems, and to define guidelines that can contribute to a better response to the challenges facing the "Technological" activity.

Table 7. Economic evolution of the company (values in euros)

Indicators	2008	2009	2010	2011	2012	2013	2014
Turnover	14 230 000	**14 308 000**	*10 438 000*	*9 132 000*	**10 161 000**	**12 281 000**	*9 359 000*
Operating Profit	1 096 000	**1 262 000**	**1 988 000**	**2 272 000**	**3 261 000**	*1 170 000*	*-41 000*
Net Profit	1 018 000	**1 250 000**	**1 431 000**	**1 546 000**	**2 593 000**	*526 000*	*-1 010 000*
Gross Value Added	7 889 000	**9 374 000**	**9 213 000**	**7 635 000**	**9 200 000**	*7 832 000*	*6 405 000*
Return On Investment	11,00%	*5,00%*	**7,00%**	**9,72%**	**12,00%**	*3,63%*	*-0,12%*
Return On Equity	22,00%	*14,00%*	*13,00%*	13,00%	**17,00%**	*3,30%*	*-7,70%*
Legend: Bod cells – positive evolution; Italics Cells – Negative evolution							

Table 8. Economic evolution of the sector (values in euros)

Indicators	2008	2009	2010	2011	2012	2013	2014
Turnover	3 002 231	**3 087 889**	*2 984 386*	*2 964 041*	**3 091 038**	**3 203 448**	**3 385 841**
Operating Profit	205 280	*170 007*	**180 128**	*152 767*	**159 778**	**198 673**	**244 943**
Net Profit	115 376	*98 921*	**101 015**	*65 160*	**69 552**	**106 458**	**132 529**
Gross Value Added	1 202 770	**1 278 529**	**1 316 858**	**1 338 648**	**1 416 576**	**1 504 036**	**1 606 597**
Return On Investment	13,66%	*10,72%*	*10,20%*	*9,00%*	*8,60%*	**9,30%**	**10,00%**
Return On Equity	18,02%	*13,39%*	*12,00%*	*7,90%*	*6,60%*	**9,10%**	**10,80%**
Legend: Bold cells – positive evolution; Italics Cells – Negative evolution							

Table 9. Company financial evolution (values in euros)

Indicators	2008	2009	2010	2011	2012	2013	2014
Assets	9 868 000	*26 819 000*	*28 086 000*	**23 376 000**	*26 512 000*	*32 275 000*	*34 826 000*
Equity	4 556 000	**9 136 000**	**10 859 000**	**12 187 000**	**15 354 000**	**16 049 000**	*13 152 000*
Liabilities	5 313 000	*17 683 000*	**17 227 000**	**11 190 000**	**11 158 000**	*16 226 000*	*21 676 000*
Financial Autonomy	44,00%	*34,00%*	**39,00%**	**52,00%**	**58,00%**	*50,00%*	*38,00%*
Financial Expenses Coverage	11,46	**11,88**	*3,94*	**4,19**	**7,32**	*3,22*	*0,31*
Legend: Bold cells – positive evolution; Italics Cells – Negative evolution							

Table 10. Evolution of the financial sector (in euros)

Indicators	2008	2009	2010	2011	2012	2013	2014
Assets	2 589 443	*2 909 487*	**2 894 688**	*2 986 505*	*3 220 523*	*3 363 952*	*3 734 300*
Equity	640 188	**738 928**	**844 079**	*826 523*	**1 046 820**	**1 169 074**	**1 231 556**
Liabilities	1 949 255	*2 170 559*	**2 050 609**	*2 159 982*	*2 173 703*	*2 194 878*	*2 502 744*
Financial Autonomy	24,72%	**25,40%**	**29,20%**	*27,70%*	**32,50%**	**34,80%**	*33,00%*
Financial Expenses Coverage	6,86	*10,89*	*9,30*	*7,20*	**8,00**	**9,00**	9,00
Legend: Bold cells – positive evolution; Italics Cells – Negative evolution							

ASSESSMENT OF THE INTERNATIONALIZATION PROCESS

The Diversification of International Markets

The company is currently in the markets of Angola, Mozambique and Brazil and is carrying out projects in other countries such as Guinea-Bissau and the Democratic Republic of Congo.

However, developing countries, along with the largest potential scales and business margins, have some specific characteristics (greater political, economic and financial instabilities), which increase the risk of activity, for example, through different economic cycles that may generate a lack of liquidity in the financial markets, or difficulty in repatriating capital or foreign exchange losses (Teixeira et al, 2017).

Thus, in order to continue to ensure activity sustained growth, the company intends to internationalize itself to new markets such as Cape Verde, Guinea-Bissau, Morocco, Tunisia and Algeria, in order to penetrate markets with different economic cycles and that could allow for the diversification of the business risk.

There are several factors that condition the internationalization decision, such as market attractiveness (market, size and growth, suppliers and customers negotiating power, type of competitors, etc.) and the company's competitive ability to successfully implement in those markets (differentiation capacity and cost leadership). Nonetheless, risk minimization also undergoes the diversification of activity to poorly correlated markets, to create the diversification effect studied by Markowitz (1952).

The option should be for markets little or negatively correlated, and the greater the range of markets little correlated with each other, the lower the risk assumed, maximizing profits, in the selected profile risk. The basic idea of this theory is the low probability that the remaining markets follow the same declining trend, avoiding potential breakage in total results (Teixeira et al, 2017).

In this sense, the correlation coefficient between the GDP growth of the different target markets of the company was calculated for 24 years (World Bank, 2012), in order to study the largest or lesser link between the Portuguese, Angolan and Brazilian economies (current markets), in view of the economies of the other countries where the group is studying internationalizing. The correlation coefficients found are presented in the table 11.

Through the analysis of the coefficients, it is possible to verify that the opportunities for diversification are immense, highlighting several negative relations.

The highest coefficient is between Angola and Algeria (both countries are producers of natural resources), but less than 50%. On the other hand, large-scale markets with a wide variety of information and communication technologies, such as Algeria and Morocco, have very little related economic cycles to markets where the company is currently present.

Thus, it is evident that the internationalization for new countries with economic potential is an opportunity for the company to diversify the risk of its business and continue to grow sustainably.

Credit Risk Management

About country risk and, according to the previous analysis, what can most penalize the business group is the credit risk associated with the Angolan market, as it represents a good part of the global business.

The fact that the main customer of this market is the Angolan government and its revenues are mainly derived from oil, has been strongly conditioning the companies' treasury that constitute the group, since the decline in fuel prices had direct impact on the country's financial capacity and on the amount of currency available for international payments. As such, the receiving terms, which were substantially lower than those normally practiced in Portugal and Europe, have widened for many months.

"*Technological*", besides seeking other markets less related to the evolution of the Angolan economy, in order to guarantee new sources of funding for markets with potential but still low in liquidity, should also try to diversify the type of Angolan customers. In Angola, the government is the main client, and its payments delay have direct impact on the business group' treasury situation. In this sense, the company

Table 11. Correlations between markets

	Angola	**Algeria**	**Brazil**	**Cape Verde**	**Guinea-Bissau**	**Morocco**	**Portugal**
Algeria	0.4934						
Brazil	0.2446	-0.0461					
Cape Verde	0.2715	0.2485	0.2126				
Guinea-Bissau	-0.0426	-0.2853	0.0931	-0.0608			
Morocco	0.1961	0.0128	-0.0342	-0.0941	-0.1350		
Portugal	0.1557	-0.0931	-0.1459	0.0313	0.0599	0.0199	
Tunisia	0.1466	0.2159	-0.3648	-0.1539	0.1074	-0.1785	-0.0650

could expand the range of customers for the local administration and the Angolan business sector, for example (Eitman et al, 2005).

However, it may also mitigate this type of risk by adhering to credit insurance services, international factoring, documentary credit or forfaiting (Porfírio, 2001).

Institutions, such as the *Compagnie Française d´Assurance pour le Commerce Extérieur* - COFACE or the Portuguese *Companhia de Seguro de Créditos - COSEC*, have financial instruments where they assume the responsibility of international credits, reducing or eliminating risk in exporting companies (Teixeira et al, 2017).

At the same time, for countries with emerging economies, institutions such as the World Bank, African Development Bank, and Angola's Bank for promotion, to safeguard Portuguese investment in the Angolan market, assume wholly or partially the risk of non-compliance of Governments and companies with public holdings. Although costly (it depends on the risk and on the amounts involved), the costs of this type of insurance are preferable to the financing costs associated with the non-receipt of customers (Teixeira et al, 2017).

The confirmed documentary credit is the safest way for the company to sell goods, because it always guarantees the transactions' receiving, although it also entails more costs for the company. However, acting in risk markets such as Angola, may require documentary credit, because it can be quite helpful, as the bank in Portugal ensures payment, regardless the Angolan entities' situation (Teixeira et al, 2017).

In this way, the company avoids both credit risk and country risk, not being exposed to the possibility of bankruptcy or lack of financial capacity of its clients and the Angolan Bank.

Forfaiting, as previously mentioned, is a way for the company to finance itself in international markets. In this case, the company will be able to have funds at the time it wants to negotiate goods' purchase, to be able to pay in cash, getting prompt payments discounts from its suppliers, reducing forfaiting operation costs.

Regarding export, by using forfaiting, the company is able to mitigate the risk associated with the political and economic situation of the importer´s country (political risks), because it sells to its bank without recourse, credit securities is accepted by the customer, usually endorsed by a bank, which assumes the commitment to pay in the event of customer default (Teixeira et al, 2017).

In international export factoring, the company grants definitive credits on its foreign customers (e.g. from Angola) to its bank in Portugal, in exchange for obtaining an advance of its associated funds (with

Figure 1. Proposed model for credit risk management

Figure 2. The confirmed documentary credit

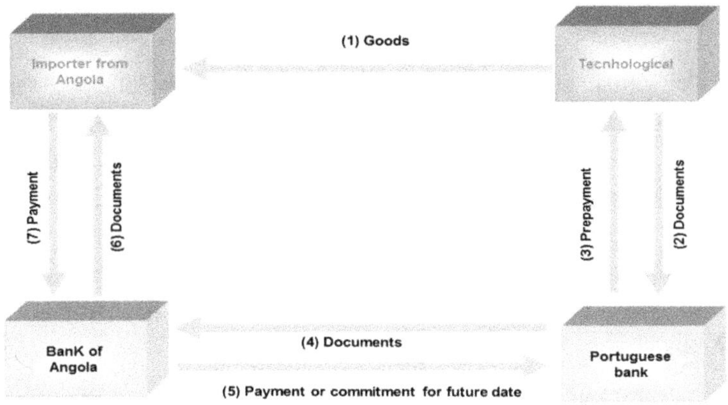

Figure 3. Forfaiting

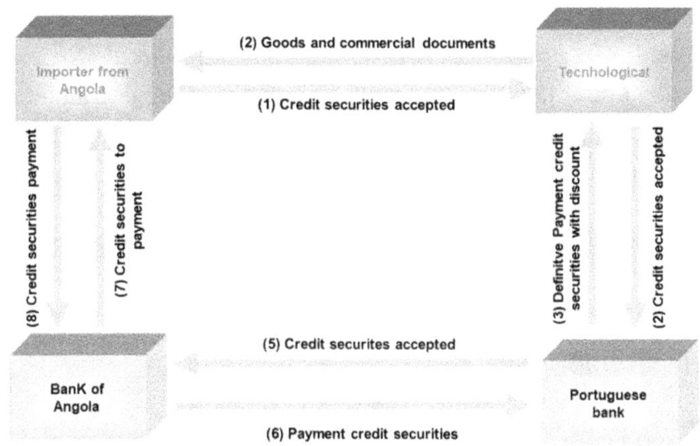

Figure 4. International export factoring

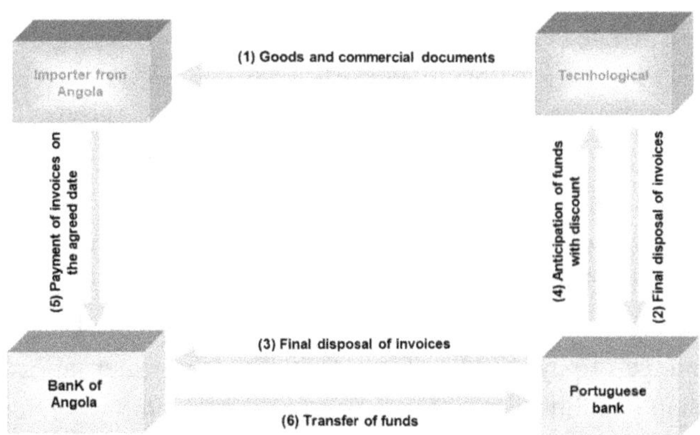

a discount for the advance period). This Bank shall send these credits to a corresponding financial entity, which will subsequently charge the importer, and carry out the transfer of funds to the Bank in Portugal (Porfírio, 2001).

Finally, in the credit risk management model, it is also proposed, that the company uses export credit insurance through official entities. As mentioned earlier, there are institutions in Portugal for this purpose, for example, COFACE and COSEC. The percentage of coverage can go up to 90% of the foreign market guaranteed credit, depending on the country. The premium rate varies according to various criteria, being defined after the customer portfolio' study of the potential insured. For commercial nature risks, as a rule, the premium rate is set at values below 1% of the insurable amounts. These costs will be compensated for, by timely receiving, improving the company's liquidity and increasing the credibility with financial institutions.

The Management of The Exchange Risk

In relation to the management of the exchange risk, are mainly the Portuguese "T*echnological*" and "T*echnological Angola*", which are subject to variations on the foreign currencies' value.

As previously mentioned, "T*echnological Brazil*" and "T*echnological Mozambique*", carry out their operations in local currency and, therefore, will only be subject to the exchange risk in results distribution in Portugal, or in the accounts' consolidation. As there is no results distribution foreseen over the coming years, as a way of achieving sustainability, a critical analysis of risk management will not be made to those companies, since it is quite residual.

Thus, the exchange risk management in the Portuguese "*Technological*" and "*technological Angola*" will be approached.

The Portuguese "*Technological*"

Internal Techniques

In relation to the Portuguese "*Technological*", within the internal techniques of exchange risk coverage, since the company makes imports in USD and GBP, it can anticipate payments whenever it foresees the valuation of the invoicing currencies.

This technique requires some treasury effort and only its execution is only possible if there is financial availability at the time of purchase or service contracting (Teixeira et al, 2017).

The company may also create a suppliers' portfolio using different invoicing currencies for the same products and services (Teixeira et al, 2017).

Depending on expected foreign currencies devaluations, suppliers are chosen considering the benefit of favorable exchange rate differences. Moreover, due to suppliers' negotiating power, is difficult to choose acquisitions currency, as well as currencies' diversification and the realization of actions on liabilities, through the change of payment deadlines (usually, large international technology providers are very rigid with payment deadlines and impose great penalties on delays that may include charging interest on arrears or interruption of service delivery).

In USD exports, clearing and matching techniques can be used, to try to match the outbound and inbound cash flows in the same currency (Eitman et al, 2005).

In stock prices, both in purchases and sales, *"Technological"* may try to negotiate with suppliers and customers, the existence of a tolerance range that will make prices fluctuate according to the changes in associated currencies' exchange, thus fixing the final value (Teixeira et al, 2017).

For example, in the case of a sale of 100.000 USD whose USD/EUR exchange rate is in 0,9 and that, at the time of receipt, three months after, the same exchange rate has been down to 0.8, the price may be adjusted so that the amount payable is strictly equal to the initially plan.

- Amount receivable in EUR: 100.000 USD x 0,9 = 90.000 EUR;
- New value receivable in EUR: 100.000 USD x 0,8 = 80.000 EUR;
- Therefore, there is a loss of EUR 10.000;
- Value to be adjusted in the starting price = 100.000 USD x adjustment x 0,8 = 90.000,00 EUR→ Adjustment = 12,5%

So, if the price was set at 12,5%, the amount to be paid would be the same as planned.

Finally, the fact that "T*echnological*" is one of the main suppliers of "T*echnological Angola*", which allows some exchange risk and interest rate management flexibility, through leading and lagging between the two companies, to influence payment and receipt deadlines negotiation and taking advantage of the exchange differences to condition both companies' results. This could be a technique to be explored both in results' management as in liquidity circulation in both companies (Teixeira et al, 2017).

For example, the fact that the income tax rate in Angola is 35%, could lead companies to choose receiving and payment deadlines in order to generate unfavorable foreign exchange differences in the country. Even generating favorable foreign exchange differences in Portugal, the tax rate on profits in Portugal is quite lower (about 21%), which will allow obtaining important tax savings.

External Techniques

In active operations, term positions' arbitrations and advances of foreign currencies may apply, using financial transactions to cover exchange risk (Teixeira et al, 2017).

Suppose that the Portuguese *"Technological"* has the following situation:

- Holds a three-month credit of 500.000 USD;
- It has a six-month debit of 600.000 GBP;
- Current exchange rate USD/GBP: 1,2.

It can set the purchase to three months OF GBP per exchange with USD, keeping the GBP applied for another three months (without ever converting them to EUR). Thus, at the end of the six months, GBP may be used for payment to the supplier. In this way, it never comes to incurring in foreign exchange differences.

As far as the advance of foreign currencies is concerned, *"Technological"* may use this technique to cover any devaluations of foreign currencies receivable in exports (Teixeira et al, 2017).

For example, if the company makes an export of 1 million USD whose receipt will take place in three months and expects the USD to devalue from 0,9 euros to 0,8 euros, it can hire a financing, at a lower cost, to pay within three months with the capital receiving from the customer.

Figure 5. Term arbitrage

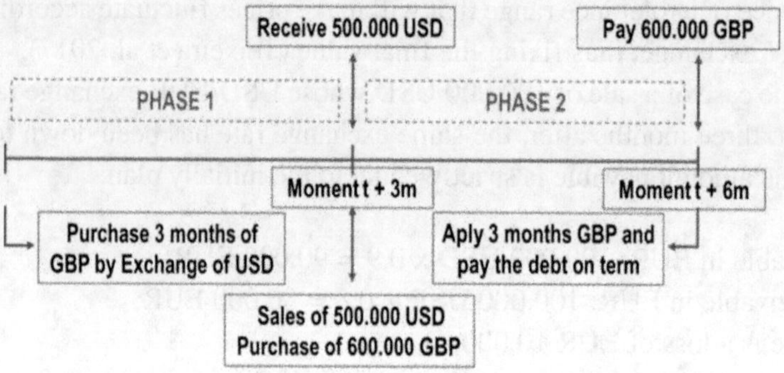

If "Technological" receives within 3 months at USD / EUR 0,8, it will obtain 800.000 euros assuming a cost of 200.000 euros.

If the company contracts a bank loan with an interest rate of 7% per year, it will have a lower quarterly cost:

- Loan amount: 1 million USD/(1 + 0,07x3/12) = 982.801 USD (updated value without the included interest of 3 months loan);
- Loan cost after 3 months: 17.199 USD →13.759 EUR with a expected exchange rate of USD/EUR 0,8.

It may also negotiate, in both active and passive operations, prompt payment discounts with customers and suppliers, when there is predictability that there are negative evolutions of foreign currencies (Teixeira et al, 2017).

Suppose that "*Technological*" will carry out an acquisition of 100.000 USD and that there are the following conditions in the exchange market: Exchange forward EUR/USD three months of 1,30; Cash exchange of 1,35; Financing cost of 5% (assuming it would have to be indebtedness). In this sense, the cash discount that "Technological" should negotiate with the supplier will at least be equal to:

Figure 6. Currency advance

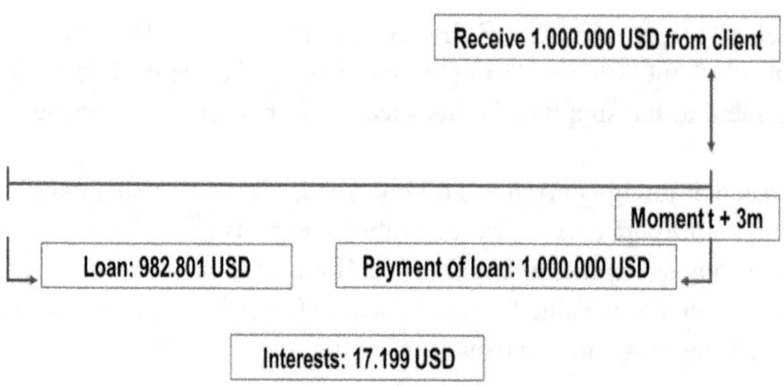

100.000 USD /1,35 x 1,05 x (1-d) = 100.000 USD /1,30 => d = 1%.

As such, the 1% discount would be the value from which "Technological" would save if it effected prompt payment.

At the level of the financial instruments used to cover the exchange rate risk, the company may use forward contracts in order to ensure the future exchange (Eitman et al, 2005).

Thus, for example, for software import worth 100.000 USD, payable within 90 days, hiring a forward to three months with a EUR/USD exchange of 1,30, the company would be protected against potential foreign currency valuations, guaranteeing the national currency equivalent of 76.923 EUR. Although it is not possible to take advantage of favorable oscillations of the EUR/USD exchange rate (eventual devaluations of USD), it would be anticipating payable amount, better controlling treasury.

For a similar situation to the above, the company may also purchase option contracts from financial institutions (Teixeira et al, 2017).

In this particular case, to guarantee an exchange rate for the importation of 100.000 USD software, the company will purchase a sales option, having the option to sell EUR, i.e. buy USD, for example, at a EUR/USD exchange of 1,30, thus paying a prize of 1,5%, the amount normally required by banks (in this case 1.154 EUR).

At the end of 90 days, one of two scenarios exists: the EUR/USD cash exchange goes down (e.g.to 1,25) and the company carries out its option, buying USD for 76.923 EUR plus the paid premium of 1.154 EUR, obtain a gain of 1.923 EUR compared to 80.000 EUR (100.000 €/1,25), which would pay at spot exchange rate.

In an opposite scenario, the spot exchange may rise, (for example, to 1,35). In this case, if the company does not choose to exercise the option, it will buy in the market in cash por 1,35, paying 74.074 EUR plus the paid premium of 1.154 EUR, obtaining a GAIN of 2.849 EUR in relation to the original situation (option at 76.923 EUR plus the prize of 1.154 EUR). However, it is essential to compare the evolution of the exchange with the costs of the instruments, since they may become costly in the face of the possibility of non-covering. Forward plus, which resemble the previous products, may also be used, but with the possibility of benefiting from the exchange rate oscillations, contrary to those originally planned, without any premium payment for exercising the right.

In the external techniques of coverage, and because they are little flexible and little available in Portugal, futures contracts are not advised to cover the exchange risk for this company.

Finally, it turns out that the company has financing and applications in USD. In this way, currency SWAP could be a great way to transform these foreign currency financial transactions into national currency, while also being protected against any changes in interest rates (Teixeira et al, 2017).

Suppose that "*Technological*" manages to obtain a financing in Angola of 10 million USD with a cost of 8% to reimburse in eight years (constant capital amortizations) and does not want to be exposed to the currency risk. In Portugal, it obtains SWAP quotation in a bank with the financial flows of 8% and 10% for the exchange of currencies between the USD and EUR, respectively (with USD/EUR 1,14 exchange rate). In scheme, we will get Figure 7.

The company obtains the initial financing in USD in the bank where it had the highest trading power, but sends that money to another bank that is available to exchange for EUR.

Over the eight years, on interest' payment date and capital reimbursement, the SWAP bank sends the equivalent value in USD for the company to fulfill its obligations. On the other hand, "*Technological*" will pay 10% for the use of EUR, property of the SWAP bank.

Figure 7. Initial cash-flows of the Swap - Year 0 - Initial Capital Exchange

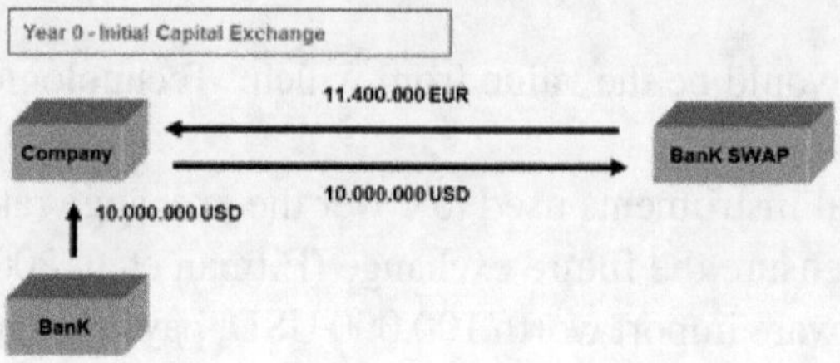

Figure 8. Periodic cash-flows of the Swap - Years 1, 2, 3, 4 - Reciprocal Payment of Interest

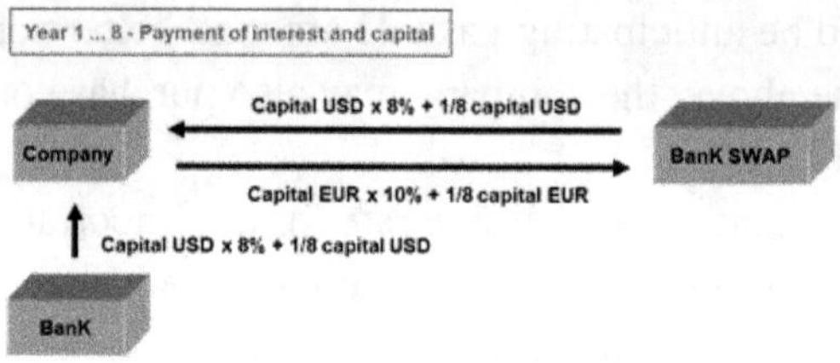

Thus, "*Technological*" will transform a financial transaction in USD, into a loan operation in EUR at a rate of 10%, having no exchange risk in the financial flows over the eight years.

The "*Technological Angola*"

Internal Techniques

In relation to the Angolan subsidiary, because it has more frequently foreign currency operations in regular activity cycle, it is first proposed to draw up a budget and control map, where all transactions verified in currency will be recorded, its expected value, its actual value verified and, finally, the result (Teixeira et al, 2017).

This map provides the origins of both positive and negative exchange differences, being a starting point for its management. Below is a sample map that can be used.

Table 12. Control map of foreign currency transactions

Date	Foreign currency operation	Specific value	Actual value	Result
DD-mm-yy	Payment X	The	B	(A-B)
DD-mm-yy	Y-Receipt	The	B	(B-A)
15-04-2011	Example: Payment. Supplier (5,000 USD)	45.000 AOA	50.000 AOA	-5.000 AOA
25-08-2011	Example: Salary pay (3,000 EUR)	33.000 AOA	32.000 AOA	1,000 AOA
20-12-2011	Example: Receiving customer (100,000 USD)	9 MILLION AOA	8.5 MILLION AOA	-500.000 AOA
	Total			-504.000 AOA

Since the company imports in USD, EUR and ZAR, it may use advanced payment as an internal technique to cover the exchange risk, if there is treasury availability, whenever it provides for the valuation of invoiced currencies. The company may also have several suppliers' options, with different invoicing currencies, choosing them according to expected foreign currencies' devaluations, avoiding those that work with currencies where valuations are foreseen.

Since the company also receives in USD, it may use the compensation and matching technique, cancelling the amounts received with the amounts payable in USD. In addition, it may also negotiate adjustments in purchase prices (as referred to in Portuguese "*Technological*"), depending on fluctuations in the involved currencies' exchange, establishing payable amount since the beginning of the contract (Porfírio, 2001).

As for wages, which are paid in USD, the company should use AOA as a reference currency, avoiding exchange risk, since workers are paid in AOA and the American currency has fairly valued against AOA.

Since the contracts with the Angolan government are based on USD but paid in AOA, the company has benefited from the constant valuations of the USD against the AOA, receiving a value higher than the initial expected.

Alternatively, if the trend towards the USD is to devalue against AOA, the company may try to contract prices' adjustments. It guarantees, thus, that the final value is the same initially negotiated, without prejudice to the parties. For example, in a USD 50 million contract, if the USD/AOA exchange value increases 10%, the contract value may be lower in the same proportion. In reverse, if the exchange rate devaluates, the value of the contract increases in the same proportion.

Since the main customer is the Angolan government, which, of course, holds a high negotiating power, it becomes difficult to choose the invoicing currency, receiving deadlines' negotiation or currencies' diversification.

External Techniques

Long-term arbitration positions and the advance of foreign currencies is also difficult in Angola, since there is always a great deal of unpredictability in receiving time by the main customer – the government.

On the other hand, even if no negotiation with the government is possible, bank financing in USD may eventually compensate for foreign exchange losses resulting from sales.

As external techniques, as suggested to the parent company, the subsidiary may rely on the negotiation of prompt payment discounts with both suppliers and customers, if a negative evolution of the currency is predicted, always considering financing cost (Porfírio, 2001).

In relation to financial instruments to cover foreign exchange risk, they are not available in the Angolan financial markets. In this sense, it is not possible to apply the options, forward, futures or swap contracts.

Next, table 13 is presented with the summary of the suggested techniques, considering the operations carried out in foreign currency.

ASSESSMENT OF THE MANAGEMENT CONTROL SYSTEM

After more than ten years since the beginning of the internationalization process, the company has become an international business group with a high diversification of the business and markets it serves, with a number of strategic business units that even work often together in projects of high scale and complexity.

Table 13. Summary of suggested techniques

Company	Type of operation	Operation	Currency	Type of technique	Suggested technique
"Technological" Portugal	Passive (payments)	Imports	USD and GBP	Internal	– Advance payment – Vendor selection depending on billing currency – Compensation/Matching – Pricing actions
				External	– Forward and Options – Ready-to-pay discounts
		Short-term loans (account cautioned)	USD	External	*-Swap Swaps*
	Active Receipts	Exports	USD	Internal	– Compensation/Matching – Pricing actions – Leading and Lagging
				External	– Forward and Options – Ready-to-pay discounts – Foreign exchange advances – Term position arbitrations
"TECHNOLOGICAL ANGOLA"	Passive (payments)	Imports, purchases in foreign currency and wages	USD, EUR and ZAR	Internal	– Advance payment – Choose currency operation – Compensation and Matching – Pricing actions – Map control
				External	Cash discount Ready
	Active (inbound deliveries)	Exports	USD	Internal	– Compensation and Matching – Map control – Pricing actions
				External	– Ready-to-pay discounts

In this way, some aspects of the management control system are identified, which, in our view, did not accompany the new reality of the company in the most convenient way. Thus, there are several suggestions for improving the management control system, once again based on the instruments previously mentioned and analyzed.

Analysis of Pilotage Instruments

Regarding budgetary planning and control, in view of the increasing size and complexity of projects carried out in Africa and Brazil, it is essential that accounting and financial information systems are capable of evidencing value creation, by Customer typology, and by Project (Jordan et al, 2011).

This is because, although business margins are very attractive, most of the time the company works directly with governments, which, through negotiating power, often delay payment deadlines, creating difficulties and obliging the company to rely on paid debt to cope with financial deficits of normal activity functioning.

In addition, the more detailed monitoring of undertaken projects would also allow highlighting each unit operational and financial contribution for the pursuit of the desired results (Anthony & Govindarajan, 2007).

Thus, the suggestion goes through the implementation of an accounting system that allows to know the income, expenses and assets associated with services' execution services (e.g., non-current assets' usage degree, receivables and required stock levels), by customer type (activity sector) and by project, always identifying the units that give rise to each heading. Thus, the company would not only be able to better understand the origin of the created value in executed services, but would also obtain a greater knowledge of the type of projects undertaken, in addition to a greater capacity to negotiate sales prices with customers, by virtue of an easier identification of necessary resources and potential margins (Jordan et al, 2011).

Thus, in addition to analyzing the internal performance of the centers of responsibility centers, it would be possible to better know the market and undertaken projects' profitability, to make decisions with greater certainty (Anthony & Govindarajan, 2007).

Using information systems, would allow obtaining a very high level of information breakdown.

Observing the previous figure, we found that there are global and specific levels of information:

- Company values;
- Contribution by SBU;
- Contribution by sectors' typology of served activity;
- Contribution by executed projects' typology;
- Contribution within each SBU, from each activity sector;
- Contribution within each SBU, for each project type;
- Contribution within each SBU and within each sector, of each project type;
- Contribution within each sector of each project type.

Currently, budgetary control is carried out monthly, through each unit financial statements' verification. Thus, it is possible for the manager and for the company to have an accurate view of the activity evolution:

- By the income statement the obtained result can be verified and compared with the expected one;

Figure 9. Levels of information to be obtained with segment definition

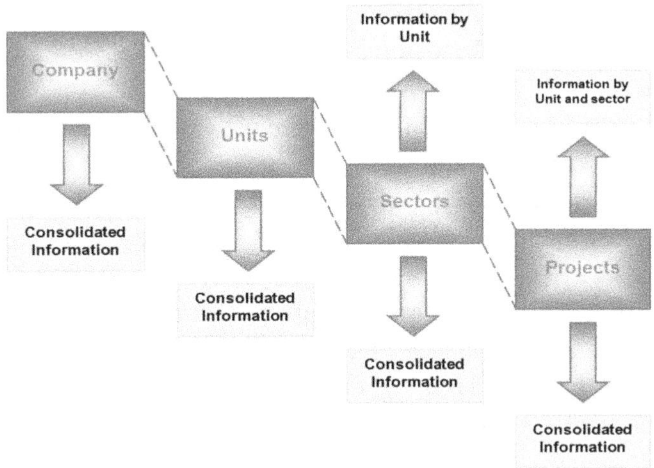

- By cash flows statement, the generated cash flow for the period is obtained, being important its knowledge to evaluate the self-financing capacity of each unit;
- By the balance sheet, the accumulated balance of net financial means is assessed, showing whether units' activity generates financial needs or resources. It is to be stressed that the company charges interest for the use of capital, on the negative balances of availabilities.

In this way, there is already a reasonable monitoring of the activity of the various units. However, the methodology of deviations is still not applicable, which makes it difficult to establish the real reasons for any existing differences.

In this sense, it is suggested that the methodology of deviations due to be applied, in order to assist decision-making, identifying why, where and who should act to correct harmful situations to the company's success (Jordan et al, 2011).

In the first phase, the deviations due' application is only proposed on the evolution of each unit's turnover, to experience the difficulties added to the information system. After being properly tested, its application on each unit's various operational headings is deemed important.

In order to verify the advantages inherent to the application of due deviations' methodology, it was made an example on the variables that normally originate turnover of strategic business units. Next, we describe the characteristics of the example:

- The main objective of the business units is the realization of software development and projects' implementation;
- There are several specific types of projects that vary depending on the products and services to be developed;
- The projects' billing is according to the number of commitment hours of required for its elaboration;
- As such, sales prices are defined according to the type of services and qualification of the technicians involved in each project.

Thus, the application of deviations due intends to show how the variation in these headings may influence turnover evolution, based on the following assumptions:

- The volume deviation is calculated according to the difference between the estimated quantity of projects to be elaborated and the number of projects effectively carried out;
- The mix deviation, is determined according to the oscillations of the number of projects carried out of each defined typology;
- The efficiency deviation is determined by the difference between the number of estimated billing hours and the actual invoices;
- The price deviation is calculated with reference to the proposed sales prices to apply and those that were actually practiced.

In the example worked, it is verified that the information for management is easily enriched by the application of deviations due, guiding managers towards the origins of turnover variations.

However, it is our understanding that in the case of projects that are more complex involving the participation of different employees' categories, with different billing prices, it will be interesting to disaggregate the deviations in each Project, by the number of hours of commitment of each level of qualification involved in its development.

An example of this methodology is presented in a Strategic business unit (SBU).

Suppose that an SBU has as its activity, the development of two types of projects:

- Each project is billed by the number of man-hours required;
- The price of the man-hours is different by design typology.

The initial budget for the turnover for the month of January was depicted as seen in Table 14.

In early February, the scope of the defined objectives was verified, and the data in Table 15 from the management accounting were withdrawn.

Thus, without accessing more data, it can only be concluded that there was a positive deviation in type A projects and a negative deviation in type B projects, being its global value positive. To learn more about the origins of the existing differences in relation to the budgeted, it is necessary to apply the methodology of deviations due (see Tables 16 through 20).

In this way, several conclusions can be drawn on the formation of the global deviation:

- On the positive side, it is verified that there were favorable deviations through the changes in the product mix, the number of billing hours and the practiced prices;
- On the negative side, there were unfavorable deviations in the scope of the Type B project, namely in sales volume, in turnover mix and prices.

Table 14.Initial budget

Projects	Volume	Mix	Efficiency	Price	Value (€)
A	3	43%	50 Hours/Man	75	11.250
B	4	57%	40 Hours/Man	5t0	8.000
Total	**7**	**100%**	--	--	**19.250**

Table 15. Real situation

Projects	Volume	Mix	Efficiency	Price	Value	Deviation
A	4	67%	52 Hours/Man	85	17.680	6.430
B	2	33%	41 Hours/Man	40	3.280	(4.720)
Total	6	100%	--	--	20.960	1.710

Table 16. Volume Deviation - Flexible Budget nº 1

Projects	Volume	Efficiency	Price	Value	Deviation
A	3	50 Hours/Man	75	11.250	0
B	3	40 Hours/Man	50	6.000	(2.000)
Total	6	--	--	17.250	(2.000)

Table 17. Mix Deviation - Flexible Budget nº 2

Projects	Volume	Efficiency	Price	Value	Deviation
A	4	50 Hours/Man	75	15.000	3.750
B	2	40 Hours/Man	50	4.000	(2.000)
Total	6	--	--	19.000	1.750

Table 18. Efficiency Deviation - Flexible Budget nº 3

Projects	Volume	Efficiency	Price	Value	Deviation
A	4	52 Hours/Man	75	15.600	600
B	2	41 Hours/Man	50	4.100	100
Total	6	--	--	19.700	700

Table 19. Price Deviation - Flexible Budget nº 4

Projects	Volume	Efficiency	Price	Value	Deviation
A	4	52 Hours/Man	85	17.680	2.080
B	2	41 Hours/Man	40	3.280	(820)
Total	6	--	--	20.960	1.260

Table 20. Total Deviation

Projects	Volume	Mix	Efficiency	Price	Deviation
A	0	3.750	600	2.080	6.430
B	(2.000)	(2.000)	100	(820)	(4.720)
Total	(2.000)	1.750	700	1.260	1.710

As such, it would be clear to the manager of this business unit that the positive evolution of the activity was mainly due to the elaboration of type A projects in favor of type B projects, generating a greater number of labor hours of and consequently a greater billing volume. In addition, the prices were higher than those foreseen in the budget.

Supposing now that the implementation of type A projects required the participation of employees with two levels of qualification and consequently, different billing prices. Thus, the sales prices of €75 and €50 presented earlier reflect the average values. As such, it is advisable to disaggregate the deviations by the different levels of qualification, making clearer their origin and more activity that is effective monitoring (see Tables 21 through 26).

It is therefore evident the contribution of each qualification level to the overall deviation value, allowing the manager to better decide on any corrections to be made in the activity and on the content of future proposals to be presented, according to projects' typology, better measuring profitability and making negotiation process more transparent.

Table 21. Initial Budget for Type A Projects

Projects	Volume	Efficiency	Price	Value
A	3	20 hours/man Level 1	80	4.800
		30 hours/man Level 2	70	6.300
Total	3	--	--	11.100

Table 22. Real Status of Type A Projects

Projects	Volume	Efficiency	Price	Value	Deviation
A	4	21 Hours/man Level 1	87	7.308	2.508
		31 hours/man Level 2	83	10.292	3.992
Total	4	--	--	17.600	6.500

Table 23. Volume Deviation - Flexible Budget n° 1

Projects	Volume	Efficiency	Price	Value	Deviation
A	3	20 hours/man Level 1	80	4.800	--
		30 hours/man Level 2	70	6.300	--
Total	3	--	--	11.100	--

Table 24. Mix Deviation - Flexible Budget n° 2

Projects	Volume	Efficiency	Price	Value	Deviation
A	4	20 hours/man Level 1	80	6.400	1.600
		30 hours/man Level 2	70	8.400	2.100
Total	4	--	--	14.000	3.700

Table 25. Efficiency Deviation - Flexible Budget n° 3

Projects	Volume	Efficiency	Price	Value	Deviation
A	4	21 Hours/man Level 1	80	6.720	320
		31 hours/man Level 2	70	8.680	280
Total	4	--	--	15.400	600

Table 26. Price Deviation - Flexible Budget n° 4

Projects	Volume	Efficiency	Price	Value	Deviation
A	4	21 Hours/man Level 1	87	7.308	588
		31 Hours/man Level 2	83	10.292	1.612
Total	4	--	--	17.600	2.200

With regard to strategic planning and control, it is observed that, although in the business plans presented in each year, objectives are foreseen in non-financial variables essential to the company's sustained success, such as innovation, quality, business risk, among other factors, in practice, there are not adequate monitorization over time.

This still becomes more relevant, if considered the enormous challenges that also arise in the internal structure adapting capacity to company's new business reality.

In fact, the Angolan internationalization process development, considering its attractiveness in terms of project size and commercial margins, strategic business units' managers began to underestimate the Portuguese market and other emerging markets' business opportunities, where it could easily be capitalized the accumulated expertise in strategic areas such as the Biometrics, where the company holds very important competitive advantages.

This phenomenon has been affecting the development of the activity, due to:

- Loss of market share in Portugal, which, at the level of risk management, does not reveal a correct decision, since they are markets with poorly correlated developments and as such, in the event of a crisis in one of those markets, losses could be compensated with another's gains;
- Overestimates of the high potential for Angolan economic and social growth, because it largely depends on its public sector and petroleum export revenues, with high exposure to international market risk for this type of products, and its impact on the financial capacity of the country and its economic agents, resulting in a dramatic pressure on the treasury of the business group;
- Less rapidity of operations with other emerging markets with equivalent needs to the work developed in Angola, which would, in the short term, lead to gains for competition, leading to opportunity loss to capitalize on accumulated expertise and ensure sustained growth in unique competitive advantages.

Thus, in response to these problems, the administration could develop efforts, in the sense of greater activity control and greater action alignment of the various business units' managers, in view of the organizational goals (Teixeira et al, 2008).

In this sense, the performance assessment system currently implemented should not only monitor the achievement of the defined economic and financial goals, but also control the evolution of certain fundamental variables to the organization's success, such as risk, quality, innovation, customer satisfaction and knowledge sharing between units, which is fundamental for optimizing the use of company resources (Teixeira et al, 2008).

For the implementation of this model, the company could resort to the Balanced scorecard' philosophy, establishing sub goals in each of the perspectives composing it. In addition, each of the perspectives could be divided, in order to understand the type of critical factor of the company's success that is intended to monitor:

- Perspective of Organizational Development: human capital, information capital and organizational capital;
- Perspective of internal processes: quality and continuous improvement and business innovation;
- Customer Perspectives: Customer satisfaction and new customer achievement;
- Financial Perspective: Orientation to value creation and evaluation of performance and risk.

Table 27. Organizational Objectives - 2014

Strategic priorities	Types of organizational Objectives	Qualitative goals	Purposes
Organizational Development	**Human Capital**	– Certification of employees – Motivation of the employees – Knowledge sharing in company newsletters	– 2 certifications per year by contributor – Employee Satisfaction Index of 85% – 300 Articles of collaborators per year
	Capital Information	– Improvement of the strategic planning and management control process	– Integration of information systems and technologies used by the end of 2014
	Organizational Capital	– Improved organizational alignment capacity	– Development of dynamic Scorecard by employee and team to the end of 2014
Internal processes	**Quality and continuous improvement**	– -Ensure excellence in the products and services provided and agreed deadlines	– Effectiveness in 80% of improvement initiatives – CMMI Level 3 Certification up to 2014 – Zero Customer Complaints
	Business Innovation	– Ensuring access to technological innovations – Creating new Solutions	– 20% of sales in new products/services – 5 intellectual property records per year
Customers	**Customer Satisfaction**	– Ensure the loyalty of current customers – Ensure the profitability of current customers	– Service level excellence rate above 90% – To ensure 20% of the tenders awarded
	Conquest of new customers	– -Ensure access to new customers	– -20% of sales in new customers
Financial Results	**Value Creation Guidance**	– Increase business margin – Reduce the level of investment	– Result of 20% on the cost of capital – VAB per worker of 75K € – Average delivery time of 90 days
	Performance and risk assessment	– Ensuring sustained growth – Assessing risk by projects and customers – Reducing the weight of strategic customers in Angola – Weight of turnover in Portugal – Weight of turnover in new markets	– Growth 10% above market – Projects with a yield of 20% on the cost of capital – Number of strategic customers at 2014:8 – 30% of total turnover – 20% of total turnover

Next, we present the organizational objectives established by the company for 2014, framed in the logic Balanced scorecard, and for which each business unit should contribute, with managers being awarded accordingly (see Table 27).

It should be emphasized that each strategic business unit and business support should contribute to the organizational goals, by obtaining properly aligned local purposes, presenting a summary map of its achievement degree Monthly Activity Reports.

Thus, for the effective implementation of the balanced Scorecard system in "*Technological*", it is essential to ensure the alignment of four decision levels, which require a lot of communication and negotiation throughout the organization:

Level 1: Organizational goals' definition and critical factors' definition that the administration needs to ensure for the business strategies' success;

Figure 10. Decision Levels to Implement Balanced Scorecards

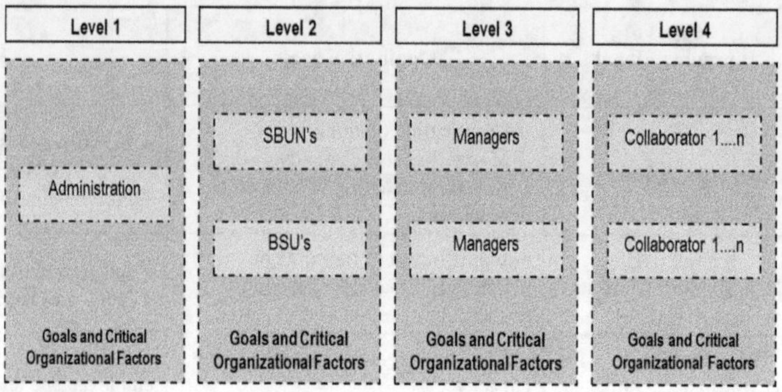

Level 2: Responsibilities' definition for each unit, including critical purposes and factors on which it needs to act, in order to ensure organizational goals' achievement;
Level 3: Definition of each manager's contribution to achieving goals and critical factors of each unit;
Level 4: Definition of each employee's contribution to achieving goals and critical factors of each unit.

In this sense, it would be important that the implementation of balanced scorecards to be complemented with strategic maps, in order to emphasize in the entire organization, the link between the different factors that condition the implementation of business' strategy. It would also matter if balanced scorecards could act in due time on events that, although are not having a direct impact on the company's results, may be able to condition the company's sustainability in the near future (Teixeira et al, 2008).

In conclusion, at the level of the pilotage instruments, the suggestions go through:

- Planning and financial control of projects and results by customer typology, in order to demonstrate its contributions to value creation and each units' performance;
- Implementation of the methodology of deviations due, for better determination of the origins of the differences between financial forecasts and financial achievements;
- Implementation of Balanced scorecard and strategic maps, to enable effective monitoring of critical business success factors.

Analysis of Behavior Guidance Instruments

At the level of the assessment of responsibility centers, it was found that only the strategic business units were evaluated and only on the evolution of the financial data. Managers were evaluated according to centers' activity on which they had authority. Although they believed that capital cost used in determining the economic income of non-current assets provided by the financial efficiency unit and interest, in case of treasury deficits, was very high in view of the financial conditions available on the market, which penalized the premiums to be received.

In this sense, the company could use the average return on investment (sector ROI) as the financial cost or the weighted average cost of invested capital (WACC) in the activity (Teixeira et al, 2013).

The option for ROI of the sector makes sense, since it evidences the profitability that similar companies in the same industry can generate by dynamizing its activity, and therefore, the value that the strategic business units should, at least, be able to generate (Teixeira et al, 2013).

In addition, ROI represents the profitability generated in the activity that is available to share by the different types of investors.

Firstly, ROI results from the flows released by the activity, whether they are of operational or financial origin that reward investors (owners and financial creditors). Let's look at the demonstration in Figure 11 (Teixeira, 2008).

At the same time, it is known that total asset (set of goods and rights belonging to the company) measures the investment performed and that, through the exploitation of these assets, a result is obtained (net results without financial leverage-NRWFL).

To place monetary values in the activity, investors (owners and financial creditors) require a remuneration, designated cost of equity, or cost of capital, as the case may be. In scheme we get what is depicted in figure 12.

Figure 11.

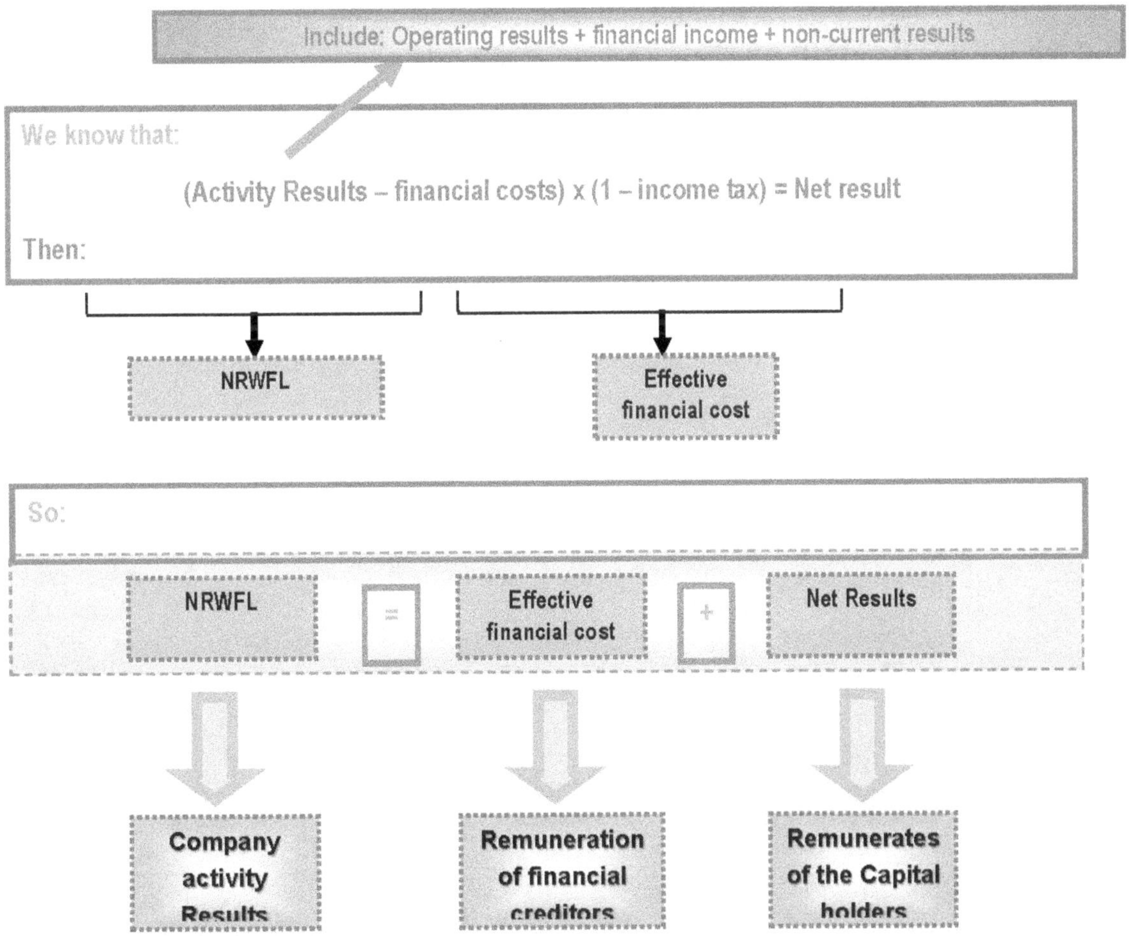

Figure 12.

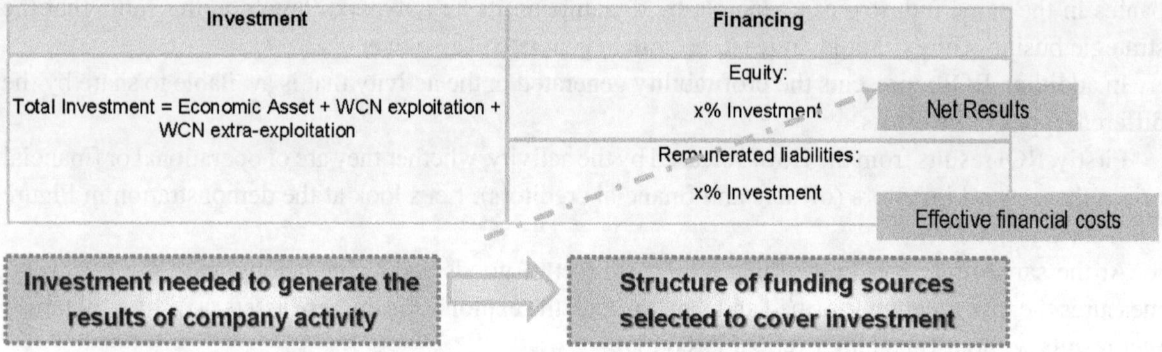

Then, when considering the result generated by the asset (NRWFL), we have the profitability generated by the company's activity; by developing the same reasoning in the remuneration of used financing sources, its cost is determined against the total amount of financial value invested in the activity (Teixeira, 2008) (see Figure 13).

Thus, it becomes possible to identify where the profitability generated is being conducted, verifying who benefits more with the created value, owners or financial creditors (Teixeira, 2008) (see Figure 14).

Thus, ROI is a benchmark for knowing the profitability available to investors, and the average value of the industry might be a standard to require as a minimum value to be generated by strategic business units.

Alternatively, and as mentioned above, the company may use as a financial cost to require strategic business units, the weighted average cost of capital (WACC), which takes into account the cost and weight of each financing source, in total invested Capital. It is then presented again its formula, as well as the assumptions that can be used in the calculation of the different headings that make up the WACC (Teixeira, 2008) (see figure 15).

Figure 13.

Figure 14.

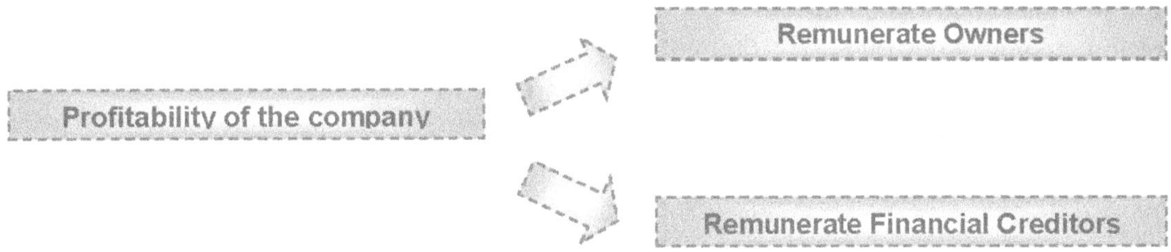

Figure 15.

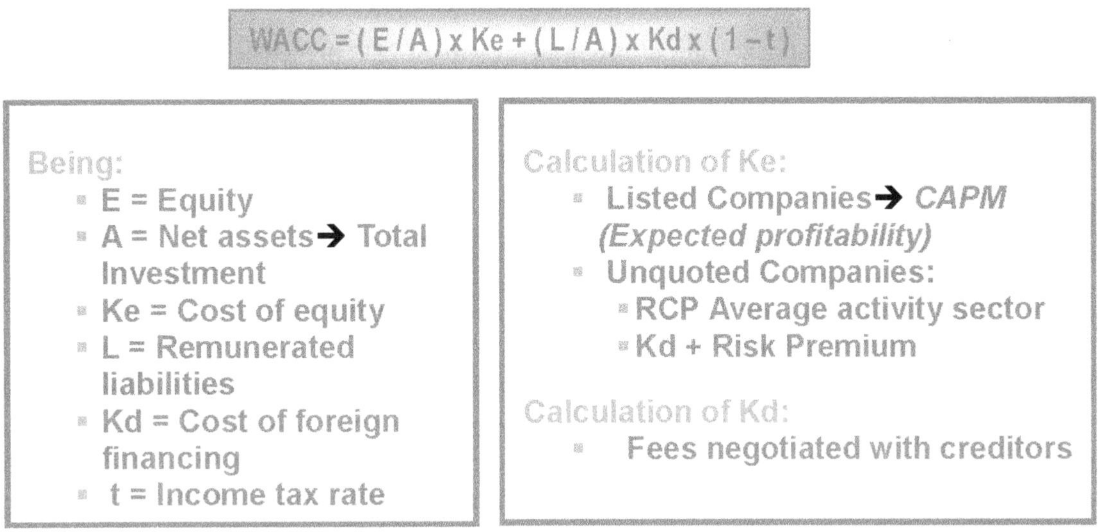

In addition to complaints regarding the amount of the financial cost charged on cash deficits, managers' opinion about non-current assets economic providing was that it was complex, in terms of logic and calculations.

In this case, the implementation of an indicator such as EVA, RCM or SAP could have the advantage of making it easier to monitor and read the valuation of value creation capacity, because it directly compares generated results against the expected, being eventually more easily understood and accepted by managers.

About economic income, it is also noteworthy that its calculation is less harsh for managers than the application of the aforementioned indicators (EVA, RCM or SAP), since it allows obtaining superior results that do not evidence, thus, the true cost of invested capital (Teixeira, 2008).

A comparative example is presented with the determination of the economic income and the Residual contribution margin.

Assuming a strategic business unit with the following values:

Operating income before amortization: 1.000.000€
Assets: 100.000€

Depreciation Rate: 12,5%
Option: Residual contribution margin
Operating income: 1 000 000 - (100.000 × 0,125) = €987.500
Capital cost rate (average ROI to the sector, or WACC): 25%
Residual contribution margin:

987.500 – [(100.000 – 12.500) × 0,25] = €965.625

Option: Economic Income
Asset Lifetime: 8 years
Capital cost rate: 25%
Acquisition value: 100.000€
Term of the arrears income for 8 years at the interest rate of 25% per period: 30.040€
Corrected Operating result:

1.000.000 – 30.040 = 969.960€

Thus, it is verified that the residual contribution margin penalizes the result of the unit more than the economic income, which also contributes to a measurement of value creation in a more correct way.

Regarding the support units, their performance was not evaluated, which created a feeling of great injustice in their various managers.

Thus, we believe that the transformation of the support units into results centers was fundamental to create higher motivation indices and to ensure a more entrepreneurial spirit in the various working areas, benefiting the efficiency in internal resources' use. That would allow these managers to be evaluated not only by the inputs of the activity but also by generated outputs (Teixeira et al, 2008).

For instance, the Administrative and accounting unit manager negotiates several sources of financing at lower costs than the market, obtains Community support for the investments to be carried out, as well as tax benefits that reduce the income tax payable. The revenues it generates for the company through these actions are higher than the turnover created by most of the strategic business units. However, there is no evaluation or award for this very important effort to the company's financial sustainability.

Simultaneously, the Administrative and accounting unit carries out several services for the units, such as treasury control, legal documents' drafting and accounting record. Therefore, working hours could easily be recorded for each unit, defining reference prices for these services, because these are activities available on the market with easily known prices. As such, by using the principles of costing based on activities, it could be attributed values for internal services' supply to the different units, avoiding the use of cost sharing rates, very criticized by managers, providing greater equity in managers' evaluation for the various areas.

Thus, the assessment of the responsibility centers could be carried out according to the table 28's indicators.

As has been described, the activity-based costing – ABC, may be very relevant in decision-making, to the extent that (Jordan et al, 2011):

- It avoids overhead costs' breakdown, since they are assigned depending on who carries out the activities and consumes the resources;

Table 28. Indicators to be used in the evaluation of responsibility centers

Unit	Type of Responsibility centre	Evaluation indicator
Units Business Strategies	Investment centers	EVA, RCM or SAP
Business Support Units	Results centers	Contribution margin or center result

- It allows highlighting the efficiency of the performed activities, identifying each one's associated costs, as well as their productivity, by comparing the necessary inputs with the outputs generated.

In the case of "*Technological*", the application of the ABC methodology will focus fundamentally on activities' management and on the structure costs' allocation possibility to business strategic units, in favor of its distribution through fees not always accepted by the managers. In fact, headings such as internal benefits and costs related to water, electricity, surveillance and safety and cleanliness, hygiene and comfort are imputed according to criteria-based allocation rates, where the number of people in each unit stands out.

To apply ABC to our case, we will use the following phases of model construction (Brimson & Antos, 1994):

- Costs' origin;
- Activities' identification;
- Assigning cost elements to activities;
- Identification of cost generators;
- Definition of measurement units;
- Common cost generators activities' aggregation;
- Formation of the generator unitary cost;
- Assigning the activity cost to the cost object.

In order to show the usefulness of the ABC model, we will apply it to the Administrative and financial support unit and to a strategic business unit.

ABC Application: Administrative and Financial Support Unit

Phase: Costs' Origin

The administrative and financial support Unit presents monthly, on average, the following costs (for example purposes, the values are fictitious):

- Human resources: three people, to which you can proportionally associate the monthly costs shown in Table 29 (if the costs were different per employee, we would have to determine the amount for each).
- Material resources: Corresponds to the diverse asset that is used by the various human resources that constitute the unit, in the activities carried out. Its monthly costs are shown in Table 30.
- Monthly costs directly attributable to the billing activity (table 31).
- Unit monthly Overhead (table 32).

Table 29. Costs of the support unit

Cost Item	Value
Personnel costs (includes salary, social charges, occupational accident insurance and food allowance	2.500€
Depreciations of the asset directly affected to each human resource (furniture, hardware and software)	2.745€
Communications (mobile phone)	100€
Fixed Asset insurance directly affected to each human resource	50€
Asset conservation directly affected to each human resource	100€
Technical books	50€
Office Supplies	50€
Communications (landline)	75€
Total costs per human resource	**5.670€**
Total Human Resources Monthly costs	**17.010€**

Table 30. Costs per asset

Cost Item	Value
I. Depreciation of the asset used by the various human resources (furniture, fax, telephone center, copier and printer)	2.500€
Asset Conservation	250€
Asset Insurance	125€
Total monthly costs for the asset	**2.875€**

Table 31. Direct costs

Cost Item	Value
Representation expenses	100€
Travel and stays	200€
Fuels	100€
Total Direct Monthly costs	**400€**

Table 32. General costs

Cost Item	Value
Electricity	50€
Office Supplies	250€
Total Monthly Overhead	**300€**

Phase: Activities' Identification

The administrative and financial unit performs the following activities:

- Accounting services to the various units;
- Collection services to the various units;
- Commercial documentation elaboration services to the various units;
- Other activities of general nature of the operation of the unit (payments to suppliers, wages processing, etc.)

Phase: Assigning Cost Elements to Activities

During the month of March, the administrative and financial unit had the following commitment to the various activities undertaken:

- Daily working hours: 8 hours;
- Number of working days in the month of March: 22 days;
- Total number of daily working hours: 8 hours × 3 persons = 24 hours;
- Total number of monthly working hours: 24 hours × 22 days = 528 Hours.

These 528 hours were consumed by the activities as seen in Table 33.

According to the working hours, monthly costs for each activity may be assigned for. It should be noted that as for the indirect costs (assets used by all activities and general activity costs) it would be divided according to the number of working hours. Next, the unit costs per hour are presented, to be assigned to each activity:

- Human Resources Working Hour unit cost: €17.010 ÷ 528 hours = €32,22;
- Unit cost of overhead working hours (asset + monthly costs): (€2,875 + €300) ÷ 528 hours = €6,01.

Phase: Cost Generators' Identification and Definition of Measurement Units

The cost generators for each activity are, depicted in Table 35.

According to the hours of commitment in each activity, we have the outputs shown in table 36.

Table 33. Hours of activities

Activities	Hours
Accounting services	190
Collection services	200
Commercial documentation elaboration services	80
Other activities	58
Total commitment hours	**528**

Table 34. Costs per activity

Activity	Direct costs	Individual overhead HR costs	Other indirect costs	Total costs
– Accounting services	-	€6.121	€1.142	€7.263
– Billing Services	€400	€6.445	€1.202	€8.047
– Commercial DOC Services	-	€2.577	€482	€3.059
– Other activities	-	€1.867	€349	€2.216
Total costs	**€400**	**€17.010**	**€3.175**	**€20.585**

Table 35. Cost generators

Activities	Cost generators	Unit of Measure
– Accounting services	– Registered documents	– Number of registered documents
– Billing Services	– Customers contacted	– Number of customers contacted
– Commercial DOC Services	– Elaborated documents	– No of elaborate documents
– Other activities	– Hours spent	– No of hours spent

Table 36. Outputs of activities

Activities	Unit of Measure	Quantities
– Accounting services	– Number of documents	100
– Billing Services	– Number of customers	20
– Commercial documentation Services	– Number of documents	150
– Other activities	– Number of hours	58

Phase: Aggregation of Activities With Common Cost Generators

If the activities identified in a responsibility center are carried out in other responsibility centers, but have the same cost generator, they must be aggregated before moving to the next phase. In our case, this situation does not apply.

Phase: Forming the Generator Unitary Cost

Table 37 depicts an example of the generator unitary cost.

Phase: Activity Cost Assignment to the Cost Object

According to the data of the unit, it is known that it provided the amount of services to the strategic business units "Tools & Solutions" and "E-Development" seen in Table 38.

Knowing the unitary costs of cost generators, the cost per unit is determined (see table 39).

Table 37. Unit costs of activities

Activities	Quantities	Costs	Unit Cost
– Accounting services	100	€7.263	**€72,63**
– Billing Services	20	€8.047	**€402,35**
– Commercial DOC Services	150	€3.059	**€20,39**
– Other activities	58	€2.216	**€38,21**

Table 38. Services per strategic business units

Activities	"Tools & Solutions"	"E-Development"	Total quantities
– Accounting services	40	60	100
– Billing Services	12	8	20
– Commercial Docs Services.	50	100	150

Table 39. Costs of activities per strategic business units

Activities	"Tools & Solutions"	"E-Development"	Total costs
– Accounting services	€2.905	€4.358	€7.263
– Billing Services	€4.828	€3.219	€8.047
– Commercial Docs Services.	€1.020	€2.039	€3.059
Total costs	**€8.753**	**€9.616**	**€18.369**

Conclusions of the Application of the ABC to the Administrative and Financial Unit

- Billing Services consume more resources and generate more costs;
- The unit cost of the collection services is much higher than that of the other services, comparing costs with generated outputs;
- The largest number of services is provided to SBU – "E-Development", and it is not surprising that the largest share of costs will go to this unit;
- Knowing carried out services' unitary costs, the administrative and financial unity has greater bargaining power before the other units, showing them clearly the resources they consume. Thus, it is natural for the SBU to try to reduce the cost-generating factors. For example, avoid negotiating more extended delivery times or decreasing the number of invoices to be issued, trying to concentrate billing orders on fewer documents;
- Knowing its activity outputs, the unit can also improve its performance by periodically comparing costs with generated outputs. This it will analyze its own productivity.

Application ABC: Strategic Business Unit – North

Phase: Costs' Origin

The Strategic business unit – Norte, presents Monthly, on average, the following costs (for example purposes, the values are fictitious):

- Human resources: 4 people to whom you can proportionally associate the monthly costs from Table 40 (if the costs were different per employee, we would have to determine the amount for each one).
- Material resources: It corresponds to the diverse asset that is used by the various human resources who constitute the unit, in the performed activities. Its monthly costs are shown in table 41.
- Direct monthly costs of trading, purchasing, production and assistance activities (table 42).
- Unit monthly Overhead (table 43).

Table 40. Costs of the strategic business unit

Cost Item	Value
– Personnel costs (includes salary, social charges, occupational accident insurance and food allowance)	€2.800
– Depreciations of the asset directly used by each human resource (furniture, hardware and software)	€3.500
– Communications (mobile phone)	€200
– Asset insurance directly affected to each human resource	€80
– Asset conservation directly affected to each human resource	€150
– Technical books	€150
– Office Supplies	€50
– Communications (landline)	€150
Total costs per human resource	**€7.080**
Total Human Resources Monthly costs	**€28.320**

Table 41. Costs of the assets

Cost Item	Value
– Depreciation of the asset used by the various human resources (furniture, fax, telephone center, copier and printer)	€3.500
– Asset Conservation	€350
– Asset Insurance	€250
Total monthly costs for fixed assets	**€4.100**

Table 42.Direct costs

Cost Item	Trading	Resource purchases	Production	Assistance
– Inventories' cost	-	€2.000		
– Representation expenses	€250	-	-	-
– Travel and stays	€250	-	€200	€200
– Fuels	€200	-	€100	€200
– Taxes	€50	-	-	-
Total Direct Monthly costs	**€750**	**€2.000**	**€300**	**€400**

Table 43. General costs

Cost Item	Value
– Electricity	€60
– Office Supplies	€340
Total Monthly Overhead	**€400**

Phase: Activities' Identification

The North Business Strategic Unit performs the following activities:

- Trading;
- Resources Purchases;
- Production;
- Technical assistance.

Phase: Cost Elements' Assignment to Activities

During the month of March, the North Business unit had the following commitment to the various undertaken activities:

- Daily working hours: 8 hours;
- Number of working days in the month of March: 22 days;
- Total number of daily working hours: 8 hours × 4 people = 32 hours;
- Total number of monthly working hours: 32 hours × 22 days = 704 Hours.

These 704 hours were consumed by the activities, as depicted in table 44.

To determine the costs of the activities, the assignment is made according to the working hours. Next, the unitary costs per hour are presented to be assigned to each activity:

- Human Resources Working Hour Unit Cost: €28.320 ÷ 704 hours= €40,23;
- Unit cost of overhead work hours (fixed Assets + monthly costs): (€4.100 + €400) ÷ 704 hours =€6,39.

Phase: Generator Costs' Identification and Measurement Units' Definition

The cost generators for each activity are, shown in table 46.

According to the hours of commitment in each activity, the outputs in table 47 were obtained.

Phase: Aggregation of Activities With Common Cost Generators

The activities foreseen for the SBU – North, are identical to those of the other units. As such, cost generators are common. Thus, in order to determine the overall cost of these activities, it is enough to aggregate

Table 44. Hours of the activities

Activities	Hours
– Trading	150
– Resources purchase	50
– Production	300
– Technical assistance	204
Total Hours of Commitment	**704**

Table 45. Costs per activity

Activity	Direct costs	HR Overhead Costs	Other overhead costs	Total costs
– Trading	€750	€6.034	€959	€7.743
– Resources purchase	€2,000	€2.011	€320	€4.331
– Production	€300	€12.069	€1.917	€14.286
– Technical assistance	€400	€8.206	€1.304	€9.910
Total costs	€3,450	€28.320	€4.500	€36.270

Table 46. Cost generators

Activities	Cost generators	Unit of Measure
– Trading	– Customer Contracts	– Number of contracts carried out
– Resources purchase	– Shopping	– Number of orders
– Production	– Projects	– Number of ongoing projects
– Technical assistance	– Contacts with customers	– Number of service requisitions

Table 47. Outputs of activities

Activities	Unit of Measure	Quantities
– Trading	– Number of contracts carried out	15
– Resources purchase	– Number of orders	10
– Production	– Number of ongoing projects	6
– Technical assistance	– Number of service requisitions	8

the values for all units. In this way, responsibility centers and activity centers will be simultaneously available. However, the objective is to identify the specific situation of the SBU – North and, therefore, no consolidation of values is made.

Phase: Formation of the Unit Cost of the Generator

Table 48 shows an example of the unit cost of the generator.

Phase: Assigning the Activity Cost to the Cost Object

According to the unit available data, it is known that it provided the amount of services to the banking and insurance and Software Houses activity sectors in table 49.

Knowing the unit costs of cost generators, the cost to be allocated to each sector can be determined (see table 50)

In addition to the data already mentioned, the accounting also allowed to know the activity of the unit by type of projects developed (see table 51).

Thus, it is also possible to know the cost associated with each type of project (see table 52).

Table 48. Unit costs of activities

Activities	Quantities	Costs	Unit Cost
– Trading	15	€7.743	**€516,2**
– Resources purchase	10	€4.331	**€433,1**
– Production	6	€14.286	**€2.381**
– Technical assistance	8	€9.910	**€1.238,75**

Table 49. Services per type of client

Activities	Banking and insurance	Software Houses	Total quantities
– Trading	9	6	15
– Resources purchase	4	6	10
– Production	3	3	6
– Technical assistance	3	5	8

Table 50. Costs per type of client

Activities	Banking and insurance	Software Houses	Total costs
– Trading	€4.645,8	€3.097,2	€7.743
– Resources purchase	€1.732,4	€2.598,6	€4.331
– Production	€7.143	€7.143	€14.286
– Technical assistance	€3.716,2	€6.193,8	€9.910
Total costs	**€17.237,4**	**€19.032,6**	**€36.270**

Table 51. Services per type of project developed

Activities	IT Tools	Outsourcing	Total quantities
– Trading	7	8	15
– Resources purchase	5	5	10
– Production	2	4	6
– Technical assistance	4	4	8

Table 52. Costs per type of project developed

Activities	IT Tools	Outsourcing	Total costs
– Trading	€3.613,4	€4.129,6	€7.743
– Resources purchase	€2.165,5	€2.165,5	€4.331
– Production	€4.762	€9.524	€14.286
– Technical assistance	€4.955	€4.955	€9.910
Total costs	**€15.495,9**	**€20.774,1**	**€36.270**

Conclusions of the Implementation of ABC to the Business Unit: North

- Production services and technical assistance consume more resources and generate more costs;
- Unitary costs of production services and technical assistance are far superior to the rest, when comparing it with generated outputs;
- The largest number of services is provided to the Software Houses activity sector and to the Outsourcing projects, and it is not surprising that the largest share of costs incurred on these headings;
- Knowing the costs for each sector of activity type and for each type of developed project, the unit has greater decision-making capacity in accepting work, because it knows in advance the level of resources and costs necessary for its realization;
- Knowing its activity outputs, the unit can also improve its performance by periodically comparing inputs and outputs, analyzing its productivity.

According to the examples presented, there are several advantages inherent in the implementation of ABC, namely (Jordan et al, 2011):

- Observing how resources are used, allowing to the managers to check the activities with higher investment volume associated;
- Identifying the unitary costs of developed activities, making planning and decision-making process easier, by giving the possibility to know in advance the associated profitability for each type of project to be ran;
- Minimizing cost allocation through imputation bases, allowing allocating indirect costs to the segments, considering the respective use of each activity. And because management decisions are reflected in the activities, ABC allows the simultaneous evaluation of these decisions and action on them;
- Achieving reliability in the management control system, better understanding the auxiliary services' values imputed to each responsibility center;
- Achieving managers' motivation in the decision process of internal transfer prices, giving ABC visibility to the unit cost of services to be provided, making it easier to negotiate among different responsibility centers;
- Enabling organizational cohesion, involving everyone in process efficiency, because the identification of the cost generators of the various activities eases decision-making on both working processes and techniques.

However, it is also true that the application of ABC requires a high organizational discipline, that is, in order to obtain the necessary data, it is essential that administrative procedures are established to ensure timely registration and accurate information.

Thus, establishing results centers at the level of the business support units and using internal transfer prices, having as reference both the values practiced in the market and the costs based on the activity, in favor of cost-sharing percentages, may contribute to greater organizational cohesion and greater alignment in the face of the strategy to be implemented Teixeira & Teixeira, 2008).

Finally, as for managers' incentive system, in addition to essential evaluating these in a support units context, it is also important that they become evaluated and rewarded for obtaining non-financial objectives, such as innovation and quality, which are fundamental for the company's sustained success and also for the contribution of its action to the global goals. That is, the incentive system should be based on the achievement of financial and non-financial goals and its impact on the activity of the center on which they have responsibility, but also on the contribution to the overall goals of the company (Teixeira et al, 2008).

Therefore, thus, evaluation of managers' system should have the dimensions shown in Figure 16.

As mentioned above, managers should be evaluated according to the purposes of the units they coordinate, but also for their contribution to achieving the organizational purposes. Thus, an effective performance evaluation model should be able to monitor the activity of managers in key financial and non-financial variables, which are fundamental to the sustained success of organizations.

We will present a work to illustrate a possible integrated evaluation system, encompassing financial and non-financial dimensions and contributing to local and global goals. It was developed for a smaller company of the "*Technological*" group, which specializes in the development of biometric solutions of the "*Technological*" group, which specializes in the development of biometric solutions.

According to the characteristics of the competitive environment and its position in the information and communication technologies sector, the company intended to achieve the organizational objectives in the years 2009 to 2011 shown in table 53.

To achieve the organizational objectives, strengthen its competitive position and mitigate the weaknesses in its internal structure, the strategic actions in table 54 were defined.

The company is constituted through two main business areas and three support areas:

- Business Area – Information Systems Services;
- Business Area – Technologies;
- Business Support area – infrastructures;
- Business Support area – quality;
- Business Support area – administrative and financial.

Figure 16. Managers' evaluation System dimensions

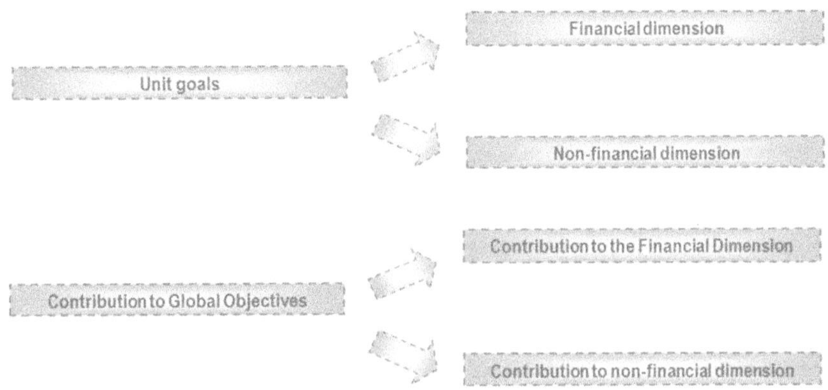

Table 53. Organizational Objectives from 2009 to 2011

Strategic priorities	Types of organizational Objectives	Goals Qualitative	Timing of objectives		
			2009	**2010**	**2011**
Process Innovation Organizational change	**Innovation**	– Ensure competitive processes – Creation of intermediate management levels by functional areas	– 1 new patent – Conception and Design – Software Factory	– 1 new patent – Quality	
Flexibility and Agility Delivered quality	**Quality**	– Ensure excellence in the products and services provided and agreed deadlines	– Service level rate > 70%	– Service level rate > 80%	– Service level > 90%
Pace of growth	**Dimension**	– Ensure the growth of turnover and access to new international markets	– Turnover100%↗ – Weight of new markets = 10%	– Turnover 40%↗ – Weight of new markets = 20%	– Turnover 19%↗ – Weight of new markets = 25%
Business Risk Management	**Risk**	– Reduce the weight of strategic customers and improve their presence in the national market	– 80% Turnover = 3 clients – National Market Weight = 5%	– 80% Turnover = 4 clients – National market Weight = 10%	– 80% Turnover = 5 clients – National market Weight = 15%
Company visibility	**Notoriety**	– Enhancing the company's image	– Notoriety rate > 60%	– Notoriety rate > 70%	– Notoriety rate > 80%
Return on investment	**Profitability**	– Ensure the return of the Capital cost set for the organization	– RCM > 15% capital Cost	– RCM > 20% capital Cost	– RCM > 25% Capital Cost

Table 54. Areas of Intervention

Performance proposals	Areas of intervention
Functional Organizational Structure	Organization and Management
Management by objectives and recruitment of employees	
Performance Assessment System	
Management control System	
Information Systems (CRM/ERP/ *Intranet*)	
Software Factory Construction	Operations and innovation
Patents	
Strengthening market share and diversification of markets (Eastern Europe) – International partnerships	Internationalization
Commercial alliances upstream	Commercial and Marketing
National partnerships	
Disclosure actions	
Institutional Site	
Quality Certification	Quality, Hygiene and safety
Vocational training	Human Resources Qualification

In addition to the areas of work that have been mentioned, there is still management, which coordinates all the company's activity.

A system of evaluation of flexible performance, immediate reading and quick action facilitator is intended, based on financial and non-financial indicators. As goals – to provide customized information to managers, according to their working area, containing data of the most diverse order, since the organizational objectives, as we have seen, are not only financial. In addition, allow the operational managers to act quickly on the existing results deviations and undertake actions, and it is vital that they are readily available.

In order to exist cohesion among different functional areas, the performance evaluation system should ensure that purposes and strategic actions of different hierarchical levels coincide. As such, in order to have a conductive line, the purposes and management-monitored actions about each working area are to be negotiated every year, with a clear commitment from managers to the defined strategy. Thus, the success of the different levels of the organization depends on the interconnection among the various areas, guaranteeing greater communication between employees and greater fluidity in the execution of the working processes (Teixeira et al, 2017).

In this sense, and according to the defined organizational goals, the responsibilities described in table 55 were established for the various areas, according to the opinions of the top managers involved in the performance assessment system.

In this way, by monitoring the performance of each work area, it allows management and operational managers to follow the activity regularly and make timely decisions about the objectives and the important variables that condition the sustained success of the company.

To give an idea of the functionality and importance of the performance appraisal system for the dissemination of the strategy and alignment of the various areas of work, the results for the first half of 2009 are given in table 56.

As such, the implemented performance evaluation system allows to highlight not only the attainment of goals, but also the identification of working areas where there should be corrections, in order to improve global organizational performance.

Thus, it can be verified that the goals less achieved are innovation, notoriety and risk, which do not reach the level of 80%. About innovation, management failed in notoriety, technologies and infrastructures working areas were those that fell short of the objectives outlined; at risk, systems area did not properly comply with predicted values. Thus, this activity monitoring system allows observing where the efforts to optimize the activity should be carried out, concentrating the managers on the goals, aligning their performance against the corporate strategy.

However, for the system to work, the role of communication within the organization must be pointed out. It is essential that there is dialogue, negotiation and alignment in the action of the various working areas, to obtain the necessary synergies and managers' commitment to the organizational objectives. For this reason, clear rules have been established regarding periodicity and realization of periodic meetings for submitting and analyzing results.

The performance evaluation system also allows analyzing the level of achievement of each working area goals. For example, see the systems business area activity summary, shown in the table 57.

Thus, it was verified that it was able to obtain a higher performance score than the company (87,8% > 80,1%). However, it is once again evidenced that there are clear improvements to be made in the objectives of risk and notoriety, being fundamental to perceive the causes of the least success in these activity areas.

Table 55. Responsibility for Organizational Goals

Type of objectives (weight in strategy)	Responsible area (weight in goal)	Indicators to be monitored (weight of area activity in the objective)
Innovation (20%)	-Management (70%)	-Creation of functional areas (60%) -Implementation of management by objectives (40%)
	- BA system (30%)	-Patent realization (50%) -Realization of technological partnerships (50%)
Quality 10	-Management (20%)	-Obtaining quality certification (100%)
	-BA Systems (25%)	-Service level (100%)
	-BA Technologies (25%)	-Service level (100%)
	-BSA infrastructures (10%)	-Service level (100%)
	-Quality BSS (10%)	-Activity mapping (100%)
	-Administrative and Financial BSA (10%)	-Quality of information (100%)
Dimension 20	-Management (40%)	-Software Factory implementation (80%) -Institutional marketing actions (20%)
	- BA system (30%)	-Increase in turnover (40%) -Increase of new markets (30%) -Marketing actions (30%)
	- BA Technologies (30%)	-Increase in turnover (40%) -Increase of new markets (30%) -Marketing actions (30%)
Risk 20	-Management (20%)	-Conducting partnerships with decision makers (50%) -Implementation of E-business (50%)
	- BA Systems (40%)	-Reduction of the weight of strategic customers (30%) -Increase in turnover in Portugal (30%) -Conducting partnerships with decision makers (40%)
	- BA Technologies (40%)	-Reduction of the weight of strategic customers (30%) -Increase in turnover in Portugal (30%) -Conducting partnerships with decision makers (40%)
Notoriety 10	- BA Systems (40%)	-Degree of notoriety (40%) -Conducting partnerships with suppliers (30%) -CRM implementation (30%)
	- BA Technologies (40%)	-Degree of notoriety (40%) -Conducting partnerships with suppliers (30%) -CRM implementation (30%)
	- BSA infrastructures (20%)	-Degree of notoriety (100%)
Profitability 20	-Management (20%)	-Implementation of the management control system (100%)
	- BA Systems (25%)	-Return on investment (100%)
	- BA Technologies (25%)	-Return on investment (100%)
	-Several BSA (30%)	-Cost control (100%)

Table 56. Degree of achievement of the organizational objectives of the 1st semester 2009

Type of objectives	Unit	Activities	Degree of achievement	Contribution to Area Score	Score area in the goal	Score of the Objective
Innovation (20%)	-Management (70%)	-Creation of functional areas (60%)	70%	42%	62%	0,7x,62 + 0,3x0,9 = **70%**
		-Implementation of management by objectives (40%)	50%	20%		
	- BA Systems (30%)	-Patent realization (50%)	100%	50%	90%	
		-Realization of technological partnerships (50%)	80%	40%		
Quality (10%)	-Management (20%)	-Obtaining quality certification (100%)	90%	90%	90%	0,2x0,9 + 0,25x1+ 0,25x0,7 + 0,1x0,8 + 0,1x0,7 + 0,1x0,8 = **83,5%**
	- BA Systems (25%)	-Service level (100%)	100%	100%	100%	
	- BA Technologies (25%)	-Service level (100%)	70%	70%	70%	
	-ASN infrastructures (10%)	-Service level (100%)	80%	80%	80%	
	-Quality BSA (10%)	-Activity mapping (100%)	70%	70%	70%	
	-Administrative and Financial BSA (10%)	-Quality of information (100%)	80%	80%	80%	
Dimension (20%)	- Management (40%)	-Software Factory implementation (80%)	90%	72%	88%	0,4x0,88 + 0,3x0,93+ 0,3x0,7 = **84,1%**
		-Institutional marketing actions (20%)	80%	16%		
	- BA Systems (30%)	-Increase in turnover (40%)	120%	48%	93%	
		-Increase of new markets (30%)	70%	21%		
		-Marketing actions (30%)	80%	24%		
	- BA Technologies (30%)	-Increase in turnover (40%)	85%	34%	70%	
		-Increase of new markets (30%)	50%	15%		
		-Marketing actions (30%)	70%	21%		

continues on following page

Regarding the incentive system, the evaluation of business area managers is carried out considering the performance in local objectives and organizational objectives. The proposal went through the following methodology:

- 70% of the evaluation should be associated with performance in the local objectives, with reference to the predicted values and the existing deviations. To emphasize the establishment of tolerance intervals in awarding, based on the deviations identified between the different quartiles of the Central balance sheet of Banco de Portugal, for the financial data, and for non-financial purposes,

Table 56. Continued

Type of objectives	Unit	Activities	Degree of achievement	Contribution to Area Score	Score area in the goal	Score of the Objective
Risk (20%)	- Management (20%)	-Conducting partnerships with decision makers (50%)	100%	50%	85%	0,2x0,85+ 0,4x0,58+ 0,4x0,93 = **77,4%**
		-Implementation of E-business (50%)	70%	35%		
	- BA Systems (40%)	-Reduction of the weight of strategic customers (30%)	30%	9%	58%	
		-Increase in turnover in Portugal (30%)	90%	21%		
		-Conducting partnerships with decision makers (40%)	70%	28%		
	- BA Technologies (40%)	-Reduction of the weight of strategic customers (30%)	80%	24%	93%	
		-Increase in turnover in Portugal (30%)	110%	33%		
		-Conducting partnerships with decision makers (40%)	90%	36%		
Notoriety (10%)	- BA Systems (40%)	-Degree of notoriety (40%)	110%	44%	86%	0,4x0,86+ 0,4x0,65+ 0,2x0,7 = **74,4%**
		-Conducting partnerships with suppliers (30%)	80%	24%		
		-CRM implementation (30%)	60%	18%		
	- BA Technologies (40%)	-Degree of notoriety (40%)	80%	32%	65%	
		-Conducting partnerships with suppliers (30%)	50%	15%		
		-CRM implementation (30%)	60%	18%		
	- BSA infrastructures (20%)	-Degree of notoriety (100%)	70%	70%	70%	
Profitability (20%)	- Management (20%)	-Implementation of the management control system (100%)	70%	70%	70%	0,2x0,7+ 0,25x1,05+ 0,25x0,8+ 0,1x0,85+ 0,1x0,9+ 0,1x1,2 = **89,8%**
	- BA Systems (25%)	-Return on investment (100%)	105%	105%	105%	
	- BA Technologies (25%)	-Return on investment (100%)	80%	80%	80%	
	- BSA infrastructures (10%)	-Cost control (100%)	85%	85%	85%	
	BSA Quality (10%)	-Cost control (100%)	90%	90%	90%	
	BSA A&F (10%)	-Cost control (100%)	120%	120%	120%	
Organizational performance		**0,2x0,7 + 0,1x0,835 + 0,2x0,841 + 0,2x0,774 + 0,1x0,744 + 0,2x0,898**				**80,1%**

Table 57. Degree of achievement of the objectives of Systems area

Type of objectives	Activities	Degree of achievement	Contribution to Area Score	Score area in the goal
Innovation (20%)	-Patent realization (50%)	100%	50%	90%
	-Realization of technological partnerships (50%)	80%	40%	
Quality (10%)	-Service level (100%)	100%	100%	100%
Dimension (20%)	-Increment turnover (40%)	120%	48%	93%
	-Increase new markets (30%)	70%	21	
	-Marketing actions (30%)	80%	24	
Risk (20%)	-Decrease in strategic clients weight (30%)	30	9	58%
	-Increment of turnover Portugal (30%)	90%	21	
	-Decision-making partnerships (40%)	70%	28	
Notoriety (10%)	-Degree of notoriety (40%)	110%	44%	86%
	-Conducting partnerships suppliers (30%)	80%	24	
	-CRM implementation (30%)	60%	18	
Profitability (20%)	-Return on investment (100%)	105%	105%	105%
Organizational performance	**0,2x0,9 + 0,1x1 + 0, 2x0,93 + 0,2x0,58 + 0,1x0,86 + 0,2x1,05**			**87,8%**

the values foreseen in the Portuguese Benchmarking index defined by the *Institute for the support of the small and medium enterprise and the investment* (IAPMEI);

- The remaining 30% of the evaluation should be associated with organizational performance, having as reference the predicted values and the deviations existing for the company.

As such, the awarding of prizes was based on the definition of tolerance intervals, in relation to the deviations occurring, taking as example the figure 17.

Finally, another substantial change that the company can implement in the short term in its internal structure, as a way of further accountability to the intermediate managers in relation to the organizational objectives: to transform the strategic business units into authentic conglomerates.

Figure 17. Example of tolerance intervals

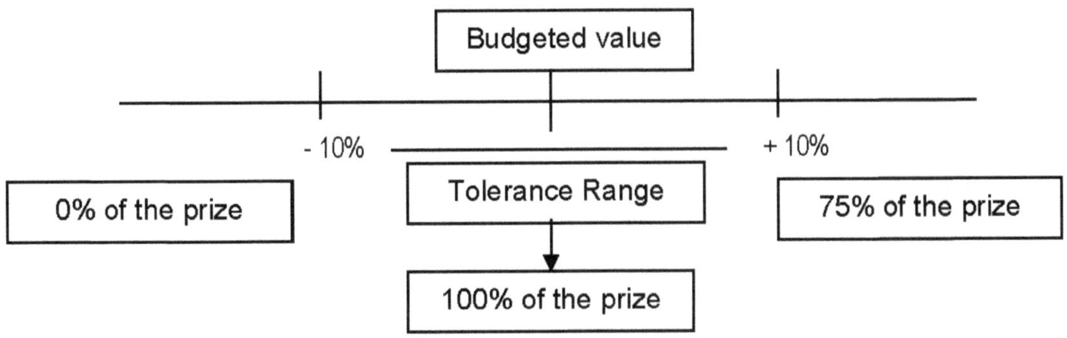

This decision will transform strategic business units into legal personality companies, whose social capital will be shared by "*Technological*" and its managers.

Thus, "*Technological*" would create a true strategic relations network among the different companies that would address different markets and industries with complementary competences, with greater autonomy degree in decisions' management for the entire activity, deciding whether to buy or sell to the old strategic and support business' units.

This transformation would oblige all previous units to become competitive in order to be sought by the other business partners, forcing managers to assume the risk of their decisions with "*Technological*", which would continue to have a central role in controlling and monitoring business, through its majority participation in the capital of each company.

Thus, "*Technological*" could eventually guarantee a greater degree of organizational adaptability. This would allow a continuous core business development, capable of creating sustainable competitive advantages over time. Simultaneously, "*Technological*" could better align the action of intermediate managers to the organizational objectives, sharing with them business risks and leading them to make decisions more according to corporate interests and not so much with the short-term results of units of which they are responsible for.

This represents great challenges for "*Technological*". Not only at competitive context level, where it should seek the most attractive international markets areas of action, but also at development and adaptation of its internal structure level, where it should be able to create the structure and business monitoring systems more adjusted to the creation of the competitive advantages and the business success of the group.

Analysis of the Instruments of Dialogue and Knowledge Management

In relation to the instruments of dialogue and knowledge management, as previously mentioned, instruments have been used to file and disseminate organizational knowledge, namely the Company Newsletter, a repository of projects made of free access and the realization of training organized by strategic business units on projects developed with enormous success.

However, in view of support units managers' dissatisfaction on the lack of evaluation of their activity, the greater effort should be in transforming these units into results centers and in distributing procedures and rules associated with the management control system' implementation (Teixeira & Teixeira, 2008).

This could be done through meetings where the assessment and transfer pricing criteria would be discussed, or through public presentations with managers and training on the procedures to be adopted at the necessary information level for operationalizing the system.

Besides, information sharing is vital to a company such as "*Technological*", which operates in a sector of activity consisting of products and services with reduced life, where innovations occur permanently.

In this sense, the organization of discussion forums for projects, among different units, as well as indicators' placement to monitoring information sharing by managers (for example, number of articles or case studies published in the company's newsletter) may be important to ensure greater fluidity of knowledge in the organization.

CONCLUSION

The evaluation of the financial performance showed that the first years of the internationalization process greatly increased the turnover and the size of the company.

However, developing countries have specific characteristics that increase business risks and, as such, the last years of the study show a big level of investment that decrease the profitability of the business and created some financial difficulties. That evolution was the result from the economic slowdown in the countries were the company developed the business (as was the case of Angola and Brazil), which had a negative impact on the average terms of receipt of international customers.

In this sense, several proposals were made for the application of payment techniques, such as documentary credit, forfaiting and factoring, to solve the cash problems that the business group has experienced in recent years.

Regarding foreign exchange risk, several alternatives were also proposed for the use of foreign exchange risk management techniques, taking into account the characteristics of foreign currency operations, the managers' level of knowledge on this issue and the conditions of the financial markets that company operates.

Finally, we examined the possibility of the company to internationalize into new countries with different economic cycles, in order to compensate possible financial difficulties in today's markets. The research showed that, within the countries that the company equates to internationalize, there are numerous opportunities, highlighting the markets of Algeria and Morocco.

In terms of management control systems, it was found that the company based its development on the implementation of instruments aimed to ensure greater decentralization of decision-making and a greater flexibility in responding to a constantly changing market. As a result, the company has managed to grow exponentially over time, internationalizing its activity and becoming a business group with dozen of business units and various business organizations.

However, growth required new challenges that were not always accompanied by the management control system implemented and as such, we identified a set of improvements that could be made on the instruments used up to the date of the work.

Among these improvements were the importance of the piloting instruments in adapting the accounting information system to create financial value per project, as well as the performance of each unit in each project carried out. In addition, an example of the application of the deviation's methodology was developed on turnover to demonstrate its contribution to the definition of the variables that influence more the financial differences in the activity.

It was also found that the implementation of the balanced scorecard and strategy maps could be very important for monitoring non-financial variables such as innovation, quality and the ability to share knowledge, which are critical success factors in a company operating in a constantly changing industry subject to global competition. At the same time, it was concluded that it was essential to implement a managers' performance evaluation system, which integrate the relevant business variables and integrate the local objectives of the strategic business units with the overall objectives of the organization. In this sense, a proposal was presented for the implementation of an integrated system for management evaluation.

With regard to the behavioral guidance instruments, it was found that at the level of alignment of the behavior of the operational managers, it was essential to transform the support units into profit centers, setting transfer prices of the internal services and allowing the assessment and establishment of incentives for all company managers. Such a measure is crucial to increase the degree of acceptance by all of the management control system implemented.

To this end, applying activity-based costing could make a strong contribution and two application examples of this methodology were presented to a strategic business unit and a business support unit. With the presented examples, several advantages inherent to the application of ABC were highlighted, namely:

- Observing how resources are used, allowing managers to verify the activities with the highest associated investment volume;
- Identification of the unit costs of the activities developed, making it easier, planning and decision-making by virtue of giving the possibility of knowing in advance the profitability associated with each type of project to be executed;
- Minimization of cost sharing through imputation bases, since it allows assigning indirect costs to segments considering the respective use of each activity. And because management decisions are reflected in activities, ABC allows both to evaluate and act on those decisions;
- Increase confidence in the management control system because managers understand better the values of internal services charged to each accountability center;
- Greater motivation of managers in the decision-making process of internal transfer prices because, through ABC is visible the unit cost of services to provide, making it easier to negotiate between different accountability centers;
- Greater organizational cohesion, due to the involvement of everyone in process efficiency, because the identification of the cost drivers of the various activities facilitates decision making about work processes and techniques.

Finally, at the level of the dialogue instruments, it was found that it was important to have greater dissemination of the rules and procedures of the management control system, as well as the implementation of events (e.g. discussion and sharing forums) to ensure greater dissemination of knowledge and, consequently, greater responsiveness to challenges posed by the market and business partners.

With regard to future challenges, we consider quite important to study on the impact of the possibility to transform the business units into conglomerates, with greater autonomy of decisions and a greater involvement of the managers in the risk. Such a decision may create greater organizational responsiveness to the market and greater alignment of managers with the organization's objectives. However, it will also bring new challenges to the organizational structure and management control systems that should be properly studied.

REFERENCES

Anthony, R., & Govindarajan, V. (2007). Management Control Systems (12th ed.). New York: McGraw-Hill.

Brimson, J., & Antos, J. (1994). *Activity – Based Management – for Service Industries, Government Entities and Nonprofit Organizations*. John Wiley & Sons, Inc.

Eitman, D. K., Stonehill, A. I., & Moffett, M. H. (2005). *International Financial Management* (9th ed.; V. Pezerico, Trans.). New York: Bookman.

Jordan, H., Neves, J., & Rodrigues, J. (2011). *O Controlo de Gestão - Ao Serviço da Estratégia e dos Gestores* (10th ed.). Lisboa: Áreas Editora.

Markowitz, H. (1952). Portfolio Selection. *The Journal of Finance, 7*(1), 77–91.

Neves, J. C. (2011). *Avaliação e Gestão da Performance Estratégica da Empresa (2nd ed.).* Lisboa: Texto Editora.

Porfírio, J. (2001). *Finanças Internacionais.* Lisboa: Universidade Aberta.

Teixeira, A., Teixeira, N., & Mata, C. (2008). *Implementação do Tableau de Bord – Estudo de caso no sector das Rochas Ornamentais.* IV Congresso de Custos do Mercosul – Montevideu.

Teixeira, N. (2008). *A rendibilidade e a criação de valor.* Aveiro: XIII Encontro AECA.

Teixeira, N., & Amaro, A. (2013). Avaliação do desempenho financeiro e da criação de valor - um estudo de caso. *Revista Universo Contábil, 6*(4), 157–178. doi:10.4270/ruc.2013436

Teixeira, N., & Jorge, N. (2016). *Avaliação do Desempenho Financeiro e criação de valor – uma visão integrada: estudo caso.* Setúbal: *I Congresso de Contabilidade Pública.*

Teixeira, N., Mata, C., Pardal, P., & Teixeira, A. (2013). A aplicação da rendibilidade supranormal para a avaliação da criação de valor. *Jornadas Hispano Lusas de Gestão Cientifica, 23.*

Teixeira, N., Pardal, P., & Rafael, B. (2017). Internationalization, Financial Performance and Organizational Challenges. In *Handbook of Research on Entrepreneurial Ecosystems and Social Dynamics in a Globalized World, EUA*. IGI Global.

Teixeira, N. & Teixeira, A. (2008). *Preços de transferência interna e a avaliação do desempenho de centros de responsabilidade.* XVIII Jornadas Luso –Espanholas de Gestão, Porto, Portugal.

Compilation of References

Abor, J. (2005). Managing foreign exchange risk among Ghanaian firms. Academic Press.

AICEP - Agência para o Investimento e Comércio Externo de Portugal. (2010). Retrieved August 31, 2018, from http://www.portugalglobal.pt/PT/Internacionalizar/Paginas/bemvindos_internacionalizar.aspx

AICEP - Agência para o Investimento e Comércio Externo de Portugal. (2015). *Portugal Global Angola – Ficha de Mercado.* Retrieved August 31, 2018, from http://www.portugalglobal.pt/PT/Biblioteca/Paginas/Detalhe.aspx?documentId=c394b4f8-db0b-4d6a-b38c-95ed9a940b5d

Alajaasko, P. (2006). *The demand for services: external but local provision.* EUROSTAT.

Almeida, J. (2001, Apr.). *Os Instrumentos de Gestão Previsional e a sua Auditoria: O Caso Português. OROC – Revisores & Empresas.*

Al-Obaidan, A., & Scully, G. (1995). The theory and measurement of the net benefits of internationalization: The case of the international petroleum industry. *Applied Economics*, *27*(2), 231–239. doi:10.1080/00036849500000029

Alonso, J., & Donoso, V. (1998). *Competir en el exterior. La empresa Española y los mercados internacionales*. Madrid: Edições Icex.

Alves, M., Teixeira, N., & Rita, R. (2006). *Foreign exchange risk: Management and disclosure of information. The case of PSI20 companies.* Paper presented at XII Encontro AECA, Córdoba.

Alves, M., Teixeira, N., & Rita, R. (2007). *A gestão do risco cambial, as fontes de risco e as técnicas de pagamento: um estudo de caso*. Paper presented at XXI Congresso Anual AEDEM, Universidad Rey Juan Carlos, Madrid, Spain.

Amaral, P., & Pedro, J. (2004). *O Capital Conhecimento – Modelos de Avaliação de activos intangíveis*. Lisboa: Universidade Católica Editora.

Andersen, O. (1992). On the internationalization process of firms: A critical analysis. *Journal of International Business Studies*, *24*(2), 209–231. doi:10.1057/palgrave.jibs.8490230

Andersson, S., Evers, N., & Griot, C. (2013). Local and international networks in small firm internationalization: Cases from the Rhône–Alpes medical technology regional cluster. *Entrepreneurship and Regional Development*, *25*(9/10), 867–888. doi:10.1080/08985626.2013.847975

Anthony, R., & Govindarajan, V. (2007). Management Control Systems (12th ed.). New York: McGraw-Hill.

Archibugi, D., Ceccagnoli, M., & Palma, D. (1996). *Innovazione e internazionalizzazione nel modello competitivo italiano. Cuaderni di Politica Industriale, 8.*

Argyris, C. (1952). *The impact of budgets on people.* Nre York: Controllership Foundation.

Arias, C., Martinez, A., & Gracia, J. (2000). Enfoques Emergentes en Torno en la Estrucutura de Capital: El caso de la Pyme. VIII Foro de Finanzas, Madrid: Asociación Española de Finanzas (AEFIN).

Azzone, G., Masella, C., & Bertelé, U. (1991). Design of performance measures for time-based companies. *International Journal of Operations & Production Management, 11*(3), 77–85. doi:10.1108/01443579110143412

BACH. (2019). *Statistics from NACE code 62.* European Central Bank. Retrieved from https://www.bach.banque-france.fr/?lang=en

Banker, R., Charnes, A., & Cooper, W. (1984). Some models for estimating technical and scale inefficiencies in data envelopment analysis. *Management Science, 30*(9), 1078–1092. doi:10.1287/mnsc.30.9.1078

Barkema, H., & Vermeulen, F. (1998). International expansion through start-up or acquisition: A learning perspective. *Academy of Management Journal, 41*(1), 7–26.

Bartol, K. & Martin, D. (1998). *Management* (3rd ed.). McGraw-Hill.

Basso, L., & Lima, A. (2002). *Análise de Processos de Gestão Voltados à Criação de valor para o Accionista – Um Estudo de Caso do GVA- FGV/SP. In 3º Encontro Ibero-Americano de Finanças e Sistemas de Informação – A Empresa do Século XXI.* Setúbal: ESCE.

Baum, M., Schwens, C., & Kabst, R. (2015). A latent class analysis of small firms' internationalization patterns. *Journal of World Business, 50*(4), 754–768. doi:10.1016/j.jwb.2015.03.001

Bausch, A., & Krist, M. (2007). The effect of context related moderators on the internationalization performance relationship: Evidence from meta analysis. *Management International Review, 47*(3), 319–347. doi:10.100711575-007-0019-z

BCP - MILLENNIUM BCP. (2015). Retrieved September 4, 2015 from http://corp.millenniumbcp.pt/pt/public/solucoesfinanceiras/riscofinanceiro/riscodetaxadejuro/Pages/OpcoesDeTaxaDeJuro.aspx

Belkaoui, A. (1998). The effects of the degree of internationalization on firm performance. *International Business Review, 7*(3), 315–322. doi:10.1016/S0969-5931(98)00013-4

Beugelsdijk, S., Kostova, T., Kunst, V. E., Spadafora, E., & van Essen, M. (2018). Cultural Distance and Firm Internationalization: A Meta-Analytical Review and Theoretical Implications. *Journal of Management, 44*(1), 89–130. doi:10.1177/0149206317729027 PMID:30443095

Bilkey, W., & Tesar, G. (1977). The export behavior of smaller Wisconsin manufacturing firms. *Journal of International Business Studies, 9*(1), 93-98.

Black, F., & Scholes, M. (1973). The pricing of options and corporate liabilities. *Journal of Political Economy, 81*(3), 637–654. doi:10.1086/260062

Boczko, A. (2005, Mar.). International Payment Risk. *Financial Management*, 35–37.

Boitani, A., & Ciciotti, E. (1992). *Innovazionne e competitivitá nell'industria italiana.* Bologna: Il Mulino.

Bolt, W., & Chakravorti, S. (2010). *Digitization of retail payments.* Working Paper, The Nederlandsche Bank.

BPI – Banco Português do Investimento. (2018). Retrieved August 4, 2018, from http://www.bancobpi.pt/empresas/internacional/solucoes-trade-finance/cheques-emitidos-sobre-o-estrangeiro

Braunerhjelm, P. (1996). The relation between firm-specific intangibles and export. *Economics Letters, 53*(2), 213–219. doi:10.1016/S0165-1765(96)00898-1

Brewer, H. (1981). Investor benefits from corporate international diversification. *Journal of Financial and Quantitative Analysis, 16*(1), 113–124. doi:10.2307/2330669

Brigs, P. (1998). *Principles of International Trade and Payments*. Oxford, UK: Blackwell Publishers.

Brimson, J., & Antos, J. (1994). *Activity – Based Management – for Service Industries, Government Entities and Non-profit Organizations*. John Willey & Sons, Inc.

Brown, M. (1996). *Keeping score: using the right metrics to drive world class performance*. New York: Quality Resources.

Bruneel, J., & De Cock, R. (2016). Entry Mode Research and SMEs: A Review and Future Research Agenda. *Journal of Small Business Management, 54*(S1), 135–167. doi:10.1111/jsbm.12291

Buckley, P., & Casson, M. (1998). Analyzing foreign market entry strategies: Extending the internalization approach. *Journal of International Business Studies, 29*(3), 539–562. doi:10.1057/palgrave.jibs.8490006

Buckley, P., Dunning, J., & Pearce, R. (1977). The influence of firm size, industry, nationality and degree of multinationality in the growth and profitability of the world's largest firms. *Weltwirtschaftliches Archiv, 114*(2), 243–257. doi:10.1007/BF02696473

Bueno, E. (2000). *De la sociedade de la Information a la del conocimiento y el aprendizaje*. Especial IX Encuentro AECA – Gestion de la Información en la Sociedade del Conocimiento y la Globalización.

Cadogan, J., Kuivalainen, O., & Sundqvist, S. (2009). Export market-oriented behaviour and export performance: Quadratic and moderating effects under differing degrees of market dynamism and internationalization. *Journal of International Marketing, 17*(4), 71–89. doi:10.1509/jimk.17.4.71

Caiado, A. (2002). *Contabilidade de Gestão* (2nd ed.). Áreas Editora.

Campbell, T., & Kracaw, W. (1993). *Financial risk management: fixed income and foreign exchange*. New York: HarperCollins Publishers.

Caves, R. (1996). *Multinational Enterprise and Economic Analysis* (2nd ed.). New York: Cambridge University Press.

Caves, R., & Mehra, S. (1986). Entry of foreign multinationals into U.S. manufacturing industries. In M. Porter (Ed.), *Competition in Global Industries* (pp. 449–481). Boston: Harvard Business School Press.

Cavusgil, T. (1980). On internationalization process of firms. *European Research, 8*(November), 273–281.

Chandler, A. (1977). *The visible hand – Managerial revolution in American business*. Boston: Harvard University Press.

Chang, Y., & Thomas, H. (1989). The impact of diversification strategy on risk-return performance. *Strategic Management Journal, 10*(3), 271–284. doi:10.1002mj.4250100306

Charnes, A., Cooper, W., & Rhodes, E. (1978). Measuring efficiency of decision-making units. *European Journal of Operational Research, 2*(6), 429–444. doi:10.1016/0377-2217(78)90138-8

Chase, R., & Aquilano, N. (1997). Gestão da Produção e das Operações – Perspectiva do Ciclo de Vida. *Monitor (Charlottetown)*.

Chiao, Y., Yang, K., & Yu, J. (2006). Performance, internationalization and firm specific advantages of SME's in a newly industrialized economy. *Small Business Economics, 26*(5), 475–492. doi:10.100711187-005-5604-6

Chiao, Y., Yu, J., Li, P., & Chen, Y. (2008). Subsidiary size, internationalization, product diversification and performance in an emerging market. *International Marketing Review, 25*(6), 612–633. doi:10.1108/02651330810915556

Chiavenato, I. (1993). *Introdução à teoria geral da administração* (4th ed.). São Paulo: Makron Books do Brasil.

Cho, K., & Padmanabhan, P. (1995). Acquisition versus new venture: The choice of foreign establishment mode by Japanese firms. *Journal of International Management, 1*(3), 255–285.

Collins, J. (1990). A market performance comparison of US firms active in domestic, developed and developing countries. *Journal of International Business Studies, 21*(2), 271–287. doi:10.1057/palgrave.jibs.8490335

Collis, D., & Montgomery, C. (1997). *Corporate Strategy – Resources and the Scope of the Firm.* McGraw-Hill.

Cornell, B., & Shapiro, B. C. (1983). Managing foreign exchange risks. *Midland Corporate Finance Journal*, 16-31.

Czinkota, M. (1982). *Export development strategies: US promotion policies.* New York: Praeger Publishers.

Czinkota, M., & Wongtada, N. (1997). The effect of export promotion on US trade performance: An analysis of industry internationalization. *The International Trade Journal, 11*(1), 5–37. doi:10.1080/08853909708523871

Damodaran, A. (2007). *Return on Capital (ROC), Return on Invested Capital (ROIC) and Return on Equity (ROE): Measurement and implications.* SSRN Electronic Journal.

Daniels, J., & Bracker, J. (1989). Profit performance: Do foreign operations make a difference? *Management International Review, 29*(1), 46–56.

Daniels, J., & Radebaugh, L. (1986). *International Business: Environments and Operations* (4th ed.). Reading, MA: Addison-Wesley Longman, Inc.

Dhanani, A. (2004). The Management of Foreign Exchange-Rate Risk: A Case from the Manufacturing Industry. *Thunderbird International Business Review, 46*(3), 317–338. doi:10.1002/tie.20011

Donnelly, J., Gibson, J., & Ivancevich, J. (2000). *Administração – Princípios de gestão empresarial* (10th ed.). McGra-Hill.

Dosi, G., Pavitt, K., & Soete, L. (1990). *The economic of technical change and international trade.* New York: Harvester.

Dragun, D. (2003). *Challenging the rhetoric: internationalization, size and financial performance.* European Retail Digest.

Drucker, P. (2001, Nov.). The Next Society – A survey of the near future. *The Economist.*

Drucker, P. (1954). *The practice of management.* New York: Harper.

Drucker, P. (1967). *The effective executive.* New York: Harper & Row.

Dunning, J. (1988). The eclectic paradigm of international production: A restatement and some possible extensions. *Journal of International Business Studies, 19*(1), 1–32. doi:10.1057/palgrave.jibs.8490372

Edvinsson, L., & Malone, M. (1997). *Intellectual Capital: Realizing your Company's true value by finding its hidden roots.* New York: Harper Business.

Ehrhardt, M. C., & Bringham, E. F. (2011). *Financial management: Theory and practice* (13th ed.). South-Western Cengage Learning.

Eiglier, P., & Langeard, E. (1999). *Servuction – A Gestão Marketing de Empresas de Serviços.* Lisboa: McGrawhill.

Eitman, D. K., Stonehill, A. I., & Moffett, M. H. (2005). *International Financial Management* (9th ed.; V. Pezerico, Trans.). New York: Bookman.

Elango, B. (2006). An empirical analysis of the internationalization performance relationship across emerging market firms. *Multinational Business Review, 14*(1), 21–44. doi:10.1108/1525383X200600002

Elango, B., & Sethi, P. (2007). An exploration of the relationship between country of origin and the internationalization performance paradigm. *Management International Review*, *47*(3), 369–392. doi:10.100711575-007-0021-5

Epstein, M., & Manzoni, J. (1998). Implementing Corporate Strategy: From Tableaux de Bord to Balanced Scorecards. *European Management Journal*, *16*(2).

Errunza, V., & Senbet, L. (1981). The effect of international operations on the market value of the firm: Theory and evidence. *The Journal of Finance*, *36*(2), 401–417. doi:10.1111/j.1540-6261.1981.tb00455.x

Esperança, J., & Matias, F. (2009). *Finanças Empresariais* (2nd ed.). Texto Editora, Alfragide.

Eusébio, R., & Rialp, A. (2002). *Innovación tecnológica y resultado exportador: un análisis empírico aplicado al sector têxtil-confección Español.* Working paper nº4, Departamento da Economia da Empresa, Universidade Autónoma de Barcelona.

Fagerberg, J. (1988). International competitiveness. *Economic Journal (London)*, *98*(June), 355–374. doi:10.2307/2233372

Felizardo, A., Félix, E., & Thomaz, J. (2017). *Organizational Performance Measurement and Evaluation Systems in SMES: The Case of The Transforming Industry in Portugal.* CEFAGE Working Paper 2017/05.

Fernandes, L., Pereira, C., Simões, D., & Moreira, A. (2019). Challenges of the Internationalization Strategy of a Technology-Based International New Venture. In N. Teixeira, T. Costa, & I. Lisboa (Eds.), *Handbook of Research on Entrepreneurship, Innovation and Internationalization* (pp. 419–438). Hershey, PA: IGI Global. doi:10.4018/978-1-5225-8479-7.ch018

Ferreira, D. (2008a). *Swaps and Credit Derivatives – Win (and lose) in the OTC markets*. Lisbon: Silabo Editions.

Ferreira, D. (2008b). *Futures and other derivatives*. Lisbon: Silabo Editions.

Filipescu, D., Rialp, A., & Rialp, J. (2009). Internationalisation and technological innovation: empirical evidence on their mutual relationship. Advances in International Marketing, 20, 125-154. doi:10.1108/S1474-7979(2009)0000020008

Filipescu, D. (2006). *Innovation and internationalization. A focus on exporting firms. Paper presented in IV Jornadas Business Economics*. Autonomous University of Barcelona.

Fitzgerald, L., Johnston, R., Brignall, S., Silvestro, R., & Voss, C. (1991). *Performance measurement in service business*. London: CIMA.

Freire, A. (1998). *Estratégia – Sucesso em Portugal*. Lisboa: Verbo.

Freire, A. (2000). *Inovação – Novos Produtos, Serviços e Negócios para Portugal*. Lisboa: Verbo.

Furtado, J., Pereira, A., Pereira, I., & Moreira, A. (2019). Does Theory fit real Life Situations? A Case Study on the Internationalization Process of a Technological Service-Based Firm. In N. Teixeira, T. Costa, & I. Lisboa (Eds.), *Handbook of Research on Entrepreneurship, Innovation and Internationalization* (pp. 419–438). Hershey, PA: IGI Global. doi:10.4018/978-1-5225-8479-7.ch016

Geringer, J., Beamish, P., & DaCosta, R. (1989). Diversification strategy and internationalization: Implications for MNE performance. *Strategic Management Journal*, *10*(2), 109–119. doi:10.1002mj.4250100202

Gerpott, T., & Jakopin, N. (2005). The degree of internationalization and the financial performance of European mobile network operators. *Telecommunications Policy*, *29*(8), 635–661. doi:10.1016/j.telpol.2005.06.003

Gogoski, R. (2012). Payment Systems in Economy - Present End Future Tendencies. *Procedia: Social and Behavioral Sciences*, *44*, 436–445. doi:10.1016/j.sbspro.2012.05.048

Gomes, L., & Ramaswamy, K. (1999). An empirical examination of the formo f the relationship between multinationality and performance. *Journal of International Business Studies*, *30*(1), 173–188. doi:10.1057/palgrave.jibs.8490065

Grant, R. (1987). Multinationality and performance among British manufacturing companies. *Journal of International Studies*, *18*(1), 79–89.

Grant, R., Jammine, A., & Thomas, H. (1988). Diversity, diversification and profitability among British manufacturing companies, 1972-1984. *Academy of Management Journal*, *31*(4), 771–801.

Greiner, L. (1972). *Evolution and revolution as organizations grow*. Harvard Business Review, July – August.

Gupta, V., & Perepu, I. (2007). *McKinsey's Knowledge Management Practices*. IBS Center for Management Research.

Håkansson, H. (1982). *International Marketing and Purchasing of Industrial Goods: An Interaction Approach*. Chichester: Wiley.

Håkansson, H., & Johanson, J. (1984). Heterogeneity in industrial markets and its implications for marketing. In I. Hagg & F. Wiedersheim-Paul (Eds.), *Between market and hierarchy*. Uppsala: Department of Business Studies.

Harrigan, K. (1988). Joint ventures and competitive strategy. *Strategic Management Journal*, *9*(2), 141–158. doi:10.1002mj.4250090205

Harzing, A. (2002). Acquisitions versus greenfield investments: International strategy and management of entry modes. *Strategic Management Journal*, *23*(3), 211–227. doi:10.1002mj.218

Hennart, J., Larimo, J., & Chen, S. (1996). *Does National Origin Affect the Propensity of Foreign Investors to Enter the United States through Acquisitions?* Discussion paper no. 189. University of Vaasa.

Hennart, J. (1982). *A Theory of Multinational Enterprise*. Ann Arbor, MI: University of Michigan Press.

Hennart, J. (2000). Transaction costs theory and the multinational enterprise. In C. Pitelis & R. Sugden (Eds.), *The Nature of the Transnational Firm* (2nd ed.). London: Routledge.

Hennart, J.-F. (2014). The Accidental Internationalists: A Theory of Born Globals. *Entrepreneurship Theory and Practice*, *38*(1), 117–135. doi:10.1111/etap.12076

Hennart, J., & Park, Y. (1993). Greenfield vs. acquisition: The strategy of Japanese investors in the United States. *Management Science*, *39*(9), 1054–1070. doi:10.1287/mnsc.39.9.1054

Hirsch, S., & Bijaoui, I. (1985). R&D intensity and export performance: A micro view. *Weltwirtschaftliches Archiv*, *121*(2), 138–251. doi:10.1007/BF02705822

Hislop, D. (2013). *Knowledge Management in Organizations: A Critical Introduction*. OUP.

Hitt, M., Hoskinsson, R., & Ireland, R. (1994). A mid range theory of the interactive effects of international and product diversification on innovation and performance. *Journal of Management*, *20*(2), 297–327. doi:10.1177/014920639402000203

Hofstede, G. (2001). *Culture's Consequences: Comparing Values, Behaviors, Institutions, and Organizations Across Nations* (2nd ed.). Thousand Oaks, CA: Sage Publications.

Hsu, C. (2005). Internationalization and performance: The S curve hypothesis and product diversity effect. *Multinational Business Review*, *14*(2), 29–46. doi:10.1108/1525383X200600007

Hsu, C., & Boggs, D. (2003). Internationalization and performance: Traditional measures and their decomposition. *Multinational Business Review*, *11*(3), 23–49. doi:10.1108/1525383X200300015

Hsu, C., & Pereira, A. (2008). Internationalization and performance: The moderating effects of organizational learning. *Omega*, *36*(2), 188–205. doi:10.1016/j.omega.2006.06.004

Huber, G. (1991). Organizational learning: The contributing processes and literatures. *Organization Science*, *2*(special issue), 88–115. doi:10.1287/orsc.2.1.88

IAPMEI. (2011). *Business Assistance - SME Academy*. Retrieved from http://www.iapmei.pt/iapmei-art-03.php?id=2498

IDC. (2019). *ICT forecasts*. Retrieved from https://www.idc.com/promo/global-ict-spending/forecast

INE. (2019). *Estatísticas do código de atividade 62*. Retrieved from https://www.ine.pt/xportal/xmain?xpgid=ine_tema&xpid=INE&tema_cod=1313

Insee - Institut national de la statistique et des études économiques. (2019*). IT statistiques*. Retrieved from https://insee.fr/fr/accueil

IQF. (2005). *O Sector dos Serviços de Informação e Comunicação. Estudos Sectoriais*. IQF.

IT Market Statistics and Trends. (2016), retrieved from https://www.ironpaper.com/webintel/articles/it-market-statistics-and-trends/

Ito, K., & Pucik, V. (1993). R&D spending, domestic competition and export performance of Japanese manufacturing firms. *Strategic Management Journal*, *14*(1), 61–75. doi:10.1002mj.4250140107

Johanson, J., & Vahlne, J. (1977). The internationalization process of the firm – a model of knowledge development and increasing foreign market commitments. *Journal of International Business Studies, 8*(1), 23-32.

Johanson, J., & Vahlne, J. (2003). Business relationship learning and commitment in the internationalization process. *Journal of International Entrepreneurship*, *1*(1), 83–101. doi:10.1023/A:1023219207042

Johanson, J., & Wiedersheim-Paul, F. (1975). The internationalization of the firm – four Swedish cases. *Journal of Management Studies*, *12*(3), 305–322. doi:10.1111/j.1467-6486.1975.tb00514.x

Jordan, H., Neves, J., & Rodrigues, J. (2011). *O Controlo de Gestão - Ao Serviço da Estratégia e dos Gestores* (10th ed.). Lisboa: Áreas Editora.

Kafouros, M., Buckley, P., Sharp, J., & Wang, C. (2008). The role of internationalization in explaining innovation performance. *Technovation*, *28*(1-2), 63–74. doi:10.1016/j.technovation.2007.07.009

Kaplan, R., & Norton, D. (1992, Jan.). The balanced scorecard – measures that drive performance. *Harvard Business Review*, 71–79. PMID:10119714

Kaplan, R., & Norton, D. (1993, Sept.). Putting the balanced scorecard to work. *Harvard Business Review*, 134–147.

Kaplan, R., & Norton, D. (1996a, Jan.). Using the balanced scorecard as a strategic management system. *Harvard Business Review*, 75–85.

Kaplan, R., & Norton, D. (1996b). Linking the balanced scorecard to strategy. *California Management Review*, *39*(1), 53–79. doi:10.2307/41165876

Kaplan, R., & Norton, D. (2001a). Transforming the balanced scorecard from performance measurement to strategic management: Part I. *American Accounting Association*, *15*(1), 87–104.

Kaplan, R., & Norton, D. (2001b). Transforming the balanced scorecard from performance measurement to strategic management: Part II. *American Accounting Association*, *15*(2), 147–160.

Kaplan, R., & Norton, D. (2004). *Mapas Estratégicos* (6th ed.). Rio de Janeiro: Editora Campos.

Keegan, D., Eiler, R., & Jones, C. (1989). Are your performance measures obsolete? *Management Accounting*, *70*(12), 45–50.

Kiederich, A., & Kraus, S. (2009). Investigating new technology-based firm internationalization: The impact on performance, the process and the antecedents. *International Journal of Business Research*, *9*(2), 1–12.

Kim, W., & Lyn, E. (1987). Reverse investments in US manufacturing industries. *Journal of International Business Studies*, *18*(2), 53–67. doi:10.1057/palgrave.jibs.8490406

Kluge, J., Stein, W. & Licht, T. (2002), *Gestão do Conhecimento – Segundo um estudo da McKinsey & Company*. São João do Estoril: Principia.

Kluge, J., Stein, W. & Licht, T. (2002). *Gestão do Conhecimento – Segundo um estudo da McKinsey & Company*. São João do Estoril: Principia.

Knight, G. A., & Liesch, P. W. (2016). Internationalization: From incremental to born global. *Journal of World Business*, *51*(1), 93–102. doi:10.1016/j.jwb.2015.08.011

Knight, G., & Cavusgil, T. (2004). Innovation, organizational capabilities and the born global firms. *Journal of International Business Studies*, *35*(2), 124–141. doi:10.1057/palgrave.jibs.8400071

Kostova, T., & Zaheer, S. (1999). Organizational legitimacy under conditions of complexity: The case of the multinational enterprise. *Academy of Management Review*, *24*(1), 64–81. doi:10.5465/amr.1999.1580441

Kuivalainen, O., & Sundqvist, S. (2006). Profitability of rapid internationalization: The relationship between internationalization intensity and firms export performance. *Journal of Euromarketing*, *16*(1-2), 59–69. doi:10.1300/J037v16n01_05

Kuivalainen, O., Sundqvist, S., Saarenketo, S., & McNaughton, R. (2012). Internationalization patterns of small and medium-sized enterprises. *International Marketing Review*, *29*(5), 448–465. doi:10.1108/02651331211260331

Kumar, M. (1984). *Growth, acquisition and investment: an analysis of the growth of industrial firms and their overseas activities*. Cambridge University Press.

Kumar, N., & Siddhartan, N. (1994). Technology, firm size and export behavior in developing countries: The case of Indian enterprises. *The Journal of Development Studies*, *32*(2), 288–309.

Kumar, V., & Singh, N. (2008). Internationalization and performance of Indian pharmaceutical firms. *International Business Review*, *50*(5), 321–330.

Lambin, J. (2000). *Marketing Estratégico*. Lisboa: MacGraw-Hill.

Larimo, J. (2003). Form of investment by Nordic firms in world markets. *Journal of Business Research*, *56*(10), 791–803. doi:10.1016/S0148-2963(02)00467-8

Laudon, K., & Laudon, J. (2002). *Management Information Systems* (7th ed.). Prentice-Hall, Inc.

Lavie, D., & Miller, S. (2008). Alliance portfolio internationalization and firm performance. *Organization Science*, *19*(4), 623–646. doi:10.1287/orsc.1070.0341

Lefebvre, E., Lefebvre, L., & Bourgault, M. (1998). R&D related capabilities as determinants of export performance. *Small Business Economics*, *10*(4), 365–377. doi:10.1023/A:1007960431147

Lourenço, I. (2001). *A informação Financeira por Segmentos*. ISCTE.

Lu, J., & Beamish, P. (2001). The internationalization and performance of SME's. *Strategic Management Journal*, *22*(6-7), 565–586. doi:10.1002mj.184

Lu, J., & Beamish, P. (2006). SME internationalization and performance: Growth vs profitability. *Journal of International Entrepreneurship*, *4*(1), 27–48. doi:10.100710843-006-8000-7

Lynch, R., & Cross, K. (1991). *Measure up – the essential guide to measuring business performance*. London: Mandarin.

March, J. (1991). Exploration and exploitation in organizational learning. *Organization Science*, *2*(special issue), 71–87. doi:10.1287/orsc.2.1.71

Markowitz, H. (1952). Portfolio Selection. *The Journal of Finance*, *7*(1), 77–91.

Martinez, J. (2006). Do industrial districts influence export performance and export intensity? Evidence for Spanish SME's internationalization process. *European Planning Studies*, *14*(6), 791–810. doi:10.1080/09654310500496115

Martin, O., & Papadopoulos, N. (2006). Internationalization and performance: Evidence from Spanish firms. *Journal of Euromarketing*, *16*(1-2), 87–103. doi:10.1300/J037v16n01_07

Matos, J. (1992). *Finanças Internacionais*. Lisboa: Editorial Presença.

Meliciani, V., & Pianta, M. (1995). Specializzazione tecnologica e crescita economica nei paesi OCSE. *Rivista Internazionale di Scienze Economiche e Commerciali*, *42*(7-8), 565–588.

Melle, M., & Raymond, J. (2001). *Competitividad internacional de las pymes industriales Españolas*. Paper presented at XI Congreso de ACEDE, Zaragoza, Spain.

Meneses, A. (2003). *Posicionamento Estratégico: Criar Valor para vencer no Mercado de Tecnologias de Informação*. Lisboa: INSAT.

Merino, F., & Moreno, L. (1996). Actividad comercial en el exterior de las empresas manufactureras españolas y estrategias de diferenciación de producto. *Papeles de Economia Española*, *66*, 107–123.

Meyer, K., & Estrin, S. (1997). Privatisation acquisition and direct foreign investment: Who buys state-owned enterprises? MOCT-MOST. *Economic Policy in Transitional Economies*, *7*(1), 159–172.

Michel, A., & Shaked, I. (1986). Multinational corporations vs domestic corporation: Financial performance and characteristics. *Journal of International Business Studies*, *17*(3), 89–101. doi:10.1057/palgrave.jibs.8490435

Mintzberg, H. (1979). *The Structuring of Organizations*. Prentice-Hall.

Montepio. (2014). Retrieved from www.montepio.pt/SitePublico/pt_PT/empresas/negociointernacional/tradefinance/creditos-documentarios

Morck, R., & Yeung, B. (1991). Why investors value multinationality. *The Journal of Business*, *64*(20), 165–187. doi:10.1086/296532

Moreira, J. (1997). *Análise de empresas – da teoria à prática*. Porto: Associação da Bolsa de Derivados do Porto.

Moreno, C. (1993). *Cambio Tecnológico y Contabilidad de Gestion*. Ministerio de Hacienda y Administraciones Públicas-Secretaría General Técnica- SGIDP.

Mota, A. G. & Custódio, C. (2006). *The company's finances*. Wall: Booknomics.

Murteira, M. (1997). *Economia do Mercado Global – Ensaio sobre condicionantes Mega e Macro das Estratégias Empresariais*. Editorial Presença.

Murteira, M. (2002). *A Economia em 24 Lições (4th ed.)*. Editorial Presença.

Neely, A., & Adams, C. (2001). *Perspectives on performance: the performance prism.* Cranfield School of Management. Retrieved from www.crandield.ac.co.uk/som/cbp

Neely, A. (2005). The evolution of performance measurement research – developments in the last decade and a research agenda for the next. *International Journal of Operations & Production Management*, *25*(12), 1264–1277. doi:10.1108/01443570510633648

Neely, A., Gregory, M., & Platts, K. (2005). Performance measurement system design A literature review and research agenda. *International Journal of Operations & Production Management*, *25*(12).

Neely, A., Mills, J., Platts, K., Richards, H., Gregory, M., Bourne, M., & Kennerley, M. (2000). Performance measurement system design: Developing and testing a process-based approach. *International Journal of Operations & Production Management*, *20*(10), 1119–1145. doi:10.1108/01443570010343708

Neves, J. (2011). *Avaliação e Gestão da Performance Estratégica da Empresa.* Academic Press.

Neves, J. (2002). *Avaliação de Empresas e Negócios.* Lisboa: McGrawhill.

Neves, J. (2012). *Análise e Relato Financeiro – Uma visão integrada de gestão (5th ed.).* Lisboa: Texto Editora.

Neves, J. C. (2011). *Avaliação e Gestão da Performance Estratégica da Empresa (2nd ed.).* Lisboa: Texto Editora.

Nordhaus, W. (2002). Productivity Growth and the New Economy. *Brookings Papers on Economic Activity*, *2002*(2), 211–244. doi:10.1353/eca.2003.0006

Nunes, J., & Cavique, L. (2001). *Plano de marketing – estratégia em ação.* Lisboa: Dom Quixote.

O'Farrell, P., Hitchens, D., & Moffat, L. (1993). The competitiveness of business services and regional development: Evidence from Scotland and the South East of England. *Urban Studies (Edinburgh, Scotland)*, *30*(10), 1629–1652. doi:10.1080/00420989320081631

Olejnik, E., & Swoboda, B. (2012). SMEs' internationalisation patterns: Descriptives, dynamics and determinants. *International Marketing Review*, *29*(5), 466–495. doi:10.1108/02651331211260340

Olve, N., Roy, J., & Wetter, M. (1999). *Performance Drivers: a practical guide to using the balanced scorecard.* Chichester, UK: Wiley.

Pangarkar, N. (2008). Internationalization and performance of SME's enterprises. *Journal of World Business*, *43*(4), 475–485. doi:10.1016/j.jwb.2007.11.009

Pennings, J., Barkema, H., & Douma, S. (1994). Organizational learning and diversification. *Academy of Management Journal*, *37*, 608–640.

Peters, T., & Waterman, B. (1995). *Na Senda da Excelência* (3rd ed.). Publicações Dom Quixote.

Peynot, D. (1987). *Gestion financière internationale des entreprises.* Paris: Montchrestien.

Pinho, C., Valente, R., Madaleno, M., & Vieira, E. (2011). *Financial risk: measurement and management.* London: Walker Editions, Ltd.

Porfírio, J. (2003). *International finance.* Lisbon: King of the Books.

Porter, M. (1980). *Competitive Strategy.* New York: Free Press.

Porter, M. (1985). *Competitive advantage*. New York: Free Press.

Prahalad, C., & Doz, Y. (1987). *The Multinational Mission*. New York: Free Press.

Ramaswamy, K. (1995). Multinationality, configuration and performance: A study of MNE's in the drug and pharmaceutical industry. *Journal of International Management, 1*(2), 231–253.

Ravenscraft, D., & Scherer, F. (1987). Mergers, Sell-Offs, and Economic Efficiency. Washington, DC: Brookings.

Reid, S. (1981). The decision maker and export entry and expansion. *Journal of International Business Studies, 12*(2), 101–112. doi:10.1057/palgrave.jibs.8490581

Ribau, C., Moreira, A. C., & Raposo, M. (2015). Internationalisation of the firm theories: A schematic synthesis. *International Journal of Business and Globalisation, 15*(4), 528–554. doi:10.1504/IJBG.2015.072535

Ribeiro, J. (2003). *Modelo de identificação de grupos estratégicos para a indústria metalomecânica de produção, por encomenda, de bens de equipamento* (Unpublished doctoral dissertation). ISCTE, Lisboa, Portugal.

Ridgway, V. (1956). Dysfunctional consequences of performance measurements. *Administrative Science Quarterly, 1*(2), 240–247. doi:10.2307/2390989

Rodrigues, J. (1992). *Custeio Baseado na Actividade*. Revista Portuguesa de Gestão.

Rodrigues, J. (2010). *Avaliação do desempenho das organizações*. Escolar Editora.

Rodriguez, D. (1999). Relación entre innovación y exportaciones de las empresas: Un studio empírico. *Papeles de Economia Española, 81*, 167–180.

Rosenzweig, P., & Singh, J. (1991). Organizational environments and the multinational enterprise. *Academy of Management Review, 16*(2), 340–361. doi:10.5465/amr.1991.4278953

Ross, S., Westerfield, R., & Jaffe, J. (1995). *Administração financeira*. São Paulo: Editora Atlas.

Rulmet, R. (1974). Diversification strategy and profitability. *Strategic Management Journal, 3*(4), 359–370.

Rupeika, A. (2005). Nowadays Approach to Foreign Exchange Risk Management. *Management of Organizations: Systematic Research, 35*, 151–164.

Salas, O. (2001). *El Cuadro de Mando Integral.* XI Congreso AECA – Empresa, euro y Nueva Economia, Madrid, Spain.

Sanchez, P. (2000). *Necesidades de Informacion en la Sociedad del Conhecimento: Especial Referencia al Capital Humano*. Especial IX Encuentro AECA – Gestion de la Información en la Sociedade del Conocimiento y la Globalización.

Santos, F. (2004). *Estratégia passo a passo*. Edições Centro Atlântico.

Scherer, F. (1980). *Industrial market structure and economics performance (2nd ed.)*. Boston: Houghton Mifflin Company.

Schueffel, P., Baldegger, R., & Amann, W. (2014). Behavioral patterns in born-again global firms. *Multinational Business Review, 22*(4), 418–441. doi:10.1108/MBR-06-2014-0029

Shahzad, F. (2019). An Analysis of Internationalization Theories and Behavior of Finnish Retail SME's in Russia. In N. Teixeira, T. Costa, & I. Lisboa (Eds.), *Handbook of Research on Entrepreneurship, Innovation and Internationalization* (pp. 419–438). Hershey, PA: IGI Global. doi:10.4018/978-1-5225-8479-7.ch019

Siddhartan, N., & Lall, S. (1982). Recent growth of the largest US multinationals. *Oxford Bulletin of Economics and Statistics, 44*(1), 1–13. doi:10.1111/j.1468-0084.1982.mp44001001.x

Silva, E. S., Qadri, M., Mota, C. & Pereira A. (2013). *International risk management and finance*. Economic Life.

Silva, F. (1979). *Contabilidade Industrial* (8th ed.). Livraria Sá da Costa.

Silva, E., & Queirós, M. (2010). *Gestão Financeira - Análise de Investimentos*. Porto: Vida Económica.

Simões, V. (1997). *Internacionalização das Empresas Portuguesas: Que papel para a cooperação?* Lisboa: Economia & Prospectiva.

Slangen, A., & Hennart, J. (2008). Do foreign greenfields outperform foreign acquisitions or vice versa? An institutional perspective. *Journal of Management Studies*, *45*(7), 1301–1328. doi:10.1111/j.1467-6486.2008.00794.x

Smithson, C. (1998). *Managing financial risk*. New York: McGraw-Hill.

Soete, L. (1987). The impact of technological innovation on international trade patterns: The evidence reconsidered. *Research Policy*, *16*(2-4), 101–130. doi:10.1016/0048-7333(87)90026-6

Sousa, A. (2006). As 100 Maiores Empresas de TI em Portugal. *Suplemento do Jornal Semana Informática, 809*.

Sterlacchini, A. (1999). Do innovative activities matter to small firms in non-R&D intensive industries? An application to export performance. *Research Policy*, *28*(8), 819–832. doi:10.1016/S0048-7333(99)00023-2

Sullivan, D. (1994). Measuring the degree of internationalization of a firm. *Journal of International Business Studies*, *25*(2), 325–342. doi:10.1057/palgrave.jibs.8490203

Taliani, E. (2001). *La Actual Concepcion de los Processos Presupuestários – Evolucion o Revolution*. XI Congresso AECA – Empresa, Euro e Nova Economia.

Teixeira, A., Teixeira, N., & Mata, C. (2008). *Implementação do Tableau de Bord – Estudo de caso no sector das Rochas Ornamentais*. IV Congresso de Custos do Mercosul – Montevideu.

Teixeira, N. & Teixeira, A. (2008). *Preços de transferência interna e a avaliação do desempenho de centros de responsabilidade*. XVIII Jornadas Luso -Espanholas de Gestão, Porto, Portugal.

Teixeira, N. & Teixeira, A. (2008). *Preços de transferência interna e a avaliação do desempenho de centros de responsabilidade*. XVIII Jornadas Luso –Espanholas de Gestão, Porto, Portugal.

Teixeira, N. (2007). A avaliação do desempenho de centros de responsabilidade – Estudo de caso. *XIV Congresso da AECA*.

Teixeira, N. (2008b). *A caracterização da estrutura financeira do sector das tecnologias de informação*. Estudo apresentado no âmbito do Concurso de provas públicas para Professor Adjunto na ESCE na área científica de Finanças (edital nº 682/2008).

Teixeira, N., Mata, C., Pardal, P., & Teixeira, A. (2012). *A aplicação da rendibilidade supranormal para a avaliação da criação de valor*. XXIII Jornadas Hispano Lusas de Gestão Cientifica, Málaga.

Teixeira, A., & Alves, T. (2003). *A Contabilidade e o Valor, na Perspectiva dos Utilizadores da Informação Financeira. In XV Encontro nacional da ADCES: Contabilidade e Valor: Novos Contextos*. Setúbal: ESCE.

Teixeira, N. (2008). *A rendibilidade e a criação de valor*. Aveiro: XIII Encontro AECA.

Teixeira, N. (2008a). *A Rendibilidade e a Criação de Valor. In XIII Encuentro AECA*. Aveiro: Universidade Aveiro.

Teixeira, N. (2013). A avaliação do risco e da criação de valor no contexto empresarial. In *Empreendedorismo, Coesão Social e Dinâmicas Empresariais. Caderno da Sociedade e Trabalho nº17*. GEP/MSESS.

Teixeira, N., & Amaro, A. (2013). Avaliação do desempenho financeiro e da criação de valor - um estudo de caso. *Revista Universo Contábil*, *6*(4), 157–178. doi:10.4270/ruc.2013436

Teixeira, N., & Carreira, F. (2008). Implementação de um sistema de avaliação do desempenho - Estudo de caso no sector português das Rochas Ornamentais. *XV Congresso Brasileiro de Custos* – Curitiba.

Teixeira, N., & Jorge, N. (2016). *Avaliação do Desempenho Financeiro e criação de valor – uma visão integrada: estudo caso*. Setúbal: *I Congresso de Contabilidade Pública*.

Teixeira, N., Mata, C., Pardal, P., & Teixeira, A. (2013). A aplicação da rendibilidade supranormal para a avaliação da criação de valor. *Jornadas Hispano Lusas de Gestão Cientifica, 23*.

Teixeira, N., Pardal, P., & Rafael, B. (2017). Internationalization, Financial Performance and Organizational Challenges. In *Handbook of Research on Entrepreneurial Ecosystems and Social Dynamics in a Globalized World, EUA*. IGI Global.

Universidade Católica – Centro de Estudos Aplicados. (2001). *O Sector das Tecnologias de Informação em Portugal*. ANETIE.

Valente, F., & Lourenço, R. (2019). Academic Entrepreneurship, Knowledge Transfer and Academic Spin-off. In N. Teixeira, T. Costa, & I. Lisboa (Eds.), *Handbook of Research on Entrepreneurship, Innovation and Internationalization* (pp. 178–206). Hershey, PA: IGI Global. doi:10.4018/978-1-5225-8479-7.ch007

Valenzuela, A. (2000). Modelo de capacidades para la internacionalización de la empresa exportadora Española. *Cuadernos de Economía y Dirección de la Empresa*, *5*, 91–109.

Vancil, R. (1973, Mar.). *What Kind of management control do you need? Harvard Business Review*.

Vernon, R. (1971). *Sovereignty at Bay: the multinational spread of US enterprises*. New York: Basic Book.

Vlacic, B., González-Loureiro, M., & Eduardsen, J. (2019). The Internationalization of SME's: Strategic Choices Under a Cognitive Approach. In N. Teixeira, T. Costa, & I. Lisboa (Eds.), *Handbook of Research on Entrepreneurship, Innovation and Internationalization* (pp. 419–438). Hershey, PA: IGI Global. doi:10.4018/978-1-5225-8479-7.ch017

Wakelin, K. (1998). Innovation and export behaviour at the firm level. *Research Policy*, *26*(7-8), 829–841. doi:10.1016/S0048-7333(97)00051-6

Wan, W., & Hoskinsson, R. (2001). Country resource environments, corporate diversification strategies and firm performance. Academy of Management Proceedings, 27-45. doi:10.5465/apbpp.2001.6133450

Wan, W. (2005). Country resource environments, firm capabilities and corporate diversification strategies. *Journal of Management Studies*, *42*(1), 161–182. doi:10.1111/j.1467-6486.2005.00492.x

Wan, W., & Hoskinsson, R. (2003). Home country environments, corporate diversification strategies and firm performance. *Academy of Management Journal*, *46*(1), 27–45.

Williamson, O. (1975). *Markets and Hierarchies: Analysis and Antitrust Implications: A Study in the Economics of Internal Organization*. New York: The Free Press.

Willmore, L. (1992). Transnationals and foreign trade: Evidence from Brasil. *The Journal of Development Studies*, *28*(2), 314–335. doi:10.1080/00220389208422234

Wolff, J., & Pett, T. (2000). Internationalization of small firms: An examination of export competitive patterns, firm size and export performance. *Journal of Small Business Management*, *38*(2), 34–47.

Young, S., & O'Byrne, S. (2001). *EVA® and Value Based Management*. New York: MacGraw-Hill.

Zander, I., McDougall-Covin, P., & Rose, E. (2015). Born globals and international business: Evolution of a field of research. *Journal of International Business Studies*, *46*(1), 27–35. doi:10.1057/jibs.2014.60

Zejan, M. (1990). New ventures or acquisitions: The choice of Swedish multinational enterprises. *The Journal of Industrial Economics*, *38*(3), 349–355. doi:10.2307/2098503

Zeng, S., Xie, X., & Wan, T. (2009). Relationships between business factors and performance in internationalization – an empirical study in China. *Management Decision*, *47*(2), 308–329. doi:10.1108/00251740910938939

About the Authors

Nuno Teixeira is a Professor at Institute Polytechnic of Setúbal. He holds a PhD in Strategic Management. Is a researcher and consulter in Strategy, Finance, Entrepreneurship, Internationalization and Management Control Systems. He is author of several papers in journals and in conferences in his areas of research.

Joaquim Silva Ribeiro is Coordinating Professor of the Business School of the Polytechnic Institute of Setúbal and Coordinator of Unit for Evaluation and Quality of the Polytechnic Institute of Setúbal (UNIQUA). He holds a PhD in Management, Master in Business Sciences and Degree in Mechanical Engineering. He was CEO and Consultant in some industrial companies. He has developed research in the areas of Management, Strategy, Operations Management and Quality Management.

Ana Bela Teixeira is a Professor at Institute Polytechnic of Setúbal. She holds a PhD in Accounting. Is a researcher in Accounting and Management Control Systems. She is author of several papers in journals and in conferences in her areas of research.

Teresa Godinho is a Professor at Institute Polytechnic of Setúbal. She holds a Master in Accounting. Is a researcher in Accounting and Finance. She is author of several papers in journals and in conferences in her areas of research.

Index

Premier Reference Source
Emerging GIS Applications for Emergency and Disaster Management

Premier Reference Source
Managerial Strategies and Green Solutions for Project Sustainability

Premier Reference Source
Comparative Approaches to Using R and Python for Statistical Data Analysis

Premier Reference Source
Solutions for High-Touch Communications in a High-Tech World

www.ingramcontent.com/pod-product-compliance
Lightning Source LLC
LaVergne TN
LVHW080528300926
849162LV00007B/1563
9781799820079